GOOD
SIMPLE COOKERY

The great English classic in a new illustrated edition

ELISABETH AYRTON

Macdonald

A Macdonald BOOK

Original edition © Rainbird, McLean Ltd 1958
Revised edition © Michael Ayrton Productions Ltd 1984

This edition first published in Great Britain in 1984
by Macdonald & Co (Publishers) Ltd

A member of BPCC plc

ISBN 0 356 10169 X

Filmset by SX Composing Limited,
Rayleigh, Essex
Printed and bound in Great Britain by
Blantyre Printing Ltd.,
London and Glasgow

Macdonald & Co (Publishers) Ltd
Maxwell House
74 Worship Street
London EC2A 2EN

GOOD
SIMPLE COOKERY

The great English classic in a new illustrated edition

ELISABETH AYRTON

Macdonald

A *Macdonald* BOOK

Original edition © Rainbird, McLean Ltd 1958
Revised edition © Michael Ayrton Productions Ltd 1984

This edition first published in Great Britain in 1984
by Macdonald & Co (Publishers) Ltd

A member of BPCC plc

ISBN 0 356 10169 X

Filmset by SX Composing Limited,
Rayleigh, Essex
Printed and bound in Great Britain by
Blantyre Printing Ltd.,
London and Glasgow

Macdonald & Co (Publishers) Ltd
Maxwell House
74 Worship Street
London EC2A 2EN

To all those with whom I live
whose differing tastes
make all cookery complex

CONTENTS

INTRODUCTION

This book was first published in 1956, soon after the food rationing necessitated by the Second World War was finally brought to an end.

The book was intended primarily for the inexperienced cook. It was received with enthusiasm by girls about to get married, and by some already married, who were trying, rather unsuccessfully, to cook in their new homes. It was also welcomed by women who had worked throughout the war, eaten mainly in canteens and restaurants, and had hardly cooked at all. They found themselves, in the years immediately after the war, trying to cook from pre-war cook books which listed ingredients, many of which were still unobtainable, and suggested procedures which they had never learnt. (Naturally, very few new cookery books had been published during or just after the war, since paper had been in desperately short supply.) This book was certainly not among the first of the post-war crop, but it filled a gap, because the recipes were simple, the methods were carefully explained, and it gave both unusual and, more important, traditional dishes. This was a time when everyone wanted to return to pre-war standards in their way of life and particularly in cooking and, if possible, to improve on those standards. By the time this book was published, the first of these desires was being realized and people were looking for ways of achieving the second.

When the decision was made to publish a version revised for the 80s, it became clear that not only our eating habits but our cooking habits had changed very markedly in the last thirty years. In the original version, the use of many ingredients which were still in somewhat short supply was reduced to the absolute minimum needed to give good results, or made optional. For instance, several recipes used one egg where today we would unhesitatingly use two; 'a little cream' was tentatively suggested as improving a sauce and the use of wine was generally followed by the phrase 'if possible'. Today, eggs and cream are used casually as required, except in households where cholesterol or calories are being carefully watched, and wine is so frequently used, both at the table and in cooking, that there is no difficulty in including a glass or two in a recipe.

On the other hand, most kinds of meat, shellfish and game have become so expensive that today most households would only serve on special occasions many of the recipes that were standard fare at the time of the first version. A prime roast of beef was the regular Sunday dinner and grilled rump or fillet steak did not seem a particularly expensive meal. Recipes for cooking joints and steaks, game and shellfish are still given because many families want to eat such food occasionally. Price and availability change from time to time and large freezer packs containing two or three good roasting joints and others for braising or stewing can often be bought very reasonably. When the book was first published, there were no domestic freezers.

The principal change in our eating habits, however, comes from the vast amount of 'convenience' food which has flooded the market in the last few years, mostly designed to save time. Twenty years ago, who would have imagined being able to buy, at a reasonable price, fillets of turkey breast covered in breadcrumbs, which can be cooked from frozen in eight minutes? Most of these pre-prepared and partly-cooked foods are very successful and very helpful to housewives who have part-time jobs and children of school age and one might think that the need for a cookery book of this basic, comprehensive kind was fast disappearing. Do people want to make their own pastry, casserole liver and bacon or steam a suet pudding? When I was first asked to revise *Good Simple Cookery*, I wondered if perhaps the time for it was past. However, my three daughters and several friends who all cling to early copies of the book, assured me that these skills are still required and very hard to find in an accessible form. When I began to go through the book, apart from the differences I have already mentioned, I found it more interesting than I had expected. I hope that, in its new form, it will prove a blessing to another generation of those who find it a pleasure to buy fresh food and cook it with the care and attention many of us remember our mothers and grandmothers giving to the dishes they prepared.

Elisabeth Ayrton

COOKING METHODS AND TERMS EXPLAINED

COOKING METHODS

Boiling If you wish to keep the flavour in a piece of meat, you put it into boiling water which seals the outside. You can then simmer it slowly, as quick boiling tends to harden it.

Quick boiling is used to reduce liquids or sauces in quantity and thus to concentrate the flavour. Meat and fish should never be boiled rapidly.

Simmering and Poaching The ingredients are placed in cold water, which is brought gently to the boil. Boiling point is never exceeded, only just reached, in this method of cooking.

Steaming This is the cooking of food by the steam or evaporation of water. It takes longer, but generally gives a better consistency and more flavour. The food is enclosed in a container above boiling water.

Stewing In this method you do not want to keep the juice and flavour inside the solid ingredients but to extract it gently into the juice in which they are cooked. You therefore simmer your ingredients just below boiling point for a long time. Naturally, the solid ingredients do not appear to have lost their flavour, but, in fact, a good deal of it has gone into the stock in which they cooked and which forms the gravy or sauce of the stew.

Roasting This is the method of exposing food to high heat without its coming into actual contact with the heat. It is another form of grilling, as the heat sears the outside of the food and thus prevents the juices from escaping. As cooking proceeds, the heat penetrates to the centre. The secret of good roasting is to baste the food with fat at frequent intervals.

Pot roasting This is a form of roasting in a pan or casserole on top of the stove. The meat is first browned, then roasted gently on a bed of vegetables. When cooked, the meat is removed and stock or wine is added to the casserole.

Baking　This is the method of dry cooking in the oven – cakes, pastries, potatoes, etc., are baked. Where meat or poultry is concerned we speak of roasting but we almost always mean baking, i.e. the meat is cooked in the oven, with hot air all round it, and not turned in front of the fire on a spit or jack as it was until the late nineteenth century.

Braising　This is a combination of roasting and stewing. The meat must first be sealed by fast cooking in the oven or in a frying pan until the outside is brown. Liquid is then added and the meat is cooked slowly in a casserole until done. Vegetables can be fried until they are slightly browned and then braised in the same way.

Frying　This is the method of cooking food in fat. You can use three methods: deep-frying, shallow-frying and sautéing.

Deep-frying　The food is plunged into enough boiling fat to cover it on all sides, usually by placing food in a frying basket and lowering this into the fat. The fat must be kept really boiling. You cannot deep-fry slowly. The food is then lifted by removing the basket, drained well over the pan and on greaseproof paper and served at once. Deep-frying is very satisfactory for such foods as fillets of fish which have been coated with batter or breadcrumbs, or for chipped potatoes, as they are cooked on all sides at once and the first side cannot become soggy or greasy while the second side is frying.

Shallow-frying　The food is cooked in a pan with enough fat to prevent it from drying, sticking or burning. You can fry very gently – 'melting' your onions, for instance, instead of frying them crisp. Never put food into the pan until the fat has reached the temperature you want for cooking it. Otherwise it will be heavy, soggy and greasy.

Sauté　This is gentle frying in very little fat. Generally butter is used. It is suitable for foods which do not need much cooking, such as mushrooms, or foods which are partly cooked and which only need heating, browning and crisping to make them attractive. Parboiled potatoes can be sautéed.

Grilling or Broiling　Grilled food is cooked over or under a fierce source of heat which is not enclosed. It is a method which is employed for comparatively small pieces of food. It has advantages over frying, because grilled foods are not at all fatty or greasy and are therefore more digestible than fried, and not fattening for those on a diet. Almost any food which can be fried may be grilled, except potatoes and onions, or food which has been coated with egg and breadcrumbs or batter. Grilled meat should never be overcooked. Steak, chops, cutlets, kidneys, fillets of fish, etc., are all good grilled. Sausages are excellent grilled instead of fried.

Searing This seals the outside of meat, fish, poultry or game, in order to keep the juices inside.

Cooking in a Double Saucepan You are, of course, really steaming: you are keeping from direct heat a delicate substance which you want to heat, and often to thicken, but which must not actually boil – often because it would curdle if it did so.

Cooking au Bain-marie You are baking in the oven, but, by standing the vessel containing the food in a larger vessel filled with water to come halfway up the food container, you ensure that the oven heat does not dry the food you are cooking, nor shrink it.

COOKING TERMS

Aspic Savoury jelly for coating cold foods.

Au Gratin Baked or roasted dishes, which are prepared with fine grated breadcrumbs and sometimes cheese sprinkled over the top. Cheese is not an essential ingredient in a dish termed *au gratin*.

Bain-marie To stand one dish in another, which contains water, for gentle cooking in the oven.

Bake Cooking by dry heat in an oven. This term is used in conjunction with roasting when applied to meat cookery. Sometimes the term is applied to cooking on griddles, hot plates, etc.

Barbecue Originally this meant an entire carcase cooked at an open fire, but this term now denotes any type of outdoor cooking of meat, and some dishes which are cooked indoors, but served with the pungent sauce which is customary in barbecue dishes.

Barding This term is sometimes confused with 'larding'. A thin sheet of bacon fat is sliced off, trimmed square to fit, and tied over the breast of a roasting bird with two or three pieces of thread. (See *Lard* below.)

Baste To moisten roasting meat by pouring over it juices and melted fat from the roasting pan.

Batter A blended mixture essentially of flour and liquid, but often with eggs and other ingredients added.

Beat To force air into a mixture by a rotary motion. This may be done with a fork, or with a rotary or electric beater. Meat is sometimes beaten with a mallet or rolling pin to tenderize it.

Beurre Noir Butter cooked dark brown, to which vinegar or lemon juice is added and the whole poured over fried or grilled fillets of fish or meat.

Bind To add sufficient liquid, water, milk, or eggs, to make a mixture hold together.

Blanch To cover with boiling water and then with cold water in order to loosen the skins of tomatoes, almonds, etc.

Bonne Femme To cook in stock with herbs, usually with mushrooms added.

Bouquet Garni Bunch of mixed herbs, used for flavouring soups, stews, etc.

Braised Lightly fried food, which is then simmered in a casserole or Dutch oven.

Canapés Small pieces of fried bread, toast or pastry, upon which savouries are served.

Caramel A sweet glaze or sauce made by boiling sugar with a little water until it is brown and syrupy.

Cereal Collective term for all farinaceous foods such as prepared breakfast cereals, rice, oatmeal, spaghetti, etc.

Cochineal A red colouring matter.

Cocottes Individual ovenproof dishes used for eggs and savouries.

Consommé Clear gravy soup.

Coquilles Cockles.

Court Bouillon Fish stock made from fish bones and trimmings and a bouquet of herbs, carrots and onion, and used for sauces in fish dishes or as a basis for fish soup.

Cream, to To work together with a spoon to a creamy consistency fat, butter, or butter and sugar.

Croquettes Small shapes of minced meat, fish, cheese or potato dipped in egg and breadcrumbs and fried.

Croûte A thick piece of bread fried in butter or deep fat. Used for dishing game and some entrées.

Croûtons Small squares of bread, toasted or fried. Served with soup or as a garnish.

Crystallize To cook fruits in hot syrup, until the sugar solidifies.

Dariole Small cup-shaped mould, usually lined with pastry, filled with a sweet cream but sometimes with a cheese cream.

Decant To pour wine or liquid which has a sediment from the original bottle to the decanter without transferring the sediment.

Devilled Grilled meat or fish cooked with mustard, cayenne pepper or other hot condiments. A highly spiced sauce is often served as an accompaniment.

Dice To cut into small cubes.

Dissolve To melt a solid food in a liquid.

Draw To remove the entrails of poultry, game, etc.

Dredge To cover with a fine, thick sprinkling – e.g. fish dredged with flour, or cakes dredged with sugar.

Dropping consistency When a spoonful of mixture raised above the bowl falls from the spoon without sticking or pouring.

Entrée A made-up dish served between the fish and meat course of a meal. Nowadays often itself the main course.

Escalope A thin slice of meat coated with egg and breadcrumbs and then fried.

Farci Stuffed.

Fillet Meat, poultry or fish, from which the bones have been removed. This term also refers to the undercut of a loin of beef, pork or lamb, etc.

Filter To strain liquid through fine muslin or linen.

Fines Herbes Mixed herbs, finely chopped and used for stuffings, omelette filling, etc.

Flambé To pour brandy or some other spirit over hot food and set light to it.

Flan Pastry case baked in a flat tin, filled when cold, either with fruit or a savoury mixture.

Florentine Meat, fish or eggs served on a bed of spinach. (Florentines are thin, rich biscuits, containing dried fruit and nuts and coated with chocolate.)

Forcemeat Stuffing.

Fricandelles Small pieces of braised meat or game.

Fritter Any piece of food, sweet or savoury, which is dipped in batter and deep-fried.

Frosting Another term for icing.

Galantine Cooked meat that has been boned, pressed into a mould with jelly and served cold.

Glacé To make smooth or glossy with icing or jelly. Also applied to crystallized or frozen foods. To give a glossy surface to food.

Glaze Meat glaze is made by reducing, by boiling, stock or gravy to the consistency of jelly. Sugar and water glaze is brushed over fruit pies, buns, etc., when they are taken from the oven. Egg and water glaze is brushed on to savoury pies before they are put in the oven.

Hors d'oeuvre Course served before soup. Generally composed of several small, cold, savoury dishes, intended to awaken the appetite.

Icing Cooked or uncooked icing. Used to decorate cakes.

Infuse To extract flavour from tea, herbs, etc., by pouring boiling liquid over them.

Jardinière Mixed young vegetables used as a garnish. Vegetables stewed down in their own juice.

Julienne Vegetables cut into thin, match-like strips.

Knead To work dough with the hands.

Kosher Foods prepared to fulfill the requirements of Jewish law.

Lace To add a dash of spirits to a beverage.

Lard To put strips of fat into lean meat or fish to prevent dryness. Properly, a larding needle is using.

Liaison The thickening element in sauces, such as flour, egg yolk, arrowroot, etc.

Line To cover the bottom and sides of a cooking utensil – such as a pie dish – with pastry, a mould with jelly, or a soufflé dish with greaseproof paper.

Macedoine A mixture of fruits or vegetables cut into small even pieces.

Macerate To soak in prepared liquid.

Maitre d'hôtel To serve garnished with parsley butter.

Marinade A mixture of seasoned oil, or seasoned vinegar (or both) or wine, or other liquid with herbs and vegetables in which food is soaked for hours or days. The purpose is to improve the flavour, to soften, and in some instances to keep fresh.

Marinate To soak in a marinade.

Mask To coat a dish completely with sauce, jelly, mayonnaise, etc.

Meunière Served fried in butter to which lemon juice and chopped parsley are added.

Mornay To serve with cheese sauce.

Mull To spice, sweeten and heat wine or ale.

Pasteurize To kill bacteria by raising to a very high temperature.

Pectin Substance contained in fruit which causes jam to set.

Portugaise To serve with tomatoes or tomato sauce.

Pound To make into a smooth paste or powder by beating with a pestle in a mortar.

Prove Term used for bread dough when it is put to rise and swell, before baking.

Purée To reduce any foodstuff to a smooth paste by passing through a sieve, moulin, or food blender.

Rare Term used to describe very underdone meat.

Réchauffer To reheat.

Reduce To evaporate liquid by fast boiling so that the quantity is reduced and the flavour increased.

Render To take raw animal fat and slowly heat so that the pure fat melts from the tissue and can be poured off for use in cooking and adding flavour to other foods.

Roux The basic mixture for all thick sauces and gravies, etc. – i.e. flour cooked for a few minutes in fat before adding the liquid part of the sauce. A white roux for white sauces is made by cooking very gently without allowing the flour to colour and a brown roux for dark sauces is made by cooking much more quickly so that the flour and fat darken.

Salt, to To preserve by covering with dry salt.

Scald To bring milk just to boiling point, but not allow it to continue to boil; to pour boiling water over any foodstuff in order to clean or to remove skin or hair.

Scallop A method of serving food by cutting into small slices, covering with sauce and breadcrumbs and baking in the oven in scallop shells or a flat ovenproof dish.

Score To cut parallel gashes over the surface of meat or fish in order to let out some of the surface fat so that it will cook crisply.

Sear To brown the surface without cooking through, by the application of intense heat. This 'seals' the juices in meat and improves the flavour.

Season To add salt and pepper, spices, herbs, condiments, etc., to bring out the flavour of a dish.

Set To leave any liquid containing a solidifying agent to become firm by cooling.

Shortening Term for fat which is used in a flour mixture – pastries, cake mixtures, etc.

Sift To shake a dry substance through a sieve or strainer.

Sterilize To kill bacteria by applying great heat.

Sweat To heat fruit or vegetables in a little fat over a low heat to soften and draw out juices.

Tartare Name given to a sharp sauce. Also minced steak is sometimes served raw and is then called 'Steak Tartare'.

Thicken To give body to liquid, as in sauces, soups, etc., by pouring on a roux and boiling, or by adding flour, cornflour, potato flour, ground rice, etc., to the liquid.

Whip To beat rapidly and so incorporate air.

Zest The yellow outer part of the skins of citrus fruits.

HERBS

Herbs are still not always given the place they should have in English cooking. This is a fairly recent development. Until the nineteenth century they were used as much in England as they have always been, and still are, on the Continent. If you have a garden or window box or a few pots on a windowsill, the majority of the most useful kinds are perfectly easy to grow and ornamental to look at.

Herbs do have great importance, for they bring out and intensify the true flavours of many foods. Long trial and error through the ages has shown which herbs go particularly well with which meats, fish and vegetables. The following table sets these out.

Remember, however, that flavouring with herbs is a subtle thing. Too strong a herbal flavour is often much worse than none at all. The table also shows which herbs are particularly strong and must therefore be used only in tiny quantities.

If you are using herbs in cooked dishes, they should be put in at the beginning of the cooking in the form of a bunch or 'bouquet garni', that is, a few sprigs of each of the herbs you want to use, bunched together and tied round with a piece of string, or tied up in muslin. This bouquet can then be lifted out when the cooking is finished or, if you suspect that they are giving too much flavour to the dish, even before. Never serve herbs which have flavoured a dish. Very finely chopped fresh herbs may be sprinkled over hot as well as cold dishes, both for flavour and decoration.

If in winter you must use dried herbs and have only powdered ones, use a teaspoon or so of the ready mixed herbs, or mix two or three separate kinds according to your recipe, and tie them up in a little bit of clean, fine muslin or linen. They can then be used and thrown away like a bouquet. At certain greengrocers you can buy dried herbs in bunches in winter and, of course, if you grow your own, in a garden, or window box, or in pots on the windowsill, you can dry any that you can spare and save them.

Herb	*Pots, window box or garden only*	*Description*	*What foods to flavour or enhance*
Balm (or lemon Verbena)	Garden only	Perennial of the nettle family. Spreads rapidly. Exquisite strong scent, but quite a mild flavour	Finely chopped, is sprinkled over salads and into soup. A bruised sprig left to steep in cider or in a jug of lemonade gives a delicious and very refreshing flavour
Basil	Pots, window box or garden	Annual	Used in many dishes, soups, casseroles, and with fish, an excellent part of a 'bouquet'. Rather strong clove-like flavour. Use very small amounts. Particularly good with tomatoes
Bay	Garden only (or in tubs)	A shrub or small tree	Should form part of most bouquets. Leaves are too tough to use chopped. Very good with fish and tomatoes. Dries well
Bergamot	Garden only	Perennial of the nettle family. Grows to 3 feet and is very ornamental	Leaves and flowers can be used in salads, and sprigs in wine cups or in iced tea
Borage	Garden only	Annual, but generally seeds itself. 3 feet, with lovely bright blue flowers	Leaves have a faint cucumber taste and are delicious over salad. Flowers can also be sprinkled over salads and floated on soup. The chopped leaves mixed into butter make a good summer sandwich filling. Traditional to put sprigs in wine cups, cider cups, etc.
Camomile	Garden or pots or window box	Perennial	Really only used to make that old-fashioned remedy, camomile tea
Chervil	Garden only	Annual, about 1 foot high	Can be used as an alternative to parsley, having a sweeter, more subtle flavour. A delicious herb for almost any purpose
Chives	Garden, pots, or window box	The smallest and most delicate form of onion. You use the leaves or 'grass' and divide the bulbs and replant each season	Excellent chopped in salads, or soups, or as part of a bouquet for fish, or in omelettes. Use anywhere, in fact, where a very delicate trace of onion would be an improvement

Herb	Pots, window box or garden only	Description	What foods to flavour or enhance
Dill	Garden only	Annual, 3 feet	Good in sauces for fish and on salads. Experiment to see if you like it
Finocchio (Sweet Fennel)	Garden only	Annual, 2 feet	Delicious in sauce for fish and some chicken dishes. Some like it chopped on salads, but experiment first, and always use very little as the flavour is very penetrating
Garlic	Garden only	Annual, 2 to 3 feet. Handsome onion heads	You can grow and dry this but in some seasons in England the bulbs do not dry out well. Of course, in Mediterranean countries, garlic goes into almost every soup and stew and most roasts are rubbed with it
Marjoram (Origano)	Garden, window box or pots	There are two kinds, perennial and annual. It is very pretty, with a dusty pink flower. Dries very well and keeps its flavour	A delicious herb, very mild – you can use quite a lot in mixed 'bouquets' or finely chopped with parsley and chives to sprinkle over salads or into soups and omelettes
Mint	Pots, window box or garden	There are many kinds, all good and delicious. The usual is Spearmint, but you can get Apple, Pineapple and several others. Mint spreads fast. A root or two in a large pot do well if well-watered and given some artificial fertilizer. In a warm room you can keep some fresh for cutting all winter	Mint is the freshest taste in the world and apart from the conventional mint sauce is good in dozens of dishes. Sprinkle it over salads and soups and over cooked vegetables, and, of course, cook with new potatoes and with peas (put it with frozen peas as well as fresh) in pea soup, in lettuce or cucumber sandwiches, or a sprig as part of a mixed 'bouquet' for any dish with mutton or lamb. Wherever you would sprinkle chopped parsley, half parsley and half mint and a few chives, will be much more interesting
Parsley	Pots, window box or garden	Perfectly easy to grow anywhere	The one herb which is used freely in English cooking, but chiefly as a garnish. Should form part of any 'bouquet'. Delicious in sauce. Particularly good with cooked, minced ham, ham mousse, etc. And, of course, on salads, in soups and sandwiches

Herb	*Pots, window box or garden only*	*Description*	*What foods to flavour or enhance*
Rosemary	Garden only	A shrub with beautiful grey lavender-like leaves and pale blue flowers	Very strong – never use too much. Its best use is with pork or mutton, which is to be roasted. Tiny sprigs stuck into the meat here and there give it a wonderful flavour and aroma. If you always use it you may tire of it, but used once in a while, when you have these roasts, it is delicious
Sage	Garden, window box or pots	Perennial	Traditional for stuffings for duck, goose and pork – in fact any rich or rather greasy meat. It is very strong. Use only a little, as it has a bitter quality if too much is used
Savory	Garden only	Summer savory is an annual and winter savory a perennial	Can be used where thyme is used and is less strong. It is particularly good with broad beans, finely chopped and sprinkled over them
Tarragon	You might get it to grow in pot or window box, but this is doubtful. It is tricky even in the garden	Perennial	One of the most delicious of all the herbs. Specially good with fish and chicken, less good with red and dark meat. Good in sharp sauces. Tarragon vinegar is good in many ways and can be made by steeping tarragon in wine vinegar. A little is good chopped over salad. It has a very pervasive flavour – be careful to use very little. Does not dry very well
Thyme	Pot, window box or garden	Perennial. There are dozens of kinds, the flavours varying slightly and the leaves and flowers very much	Traditional in stuffing for chicken and fish. Very good with veal, particularly lemon thyme. Good in a bouquet garni. Very good if a few sprigs are stuck into a roast of lamb and cooked with it. Also sprinkled over salads. Very pervasive. Use very little

Drying and Storing Herbs

Pick whatever you can spare of each herb just before it flowers. All herbs, except parsley, can be dried on the rack over a stove. Wash them and shake them well, then lay them on a piece of muslin on the rack. Cover with a piece of muslin to protect them from dust. Dry until crisp, about half a day. Parsley should be washed, shaken well and then placed in a very hot oven for 2 minutes only. It can then be finished off on the rack in the same way as the other herbs. Both the colour and flavour of dried parsley are much better if dried like this, but it is never so good as fresh, which you can usually manage to have available from a pot indoors.

When the herbs are dry, put them, each kind separate, in airtight glass jars – bottling jars or jam jars with lids – leaving the sprigs whole, so that you can easily make a 'bouquet' – which, if they are dried, should have muslin round it, as the crisp herbs tend to break up where fresh ones do not.

If you have no storage space for the jars, tie the herbs in muslin bags and hang in a dry place. This was the method used in the old days and works very well.

Cultivation

The cultivation of herbs in a garden is very simple. They nearly all spread and must be kept in control. They all like sunshine and a well-drained and not too rich soil (except mint, which is a gross feeder) but fortunately they are not very particular and will adapt themselves and grow almost anywhere except in complete shade.

Tarragon is apt to be a little difficult where the soil is heavy and not well drained and thyme sometimes gives up in these conditions. Our ancestors used to grow them in a formally arranged herb garden, each kind separated from another by dwarf box hedges. Such a garden is a great pleasure to look at and smells delicious in the sun, but it requires a great deal of labour and most people nowadays must content themselves with a herb patch, which should be as near the back door as possible for convenience. Plant them all together but fairly well spaced with the taller at the back, and simply keep the more rampant (balm, bergamot, mint and so on) from choking the rest.

If you are growing your herbs in pots or window box:

1 Arrange for good drainage by having a thick layer of stones, shards, etc., at the bottom.

2 Give them some humus of compost or peat or leaf mould. Then use earth with some sand.

3 Give them some artificial fertilizer from time to time.

4 Give them a soil depth of about 6 inches (15 cm).

5 Have them in a sunny window – really sunny – otherwise they won't do anything for you.

6 Don't pick too much off the small plants at a time – leave plenty of leaves and young shoots.

7 In the case of mint and parsley, be prepared to use up the plants you have and start again every few months.

The best, easiest and most generally useful herbs for pots and window box are:

Chives	Mint
Parsley	Marjoram
Basil	Thyme
Sage	

APPETIZERS, HORS D'OEUVRE AND SAVOURIES

APPETIZERS

Appetizers are served with drinks before a meal starts and not, as in the case of hors d'oeuvre, at the table. In many countries, Russia, Scandinavia, Spain and Greece, for example, spirits have never been served without a few small savouries to eat in the fingers. In America, nuts, olives or crisps are almost always offered and very often canapés, cubes of cheese, etc. In England drinks are often served without any food, except on special occasions, but when they are available appetizers are always much appreciated, from simple peanuts to elaborate hot canapés.

They must be small, and it must be possible to eat them as you stand up, without fear of making your hands or your clothes dirty. They should be of a size that can be put whole into the mouth.

For this reason, all kinds of savouries stuck on cocktail sticks are a usual form of appetizer, and canapés where the savoury is mounted on a tiny piece – not more than an inch (2½ cm) square – of thin toast, fried bread, puff pastry, or a small salt biscuit. Tiny sausage rolls, and patties and puffs may be served as appetizers, and cheese straws and all kinds of salted nuts, olives and small gherkins.

Dips

A bowl of fondue (see page 184) or of the special sauce given for Prawn Cocktail (see page 28) made rather thick by using a thick mayonnaise. May be served with potato crisps, fingers of toast, small salt biscuits or strips of raw carrot, cucumber or celery to dip into it. The bowl of sauce and the plates of toast or biscuits should be arranged on a tray, in case any of the sauce is splashed.

A bowl of mustard sauce may be served in the same way, with small hot cocktail or frankfurter sausages to dip into it.

Appetizers served on cocktail sticks

(1 to each stick)

Cooked prawn

Chipolata sausage, twisted to make 2, or cocktail sausage

Button mushroom, filled with parsley butter (chilled)

Cube of cheese, such as Cheddar, Cheshire, Gruyère or a blue cheese with, or without, a cube of tinned pineapple

Cube of cucumber

Roll of lean ham with cream cheese or asparagus inside (very small)

Roll of smoked salmon

Tiny firm rissoles or meat balls

Canapés

Garnishes

Chopped parsley

Chopped mint

Small piece of tomato

Small piece of red or green pepper

Sprinkling of cayenne or paprika

Tiny piece of black or green olive

Finely chopped hard-boiled egg

Toppings

Finely minced cooked ham

Finely minced cooked chicken

Finely minced cooked kipper

Finely minced cooked herring fillet

Finely minced cooked smoked haddock

One inch (2½ cm) squares of toast, fried bread, puff pastry, or a small salt biscuit. Can be piled or thickly spread with any savoury mixture, which can then be decorated with one of the suggested garnishes.

Work any of the toppings into an equal quantity of butter, with a little finely chopped parsley or paprika added, to make a smooth highly seasoned cream. Spread the canapés thickly. Smooth off neatly, decorate and chill a few minutes in refrigerator. Or use any of the savoury butters, (see Chapter 10) such as Green Butter, Anchovy Butter.

More Expensive Canapés

Cut with scissors exactly to fit buttered toast, biscuit or pastry. Sprinkle very lightly with cayenne.

Smoked Salmon

Butter the toast or biscuit, and press the shrimps well down with knife blade into the butter.

Potted Shrimps

Celery Boats

1 or 2 heads of celery

½ lb (240 g) cream or blue cheese

Pepper and salt

Worcestershire sauce

Cayenne

Cut the white and tender inside stalks of well washed celery into 1½ inch (3¾ cm) lengths. Pipe over them the cream or blue cheese, well beaten with a fork, and seasoned with pepper, a little salt, and a dash of Worcestershire sauce, if liked. Sprinkle lightly with cayenne and chill slightly.

Stuffed Mushrooms

2 or 3 mushrooms per person
½ oz (15 g) Green Butter for 3
    mushrooms
Butter to sauté mushrooms

Very lightly sauté small or medium-sized mushrooms. Drain, cool and chill slightly. Pipe around and over the trimmed stalks with Green Butter (see Chapter 10). Stick a cocktail stick in the centre of each.

Salted Almonds

½ lb (240 g) almonds in skins or
    blanched
1 tbsp pure olive oil, or 1 oz (30 g)
    fresh butter
Salt

If in skins, blanch and dry them well. Fry in the oil over a gentle heat until they are a pale brown. Drain well on salted kitchen paper.

HORS D'OEUVRE

Hors d'oeuvre are served at the table. They must be small and appetizing, in fact very much like appetizers, and can be eaten with knife and fork, or teaspoon, so they need not be so dry and crisp. Hors d'oeuvre are a blessing to the hostess who is also the cook, because they can be completely prepared before guests arrive and kept in the refrigerator. In most cases, they can be arranged beforehand in serving dishes or on plates. On the whole, if you are serving appetizers before the meal, it is a mistake to begin it with hors d'oeuvre. Do not serve a cheese hors d'oeuvre if you are going to serve cheese later in the meal. A mixed hors d'oeuvre is always a good start, and can consist of any combination of the following, but should contain one or two meat, one or two fish, and one or two vegetable ingredients, not all vegetable or all meat or fish.

Mixed Hors d'oeuvre

Vegetables
Olives, black, green, or stuffed
Pimentoes, tinned or fresh, finely
    sliced
Cocktail onions
Radishes
Cucumber, sliced and sprinkled
    with salt, lemon juice and
    chopped parsley
Tomatoes, blanched, sliced and
    sprinkled with parsley, thyme,
    and a little sugar and salt
Haricot or butter beans
Beetroot, diced

Gherkins
Celery – finely shredded, chilled to
    make it curl and lightly folded
    into a good mayonnaise
Russian salad (see Chapter 12)
Grated raw carrots
Potato salad (see Chapter 12)
Fish
Herring fillets
Rollmops
Sardines
Anchovies
Smoked salmon
Prawns

Shrimps
Potted shrimps
Cold cooked kipper fillets
Cold cooked salmon or salmon
    trout
Meat
Cold chopped cooked chicken,
    lightly mixed with mayonnaise
Sliced sausage – salami, liver
    sausage, ham sausage,
    mortadella, etc.
Cooked ham
Raw smoked ham
Any pâté or terrine

Galantine
Smoked goose or turkey
Chopped cooked chicken livers
* served with chopped hard-*
* boiled egg and parsley*
Cheese
Cubes of hard cheese – Cheddar,
* Gruyère, Emmenthal, etc.*

Eggs
Hard-boiled, quartered, and
* lightly covered with*
* mayonnaise, or chopped to*
* decorate potato salad, etc.*

A mixed hors d'oeuvre should contain any six of the above ingredients as a minimum, and as many more kinds as you like. Each person needs very little of any one ingredient – about a dessertspoon of any chopped or diced mixture or one or two small slices – say 2 in (5 cm) square – of any sliced ingredient. A ¼ lb (120 g) of any ham or sausage is enough for 6 or 8 people if the hors d'oeuvre is a mixed one.

The hors d'oeuvre can be served in a special hors d'oeuvre dish with divisions or in small, pretty bowls and dishes arranged on a tray, or a plate can be arranged for each person, in which case, be careful to keep the different things well separated, so that the mayonnaise from the Russian salad does not run over the sausage, and so on.

Traditional Separate Hors d'oeuvre

Where one dish is served, with one or two ingredients only.

Raw Smoked Ham

Served alone with very thin brown bread and butter, or with a few black olives, or excellent as a summer hors d'oeuvre with a small slice of melon, or with a ripe green fig. Often served like this in France, Italy and Spain.

Ham – 1 oz (30 g) per person

Celery Rémoulade

Very finely shredded or coarsely grated celery, the white part only, stirred into a good mayonnaise, to which cream has been added. Serve alone in individual dishes or with a few olives.

Serves 4
½ lb (240 g) celery
3 tbsp mayonnaise
* (see Chapter 12)*
2 tbsp cream

Avocado

Serve half per person, stoned, sprinkled with salt and lemon juice and chilled. Can be served plain, or with French dressing, or filled with cooked shrimps or prawns or potted shrimps.

½ avocado per person
Salt
Lemon juice

Serves 4
¾ lb (360 g) mushrooms
1 tbsp white wine
1 clove garlic
1 bay leaf
1 stick celery
1 tbsp oil
Juice of ½ lemon
Sprig of thyme
6 peppercorns
Salt

Prawns or shrimps
Mayonnaise (see Chapter 12)
Tomato purée
Lemon juice
Tomato ketchup (optional)

Champignons à la Grecque

Simmer all the ingredients together very gently for 15 minutes. Allow to cool with the lid on, then remove the thyme, bay leaf, and celery stalk, and serve cold in the liquid in which they cooked.

Serve in individual ramekins with crusty French bread as an accompaniment.

This makes a deliciously refreshing and satisfying starter.

Prawn or Shrimp Cocktail

Mix mayonnaise with a little tomato purée, stirring until it is a pale pink, add a squeeze of lemon juice and some tomato ketchup, if liked. Stir in shelled prawns or shrimps.

A hotter and sharper sauce for these shellfish cocktails can be made by stirring into ¼ pint (150 ml) mayonnaise (which should be home-made) 1 tablespoon sherry, juice of ½ lemon, a drop or two of tabasco and ½ teaspoon French mustard. Beat well together, and stir the prawns, lobster or shrimps into it. Serve in glasses which you have lined with one or two crisp, pale lettuce leaves.

Pâtés, Terrines and Potted Shrimps

Any one of these makes an excellent and traditional hors d'oeuvre, served with plenty of hot toast.

Plate of Varied Sausages and Ham

One slice each of liver sausage, mortadella and salami – or any other kinds preferred, small thin slice of cooked ham and thin slice of raw smoked ham. Serve with thin brown bread and butter. This is a good hors d'oeuvre to serve before a main course of fish. Decorate with small gherkins or olives.

SAVOURIES

A savoury is a very small mouthful of something hot or cold, but usually hot, which comes at the end of a meal. It is designed to take away the sweet, cloying taste of the sweet course. It must be salted and either sharp or hot, i.e. curried or seasoned with cayenne pepper. It must be only very small as it will come at the end of a filling meal and, for the same reason, it must be attractive to tempt people. A savoury can, of course, be served instead of a sweet. Curiously, the savoury is an entirely English conception. Below are a few traditional ones.

Angels or Devils on Horseback

Trim the oysters. Remove the rind from the bacon and smooth each rasher with a knife to flatten it. Wrap the oyster in the bacon, and run a skewer through. Four or six can be threaded on one skewer. Grill slowly, turning frequently until the bacon is cooked through. Serve one roll for each person on a croûte of fried bread which neatly fits under the Angel. Place a small slice of lemon on top, or decorate with watercress. Devils are made in the same way using chicken livers instead of oysters.

For each person
1 oyster, or ¼ chicken liver
1 thin rasher bacon
1 croûte of fried bread, about 2×1 in (5×2½ cm)
Small, very thin slice of lemon, or bunch of watercress

Cheese Straws

Into the short pastry which should be very good (see Chapter 17) roll the grated cheese. Parmesan is best, but Cheddar will do. Roll out thinly. Cut into strips ¼ in (½ cm) wide and divide these into 3 in (7½ cm) lengths. Make a ring about 2 in (5 cm) diameter for each person. Bake in 400°F/200°C/Gas Mark 6 oven for 5-10 minutes. To serve, place a small bundle of straws through a ring and serve either lying flat on a dish or standing up.

Serves 4-6
½ lb (240 g) short pastry
¼ lb (120 g) grated cheese

Scotch Woodcock

Spread the fingers of toast with a little butter, and then, rather thickly with the pâté or paste you are using. Scramble the eggs till just creamy and set. Pile them on the fingers of toast. Sprinkle with cayenne pepper or chopped parsley and serve at once.

Serves 4
1 finger of toast for each person
A little butter
1 oz (30 g) of pâté de foie or pâté maison, or 1 oz (30 g) of anchovy butter and some fillets of anchovy, or 1 kipper fillet pounded to a paste with butter
2 eggs
Cayenne or chopped parsley

STOCKS AND SOUPS

STOCKS

Good soups are very important. They are the traditional beginning to a formal meal, hearteningly hot in winter, refreshingly cool in summer.

In informal cookery, soup is more important still, because it is the housewife's standby, ensuring that the meal is substantial enough (if she has doubts of this) or changing it, if necessary, from an all-cold meal to one with a hot beginning.

In poor countries, soup forms the main dish of the day for many people. The stock is made from the bones and trimmings of the meat, or chicken, which is often served on Sundays, and the soup is made filling and appetizing with many vegetables, which in this kind of potage are not puréed, or strained, but cut up and served in the broth. Eaten with plenty of bread and followed by some cheese, this kind of soup makes a nourishing and sustaining meal.

Meat, Poultry or Game Stock

Every bone you have in the house should be put in a large, heavy saucepan and boiled for at least an hour or better still, for two or three.

For very good and careful cooking, you should keep different kinds of stock separate: mutton and lamb stock for dishes made with these; beef stock for beef dishes; and veal or chicken stock, which are generally interchangeable, for dishes requiring white stock. On the whole, it may be taken that lamb or beef may be used interchangeably for meat or brown stock, and chicken or veal for white stock, except for special dishes and certain soups where the kind of meat stock necessary is stated, because any other would alter and spoil the flavour.

In summer a cold soup makes a delicious start to a meal or, followed by a salad or by bread and cheese, is enough for luncheon or supper. Cold soups may be clear, either liquid or jellied, or may be a thick purée, like the famous Vichysoisse.

If you want to make a special soup and have no stock ready, bouillon or stock cubes (beef, chicken, etc.) are excellent and can be made up in a few minutes. Any stock or soup made with meat bones or the carcase of a bird must be degreased. When possible, cool and then chill the liquid so that the fat can be lifted off the top as a solid, whole or in pieces.

Vegetable Stocks

These are the bases, alone or mixed with meat stocks, of many good soups. They can be made specially by boiling the vegetable you require in salted water for a little longer than if you were cooking it to serve, discarding the solids and saving the stock. Never keep a vegetable stock for more than 3 days even in a refrigerator. Old and coarse vegetables and outside leaves may be used for stocks, but should, of course, have been well cleaned first.

On the whole, however, all you need do is save the liquid you drain from vegetables before dishing them up. There will probably not be a large quantity if you stick to the quantities suggested on the boiling chart for vegetables given in Chapter 11, but it will be strong and well flavoured and can be thickened and diluted according to the recipe you are following.

Vegetable Purées

A purée simply consists of well-cooked vegetables (with or without the addition of the liquor in which they cooked, according to the consistency wanted) which are put through a sieve, food mill, blender or liquidizer. Any type of vegetable or fruit can be made into a purée. Meat is too fibrous to make a true purée in this way, and must be minced and pounded in a mortar instead.

The purée can be thickened with eggs, a roux, cornflour, or a sauce base; or thinned with water, wine or stock or milk, according to the recipe. Plain vegetable purées, apart from being the basis of many excellent soups, form an important part of a baby's diet and also of various invalid diets.

Fish Stocks

Fish stock or Court Bouillon is the basis of many good fish soups, bisques, the famous bouillabaisse of Marseilles, soups made with shellfish, and so on. Ask for some bones and heads when buying your fish. Put about 1 pint (600 ml) of cold water to ½ lb (240 g), add a bouquet of herbs (parsley, thyme, fennel, basil, marjoram, bay leaf – any or all of these) and 1 onion. Bring to the boil and simmer for 30 to 40 minutes. Strain. A fish stock made like this usually makes a slightly milky-looking jelly when chilled. It may be kept in the refrigerator for a few hours till wanted.

SOUPS

Soups may be divided as follows:
1 Clear soups, or consommés
2 Thick soups based on purées
3 Thick cream soups based on roux
4 Broths
5 Fish soups

Clear Soups or Consommés

For a proper clear soup, or consommé, you need a special brown stock, which you then clarify and strengthen at the same time. The stock you may make from bones and trimmings will not really do for this. You need what is called first stock, brown or white, according to whether it is made from beef, or veal and chicken. It is then strengthened and cleared with fresh beef, egg shell, and egg white. However, though described here for those who want to make them, the proper preparation of First Brown and White Stocks is elaborate and time-consuming and is only necessary in home cooking on very special occasions. For most occasions, stock poured off meat bones or chicken carcase after prolonged boiling, cooled and chilled, and then fat removed, is an excellent basis for all soups.

First Brown Stock (Basic Recipe)

2 lb (1 kg) shin of beef
Dripping
4 pt (2 l) cold water
½ tsp salt
12 peppercorns
2 bay leaves
1 medium-sized carrot
1 medium-sized onion

Wipe the meat and remove all skin and fat. Cut the lean into small pieces and scrape the bones. Heat a little dripping and fry the pieces of meat and the bones quickly until all are a good brown colour. This improves the flavour and the colour of the stock. Strain off any surplus fat, as grease must be avoided. Add cold water and leave to soak for ½ hour. Bring slowly to boiling point, add the salt and remove any scum. Add the peppercorns and bay leaves, and simmer for 4 hours; then add the prepared vegetables. Simmer the stock for 4 hours more and then strain into a bowl and leave standing overnight to allow time for any fat to solidify. Remove all traces of fat the following day.

First White Stock (Basic Recipe)

Use knuckle of veal, chicken carcase, skin, etc., instead of beef. Omit the frying of the meat and bones; otherwise follow the method given above.

Clarifying (Basic Recipe)

You now clarify and strengthen your prepared first stock, whether brown or white, as follows.

Shred the beef finely and soak it in ¼ pint (150 ml) cold water to extract the protein for 1 hour. Then put it with all the ingredients, including unbeaten egg white and crushed shell, into a large, deep pan. Whisk steadily over gentle heat until boiling point is almost reached. Remove the whisk and allow the stock to boil up two or three times. Leave the covered pan in a warm place and allow the stock to infuse for about 15 minutes. Strain the stock through a dry cloth twice. (The egg shell and partially coagulated egg white act as a filter.) Reheat the strained stock, but do not allow it to boil, as this makes it cloudy. Season, and serve very hot, or chill 2 or 3 hours in refrigerator or cold larder and serve cold and jellied.

2-3 oz (60-90 g) lean stewing beef
2 pt (1 l) first stock
1 egg white and shell (crushed)
1 small onion
2 tsp salt
6 white peppercorns
1 piece celery
1 large carrot

Beetroot Soup (Iced)

Cook 2 large beetroots in the oven (like potatoes baked in their jackets) for 2 hours. Peel and then grate them into the aspic jelly, add a teaspoon of vinegar or lemon juice, season highly, and simmer very gently for 10 minutes. Pour through a fine strainer and put into a bowl to set. This soup should be served piled in spoonfuls in shallow bowls. It is a beautiful bright red. Sprinkle the jelly with chopped parsley or chives.

The grated beetroot can be reheated and served at another meal. An ounce (30 g) of butter and some black pepper should then be stirred into it.

Serves 4
2 large beetroots
1 pt (600 ml) aspic jelly (made up according to directions on pkt)
1 tsp vinegar or lemon juice
Salt and pepper
Chopped parsley or chives

Chicken Consommé

Roast a boiling fowl (or 6 defrosted chicken joints) in a hot oven for 10 minutes, to seal and concentrate the flavour.

Then boil gently 1½ to 2 hours in 4 pints (2 l) of unclarified first white stock, as above.

Remove chicken and serve hot or cold as main course. Leave stock overnight and next day clarify as explained above.

Serves 6-8
1 boiling fowl
4 pt (2 l) first white stock

Chicken and Tomato Consommé (Iced)

Cook tomato juice gently for 5 minutes with the garlic, sugar, basil and seasoning.

Strain well and add the stock and white wine. Heat again, and then put in refrigerator to chill.

Serves 6-8
1 pt (600 ml) fresh or canned tomato juice
1 clove garlic
1 dessertsp sugar
Sprig of basil
Salt and pepper
1 pt (600 ml) chicken stock
¼ pt (150 ml) white wine

Julienne Soup

Serves 6-8
1 carrot
1 small turnip
1 stick white celery
1 leek
1 onion
2 oz (60 g) butter
2 pt (1 l) clarified stock
1 tsp sugar
Salt to taste
Heart of small lettuce
Sprig of tarragon

Shred the carrot, turnip, celery, leek and onion. Melt the butter in a saucepan, put in the vegetables, and fry them until they are just lightly browned. Bring the clarified stock to the boil and pour it on the vegetables, stirring in the sugar and salt to taste, if the stock is not already seasoned. Cook gently, skimming at intervals. When the vegetables are tender, after about 15 minutes, add the heart of the lettuce and the tarragon, both very finely shredded. Boil gently for 5 minutes and serve.

When lettuce is not available, the soup may be served without it, or a few shreds of the heart of a cabbage may be fried with the other vegetables.

Thick Soups Based on Purées

These are vegetable soups, made with a purée (see page 31), which is then diluted with milk, stock, or water. The purée sometimes requires binding by adding it to a roux.

Artichoke Soup

Serves 8
2 lb (1 kg) Jerusalem artichokes
1 dessertsp lemon juice
2 oz (60 g) butter or margarine
1 medium-sized onion
Salt and pepper
1 ½ pt (900 ml) white stock
1 pt (600 ml) milk
Small squares of toast
Parmesan cheese

Put the lemon juice into a basin of cold water. Wash the artichokes, peel and put at once in the acid water in order to keep them white. Melt the butter in a saucepan and, as soon as it is hot, drain the artichokes well and add them to the butter with the peeled and sliced onion. Sprinkle with salt and pepper and cook gently for 5 minutes; they must not brown at all.

Add the stock gradually. (This need not be first stock, an ordinary white bone stock will do, or this soup may be made with water only, as the artichokes have a very definite flavour.) Simmer gently until the vegetables are quite soft. Do not drain. Put through a blender, return to the saucepan, and add the milk. Season well. Bring just to boiling point and serve very hot with small squares of toast and finely grated Parmesan cheese.

Butter Bean or Haricot Bean Soup

Serves 8-10
1 lb (½ kg) dried haricot beans
1 onion
6 cloves
1 carrot
2 rashers fat bacon or ham bone
Milk, as required
Salt and pepper
½ oz (15 g) butter
Croûtons
1 tsp chopped parsley

Soak the dried haricot beans in cold water overnight, then boil them in 4 pints (2 l) of water, together with the onion studded with cloves. Add the carrot and the rashers of bacon or a ham bone. When tender (2-3 hours) remove the onion, carrot and the ham bone or bacon and put the beans and the liquid through a blender. Dilute with milk if too thick. Season to taste with salt and pepper. Add a nut of butter at the last moment, and garnish with croûtons and chopped parsley.

Carrot Soup

Serves 8

1 lb (½ kg) carrots
1½ oz (45 g) butter
1 onion
1½ pt (900 ml) stock or water
Salt and pepper
Pinch of sugar
3 oz (90 g) rice
1 pt (600 ml) milk
Croûtons
1 tbsp chopped parsley

Slice the carrots and cook them gently in 1 oz (30 g) of the butter, together with the sliced onion, for 2 to 3 minutes. Add the stock or water and season with salt, pepper and a pinch of sugar. Now add the raw rice. Cook gently until tender. Sieve without draining, and dilute the purée with the milk. Check the seasoning. Stir in the rest of the butter at the last moment. Garnish with croûtons and chopped parsley.

The sieved rice thickens and binds the purée.

Chestnut Soup

Serves 6-8

1 lb (½ kg) chestnuts
1 onion
2 cloves
2 pt (1 l) white or bone stock
1½ oz (45 g) butter
1½ oz (45 g) flour
Salt and pepper

Prick chestnuts well and roast at 400°F/200°C/Gas Mark 6 until shells crack. Remove shells and inner skin and pound chestnuts lightly. Put into pan with the onion, cloves, and flavoured stock, and simmer until tender for about 1½ hours. Put through a blender. Make a roux with the butter and flour and stir the liquid into it. Bring to the boil. Check seasoning before serving.

Crécy Soup

Serves 6-8

4 large carrots
2 onions
2 sticks celery
1 turnip
1 oz (30 g) butter
2 pt (1 l) second stock
¼ lb (120 g) rice
1 oz (30 g) ham or a ham bone
12 peppercorns
Seasoning

Prepare and slice the vegetables, and sauté for 10 minutes with the butter. Add stock, rice, ham, and peppercorns, and simmer for 1½ to 2 hours. Put through a blender without draining, but removing peppercorns. Add seasoning, reheat, and serve.

Crème Vichyssoise

Serves 8

4 leeks
2 small onions
1 oz (30 g) butter
3 large potatoes
2 pt (1 l) chicken consommé
1 tsp salt
1 pt (600 ml) milk
Salt and pepper
½ pt (300 ml) whipped cream
Chopped chives

Slice whites of leeks and onions, and fry in butter without allowing them to brown at all. Peel and slice the potatoes, then add them to the other vegetables, with the chicken consommé and salt. Boil for 30 to 35 minutes. Put the mixture through a blender or sieve, return it to the heat, and add the milk. Season and bring to the boil. Chill and fold in the whipped cream. Leave in refrigerator at least 2 hours and serve sprinkled with chopped chives.

Lentil Soup (White)

Serves 8
½ lb (240 g) lentils
1 ham bone or rasher fatty bacon
1 blade mace
6 peppercorns
Sprig of parsley
1 stick celery
1 onion, sliced
1½ pt (900 ml) water
1½ oz (45 g) flour
1½ oz (45 g) butter
1 pt (600 ml) milk
A little cream
½ tsp sugar
Salt and pepper

Put the lentils, ham bone or bacon, flavourings and vegetables in the water to cook until tender (2-2½ hours); remove ham bone or bacon and blend without draining. Make a roux with the flour and butter. Stir in milk and then add purée of vegetables and bring to the boil. Cool slightly, add the cream and sugar, reheat, without allowing to boil, season and serve.

This is a warming starter for a winter's day, or can be served with crusty French bread, perhaps spread with a flavoured butter (see Chapter 10), as a filling snack.

Pea Soup (Dried Peas)

Serves 8-10
1 lb (½ kg) dried peas
1 bay leaf
Sprig of thyme
Mint
1 onion
1 carrot
1 rasher bacon
1 leek
1 pt (600 ml) hot milk
1 oz (30 g) butter
Croûtons

Soak the dried peas in cold water overnight. Place the soaked peas in a saucepan with 2 pints (1 l) of water and the bay leaf, thyme and some mint, chopped onion, sliced carrot, finely chopped rasher of bacon and a leek. Bring to the boil and cook until tender (about 2 hours). Blend peas and other vegetables, and return to the liquor and add the hot milk to the purée. Stir in butter just before serving, and garnish with croûtons and some more chopped mint.

Pea Soup (Fresh Peas)

Serves 4
1 lb (½ kg) peas, shelled
1 pt (600 ml) hot milk
1 oz (30 g) butter
Croûtons
Fresh mint
Parsley

Cook the shelled fresh peas (or frozen peas) until tender. Put through a blender without draining, then add the hot milk. Add 1 oz (30 g) of butter when serving and top with croûtons and chopped fresh mint and parsley.

Potato and Watercress Soup

Serves 6-8
2 lb (1 kg) potatoes
2 large onions
½ pt (300 ml) milk
Salt and pepper
Large bunch of watercress
2 tbsp double cream

Boil the peeled potatoes and onions in 2 pints (1 l) of water. When soft (30 minutes), put through a blender with the water in which they cooked. Add the milk and bring to the boil. Season highly and stir in the watercress, washed and finely chopped – all except the pieces of root and very hard stalk, and then add the cream. Serve at once. The watercress gives a delicious tang to the soup. Dilute with a little more milk if too thick.

Potato Soup

Cook the finely shredded whites of the leeks in the butter for a minute. Add the peeled and quartered potatoes. Cover with 2 pints (1 l) of water. Season and cook until tender. When the vegetables are cooked, mash and sieve them without draining. Return them to the liquid and add the hot milk. Add a good piece of butter just before serving and top with grated cheese and croûtons.

This soup can be varied with the following additions: half the quantity of turnip purée; a few small sprouts, cooked separately and added at the last minute; shredded sorrel leaves and a sprig of chervil; celeriac purée and diced carrots and celery.

Serves 6-8
2 leeks
1 oz (30 g) butter
1 lb (½ kg) peeled potatoes
Salt and pepper
½ pt (300 ml) hot milk
Extra butter
2 oz (60 g) grated cheese
Croûtons

Thick Soups Based on a Roux

If a thick soup is not based on a purée of vegetables, it must be thickened with flour. This is generally done by making what is called a roux. For this you melt butter in a heavy saucepan, add flour, and stir over gentle heat until it is a smooth paste, then very gradually stir in the liquid from which the soup is made, being careful to keep the mixture smooth.

Asparagus Soup

Wash and prepare asparagus, reserving tips (cooked separately) for garnish. Cut remainder into 1 inch (2½ cm) lengths. Cook in the boiling stock or water with peas or spinach, sugar and seasoning until tender. Put through a blender without draining. Make a roux with the butter and flour, add purée and bring to the boil, stirring in the milk. To serve, add the asparagus tips, a few to each bowl, and stir in cream.

Serves 6
20 asparagus heads
1 ½ pt (900 ml) white stock or water
½ lb (240 g) green peas or spinach
1 tsp sugar
Seasoning
1 oz (30 g) butter
1 oz (30 g) flour
½ pt (300 ml) milk
3 tbsp double cream

Barley Cream Soup

Blanch the barley for a minute in boiling water, drain and simmer in the stock for 2 hours. Pass through a blender, add the milk and cream, seasoning and butter. Stir well. Reheat and serve sprinkled with chopped parsley.

Serves 6-8
3 oz (90 g) pearl barley
2 pt (1 l) white stock
¼ pt (150 ml) milk
¼ pt (150 ml) cream, or ½ pt (300 ml) milk, if no cream available
Seasoning
1 oz (30 g) butter
Chopped parsley

Serves 6-8
1 or 2 heads of celery
1½ pt (900 ml) white stock or
*   water*
Bouquet garni
1½ oz (45 g) butter
1½ oz (45 g) flour
1 pt (600 ml) milk
Salt and pepper
Croûtons

Celery Soup

Wash celery thoroughly, and cut into pieces. Cook in stock or water with bouquet garni until tender – about 40 minutes. Remove bouquet garni and put through a blender without draining. Then rub lightly through a sieve so that the celery strings are kept back. Make a roux with the butter and flour, add purée and milk gradually. Stir until boiling and season. Serve with croûtons of toast.

Serves 6
2 large cucumbers (ridge or
*   hothouse)*
2½ oz (75 g) butter
Salt and pepper
Pinch of sugar
2 oz (60 g) flour
1½ pt (900 ml) white stock
¼ pt (150 ml) cream
2 egg yolks
Croûtons
Chopped chives

Cucumber Soup

Peel the cucumbers, remove seeds, cut into 2 inch (5 cm) pieces and boil for 10 minutes in salted water. Strain and rinse in cold water to preserve colour. Sweat in a pan with ½ oz (15 g) of butter, salt and pepper, and a pinch of sugar for about 20 to 30 minutes. Make a roux with the rest of the butter and the flour, add stock and boil for 5 minutes. Add cucumber pushed through a fine sieve, stir in cream and beaten egg yolks and reheat but do not allow to boil. Serve with croûtons of toast, not fried bread, and sprinkle with chopped chives.

Serves 6
½ lb (240 g) mushrooms
1 onion
1 oz (30 g) butter
1½ oz (45 g) flour
1½ pt (900 ml) boiling milk
Salt and pepper
Croûtons
Cream

Mushroom Soup

Cook the finely sliced mushrooms and chopped onion gently in the melted butter in the bottom of a deep saucepan for 3 minutes or until tender, without allowing them to become coloured. Sprinkle in the flour, stir well, and simmer for 3 minutes over a very low heat. Gradually add the boiling milk and stir and simmer for 5 minutes. Season well.

Serve very hot with fried croûtons and a teaspoon of cream put on top of each bowl as you carry it to table.

Serves 6-8
1 lb (½ kg) onions
1½ oz (45 g) dripping or
*   margarine*
Salt and pepper
2 pt (1 l) stock
1½ oz (45 g) flour mixed with
*   cold milk*
Croûtons
Grated cheese

Onion Soup (1)

Peel and slice onions and toss in melted dripping but do not brown. Add salt and pepper. Heat stock and add onions. Bring to the boil, simmer gently for 1 to 1½ hours. Add blended flour, reboil and serve very hot with croûtons of fried bread and grated cheese.

Onion Soup (2)

Cut onions into eighths vertically. Put in saucepan with the cloves and add stock. Bring to the boil and simmer for 2 hours. Pour into bowl and make a roux with 2 oz (60 g) of butter and the flour in the saucepan in which they cooked. Gradually stir into it the onions and stock and bring to the boil. Stir in the milk till all is boiling again. Add the rest of the butter and serve very hot with fried croûtons and grated cheese.

Serves 6-8
1 lb (½ kg) onions
2 or 3 cloves
1½ pt (900 ml) stock
3 oz (90 g) butter
1½ oz (45 g) flour
½ pt (300 ml) milk
Croûtons
Grated cheese

Spinach Soup

Frozen spinach is excellent for this soup. Defrost and then cook gently in the melted butter over a low heat for 2 minutes. Sprinkle in the uncooked rice and cover with ½ pt (300 ml) of water. Boil for 25 minutes, then put rice and spinach through a blender with the liquor the spinach has made. Stir in the hot milk, season and serve very hot, garnished with croûtons.

A little cream, added at the last moment to each helping, and allowed to float, is an improvement.

Serves 4-6
1 large pkt frozen spinach, or 1 lb (½ kg) cleaned spinach
1 oz (30 g) butter
1 oz (30 g) rice
½ pt (300 ml) hot milk
Salt and pepper
Croûtons

Tomato Bisque

Quarter the tomatoes, put them in a saucepan with the salt, pepper and ½ pint (300 ml) of cold water. Cover and cook over gentle heat until they are a soft pulp. Rub them through a fine sieve. Melt the butter in the saucepan, add the flour and stir over gentle heat until it is a smooth paste, then very gradually stir in the milk, being careful to keep the mixture smooth. Slowly add the tomato purée and stir until it just comes to the point of boiling. Do not let it actually boil. Stir in the cream, and serve each helping with a sprinkling of chopped parsley and mint, and fried croûtons.

Serves 6-8
1½ lb (¾ kg) tomatoes, skinned
1 tsp salt
Good sprinkling of pepper
1 oz (30 g) butter
1 oz (30 g) flour
1½ pt (900 ml) milk
¼ pt (150 ml) cream
Chopped parsley and mint
Croûtons

Tomato Soup

Put tomatoes, stock, onion and bouquet garni into a pan. Simmer till tender for ¾ to 1 hour, then rub through a fine sieve. Make a white roux with the butter and the flour, add the purée gradually and stir until it comes to the boil. Simmer gently for 2 or 3 minutes. Stir in the thin cream or top of the milk and add a small piece of butter just before serving. Serve with chopped parsley and croûtons of fried bread or, simply, sprigs of mint.

Serves 4-6
1 lb (½ kg) tinned or fresh tomatoes
1 pt (600 ml) white stock
1 small onion
Bouquet garni
1½ oz (45 g) butter
1½ oz (45 g) flour
¼ pt (150 ml) thin cream or top of milk
Extra butter
Chopped parsley and croûtons or sprigs of mint

Vegetable Soup (White)

Serves 5-6
1 carrot
1 small turnip
1 stick celery
1 large onion
½ oz (15 g) hot dripping
1½ pt (900 ml) white stock or water
¼ lb (120 g) shelled peas or broad beans
1 bay leaf
2 oz (60 g) flour
½ pt (300 ml) milk
Salt and pepper

Prepare the carrot, turnip and celery, cut into 1 inch (2½ cm) long blocks then into strips the thickness of a match. Chop onion finely, sweat with the vegetable strips for 5 minutes in the hot dripping. Add stock or water, peas or broad beans and bay leaf, then simmer until tender for about 1 hour. Mix flour and milk smoothly, add to soup and stir until boiling. Simmer for 5 minutes, season, and serve.

Serve a bowl of crunchy croûtons of fried bread separately, or sprinkle each helping with grated Parmesan cheese.

Broths

These are generally made from the liquor from meat and vegetables which have been boiled together. In most cases, pieces of meat or poultry and vegetables are served in the soup, which is not strained or clarified.

Beetroot Bortsch

Serves 8
Duck carcase
½ lb (240 g) stewing beef
1 onion
1 small cabbage or 3 sprouts
4 mushrooms
A little fat
2 pt (1 l) good stock (first or good bone stock)
1 beetroot, peeled and shredded
Parsley, marjoram, bay leaf and clove
Salt and pepper
3 tsp cornflour
4 tbsp sour cream

Bortsch comes from Russia and this is a traditional recipe. It is very delicious and quite unlike any other soup. It should be made with duck, as nothing else gives the same flavour, but you can make the following recipe with a different bird and it will still be delicious.

Lightly fry the beef with the shredded vegetables in a little fat until they are a nice light colour. Stir in the stock and shredded raw beetroot. Add the duck carcase and herbs, cover and simmer gently for 2 hours. Take the meat, carcase and herbs out of the soup and dice finely the lean of the beef and any bits of duck. Season the liquor with salt and pepper. Stir in cornflour blended to a cream with a little water. Bring to the boil and simmer for 5 minutes. Stir in the sour cream. (This may be bought sour cream, or thin cream into which you have stirred a spoonful of lemon juice to sour it. In either case it should be well whipped up before adding, or you may use yoghourt.) Add the small pieces of beef to the soup just before serving.

The soup should be a beautiful lilac-fuschia colour. It may also be chilled and served iced, after adding the sour cream. In this case omit the pieces of meat.

Chicken or Veal Broth

Break up carcase and put in large saucepan with all skin and trimmings. Add vegetables, bouquet garni and seasoning. Cover with water or with the liquor in which chicken was boiled or any white stock you have. Simmer for 2 hours. Stir in the uncooked rice. Cook 30 minutes more. Strain and serve very hot. The rice will have thickened the soup a little. Serve this with chopped parsley and squares of toast.

For Veal Broth, use a knuckle of veal or about 2 lb (1 kg) veal bones instead of chicken.

Serves 6-8
Carcase of roasted or boiled chicken
1 onion
1 stick celery
1 carrot
Bouquet garni
Seasoning
2 oz (60 g) rice
Chopped parsley
Squares of toast

Kidney Soup

Remove all fat from kidney, wash, dry and cut into slices. Fry quickly in hot butter or margarine together with the onion. Drain and add to stock with vegetables and bouquet garni. Simmer for 2 hours, then strain and cut the kidney into dice. Return stock to pan, thicken with cornflour and boil for a few minutes. Add kidney, seasoning and sherry, and serve very hot with croûtons of toast.

Serves 6
½ lb (240 g) ox kidney
1 oz (30 g) butter or margarine
1 small onion
2 pt (1 l) bone or brown stock
1 small carrot
½ turnip
Bouquet garni
1 oz (30 g) cornflour
Seasoning
¼ pt (150 ml) sherry (if desired)
Croûtons

Minestrone

Melt the fat in a large saucepan, add the diced bacon and onion and simmer for 5 minutes. Add 2 pints (1 l) of water, and bring to the boil. Add the finely diced carrot, turnip, potato and celery stalks. After 10 minutes, add the shredded cabbage and the skinned, seeded, drained and chopped tomatoes. Cook for 25 minutes, then add the diced French beans or fresh peas and rice or vermicelli. Allow to simmer gently for 45 minutes. Skim carefully from time to time. Pound a clove of garlic with salt, a pinch of basil or marjoram, and a pinch of chopped parsley. Add this to the soup, boil for 5 minutes, then serve very hot, with grated cheese.

Serves 6-8
2 oz (60 g) margarine or dripping
2 oz (60 g) bacon
1 large onion
1 carrot
1 turnip
1 potato
2 celery stalks
½ small cabbage
4 large tomatoes
2 oz (60 g) French beans or fresh peas
2 oz (60 g) rice or vermicelli
1 clove garlic
Salt
Basil or marjoram
Parsley
3 oz (90 g) grated cheese

Mutton or Scotch Broth

Serves 6-8
*½ lb (240 g) scrag end of mutton
   or mutton bones and trimmings
1 onion
1 carrot
1 leek
1 stick celery
Sprig of thyme
Salt and pepper*

Put the meat, vegetables and thyme into a large saucepan and cover with water. Simmer 2 to 3 hours. Strain, degrease and season. Put back the lean meat, finely cut, and the onion, carrot and leek, chopped. Season and serve very hot.

For Scotch Broth, cook as above but add 2 oz (60 g) pearl barley with the meat. Ten minutes before serving, also add 2 large carrots, coarsely grated. Lift out the meat, the whole vegetables and thyme, but carefully leave the barley and grated carrot. The lean meat may be chopped and put back as before.

Onion Soup (Brown)

Serves 6-8
*1½ lb (¾ kg) onions
2 oz (60 g) butter
2 pt (1 l) brown stock or vegetable
   stock from stockpot – need not
   be first stock
1 small slice ham or bacon,
   chopped
Salt and pepper
1 slice of bread per person
¼ lb (120 g) grated cheese*

This is the superb onion soup traditional in France. The bread and cheese make the soup a full meal in itself and the final grilling and serving only takes 5 minutes, providing you have the cheese grated and the bread cut and toasted.

Peel and chop the onions finely. Melt the butter in a saucepan, add the onions and gently fry until well browned, but not crisp. Cover and cook very gently for ½ hour. Add the stock, ham, and a good sprinkling of salt and pepper. Cover and simmer for an hour. Serve in deep bowls, filling each bowl with soup, but not too full. On top of the soup, place a slice of white bread ¼ inch (½ cm) thick with crust left on, and toasted only on the side put in the soup. Cover the upper side thickly with grated cheese, stand the bowl under a hot grill till the cheese is stringy and sizzling (2 minutes) and keep in warming drawer or cool oven till all are ready.

Orange and Tomato Soup

Serves 6-8
*6 oranges
1 pt (600 ml) tin tomato juice, or
   1 lb (½ kg) tomatoes
2 tsp sugar
Salt and pepper
Juice of ½ lemon
¼ pt (150 ml) cooking sherry
1 tbsp brandy
Mint
Croûtons*

This is an unusual and very stimulating soup. Very good if the main course is rather rich and heavy. If using fresh tomatoes, skin them, stew in 1 pint (600 ml) of water until soft, then pass through a fine sieve.

Squeeze all the juice from the oranges and put it in a saucepan with the tomato juice or purée. Stir in sugar, salt and pepper and lemon juice. Bring to the boil and add the sherry and brandy. Boil, stirring, for 1 minute. Serve at once with freshly chopped mint sprinkled on top and fried croûtons.

Oxtail Soup

Serves 8-10

½ oxtail
2 carrots
1 large onion
3 cloves
Bouquet garni
2 oz (60 g) margarine
3 oz (90 g) flour
1 tsp tomato purée
1 tsp redcurrant jelly
2 tbsp sherry
Salt and pepper

Put the oxtail, cut by your butcher into joints, into a large saucepan with the carrots, onion stuck with the cloves, bouquet garni and 4 pints (2 l) water. Bring to the boil, skim, and simmer 2 hours. Remove the oxtail, take off all the meat and cut into dice. Remove vegetables and herbs. It is important to allow the liquid to stand at this point so that all grease can be removed. Make a roux with the margarine and flour and add the oxtail stock, stirring till it boils. Then simmer 2 or 3 minutes and stir in tomato purée, redcurrant jelly and sherry, season well and add diced meat. Serve very hot.

Potage du Jour

Serves 6-8

1 lb (½ kg) potatoes – small ones
   cooked whole are best
1 lb (½ kg) carrots, halved
2 small turnips, cut in pieces
4 small onions, cut in halves
½ lb (240 g) piece of boiling bacon
Bouquet garni
Salt and pepper
Any of the following: ½ lb (240 g)
   shelled peas, broad beans,
   prepared French beans, diced
   marrow or cucumber
½ lb (240 g) cabbage

This is a very simple everyday soup which is varied according to what vegetables are in season.

Put root vegetables, onions and bacon in heavy saucepan with the bouquet garni and seasoning. Cover with 2 pints (1 l) of water, bring to the boil and simmer gently for 30 minutes. Add your choice of vegetables and simmer another 20 minutes. Add finely chopped cabbage and simmer 10 minutes more. Season again. Lift out bacon and divide so that there is a piece for each plate. Remove bouquet garni. Ladle out vegetables and soup so that each plateful contains some of every kind. Serve with crusty French bread.

Fish Soups

These are made on the same principle as meat soups, using fish in place of poultry or meat and fish stock instead of beef or chicken stock.

Fish Soup

Serves 4-6

2 lb (1 kg) any white fish
1 cod's head
1 onion
1 leek
1 stick celery
¼ pt (150 ml) white wine
3 tbsp tomato purée
2 tbsp flour
½ pt (300 ml) milk
Sprig of parsley
A little fennel
1 clove garlic
Lemon peel

Put the fish and vegetables into a pan and cover with water. When the fish is cooked, remove it carefully, take out any bones, and cut the flesh into quite large pieces. Cook the rest of the stock for 20 minutes more, then strain it through a sieve and return to the pan. Add the white wine and tomato purée and thicken with the flour mixed into the milk. Pour the soup on this, stirring all the time and simmer for 3 minutes. Then add the pieces of cooked fish, and a large handful of chopped parsley, the chopped fennel and garlic, and some finely grated lemon peel. (The fennel and garlic can be omitted.)

This is almost a fish stew and makes a very good luncheon or supper dish.

Lobster Bisque

Serves 4-6

1 small lobster or half a large one
1 oz (30 g) butter
1 bay leaf
Sprig of parsley
Seasoning
1 ½ oz (45 g) cornflour
1 ½ pt (900 ml) fish stock
¼ pt (150 ml) cream
Lemon juice

Remove lobster from shell and keep claw pieces for garnish. Wash and pound the shell with the butter and put into a saucepan with the bay leaf, parsley, seasoning and cornflour. Cook very gently without allowing it to colour, for 10 minutes. Add stock and roughly chopped lobster and simmer gently for 40 minutes. Pass through a fine sieve and then strain again through muslin to make sure the gritty shell pieces are cleared. Add cream and garnish with diced claws. Finally, add some lemon juice. Do not allow to boil again.

Mussel Soup

Serves 4

2 pt (1 l) mussels
1 stick celery
1 small onion
2 oz (60 g) butter
2 tbsp flour
¼ pt (150 ml) milk
1 clove garlic
Salt
¼ pt (150 ml) white wine
Sprig of parsley

Cook the mussels in water with the chopped celery and onion, and, when they have opened, take them out of their shells and keep them aside. Strain the liquid in which they have cooked through muslin. Make a roux with the butter and flour. Stir in the milk and boil for 3 minutes. Gently add the stock and clove of garlic, crushed with salt, and the wine. Simmer for 5 minutes, stirring continually. Add the mussels and the parsley and serve at once.

PÂTÉS AND TERRINES

Home-made pâtés and terrines make a good start to a dinner and an excellent main dish for lunch or supper. They take a little time to make but they always keep well in a cool place and improve in flavour and consistency, so they can be made at a convenient time. Livers can be saved from game and poultry or bought specially from large stores. Old birds, hares, rabbits, etc., can be used up in this way, or meat left over from a game casserole or a boiled fowl. Pigeons, which are generally cheap and plentiful, make excellent pâtés.

PÂTÉS

Liver Pâté (1)

Serves 4
½ lb (240 g) chicken livers, or duck, goose or game-bird liver, or a mixture
½ pt (300 ml) water
A little sherry
Salt
Pinch of freshly ground black pepper
1 dessertsp brandy
3-4 rashers fatty bacon

Stew the livers very gently in ½ pint (300 ml) of water for 20 minutes, with some sherry and a little salt. Remove and drain, keeping the liquid. Grind the livers finely through a food mill (carefully removing all skin, gristle, etc., first). Then put the finely ground livers into a mortar (or a bowl) and pound them with a pestle or a wooden spoon until quite smooth and blended into a paste. Season with black pepper and add the brandy and a little of the liquid in which the livers cooked – just enough to leave them solid but a little wet. Line a small earthenware casserole with 2 or 3 rashers of rather fatty bacon and press the liver mixture well down into it. Cover with another piece of bacon. Put lid on. Stand in a tray of water and cook in oven at 300°F/150°C/Gas Mark 2, for 1½ hours. Remove and take off lid. Put a weight on, and leave overnight. To serve, strip off all the bacon, which will have flavoured and salted the pâté. Serve cold with very hot toast and butter.

Serves 4

½ lb (240 g) livers of poultry or
*   game*
3 ½ oz (105 g) butter
1 tbsp brandy
1 tbsp sherry
1 clove garlic
Salt and pepper
Sprig of thyme

Liver Pâté (2)

Melt 1 oz (30 g) butter in a frying pan. Put in the cleaned and trimmed livers and fry very gently for 6 or 7 minutes. Remove, and put in mortar (or bowl) and pound with pestle or wooden spoon till smooth. Add brandy and sherry to the butter in the frying pan and simmer for a moment. Then add garlic crushed with salt, black pepper and a pinch of chopped thyme. Stir for a moment, and pour into livers in the mortar. Stir and pound all together and work in another 1 oz (30 g) of unmelted butter. When all is evenly and smoothly mixed, put it in a small earthenware casserole which it should almost fill. It needs no further cooking. Melt another 1½ oz (45 g) butter in a small pan and pour over the top of the pâté which should be covered at least ⅛ in (¼ cm) thick and well sealed by this means. Cover tightly with foil and lid. It will keep in a refrigerator for a month or so and in a larder for a week. Do not eat for a day or two after making.

Serves 6

Livers from hare, rabbit or birds,
*   or ¼ lb (120 g) calves liver*
A little butter
1 lb (½ kg) cooked hare, rabbit,
*   any game meat, or a mixture*
2 rashers bacon
¼ lb (120 g) breadcrumbs
Salt and pepper
1 clove garlic
Thyme
1 bay leaf

Pâté Maison

Cook the liver by lightly frying in a little butter. Mince the meat and the raw bacon and the liver and mix well with the breadcrumbs. Season rather highly with salt and pepper. Rub around suitable earthenware casserole with a clove of garlic, and sprinkle with a very little finely chopped thyme. Press the meat down into the dish, and put a bay leaf on top. Cover, and stand in a tray of water and cook in oven at 300°F/150°C/Gas Mark 2 for about 2 hours. If a skewer stuck into the pâté comes out clean, it is ready. Put a weight on it when cold and leave overnight.

TERRINES

Serves 4

½ a rabbit
1 onion
2 oz (60 g) fatty bacon
Black pepper
Salt
Pinch of finely chopped fresh sage
Pinch of thyme
1 tbsp brandy
4 rashers bacon
1 bay leaf

Terrine of Rabbit

Cook the rabbit gently in water with the onion until tender. Remove all the flesh and mince finely. Mince the uncooked bacon and mix with the rabbit. Season with pepper but not much salt, because of the bacon. Stir in the sage and thyme. Add the brandy, mixing well. Put rashers of bacon over the bottom and up the sides of a small earthenware casserole. Press the mixture well on to these and down into the casserole. Fill up with the liquid in which the rabbit cooked. Stand in a tray of water and cook covered for 40 minutes at 300°F/150°C/Gas Mark 2. Remove and leave overnight with a weight on top. Turn out, strip off the bacon rashers and place the bay leaf on top, pressing in slightly, before serving.

Terrine of Grouse

Roast the grouse quickly for 10 minutes, then allow to cool, remove the breasts and set aside. Place the carcases in a saucepan. Fry the onion with the diced bacon and add this to the grouse, together with the stock and sherry. Bring to the boil and simmer very gently for 1 hour. Allow to cool, then remove the flesh from the grouse carcases and mince it. Strain off ½ pint (300 ml) of stock and add bay leaf, the mushrooms, and a sprig of thyme. Boil for 10 minutes, then dissolve gelatine and butter in it. Cut the breasts of the grouse into thin slices, coat them with the minced grouse, and sandwich 2 slices together. Place them in an earthenware casserole, pour over the boiling liquid, removing the thyme and bay leaf, but not the mushrooms. Stand in a tray of water and cook at 350°F/180°C/Gas Mark 4 for 45 minutes. Press with a weight overnight and serve the next day or the day after. Very good and rich.

Serves 4-6
2 mature grouse
1 small onion, finely sliced
3 oz (90 g) bacon
1 pt (600 ml) stock
¼ pt (150 ml) sherry
1 bay leaf
2 oz (60 g) mushrooms, finely chopped
Sprig of thyme
1 tbsp gelatine
1 oz (30 g) butter

Terrine of Pigeon

Roast the pigeons for about 10 minutes. Remove all flesh from bones. Reserve the breasts and chop the rest with the bacon. Arrange the chopped mixture in layers, alternating with small slices of the breasts in a fairly deep earthenware casserole or pie dish. Strain the giblet jelly sauce (given below) over it to fill up the dish.

To make the sauce, stew the giblets and livers for 40 minutes. Remove the livers and crush them with a wooden spoon and grind them through a fine food mill. Stir the brandy with the pounded livers, mixing well. Melt the gelatine in ½ pint (300 ml) of hot giblet stock and bring to the boil. Stir in the liver mixture. Add the seasoning, crushed garlic and thyme. Cook for 10 minutes.

Put the bay leaf on top, cover the dish, stand it in a pan containing water and cook in the oven at 350°F/180°C/Gas Mark 4 for 2 hours. Leave until cold. Better the next day. Will keep a week.

Serves 6
2 pigeons (with livers and giblets)
¼ lb (120 g) bacon
2 tbsp brandy
½ oz (15 g) gelatine
Salt and pepper
1 clove garlic
Sprig of thyme
1 bay leaf

FISH AND SHELLFISH

Fresh fish, known in the trade as 'wet fish' is not as easily available as it was even ten years ago. This is because fish freezes particularly well and frozen fish saves both the shopkeeper and the housewife a great deal of time and trouble. Very few supermarkets sell anything but frozen fish and specialist shops selling fish, poultry and game are few and far between. However, most fairly large towns have at least one shop which does sell fresh fish and most food markets include a fish stall.

Frozen fillets of cod or haddock or plaice, ready crumbed or covered in batter are excellent and fillets of any of the above, frozen in their natural state, can be skinned while half frozen (which makes skinning very easy) and rolled and stuffed, baked, made into fish pie or steamed and served with a shrimp sauce. Larger cuts, however, are not sold frozen and large fish such as turbot, halibut or hake must be bought fresh.

Of freshwater fish, only trout is available frozen. Good fish to buy are salmon, salmon trout or carp (which often has to be specially ordered) or pike.

Shellfish also freeze well but only prawns are readily available, though some supermarkets do sell crabs and sometimes frozen lobsters and crayfish tails.

A piece of fresh fish carefully cooked and seasoned and served with a good sauce makes a very fine dinner indeed. Though frequently served by our ancestors, fish is cooked rather more rarely today. When buying fresh fish, look out for the following signs:

1 The eyes of a fish should be bright and full. They should not be sunken or dull.
2 Flesh should be firm and should not show dimples or indentations.
3 Of course, there should be no trace of an unpleasant smell.
4 The gills of a fish should look red.
5 Fresh fillets which are ready on the slab, should look firm and full, not shrunken and watery, or yellow.

Quantities to buy per person

Large fish (cod, ling, hake, large fresh haddock, salmon, trout, bream, etc.) Allow ½ lb (240 g) per person, as there will be a certain amount of wastage of skin, bones and trimmings.

Fillets 1 large or 2 small per person. Dabs, flounders, slip soles, trout, small mullet, etc. – 1 to each person.

Smelts 3 to 6 according to size.

Whitebait ¼ to ½ pt (150-300 ml) per person.

Mackerel, Herrings ½ very large or 1 small. The small usually have the best flavour.

Scallops 2 or 3 per person.

Oysters 6; 12, if very fond of them, and if you are feeling very extravagant.

Dublin Bay Prawns or Scampi Allow about 6 to 8 per person.

Crabs A small one is generally enough for 2 and a large one for 3 or even 4.

Mussels About a dozen per person.

Prawns or Shrimps ¼ to ½ pt (150-300 ml) per person.

Lobster Small – 1 between 2 people. Large – 1 between 3 or 4 people.

Cooking and Serving

All fish really need a sauce of some kind as an accompaniment, generally something slightly sharp or, in some cases, smooth and creamy.

Not all fish are suitable for every method of cooking. For instance, most people would hesitate to poach mackerel but would fry or grill it in preference. On the whole, the kinds of fish which may be offered you at your fishmongers divide as follows.

For baking (that is, cooked in the oven in a covered ovenproof dish, with a little butter and milk; or wrapped in greaseproof paper, or foil; or cooked on a roasting tray) Sea bream, cod, haddock, halibut, mullet, salmon, salmon trout, trout, John Dory, sole, gurnet, brill, turbot.

For poaching and steaming Cod, haddock, herring, sea trout, river trout, herring roe, carp, halibut, hake flounders, salmon, John Dory, gurnet, eels, brill, skate, bream, turbot.

For grilling and frying Bloaters, kippers, flounders, river trout, salmon steaks, cod steaks, cod roe, John Dory, herring, smelts, skate, halibut steaks, sole, plaice, sprats, gudgeon, eels, mullet, sea bream, mackerel, whiting, whitebait, megrims.

For fishcakes, kedgeree, soufflés, fish pies, etc. Haddock, sea bream, turbot, hake, halibut, salmon, cod, brill, gurnet.

Sauces and Garnishes

Sauces for poached or steamed fish

Egg	Maître d'hôtel	Hollandaise	Lobster
Parsley	Shrimp	Melted butter	Tomato
Caper	Anchovy	Tartare	Mushroom
Mustard			

Garnishes

Poached white fish can be garnished with:
A sprinkling of parsley
Slices of lemon or cucumber arranged round dish
Chopped olives sprinkled over fish
Shrimps arranged round dish, a small heap for each person
Croûtons of fried bread or puff pastry arranged round the dish
A few small sautéed button mushrooms.
Salmon is generally garnished with thin slices of cucumber.

Sauces for fried, baked or grilled fish

Tartare	Green Butter	Anchovy Butter
Hollandaise	Mushroom	Horseradish

Garnishes

Fried, baked or grilled fish is generally garnished with:
Sprigs of parsley, fresh or fried crisp
Sprigs of watercress
Slices of quarters of lemon
A thin sprinkling of very finely chopped fennel.
Fried trout is sometimes garnished with fried almonds.

Recipes

Poached Fish

This is a basic recipe and applies to all large fish, i.e. cod, fresh haddock (large), bream, brill, halibut, turbot, salmon, sea trout, John Dory and gurnet, which you propose to cook. The important thing to remember is *never boil any fish* – poach it, that is, simmer it just below boiling point in salted water, if you must, but if possible in a Court Bouillon, or basic fish stock, which is the proper stock for all fish. You can, for certain dishes, poach your fish in a quarter water to three-quarters milk and make your sauce from this liquor when you have lifted the fish out. Any of the liquor in which the fish was poached may be put aside in the refrigerator for 24 hours and used as the bouillon in which to cook another fish or as the basis for fish soup, bisque, bouillabaisse, etc.

Court Bouillon

*Head and trimmings (fins, etc.)
  from the fish you are going to
  cook or fish bones (ask your
  fishmonger for some)
1 carrot, sliced*

*1 onion, sliced
1 leek
1 shallot
1 clove garlic
Bouquet of herbs*

*Salt and pepper
2 tbsp vinegar (wine vinegar is
  best)
1 ½ pt (900 ml) water*

Simply boil all together for 20-30 minutes and strain. If convenient, this can be made in advance and kept in a cool place till you are ready to cook the fish.

Grilled Bloaters

Serves 4

*4 bloaters
1 oz (30 g) butter or margarine*

Wash the fish thoroughly. If you do not like them very salty soak in hot water for an hour first. Brush with melted butter or margarine. Put under a hot grill and brown on one side for a minute, turn over and brown the other side. Serve very hot.

Baked and Stuffed Cod

Serves 4-6

*2 lb (1 kg) piece of tail end of cod
Salt and pepper
¼ lb (120 g) breadcrumbs
1 tbsp finely chopped onion
2 oz (60 g) margarine or butter
1 tbsp chopped parsley
Rind and juice of ½ lemon
1 egg
Extra butter or margarine*

Fresh haddock, hake, brill and bream are also good cooked in this way.

Remove bone from the fish with sharp pointed knife, open one side and rub in salt and pepper. Put the breadcrumbs and onion in a bowl and stir in melted margarine or butter, chopped parsley, lemon and a sprinkling of salt and pepper. Bind with the egg. Lay the fish out flat and spread the stuffing on one side of the fish and fold over. Sew up open side with needle and thread. Grease an ovenproof dish with butter or margarine, and lay the stuffed fish on this. Place in oven at 375°F/190°C/Gas Mark 5, bake 10 minutes uncovered. Then baste with juice and fat from pan and cover closely and continue to cook for 20 minutes.

Remove from oven and serve at once in the dish in which it cooked. If liked, a little grated cheese can be sprinkled over the cod 10 minutes before serving. Halves of tomatoes may be placed round it before covering, or it is excellent served with a separately made tomato sauce.

Cod Cutlets with Cheese

Serves 4

*4 cod cutlets
About 2 oz (60 g) butter or
  margarine
Salt and pepper
Breadcrumbs
3 oz (90 g) grated cheese*

Grease an ovenproof dish and lay the cod cutlets in it. Season with salt and pepper and sprinkle thickly with breadcrumbs and the grated cheese. Dot all over with butter or margarine. Bake in an oven for 25 minutes at 350°F/180°C/Gas Mark 4. Serve with creamed potato.

Serves 4-6

1½ lb (¾ kg) cod, cooked
1 oz (30 g) butter or margarine
1 tbsp flour
2 tbsp curry paste
2 tsp chutney
1 oz (30 g) sultanas
Pinch of cayenne
1 medium-sized onion
½ pt (300 ml) fish stock or white stock, or water
Salt and pepper
Lemon juice
½ tsp paprika

Curried Cod

Melt the butter or margarine in a deep saucepan, add the flour, curry paste, chutney, sultanas, cayenne and the onion, finely chopped. Cook for 3 minutes, then add the stock and stir until it boils. Add the salt and pepper and a dash of lemon juice and simmer gently for 15 minutes.

Flake the cod and add it to the curry sauce, removing all skin and bones. Simmer gently for 10 minutes, stirring often.

Just before serving, stir in the paprika. Serve in a shallow dish with plain boiled rice.

Serves 4

4 thick cod or hake cutlets
1 onion, thinly sliced
1 clove garlic, crushed
2 oz (60 g) butter or margarine
Salt and pepper
A little grated nutmeg
3 large parboiled potatoes, cut in quarters
1 bay leaf
Sprig of thyme
6 peppercorns
About 3 slices of lemon
Extra butter
¼ pt (150 ml) Hollandaise Sauce

Cod, Hake or Fresh Haddock Cutlets

Lightly fry the onion and garlic in the butter or margarine until the onion is just soft, but not crisp. Put the onion, and the butter it was cooked in into a well-buttered ovenproof dish. Put the fish cutlets on top of the onion, add seasoning and nutmeg, then put in the potatoes, bay leaf, thyme and peppercorns. Put lemon slices and dabs of butter on top of the fish. Cover with buttered foil. Bake in a fairly hot oven, 400°F/200°C/Gas Mark 6, until the fish is done (about 20 minutes). Baste several times during cooking.

When cooked, serve on a hot dish, surrounded by the potatoes and onion. Pour Hollandaise Sauce (see Chapter 10) over the fish.

Serves 4

4 thick cod steaks
Flour
Salt and pepper
A little butter
¾ pt (450 ml) milk
3 oz (90 g) grated cheese

Cod Steaks au Gratin

Dip the steaks in flour, seasoned with salt and pepper. Place in a greased baking dish. Pour the milk round, sprinkle lightly with salt and pepper, and cover with lid or buttered foil. Bake in a moderate oven, 350°F/180°C/Gas Mark 4, for about 30 minutes. Remove lid or foil, sprinkle with the cheese, increase heat and bake until cheese is melted and browned, or finish under grill to brown cheese quickly. Crumbs as well as cheese, may be sprinkled over the cooked fish and browned, if liked.

Fried Cod's Roe

Boil the roe for about 15 minutes. Drain and cut into slices. When cold, dip in seasoned flour, brush with beaten egg, roll in breadcrumbs and fry until golden brown.

Serve with crisply fried bacon and slices of lemon.

Serves 4
1 lb (½ kg) cod's roe
Flour, salt and pepper
1 egg, beaten
Breadcrumbs
Fat for frying

Boiled or Stewed Eels

Skin, remove heads and clean eels. Cut into 4 inch (10 cm) lengths. Put them in a saucepan with enough cold water to cover them. Bring to the boil and stew gently for 20 minutes, or longer, according to thickness. Strain into a fresh saucepan a pint (600 ml) of the eel liquor. Mix the flour until smooth with the cream or top of the milk. Stir this into the stock and add the parsley and salt and pepper. Simmer gently for 5 minutes. Add the butter or margarine and stir until this has melted. Drain the eels, arrange on a hot dish and pour the sauce over.

Serves 6
2 lb (1 kg) eels
1½ tbsp flour
¼ pt (150 ml) cream or
*   top of the milk*
1 dessertsp minced parsley
Salt and pepper
¼ oz (7½ g) butter or margarine

Jellied Eels

Clean, skin and remove heads from the eels and put them in a saucepan with a good sprinkling of salt and pepper, the onion with the cloves stuck in it, bay leaf, vinegar and 1½ pints (900 ml) of cold water. Simmer until the eels are quite tender, then take out the bones and cut the eels into small pieces. Strain the juice into a clean pan and boil it rapidly until it is clear, removing any scum as it rises. Add the gelatine and boil gently for a minute. Strain the liquor into a bowl.

Arrange pieces of eel in mould or basin. Pour in liquor. Allow to set, turn out and serve, garnished with parsley.

Serves 4-6
1½ lb (¾ kg) eels
Salt and pepper
1 medium-sized onion
2 cloves
1 bay leaf
1 dessertsp vinegar
½ oz (15 g) powdered gelatine
Parsley

Kedgeree with Haddock

This is an excellent breakfast, or supper dish, which may be prepared ahead of time and reheated by stirring over low heat in a little melted butter. It must be served very hot to be good.

Hard-boil the eggs, shell and chop. Drain the fish well and flake it, removing all bones and skin very carefully. Melt the butter, then add the rice, eggs, fish and seasoning. Mix well together and serve very hot, sprinkled with chopped parsley, if liked.

Serves 6
1 lb (½ kg) cooked smoked
*   haddock*
3 eggs
¼ lb (120 g) butter
¼ lb (120 g) cooked rice
Salt and pepper
Chopped parsley (optional)

1 fillet per person (or ½ if large)
2 eggs
2 tbsp milk
Salt and pepper
¼ lb (120 g) fresh breadcrumbs
  (or pkt prepared breadcrumbs)
2 oz (60 g) butter or margarine

Haddock Fillets Fried with Egg and Breadcrumbs

Also
Plaice fillets
Whole dabs or small plaice
Lemon sole fillets or small
whole fish
Hake fillets

Bream fillets
Brill fillets
Skate fillets
Whiting (whole or filleted)
Cod steaks or cutlets – these are
inclined to be dry

Beat the eggs well with the milk and season with salt and pepper. Sprinkle a layer of breadcrumbs thickly on a plate, dip a fillet of fish into the egg and milk mixture see that it is covered on all sides (or you can brush it over with a pastry brush). Lay it on the layer of breadcrumbs, sprinkle more over the top and press them firmly on. Lift fillet, which should be evenly coated on both sides, and fry exactly as in previous recipe. Smaller, thinner fillets naturally need a minute or two less time for frying after they have browned.

Very good served with Tartare Sauce (see Chapter 10), egg and lemon, or any sharp sauce.

1 haddock fillet per person
  (if large, cut across and use 1
  for 2 people)
1 egg
1½ tbsp flour
¼ pt (150 ml) milk
Salt and pepper
2 oz (60 g) butter or margarine
2 tbsp frying oil

Haddock Fried in Batter

(Also hake, bream, brill, cod, steaks or fillets)

Break egg into a bowl, stir in the flour to make a smooth thick paste. (If too dry, moisten with a little of the milk.) Gradually beat in the milk till you have a thick creamy batter which coats your spoon. Season with salt, then beat well with a rotary beater or with a fork in order to aerate the batter. Heat the butter or margarine and oil in a pan until it is very hot and smoking. Rub each fish fillet with salt and pepper, dip in the batter and place at once in the pan. Fry for 2 minutes on each side, not too fast, as the batter easily catches. It should swell, and be a light golden brown. Then reduce heat and fry very slowly for 4 minutes more on each side (total frying time 4 minutes fast plus 8 minutes slow frying) so that the fish is cooked through.

Haddock, hake or bream fillets are very good cooked like this, as the batter is crisp and light and the fish inside flaky and yet juicy and well-flavoured. All these fish are inclined to be dry if cooked without the protection of the batter, or of egg and breadcrumbs.

Smoked or Dried Haddock

Smoked haddock is best cooked in milk, which takes on its delicious flavour and acts as a simple sauce.

Put the haddock in a clean frying pan or any shallow pan. Pour the milk over so that it just covers the fish. Do not season. Simmer very gently indeed for about 10 minutes. Place the fish on a hot serving dish and pour the milk round. Shake a little pepper over the fish and put dabs of butter on it. Serve at once.

Can be cooked in exactly the same way in a moderate oven, 350°F/180°C/Gas Mark 4, in an ovenproof dish, but in this case it must be closely covered and will require about 20 minutes cooking time.

It is traditional, when you want a more substantial dish, to divide the haddock, if whole, into portions, removing the backbone and to serve a poached egg on each piece. The egg can be poached separately, or poached in the milk in which the haddock was cooked.

1 smoked haddock (see that it is plump and moist-looking and pale in colour) or 1 fillet of smoked haddock per person
½ pt (300 ml) milk
Pepper
1 oz (30 g) butter

Grilled Halibut

(Also for Turbot)

Sprinkle slices of fish with salt and pepper. Brush with melted butter. Place about 1 inch (2½ cm) below hot grill, allowing 5-7 minutes a side according to thickness of slice. Baste with butter two or three times while each side is grilling, using juices in pan or a little more fresh butter if necessary.

Excellent served with Green Butter, Maître d'hôtel Sauce or Tartare Sauce (see Chapter 10).

1 slice – about ¾ in (1 ¾ cm) thick – of halibut or turbot for each person (if fish is very large, allow ½ slice, cut across)
Salt and pepper
Melted butter

Grilled Herrings

The fish may be grilled just as they are, or rubbed with flour, pepper and salt, or dusted over with oatmeal. They may be split and opened flat or grilled closed.

Place fish on grill topped with several small pieces of butter, margarine or dripping and grill for 3 minutes each side if opened flat, or 4 if closed. Spoon a little of the fat which falls into pan over them once or twice.

Very good served with Mustard Sauce (see Chapter 10).

1 herring per person
Flour, pepper and salt, or oatmeal (optional)
1 oz (30 g) butter, margarine or dripping

Poached Herrings

1 herring per person

Cook slowly in boiling salted water for 5 minutes. Serve with boiled potatoes and Mustard Sauce (see Chapter 10).

Fried Herrings

1 herring per person
Oatmeal, or flour, salt and pepper
Fat or oil for frying

Make 4 gashes across each side of the fish. Roll in oatmeal or seasoned flour, and fry in smoking hot fat or oil – 2 oz (60 g) for 4 herrings – for about 3 minutes on each side.

Soused Herrings or Mackerel

Serves 4
4 fresh herrings
¼ tsp salt
1 dessertsp brown sugar
1 blade mace
1 bay leaf
6 peppercorns
2 cloves
About ¼ pt (150 ml) vinegar
About ¼ pt (150 ml) water

Cut down from the opening already made for cleaning the fish to the tail. Lay them on their backs and remove all possible bones. Sprinkle all over with salt. Roll them up, starting at the tail end. Place them in a small pie dish with the sugar, mace, bay leaf, peppercorns and cloves. Pour over them enough vinegar and water to cover. Bake in a moderate oven, 350°F/180°C/Gas Mark 4, for 35 minutes. Remove and allow to get cold before serving with the strained liquor in which they cooked.

Baked John Dory

1 John Dory
Butter for greasing
Salt and pepper
Grated lemon rind
½ pt (300 ml) white wine or milk
1 oz (30 g) butter
1 oz (30 g) flour
Lemon juice
1 egg yolk

A very good fish with an ugly head. Not always available, but worth buying when it is. It is best filleted and cooked as sole, but the following is a delicious way of serving the whole fish.

Grease an ovenproof dish well with butter and put the fish in it. Sprinkle with seasoning and lemon rind. Cover with wine or milk. Bake 25 minutes in oven preheated to 350°F/180°C/Gas Mark 4. Lift fish on to a serving dish. Make a roux with the butter and flour. Cook 1 minute. Add some lemon juice and the beaten egg yolk. Do not allow to boil again. Pour round fish or serve in sauceboat immediately.

The wine gives a slightly sharp sauce and the milk a rich creamy sauce slightly sharpened by the lemon. Either is good.

Fried Mackerel

4 medium-sized mackerel
3 oz (90 g) fat

Treat exactly as for grilled mackerel but fry, putting them into smoking hot fat for about 3 minutes on each side.

Poached Mackerel

Simmer very gently in a Court Bouillon (which, if possible, contained some fennel, as the flavour of this herb is very good with mackerel) for 10-15 minutes. Drain very carefully and serve hot with Béchamel Sauce containing chopped fennel or tarragon leaves, or a Gooseberry Sauce (see Chapter 10). Green gooseberries, like fennel, go particularly well with mackerel.

1 mackerel per person
½ pt (300 ml) Court Bouillon per fish
Béchamel or Gooseberry Sauce

Grilled Mackerel

Split the fish lengthwise so that they will lie flat or leave whole and score each side deeply. Wash and dry. Rub with flour or oatmeal, salt and pepper. Lay flat on grill, dotted with pieces of butter. Grill each side for about 4 minutes, adding a little more butter if necessary. Serve with slices of lemon, Gooseberry Sauce, Maître d'hôtel or Green Butter (see Chapter 10).

Serves 4
4 medium-sized mackerel
Flour or oatmeal
Salt and pepper
1 oz (30 g) butter or margarine

Baked Fillets of Mackerel

Butter a flat, ovenproof dish and lay the fillets, rubbed with flour, salt and pepper, in it. Sprinkle with parsley and chopped onion, place the skinned and quartered tomatoes over the fillets. Pour in wine or cider and sprinkle breadcrumbs all over. Dot with pieces of butter. Bake at 375°F/190°C/Gas Mark 5 for 30 minutes. Serve with plain boiled rice or mashed potatoes.

Serves 4
2 large mackerel, filleted
About 2 oz (60 g) butter
Flour
Salt and pepper
1 tbsp chopped parsley
1 small onion, chopped
½ lb (240 g) tomatoes
¼ pt (150 ml) white wine or rough cider
¼ lb (120 g) breadcrumbs

Red Mullet

This is a very delicate and beautiful fish. Your fishmonger will prepare it by pulling out the gills. The liver is very good. The skin is easily broken and it should be handled lightly. It is best grilled or baked or cooked 'en papillote', but tends to break up if fried and is not good poached.

See Trout for methods of cooking but allow an extra 5-7 minutes when cooking 'en papillote' and 2-3 minutes extra each side when grilling.

Baked Pike

1 pike
Herb forcemeat
4 rashers fatty bacon
2 oz (60 g) butter or dripping

A pike really needs stuffing as it is inclined to be cotton-woolly if served plain.

Fill the fish with herb forcemeat and sew it up carefully with needle and thread. Cover with the bacon. Grease a large sheet of paper or foil and wrap the whole fish in it and lay in roasting tray. Bake in a 400°F/200°C/Gas Mark 6 oven for ½ hour. Remove the paper and cook for a further 10 minutes. Serve on a hot dish. Tartare or Caper Sauce (see Chapter 10) is best with a pike.

Plaice or Flounders Fried Whole or Filleted

1 lb (½ kg) fillets of plaice
Salt and pepper
1 tbsp flour
½ oz (15 g) butter or margarine

These may be fried in a coating of batter or dipped in egg and breadcrumbs (see Fried Haddock recipes), or as follows.

Wash and dry the fillets, sprinkle with salt and pepper, and flour each fillet. Put the butter in a frying pan, and when it is really hot, put in the fillets and reduce the heat to moderate. Fry gently until nicely browned, 2 minutes each side. Drain well and serve on a hot dish.

Prepare for grilling in the same way, but brush with melted butter when you have arranged fillets on the rack. Cook about 3 minutes each side.

Salmon

Scotch salmon is always the best and most expensive; frozen Canadian salmon is quite good and cheaper and Pacific salmon, which is sometimes offered in large shops, is not so good but much cheaper than either. It makes a nice dish, however, but should always have a good sharp sauce served with it, or it is apt to be oily and tasteless.

Grilled Salmon

Serves 4-8
4 slices of salmon ¾ in (1 ¾ cm)
thick (½ or 1 per person,
according to size of fish)
2 oz (60 g) butter

Brush fish with the melted butter. Place on rack and cook under a moderate grill for about 10 minutes. Turn, brush other side with butter and cook for a further 10 minutes. Serve at once on a hot dish with thin slices of cucumber, Tartare Sauce, Hollandaise Sauce, Maître d'hôtel Butter or Green Butter (see Chapter 10).

Poached Salmon

1 salmon
Salt
Garnishes

Leave the fish whole. Salmon should be simmered in plain salted water and not in a Court Bouillon. Have a fish kettle with sufficient simmering salted water barely to cover the fish and cook very gently. Never let it come to the boil. Allow 10 minutes to each pound (½ kg) and 10 minutes over. Drain thoroughly and serve, lifting it out very carefully so that you do not break the fish, on to a hot dish.

Serve with slices of cucumber, Hollandaise Sauce or Tartare Sauce (see Chapter 10). Plain boiled potatoes and green peas are the best vegetables to accompany this fish.

A slice of salmon is cooked in exactly the same way as the whole fish.

Salmon Trout or Sea Trout

1 salmon trout
½ oz (15 g) butter
Flour
Salt and pepper
Lemon juice
Herbs (varied)

This excellent fish, thought by many people to be more delicate than salmon, is cooked in exactly the same way. It is smaller than salmon and generally a little cheaper. A whole salmon trout, however, big enough for 4 to 6 people, is probably best of all cooked *en papillote* as follows.

Have a very large sheet of greaseproof paper, or lay two sheets or three overlapping; or a large piece of aluminium foil. Butter the paper or foil well and sprinkle with flour, salt and pepper. Lay the fish in the centre. Rub the cavity where the fish was cleaned with salt and pepper. Squeeze in a little lemon juice and put inside a bunch of parsley, fennel, marjoram and a piece of tarragon (but very little of the last, as it is strong). Any or all of these herbs may be used. Also put in a lump of butter (about ½ oz (15 g)). Wrap up the fish, making a close parcel that will let no juice run out. Tie round with string in several places if necessary. Lay on a baking tray and put in oven preheated to 400°F/200°C/Gas Mark 6. Cook for 30 minutes.

Remove from oven and undo parcel, letting juice run into baking tray. Lift fish very carefully, using slice and palette knife to support it, so that it does not break, on to a hot, ovenproof dish. Strain the juice and pour it all over the fish. Remove herbs and discard. Put back into oven on dish for 4 minutes to reheat and slightly crisp the top of the skin. Serve with slices of cucumber and quarters of lemon.

Skate

Skate should be soaked in cold water for an hour before using. Remember that this fish does not keep well.

Poached Skate

Serves 4
1 ½ lb (¾ kg) skate
Salt
1 tbsp lemon juice or vinegar

This does not need a Court Bouillon. Cook in boiling salted water, with a tablespoon of lemon juice or vinegar added, for about 20 to 30 minutes. Drain well.

Serve with Caper Sauce or Cheese Sauce (see Chapter 10).

Skate in Black Butter

Serves 4
1 lb (½ kg) skate
2 onions
1 carrot
2 lemons
3 oz (90 g) butter
1 tbsp vinegar or lemon juice
1 oz (30 g) capers

Cut the skate into neat pieces and boil in 1 pint (600 ml) water with the onions, carrot and the juice of 2 lemons. When the fish is cooked, strain it, remove the skin, and place it in a dish. Cook the butter until brown, add a little vinegar or lemon juice. Stir in the capers, pour over the fish and serve at once very hot.

Dover Sole

Apart perhaps from Scotch salmon, Dover sole is certainly the best British fish, and is one of the best fishes of the world. There are literally dozens of ways of serving it, based on frying, grilling, steaming or poaching the whole or filleted fish, and accompanying it with different sauces, shellfish, vegetables and fruits. On the whole, connoisseurs agree that a good, fresh sole is best cooked as simply as possible. A properly grilled sole served with Tartare Sauce or Maître d'hôtel Sauce, or a good Sole Meunière is hard to beat. Whether the addition of cream, grapes, lobster, apple, oysters, truffles, etc., really improves on these plain, traditional ways of serving the sole, is doubtful, but the more complicated ways are always delicious and interesting to cook and eat for a change.

Dover soles are always expensive, but no other fish can really substitute for them. However, Lemon soles, sometimes called Witch soles, which are always much cheaper, are in themselves very good. Grilled, fried, steamed or poached or cooked Meunière or Bonne Femme, they should be treated in the same way as Dover soles and are excellent. It is not advisable to attempt the more complicated recipes with them as they have a much looser consistency and less definite flavour than Dover soles.

Sole Bonne Femme

Ask your fishmonger to give you the head, skin, bones and trimmings of the sole when he has filleted it for you, and boil in 1 pint (600 ml) water with herbs, etc., to make a Court Bouillon.

Grease the bottom of a shallow ovenproof dish. Sprinkle with chopped shallots, parsley and sliced mushrooms. Lay the fillets on top, side by side. Mix the wine and fish stock, then pour over the fillets. Bake in a slow oven, 325°F/160°C/Gas Mark 3, for 12 to 16 minutes, basting occasionally with the liquid. When fish is cooked, pour off the liquid into a saucepan. Cook quickly till reduced by half. Remove from heat and pour into bowl. Make a white roux in the saucepan with ½ oz (15 g) butter and the flour and season. Cook 2 minutes and stir in fish stock. Boil for 3 minutes, stirring. Allow to cool for 1 minute and stir in the remaining butter, softened and in small pieces. Stir gently but well, holding pan over low heat. When all the butter is incorporated, pour over fish and brown for 1 minute under grill to glaze. Serve with Duchesse or creamed potatoes.

Serves 4
4 large fillets of sole
2 shallots or 1 onion, peeled and chopped
2 tsp minced parsley
2 oz (60 g) mushrooms, finely chopped
¼ pt (150 ml) white wine
¼ pt (150 ml) fish stock
3 oz (90 g) butter
1 dessertsp flour
Salt and pepper

Sole Meunière

You can use whole small soles, well trimmed, or a filleted sole.

Melt the butter in the frying pan. Dredge the fish with flour and season. Put it into the hot butter and, shaking the pan carefully, fry very gently on both sides, for about 2 to 4 minutes a side. Take the fish out, and keep it hot on serving dish. Make the butter boil in the frying pan until it darkens, stir in quickly the lemon juice and wine, or all lemon juice, and bring to the boil again. Stir in chopped parsley, pour over sole and serve at once.

Serves 4
4 small sole or 4 fillets
2 oz (60 g) butter
A little flour
Salt and pepper
1 dessertsp lemon juice
A very little white wine
Chopped parsley

Fried Dover Sole

Beat the egg on a plate and stir in the milk. Dip the soles in flour, salt and pepper. Lay on the plate with the egg and turn. Then dip in breadcrumbs and press gently. Fry in hot, deep fat to a golden brown, about 4 to 6 minutes, or in shallow hot fat, turning once, about 3 minutes a side. Half butter, half frying oil is very good for the shallow-frying method. In any case, do not put the soles in until the fat is really hot, and drain well before serving.

Serves 4
4 Dover soles
1 egg
1 tbsp milk
Flour
Salt and pepper
Fine breadcrumbs
Fat for frying

Grilled Dover Sole

Rub flour, salt and pepper into the fish on both sides. Melt the butter and brush over the fish or fillets, so that they are evenly coated. Grill under hot grill about 4 minutes a side if whole fish or 3 minutes if fillets. Pour more hot butter over fish once or twice.

Fillets or whole small soles
A little flour
Salt and pepper
2-3 oz (60-90 g) butter

*Fillets or whole small soles
(remember the size of your
steamer)
Very little butter
Salt and pepper*

Steamed Sole

Place the fillets or the whole fish in a perforated steamer over a saucepan of boiling water and cover tightly. Put a few dabs of butter on the fish and a sprinkling of salt and pepper. Steam for about 20 minutes for fillets, or 30 minutes for whole fish.

Serves 4
*4 whole sole or fillets
About 2 oz (60 g) butter
Salt and pepper
½ pt (300 ml) dry white wine or
milk
½ oz (15 g) flour
Lemon juice and chopped parsley,
or pinch of grated nutmeg*

Sole Poached in Wine or Milk

Grease an ovenproof dish with butter, lay the fish in it with a few dabs of butter on them and a sprinkling of salt and pepper. Pour over the white wine or the milk. Place in oven preheated to 350°F/180°C/Gas Mark 4, and cook for 25 to 30 minutes, covered with lid or buttered greaseproof paper or foil. The fillets or whole fish are removed to serving dish and the liquor, wine or milk, used to make a sauce.

Stir the flour into ½ oz (15 g) melted butter, to make a white roux. Boil 1 minute. Gently stir in the hot wine or milk in which the fish cooked. Boil 2 minutes. Season to taste. If wine was used, a squeeze of lemon juice and a teaspoon of chopped parsley may be stirred into sauce. If milk, a pinch of grated nutmeg may be liked. In either case, 1 oz (15 g) butter, stirred in small pieces into the sauce enriches and improves it. Pour over fish and serve.

Other Traditional Ways of Serving Sole

Sole Colbert Fried, opened flat (floured, egged and breadcrumbed); 2 pats maître d'hôtel butter on each sole.

Sole Sicilian Meunière with anchovy fillets and beurre noir.

Sole Française Steamed with white wine sauce and asparagus tips.

Sole Pommery Meunière with apples, quartered and poached, and beurre noir.

Sole Maryland Steamed with white wine sauce, tomato, truffles and asparagus tips.

Sole Mornay Steamed with cheese sauce.

Sole Florentine Steamed and served on a bed of well-drained leaf spinach with cheese sauce over the fish.

Sole Portugaise Steamed with sauce of tomato, white wine and shallots.

Sole Cardinal Steamed with piece of lobster claw and lobster sauce, and a few mushrooms.

Sole Véronique Steamed with peeled white grapes and white wine sauce.

Sole Au Gratin Steamed with cream and white wine sauce, cheese grated over and lightly browned.

Trout

As sole is the king of sea fish, so trout is the king of freshwater fish. Like the sole, there are many ways of cooking it, but it has its own elegant texture and flavour and needs little garnishing. It tastes best of all, as all freshwater fishermen know, if it is grilled or fried over hot coals minutes after it has been caught, and eaten very hot with a rasher or two of bacon. Nowadays you can often buy trout direct from trout farms or frozen from most supermarkets and the flavour and texture are excellent.

Grilled Trout (1)

1 trout per person
A little flour
Salt and pepper
2 oz (60 g) butter

Split the trout and rub all over with seasoned flour. Brush with melted butter and cook under a hot grill with the fish opened flat, for 3 minutes on each side. Baste with the butter once or twice. Serve with lemon or Tartare Sauce (Chapter 10).

Grilled Trout (2)

1 trout per person
Flour
Salt and pepper
½ oz (15 g) Green Butter

Split trout and rub outsides with seasoned flour. Lay on the inside the pat of Green Butter (see Chapter 10). Close trout over this and grill as above, about 4 minutes a side, basting with the butter and herbs that run out of the fish into the pan. Pour all this liquor over them on serving dish. Very good served with bacon rolls, one to each fish.

Fried Trout

Serves 4
4 trout
Milk
Salt and pepper
2 oz (60 g) oatmeal
Fat for deep-frying, or butter

Trout should never be dipped in egg and breadcrumbs, which does not suit their flavour or consistency. They are much better dipped in milk, seasoned, and then rolled in oatmeal. Deep-fry about 4 minutes in hot fat, or shallow-fry 3 minutes a side in butter. Or they may be simply floured and fried. They are very good served with a rasher of bacon for each fish.

Serves 4
4 small trout
3 or 4 thin slices fatty bacon
Salt and pepper
Parsley
Butter

Baked Trout

Split trout open and remove the bones. Lay the slices of bacon on the bottom of a baking dish. Lay the trout on them, skin side uppermost, and sprinkle with a little salt, pepper and chopped parsley. Dot with pieces of butter. Bake in oven preheated to 450°F/230°C/Gas Mark 8 for about 10 to 15 minutes. Serve at once.

Serves 4
4 small trout
1 tbsp flour
Salt and pepper
2 oz (60 g) butter
1 dessertsp lemon juice
Parsley, finely chopped

Trout Meunière

Toss fish in seasoned flour. Heat half the butter in a pan and fry the fish in it until a golden brown colour on both sides and well cooked – about 3 minutes a side. Keep hot on dish. Add the rest of the butter to that already in the pan and heat it until brown. Add the lemon juice and boil again. Sprinkle in parsley, pour over fish and serve.

Serves 4
4 trout
Flour
Salt and pepper
2 oz (60 g) butter
2 oz (60 g) blanched almonds split in two

Trout with Almonds

This is a traditional recipe of the hill districts of France, where almonds are grown and trout are plentiful in the streams. The crisp almonds are excellent with the fish.

Rub the fish with seasoned flour and fry in some hot butter until cooked. Then keep hot on a flat dish. Put rest of butter in pan, toss the blanched, split almonds in a little salt and throw them into the hot butter. Fry quickly for 1 minute, turning and moving them in the pan. Pour all the nuts and butter over the fish and serve at once.

Serves 4
4 trout
2 oz (60 g) butter
Salt and pepper
Chopped parsley
Chopped fennel (optional)

Trout en Papillote

This is the simplest of all ways to cook fish, and one of the best as the flavour is preserved.

Have a sheet of greaseproof paper ready for each fish, of a size to wrap it completely. Butter the paper and sprinkle it with salt and pepper and a little chopped parsley, or chopped parsley and fennel, if liked. Lay each fish on its paper and make into a parcel, screwing the ends of the paper so that they will hold. Lay the little parcels on a baking tray and bake in a preheated oven at 400°F/200°C/Gas Mark 6 for 20 minutes.

You can serve the parcels at the table, so that everyone unwraps his own, and smells the delicious aroma, or unwrap in the kitchen and carefully lift trout from paper and lay on a hot dish. Good served with quarters of lemon or Tartare or Lemon or Hollandaise Sauce (Chapter 10), but also nice plain.

Opposite: *Stuffed Mushrooms (see page 26) and Celery Boats (see page 25)*

Left: *Angels on Horseback (see page 29)*

Opposite: *Tomato Soup (see page 39)*

Below: *Fish Soup (see page 43)*

Skate in Black Butter (see page 60) *Grilled Mackerel (see page 57)*

Above: *Stewed Mussels (see page 70)*

Opposite: *Pâtés (see page 45)*

Prawns à l'Orange (see page 71)

Coq au Vin (see page 81)

Above: *Roast Goose (see page 83)*

Right: *Jugged Hare (see page 94)*

Fried Whitebait

Serves 4
1½lb (¾kg) whitebait
Flour
Fat for frying
Lemon
Brown bread and butter

(Also for Sprats.)

Frozen whitebait are often available and are very good. If fresh are to be used, wash them and dry in a clean cloth. Sprinkle well with flour. Toss them in a wire sieve or in a colander to separate them from each other and get rid of surplus flour. Put them in frying basket, and lower into deep fat which is really hot, still and smoking. Fry them for 2 minutes only. Lift out basket and drain well – serve on a very hot dish with quarters of lemon and thin brown bread and butter.

Make sure the fat is really hot or the whitebait won't be crisp. If you have to fry them in two lots, bring the fat up to temperature each time.

Baked Whiting

4 whiting
Salt
Juice of ½ lemon
1 oz (30 g) butter
2 tsp chopped parsley

Place fish in a greased, shallow ovenproof dish. Sprinkle with a little salt, and the lemon juice. Dab with the butter, sprinkle with chopped parsley and bake 10 minutes in a 350°F/180°C/Gas Mark 4 oven. Serve at once.

Fried Whiting

4 whiting, skinned
1 dessertsp flour
1 egg, beaten
Breadcrumbs
Salt and pepper
Fat for frying
Parsley
Lemon

Pull the tail of fish through the eye-holes. Dredge lightly with flour. Dip in beaten egg and coat with breadcrumbs and season. When the deep fat in the pan is smoking hot, fry the fish until golden brown. Drain and garnish with fried parsley and pieces of lemon.

General Fish Dishes

Fish Cakes (1)

Serves 6
Equal quantities of cooked,
  flaked fish and mashed potato
Salt and pepper
Chopped parsley (optional)
Flour
Egg and breadcrumbs (optional)
2 oz (60 g) fat for frying

Mix the cooked, flaked fish and the mashed potato well together with a fork. Season rather highly, adding chopped parsley, if liked. Divide into portions about the size of golf balls. Flour well all over and shape into flat cakes with the hands. Plunge into shallow, smoking hot fat and fry quickly till golden brown, turning once. Or dip in egg and breadcrumbs and fry as for haddock fillets (see page 54). Serve very hot on heated dish

Tomato sauce is very good with fish cakes. If liked, 1 teaspoon tomato purée may be worked into the fish and potato mixture.

Serves 6

1 lb (½ kg) cooked, flaked white
*   fish*
¼ pt (150 ml) white sauce
½ lb (240 g) mashed potatoes

Fish Cakes (2)

Many people much prefer fish cakes made like this.

Mix the fish with the white sauce and stir in the mashed potatoes. Then proceed as in previous recipe. This gives a more moist consistency to the fish cakes. If made by this method, the cakes should be both floured and dipped in egg and breadcrumbs as, if flour alone is used, the softer texture is apt to break and stick when frying.

Serves 4

1 whiting
1 lemon sole
2 fillets of fresh haddock
1 mackerel
2 onions
4 tomatoes, skinned
2 cloves garlic
Bouquet garni containing fennel
Strip of lemon peel
2 tbsp olive oil
Salt and pepper
Saffron
½ pt (300 ml) prawns, shelled
4 Dublin Bay prawns
6-8 slices of bread, ¼ in (½ cm)
*   thick*
Chopped parsley

Bouillabaisse

This famous soup-stew, which belongs to Marseilles and all the South of France, is adapted to the fish likely to be available in England. It is a meal in itself and should be served in generous helpings. The saffron gives the fish a characteristic and exciting flavour.

Put the peeled and sliced onions in a saucepan with the tomatoes, garlic, bouquet garni and lemon peel. On top of this lay the cleaned whiting, lemon sole, haddock and mackerel. Add the olive oil, then pour over boiling water so that it more than covers the fish. Season with salt and pepper and a good pinch of saffron. Boil fiercely for 10 minutes, then add the shelled prawns and Dublin Bay prawns. Boil more gently for a further 10 minutes. Arrange the slices of bread in a large bowl and pour the liquid on to them. Pile all the fish on another flat dish. Sprinkle with parsley and serve at once.

Everyone takes some of each fish – or whatever he fancies – and then ladles the soup and bread over it. Very good with a rough, red wine.

Bouillabaisse can be made successfully with frozen fish using 2 fillets of haddock, 1 cod fillet, 1 fillet of plaice, 2 fillets of smoked mackerel (or smoked haddock) and frozen prawns.

Serves 4

¾ lb (360 g) cooked, flaked fish
½ pt (300 ml) white sauce
Salt and pepper
½ lb (240 g) flaky pastry
*   (see Chapter 17)*

Russian Fish Pie

Prepare the white sauce as for fish pie below, add the fish and season. Line a shallow ovenproof dish with flaky pastry. Fill with the cold fish mixture in its sauce, cover with pastry lid and bake in a hot oven, 450°F/230°C/Gas Mark 8 for 20 minutes. Then cover with foil and put the dish back in the oven for a further 15 minutes.

Fish Pie

Fish pie can be made from any white fish which has been simmered in stock or in milk with a little water. Smoked haddock can be used, but is apt to be a little too salty – it is better to use partly fresh fish and partly smoked.

Make the white sauce with equal quantities of milk and liquor in which the fish was cooked. Flake the fish, being careful to remove all skin and bones. Stir the fish lightly into the hot sauce and bring to the boil again. Season to taste. Pour into a shallow ovenproof dish and top with a thick layer of breadcrumbs, or breadcrumbs mixed with grated cheese. Dab with butter and put under hot grill till top is browned and serve at once.

If you wish to, top with creamed potatoes, allow the fish to get cold in the sauce leaving it in the dish, so that it solidifies slightly and forms a skin on which the potato can rest. Lightly smooth over the fish some well-seasoned creamed potatoes (not too dry). Mark all over with fork, dot with butter and let the pie heat in oven at 375°F/190°C/Gas Mark 5 for 20 minutes.

Serves 4-6
1 lb (½ kg) cooked fish
¾ pt (450 ml) white sauce
Salt and pepper
Breadcrumbs, or breadcrumbs
  mixed with grated cheese, or
  creamed potatoes
A little butter

Risotto with Seafood

Put the rice in a heavy pan with the oil, green pepper, onions, salt and pepper, and cook gently without browning on a low heat for 5 or 6 minutes, stirring constantly. Then add the hot stock and water and simmer about 20 to 30 minutes until rice is tender.

Flake the meat from the lobster, add the prawns and heat for 3 minutes in the butter, nutmeg and lemon juice. Then stir in the cream and half the cheese. Put the hot rice in a big serving dish, place the seafood in the centre, and sprinkle with the rest of the cheese.

This is a very good supper dish. The lobster can be replaced with crab meat, or you can use cooked and flaked dried haddock, or a fresh white fish, such as hake. A few sliced, cooked mushrooms are also good.

Serves 4-6
½ lb (240 g) rice
2 tbsp olive oil (optional)
1 green pepper, sliced
2 large onions, finely chopped
Salt and pepper
1 pt (600 ml) hot stock
1 pt (600 ml) water
1 small lobster
½ pt (300 ml) prawns, shelled
¼ lb (120 g) butter or margarine
½ tsp nutmeg
Juice of ½ lemon
¼ pt (150 ml) cream or top of milk
3 oz (90 g) grated cheese

SHELLFISH

Buying

Cockles and Mussels Sold cooked or raw. If raw, they *must* be tightly closed. Discard any that are open. Buy only from a good shop that you can trust. If you boil them yourself, throw away any that float.

Oysters Must have their shells closed. Fishmongers will open them for you, but see them closed first.

Prawns and Shrimps Can be bought boiled or unboiled, but are generally sold boiled. Frozen prawns can be obtained from any supermarket and are very good.

Crayfish and Lobsters Generally sold boiled.

Scallops Must be very fresh. Should be very white and the roe very bright orange.

Crabs Generally sold boiled and dressed. The male has larger claws and is better than the female. Frozen dressed crab is often available and is excellent.

Scampi Nowadays most often bought frozen and ready crumbed, these are excellent.

Never keep shellfish more than a few hours before eating, or more than one night in refrigerator.

Seasons

Crabs No close season, but best and most plentiful in April, May and June.

Lobsters Most plentiful during the summer, mostly because of difficulty of catching in rough weather.

Mussels Best August to November.

Scallops Best December to March. Not many available in summer.

Oysters 'When there is an 'R' in the month', i.e. from September to the end of April. Imported ones can, however, be bought and eaten all the year round. English oysters, known as natives, are the best, but nowadays almost prohibitively expensive.

Prawns and shrimps All the year round, but scarce in winter because of difficulty of catching in rough weather.

Recipes

Boiled Cockles

Cockles which do not open by themselves after cooking are unfit to eat. Throw these away.

Wash the cockles well in two or three changes of water with salt added and scrub the shells. Leave them to soak in salt and water. Then put them in a saucepan with a little water at the bottom and lay a clean cloth over them. Shake the pan constantly to prevent their burning. As soon as the shells open they are cooked enough. Drain them and serve in their shells on a hot dish.

Cockles
Water
Salt

Crab Croquettes

Remove the meat from the cooked crab and chop it finely. Melt the butter in a saucepan, stir in the flour and add the milk gradually. When the sauce is smooth, season to taste with salt, pepper and paprika and add the crab. Turn on to a plate, leave till cold, then shape into ovals. Dip in flour, then in egg and breadcrumbs. Fry in deep, smoking hot fat till golden brown. Drain and serve at once.

Serves 4
1 large pkt frozen, dressed crab,
* or 1 large fresh crab*
1 oz (30 g) butter or margarine
1 oz (30 g) flour
¼ pt (150 ml) hot milk
Salt, pepper, paprika
Flour, egg, breadcrumbs
Fat for frying

Scalloped Crab

Flake the crab meat and season with salt, pepper and nutmeg. Stir in the breadcrumbs, softened butter and eggs. Wash the crab shells and half fill with the mixture. Sprinkle with grated cheese.

There should be a thick coating of cheese, as it brings out the flavour of the crab. Put a few dabs of butter on top and brown in a hot oven for 10 minutes.

Serves 4
½ lb (240 g) crab meat
Salt, pepper, nutmeg
2 tbsp breadcrumbs
2 tbsp butter
2 eggs, well beaten
2 oz (60 g) grated cheese
Extra butter

Lobster au Gratin

Clean the lobster shell, cut it down the back, then remove and chop the meat and roe or coral. Melt butter in a saucepan, stir in chopped shallot, lightly brown and then add lemon juice, sauce, lobster meat, tarragon, parsley and seasoning. Return mixture to halves of shell, sprinkle with breadcrumbs and dot with butter. Bake in a 350°F/180°C/Gas Mark 4 oven for 15 minutes.

The tarragon may be omitted but gives a distinctive flavour which is very good with the lobster meat.

Serves 2
1 medium lobster
1 oz (30 g) butter
1 shallot, chopped
1 dessertsp lemon juice
¼ pt (150 ml) white sauce
¼ tsp chopped tarragon
1 tsp minced parsley
Pepper, salt, paprika
Breadcrumbs
Extra butter

Lobster Newburg

Serves 2
1 lb (½ kg) lobster
2 oz (60 g) butter
1 tbsp brandy
3 tbsp sherry
1 tbsp cream
1 egg yolk
Salt and pepper

Split the lobster in half and remove the meat from the body and from the claws. Melt the butter in a saucepan and add the diced lobster. Heat for 1 minute. Add the brandy and set it alight. Add the sherry, mix the cream and egg yolk together in a basin and gradually stir into the lobster, and season. Slowly heat it but on no account allow it to boil, as the cream and egg will curdle. Put the lobster in a serving dish with plain boiled rice.

Lobster Thermidor

Serves 2
1 lobster
2 shallots
½ oz (15 g) chopped parsley
Salt and pepper
¼ pt (150 ml) white wine
¼ pt (150 ml) white sauce
1 tbsp grated cheese
Cayenne pepper
A little lemon juice
French mustard

Halve the lobster lengthwise, removing the meat. Stew the shallots, parsley, salt and pepper, in the white wine. Mix all this into the white sauce and bring to the boil for 5 minutes, stirring all the time. Add a little grated cheese and the diced lobster, plus a pinch of cayenne pepper and a squeeze of lemon juice. Coat the inside of the half shells with a very little French mustard and quickly pour in the lobster mixture. Sprinkle with the rest of the grated cheese and brown under a hot grill.

Stewed Mussels

Serves 4-6
4 pt (2 l) mussels
Pepper
Sprig of parsley, plus a little chopped parsley
Sprig of thyme
2 shallots, chopped
¼ pt (150 ml) white wine
¼ pt (150 ml) water
¼ lb (120 g) butter

Scrape the mussels and wash them thoroughly in several changes of water. Throw away any that are already open and any that float. Put in a large pan with pepper to taste (no salt), sprig of parsley, thyme and shallots. Pour in the white wine and water. Bring to the boil with lid on pan while mussels open. Stir well. When the mussels are open, take them out, discard the empty half of the shell and keep hot. Boil stock until reduced by half, add parsley and butter. Pour melted butter on the mussels and serve hot.

Mussels au Gratin

Serves 4-6
4 pt (2 l) mussels
½ pt (300 ml) water
¼ pt (150 ml) wine
¼ lb (120 g) breadcrumbs
Finely chopped parsley
Finely grated cheese (Parmesan if possible)

Scrub the mussels well and remove beards. Place them in a deep pan, add the water and wine. Cover the pan, bring to the boil for 2 minutes. Remove the mussels from the heat, and let them stand for 5 minutes. Drain off the liquor, strain it and set aside. Remove any remaining beards.

Arrange each mussel on the half shell and place closely together in a shallow ovenproof dish. Sprinkle liberally with breadcrumbs, then with parsley and finally with cheese. Pour over half the strained liquor, being careful not to disarrange the mussels. Bake in a moderate oven, 350°F/180°C/Gas Mark 4, for 15 minutes before serving.

Prawns or Shrimps à l'Orange

Carefully cut the tops off oranges. Scoop out all the pulp, being careful not to break or pierce skin. Put the pulp through a sieve or strainer to extract juice. Grate some orange peel from the tops cut off the oranges. Mix the prawns or shrimps into the cold white sauce. Stir in cream and grated orange rind, and season. Add about 2 tablespoons of orange juice, until of the consistency of good raw cream, and pour into the orange skins. Chill for an hour or two. Serve one for each person, standing the filled oranges on crisp lettuce with a sprig of mint laid across the top of each.

Serves 4
1 pt (600 ml) prawns or shrimps
4 oranges
¼ pt (150 ml) good white sauce, fairly thick
¼ pt (150 ml) cream
Salt and pepper
Lettuce
Sprigs of mint

Prawns in Cream

Stir the shelled prawns or shrimps into the white sauce. Add the cream, seasoning and lemon or orange rind. Chill and serve on a piece of lettuce. Decorate with chopped hard-boiled egg, if liked.

Serves 4
1 pt (600 ml) prawns or shrimps
¼ pt (150 ml) good white sauce
¼ pt (150 ml) cream
Salt and pepper
A little grated lemon or orange rind
Lettuce

Prawns in Aspic

Make up the aspic jelly according to directions on packet. Allow to cool a little. Pour about half into a mould, or individual moulds. When beginning to set, put into each mould a few prawns, half a hard-boiled egg, olives, cut in half, or peas, and pack remainder of prawns around egg. Pour over rest of jelly to fill up moulds. Allow to set and chill, if possible. Turn out and serve on a bed of lettuce or watercress.

Serves 4
½ pt (300 ml) prawns
½ pt (300 ml) aspic jelly
2 hard-boiled eggs
A few olives or cooked peas
Lettuce or watercress

Curried Prawns

Fry the sliced onion in the oil until tender. Add the curry paste, stir for a few minutes, then add the skinned and chopped tomatoes, chopped garlic and chillies. Cook for 5 minutes. Add the prawns and simmer for 5 minutes. Beat the egg together with the cream and add vinegar, or lemon juice, and salt. Stir into the prawn mixture, reheat, but do not boil, and serve with plain, boiled rice.

The chillies can be omitted. 2 oz (60 g) of sultanas, or 2 oz (60 g) blanched almonds, or 1 large cooking apple, peeled and cut in rings which are lightly fried but soft, or 2 oz (60 g) fresh chopped pineapple, or drained, chopped pineapple chunks are all excellent additions to this curry.

Serves 4
1 pt (600 ml) shelled prawns (fresh or frozen)
1 onion
4 tbsp olive oil
1 tbsp curry paste
4 ripe tomatoes
1 clove garlic
6 small red chillies
1 egg
2 tbsp cream
3 tbsp vinegar or lemon juice
1¼ tsp salt

Scallops au Gratin

Serves 3-4

6 scallops
½ pt (300 ml) milk
1 onion, sliced
Butter or margarine
2 tbsp flour
2 oz (60 g) mushrooms
1 tbsp minced parsley
Salt, paprika
Breadcrumbs
1 tbsp grated cheese

Put cleaned scallops in a saucepan. Cover with cold water and bring slowly to the boil. Drain and cut into 4 pieces. Grease 4 scallop shells. Heat milk slowly in a saucepan with the onion. Melt 1 tablespoon butter or margarine in a saucepan, stir in flour, cook for 2 minutes and pour in hot milk. Stir till smooth and boiling. Chop mushrooms and fry them in butter or margarine. Add scallops, mushrooms, parsley and onion to the white sauce. Bring to the boil, season with salt and paprika and cook for 2 or 3 minutes. Pour into shells and sprinkle with breadcrumbs, then with cheese and brown under grill for 2 minutes. Reheat for 5 minutes in a 350°F/180°C/Gas Mark 4 oven, if not totally hot.

Fried Scallops

Serves 3-4

Scallops, 1 per person
Flour, salt and pepper
Fat for frying
½ lemon, sliced
1 dessertsp finely chopped parsley

Roll the washed and dried scallops in seasoned flour. Drop into smoking hot fat and then reduce heat and fry gently till golden brown, about 8 minutes. Lift with perforated spoon, drain well and serve with lemon slices and chopped parsley.

Stewed Scallops

Serves 3-4

6 scallops
A little butter or margarine
Flour
A little milk
Salt and pepper

Wash the scallops well. Put them into a saucepan with enough water to cover them. Simmer gently till tender. Lift out on to a buttered ovenproof dish. Thicken the liquor in which they were cooked, by adding to it a white roux made with butter or margarine and flour and mixed with a little milk, salt and pepper. Cook the sauce for 2 or 3 minutes and pour it over scallops to serve.

Coquilles St Jacques

Serves 4

6 scallops, boiled
1½ oz (45 g) butter
1 oz (30 g) flour
½ pt (300 ml) milk
¼ lb (120 g) mushrooms, finely
  sliced and sautéed
Salt, pepper, mace
Breadcrumbs and grated cheese

Cut each of the boiled scallops into 3 slices. Melt 1 oz (30 g) butter in the saucepan, stir in the pieces of scallops and fry for a minute. Stir in the flour. Boil for a minute, but do not allow to brown. Stir in the milk gradually and add the mushrooms. Season well with salt, pepper and a pinch of mace. Put into 4 to 6 scallop shells or shell dishes. Sprinkle with a mixture of breadcrumbs and grated cheese and dot with the rest of the butter. Brown under grill and then reheat in a 350°F/180°C/Gas Mark 4 oven for 5 minutes. Serve very hot.

Scallops à la Provençale

Cut each of the boiled scallops into 3 slices and roll them in flour. Place the chopped onions in a saucepan with a little butter or oil and toss lightly. Add the scallops and fry for a few minutes, then add the wine, tomatoes, crushed garlic, salt and pepper and chopped parsley. Cook for 20 minutes. Serve piled in the centre of a very hot dish and surrounded with plain boiled rice.

Serves 4
6 scallops, boiled
A little flour
2 onions, chopped
Oil or butter for frying
¼ pt (150 ml) white wine
6-8 tomatoes, skinned and chopped
1 clove garlic
Salt and pepper
Chopped parsley

Potted Shrimps

Put the shrimps into a saucepan with 1½ oz (45 g) of the butter. Season with a pinch of ground mace, grated nutmeg and cayenne and place the saucepan over a low heat just enough to melt the butter. Turn mixture into small jars or pots, pressing the shrimps down firmly. Melt the rest of the butter, and pour some over the top of each jar to seal.

These will keep some days in a refrigerator. They should be served as an hors d'oeuvre with hot, thin toast.

Serves 8
1 pt (600 ml) shrimps, shelled
3 oz (90 g) butter
Ground mace
Grated nutmeg
Cayenne pepper

Shrimps or Prawns in Coquilles

Grease a scallop shell or small dish for each person. Mix the shrimps, parsley and mushrooms into the sauce and pour into the shells. Do not fill them quite full. Sprinkle each thickly with grated cheese and then with breadcrumbs. Dot with pieces of butter. Bake in a moderate oven, 350°F/180°C/Gas Mark 4, for 7 minutes. Brown tops under hot grill. Serve very hot.

Serves 4
1 pt (600 ml) cooked, shelled shrimps or prawns
1 tbsp chopped parsley
2 oz (60 g) sliced, cooked mushrooms (optional)
½ pt (300 ml) béchamel sauce
2 oz (60 g) grated cheese
2 oz (60 g) breadcrumbs
A little butter

POULTRY AND GAME

POULTRY
Recipes

Roast Chicken

Serves 4
1 chicken
Flour, salt and pepper
¼ lb (120 g) butter, lard,
    dripping or cooking fat
3 or 4 bacon rinds or a rasher of
    fat bacon

Birds suitable for roasting vary in size from a young bird which weighs about 2½ lb (1¼ kg) and will feed 2 or 3 people to a capon or Christmas cockerel which weighs 8 lb (4 kg) or so and will feed 6 or 8 people.

Preheat oven to 450°F/230°C/Gas Mark 8. Rub breast and legs of chicken with flour and salt and pepper and place in baking tray. Press fat on to breast and legs with knife. Place 3 or 4 bacon rinds or a rasher of fat bacon over the breast. Put on middle shelf of oven. Potatoes for roasting may be placed round the bird. After 10 minutes, baste, and turn oven down to 400°F/200°C/Gas Mark 6. Baste occasionally. A few minutes before chicken is done, remove bacon from breast to allow it to brown. If you cook bird with breast uncovered from the start, and it begins to darken too much before the bird is done, cover breast with a piece of foil.

A roasting bird of 2½-3 lb (1¼-1½ kg) will need 45 minutes.
A roasting bird of 3-5 lb (1½-2½ kg) will need 45 minutes to 1½ hours.
A roasting bird of 5-8 lb (2½-4 kg) will need 1½ to 2 hours.

It is traditional to serve with roast chicken, any of the following:
   Bread Sauce (see Chapter 10).
   Watercress – simply wash well and arrange 2 or 3 sprigs per person round the bird.
   Gravy – make as for all roasts, but not very thick for chicken.
   Small sausages. These and bacon rolls may be placed in the baking tray with the chicken and potatoes a ¼ hour before bird is ready.
   Any green vegetable goes well with chicken, but if you serve several of the accompaniments suggested, a plain green mixed salad with a French dressing (see Chapter 12) is probably best of all, unless you intend to serve watercress.
   A chicken may be stuffed or not, just as you like.

Poultry and Game 75

Mix everything together in bowl. Lift flap of breast at neck end of chicken carcase. Work the stuffing in, mould the breast to a good plump shape, pull down flap of loose skin and stitch up with needle and thread.

Stuffing
3 oz (90 g) fine breadcrumbs
1 dessertsp chopped parsley
½ tsp chopped thyme
Salt and pepper
Egg to bind
1 tsp lemon juice

Boiled Fowl

Serves 4-6
1 fowl
1 onion
1 carrot
Sprig of parsley and thyme
4 white peppercorns
1 tsp salt

Put bird in a pan of cold water with the quartered onion and carrot, the parsley, thyme, peppercorns and salt. As soon as it comes to the boil, remove the scum. Then simmer gently until quite tender (about 1½ to 2 hours). Remove bird and place on a hot dish and keep warm.

For the sauce, melt the butter, stir in the flour, cook gently for 3 minutes, stirring all the time. Gradually stir in the milk, add the salt and stir while it boils gently. Add 1 pint (600 ml) of stock in which the chicken was cooked and boil 2 or 3 minutes. Use remainder of stock for soup. Pour sauce over bird.

Very good served with plain boiled rice. Two chopped hard-boiled eggs or 1 tablespoon of finely chopped parsley may be stirred into sauce before it is poured over bird.

For the Sauce
2 oz (60 g) butter
2 oz (60 g) flour
½ pt (300 ml) milk
¼ tsp salt
1 pt (600 ml) stock

Fried Chicken and Chicken Maryland

Serves 4
1½-3 lb (¾-1½ kg) chicken
Flour
Salt and pepper
2 oz (60 g) butter
2 tbsp olive oil, or 2 oz (60 g) fat

You need a very young bird of about 1½ to 3 lb (¾-1½ kg) in weight. Cut into 8 pieces and rub each piece with flour and salt and pepper. Or buy frozen chicken joints.

Put the butter into a thick frying pan together with 2 tablespoons of olive oil or the cooking fat. Heat until smoking hot. Fry your pieces of chicken till light golden brown on all sides, turning them with a spatula so that every part is fried for 2 minutes in the hot fat.

The following accompaniments are good with fried chicken and make one small young bird into a substantial meal for 4 people.

Small sausages, mushrooms, bacon rolls and tomatoes.

Small cobs of corn – 1 per person.

Fried bananas – half a banana, cut longways for each person dipped in flour and fried when the chicken is removed from pan for 2 minutes on each side.

For the famous Southern American dish, Chicken Maryland, the fried chicken is served accompanied by corn cobs, fried bananas and bacon rolls.

Sauté potatoes and peas or green beans are the best vegetables for serving with fried chicken.

Serves 4
1 chicken per person
2-3 oz (60-90 g) butter
2 oz (60 g) margarine
4 bacon rinds or pieces of fatty bacon

Stuffing
¼ lb (120 g) fine breadcrumbs
2 oz (60 g) mushrooms, chopped and lightly sautéed
1 dessertsp finely chopped parsley
1 egg yolk.

Spring Chickens (Poussins)

A whole spring chicken for each person is considered a delicacy. For 4 people it makes a rather expensive meal, but in spring and early summer, you can sometimes buy 4 plump little birds for not very much more than 1 large roasting bird.

You can stuff the small birds or not, as you like. The following stuffing, which is not too strong for their delicate flavour and texture is very good.

Mix everything for stuffing together and insert in breasts of poussins. Stitch up flap of each breast with needle and thread. Alternatively, put the stuffing inside, inserting from the tail end.

Place the little birds, empty or stuffed, in roasting tray, preferably on a grid, though they may lie on the bottom. Cover the breast of each with fatty bacon or rinds. Melt 2-oz (60 g) of butter and the margarine in a small saucepan and pour over the birds so that each is well coated. Put into preheated oven, 400°F/200°C/Gas Mark 6. After 5 minutes, baste with butter which has run down into pan. If not enough, melt 1 oz (30 g) more and pour over. Repeat after 10 minutes and remove bacon from breasts. Repeat basting after 5 minutes. After a further 10 minutes the birds should be nicely browned and cooked exactly enough. Keep hot while you make a rather thin gravy in the pan in which they cooked, after pouring almost all the butter off. Serve as soon as possible.

French fried or straw potatoes or very good creamed potatoes are best with spring chickens and a plain green salad, particularly if it contains some watercress, is better than a cooked green vegetable. Do not serve sausages or bacon rolls with these, the flavours are too strong for the delicate young chickens.

Serves 4
½ to 1 chicken
Salt and pepper
3 hard-boiled eggs
¼ lb (120 g) mushrooms
1 oz (30 g) butter, lard or margarine
¼ lb (120 g) bacon
Parsley
1 lb (½ kg) puff pastry, or raised pie pastry (see Chapter 17)
½ pt (300 ml) white stock
Beaten egg

Chicken Pie

Cut the chicken into small joints, and season these with salt and pepper, cut the hard-boiled eggs in quarters. Slice the mushrooms and sauté them in the fat. Chop the bacon and the parsley. Roll out the pastry and lay a thin strip round the edge of a pie dish. Fill dish with prepared ingredients, then pour in stock so that it does not quite cover top layer. Wet strip of pastry on dish rim with water. Cover with the rest of the pastry, pressing down and trimming the edges. Brush with beaten egg and make a hole in the centre. Decorate with 3 pastry leaves and a rose. Bake in a moderate oven for about 1½ hours. Allow 20 minutes at 450°F/230°C/Gas Mark 8 for pastry to cook, then reduce to 300°F/150°C/Gas Mark 2. If pastry browns too much, cover with foil or greaseproof paper. More hot stock can be poured in through the hole in the pastry before serving.

Boiled Chicken with Rice

Serves 4-6

1 fowl
3 carrots
2 onions
1 bayleaf
Sprig of thyme
1 clove garlic (optional)
½ lb (240 g) rice – Patna or any
long-grained rice
1 oz (30 g) butter
1 oz (30 g) flour
½ pt (300 ml) milk
Salt and pepper

(Poule au Riz – traditional French chicken dish.)

Boil the fowl with the carrots, onions, bayleaf, thyme and garlic, until cooked (1½ to 2 hours). Remove the cooked fowl. Strain the liquid, keeping the vegetables on one side. Boil the rice in the strained liquid for 20 minutes, then strain it, reserving liquid, and keep hot, covered with buttered paper or foil. Melt the butter in a small saucepan and stir in the flour. Cook for a few moments, stirring with a wooden spoon, then add ¾ pint (450 ml) of strained liquid and the milk. Stir, and allow to simmer for 5 minutes. Season to taste.

Remove all the skin from the fowl, carve it into joints and pieces, then pour sauce over. Serve the rice and vegetables separately, or arrange rice in a border round the fowl.

Chicken of the Dukes of Burgundy

Serves 4

1 young roasting chicken cut into 8
pieces or 4 breast portions
Flour
Salt and black pepper
¼ lb (120 g) butter
2 onions
¼ lb (120 g) button mushrooms
¼ pt (150 ml) cooking brandy
½ pt (300 ml) white stock or
chicken stock cube with water
3 tbsp cream
2 egg yolks

Lightly flour, salt and pepper the chicken, and sauté in butter which you have heated in an ovenproof casserole on top of the stove. Turn all the pieces in the butter till they are lightly browned on every side. Add the finely cut onions, and turn lightly in the butter with the chicken for 2 minutes only. Cover the dish closely with lid or foil and place in preheated oven, 350°F/180°C/Gas Mark 4 for 30 minutes. Remove from oven, add small mushrooms. Replace and cook for a further 10 minutes. Take out dish, pour brandy over the pieces of chicken, being careful to cover them as much as possible in pouring. Quickly set light to brandy and after a minute, if still burning, blow out. Lift pieces of chicken and mushrooms on to serving dish and keep hot.

Season the butter, brandy and juice in pan with a little salt and black pepper and stir in stock. Add the cream and egg yolks, mixed together but not beaten. Stir them well in pan and reheat very slowly but do not allow to boil. Pour over chicken and serve. The burnt brandy and cream gives the chicken and the sauce a superb flavour. Serve with plain boiled rice or purée of potatoes and a salad.

Serves 4-6

1 large chicken, 3½-4 lb
(1¾-2 kg), or 8 chicken joints
or breasts
Salt
2 carrots
2 turnips
1 head of celery
Sprig of thyme
Parsley
1 bay leaf
4 cloves
6 peppercorns

Sauce

1 oz (30 g) butter
1 oz (30 g) flour
1 pint (600 ml) chicken stock
¼ pt (150 ml) cream
¼ pt (150 ml) sherry
3 egg yolks
Salt, cayenne pepper
Juice of ½ lemon

Serves 6-8

1 large chicken, 4-6 lb (2-3 kg)
2 onions
4 carrots
2 tomatoes, blanched
2 hard-boiled eggs
1 pkt aspic jelly
Peas, mushrooms, asparagus tips
(optional)

Chicken à la King

Boil the chicken in slightly salted water together with the carrots, turnips, celery, thyme, parsley, bay leaf, cloves and peppercorns. Simmer gently for 1½ to 2 hours, then allow to cool in its own liquid. When cold, discard the skin and carve the breast into thin slices. If joints are used, simmer gently for 40 minutes; if fillets are used, for 25 minutes. Cut and dice the meat from the legs and thighs and place all the pieces of chicken in a dish.

For the sauce, melt the butter in a saucepan, add the flour, stir well, then pour in 1 pint (600 ml) of boiling chicken stock. Simmer for 10 minutes gently, then add the cream and the sherry. Whisk the 3 egg yolks and gradually stir in the sauce a little at a time, until all has been used. Season to taste with salt, cayenne pepper and the lemon juice.

Pour the sauce over the chicken and reheat, but do not allow to boil. Sliced mushrooms sautéed in butter may be added to the chicken before the sauce is poured over.

Chicken in Aspic

Boil the chicken with onions and carrots as in recipe for Chaud-froid of Chicken. Allow to cool in liquor. Remove the chicken, take off skin and carve the breast into neat slices. Arrange these over the bottom and sides of a medium-sized basin which you have previously rinsed with cold water or place a small slice in each of 8 or 9 small individual cocottes or small moulds.

Press a few slices of thinly cut tomatoes and rings of hard-boiled egg against sides of moulds between pieces of chicken. Make up aspic jelly according to directions. Cut the rest of the meat from the chicken, remove skin and dice meat, so that each piece is about ¼ inch (½ cm) square. Place a layer in the moulds or basin on top of the slices of breast. Pour in aspic just to cover. Next put a layer of the cooked carrots diced with cooked peas, mushrooms (previously sliced and sautéed), or cooked asparagus tips. Also add a few slices of tomato and hard-boiled egg. Cover with aspic, add another layer of diced chicken and so on till moulds, or basin, are full, ending with a layer of chicken. The aspic should just cover it.

Leave in refrigerator or cool place to set and serve on a bed of crisp lettuce accompanied by potato salad.

Chicken with Almonds

Cut the chicken into 8 portions. Lightly flour and season with salt and pepper. Melt butter in frying pan, and fry finely sliced onions, without allowing them to brown. Remove and place in the bottom of a wide, shallow casserole with a lid. Put the joints of chicken in the pan and brown on all sides. Remove and arrange in casserole on top of onion. Tip blanched almonds into pan and fry very fast for 2 minutes, shaking pan off the heat. Turn into the casserole over chicken. Stir 1 tablespoon flour into the butter remaining in frying pan. Work it in well, but let it only brown slightly. Stir in stock, adding it slowly and allowing it to thicken smoothly. Add brandy or sherry. Pour sauce over chicken in casserole, cover closely and place in oven at 350°F/180°C/Gas Mark 4 for 45 minutes. Serve at once, having checked the seasoning of the sauce in the casserole.

Serves 6-8
1 roasting chicken or 8 portions
Flour
Salt and pepper
3 oz (90 g) butter
2 medium onions
*3-4 oz (90-120 g) blanched
    almonds*
*½ pt (300 ml) white stock
    (or stock cube and water)*
2 tbsp brandy or sherry

Chicken with Pineapple

This is made exactly as chicken with almonds in the previous recipe, except that the almonds are omitted. While the casserole is cooking in the oven, peel and slice the pineapple, and cut the slices into small wedges, as you would cut a cake. Unless the centre core is very hard, this need not be removed. Fifteen minutes before the casserole is finished, remove from the oven, drop in the pieces of pineapple, stir very lightly so that the sauce covers or coats them, cover the casserole again and put back into oven for the last 15 minutes.

*Same ingredients as recipe above,
    but omitting almonds, and
    adding a small pineapple*

Devilled Chicken Legs

The cooked legs and thighs of any of the larger birds, chicken, turkey, goose, duck, etc., are very good devilled.

In a saucer put the dry mustard, salt, a pinch each of cayenne and black pepper, paprika and curry powder. Mix together, add French mustard and work into a paste. Add 1 oz (30 g) butter and work smooth. Make 4 slits down the lengths of each of the joints to be devilled and work a little of the paste into each. Spread the cut, skinless sides with a little more. Dust the joints with flour, salt, cayenne and black pepper. Place on grill and pour or brush a little melted butter over each.

Grill for 6 minutes, turning so that all sides are grilled. Baste with more butter or with juices from pan two or three times. The danger in grilling cooked joints is that they will be dry.

Serve each joint at once, piping hot, on a strip of buttered toast. A green salad is the best accompaniment and a little plain boiled rice, if liked.

*1 cooked chicken leg per person or
    1 turkey leg between 2*
1 tsp dry mustard
1 tsp salt
Cayenne pepper
Black pepper
½ tsp paprika
½ tsp curry powder
1 dessertsp French mustard
2 oz (60 g) butter
Flour

Serves 6

1 large chicken, 5-6 lb (2½-3 kg)
4 carrots
1 onion
3 or 4 cloves
1 clove garlic (optional)
1 bay leaf
Sprig of thyme
Salt
6 peppercorns
Juice of 1 lemon

Sauce

1 pt (600 ml) white sauce
1 oz (30 g) powdered gelatine
1 tbsp cream
Salt and pepper
Mint or tarragon (optional)
1 pkt aspic jelly

Chaudfroid of Chicken

Place the bird in a large saucepan with the carrots, onion studded with cloves, garlic, bay leaf, thyme, salt and peppercorns, and cover with the lemon juice and 3 pints (1½ l) of water. Bring to the boil. Remove the scum from the surface, reduce the heat and allow to simmer for 1½ to 2 hours. When the bird is cooked, remove it from the heat and allow it to cool in liquid. When cold, remove the bird and take off all the skin. Place the vegetables on one side, and strain the liquid through a fine sieve.

Make 1 pint (600 ml) of white sauce according to the recipe given in Chapter 10, and stir in the powdered gelatine melted in a tablespoon hot water. Bring just to the boil, allow it to cool, then add the cream and salt and pepper to taste.

When tepid, coat the chicken with this sauce. Cut from the cooked carrot a few thin slices and arrange on the breast and legs of the smoothly coated bird. If you have a little young mint or tarragon, a few leaves of these may also be arranged.

Make up the packet of aspic jelly according to directions, allow to cool but not to set, and pour gently over the decorated bird, so that you do not disturb the arranged vegetables. Set in refrigerator or cool place for several hours or overnight. Any surplus aspic which has run off the bird or is left over can be beaten up with a fork and arranged in piles round the bird on its dish. Serve with a good green or mixed salad and potato salad.

This is not a very difficult cold dish, but it looks impressive for a summer luncheon or supper.

Serves 6

1 boiling fowl or large chicken or
*   capon*
2 onions
2 cloves
4 carrots
2 turnips
2 sticks celery
1 clove garlic (optional)
1 oz (30 g) salt
A few peppercorns
1 bay leaf
Sprig of thyme

Sauce

2 oz (60 g) onions
2 oz (60 g) fat
¼ lb (120 g) mushrooms
2 oz (60 g) bacon
1½ oz (45 g) flour
3 tbsp sherry

Casserole of Fowl with Mushrooms

Place the fowl in a very large saucepan. Add the onions, studded with cloves, the carrots split lengthwise, turnips, celery, garlic, salt, peppercorns, bay leaf and thyme. Bring to the boil gently, removing the scum from the surface. Boil gently for 1½ to 2 hours. A 5-6 lb (2½-3 kg) chicken or capon will need about 1½ hours and a boiler about 2 hours. Equally good, and much quicker, buy large chicken portions and simmer for 30-40 minutes. In this case, slice the vegetables finely. When cooked remove from heat and allow to cool in the liquid. Remove solidified fat, take out the fowl, remove all skin and carve it into 8 to 12 pieces. Keep warm. Strain the liquid.

To make the sauce, fry the chopped onions in the fat until brown, together with the sliced mushrooms and diced bacon. Stir in the flour, stir well and moisten with 1 pint (600 ml) of the strained liquid. Add sherry. Place the chicken portions in deep casserole dish, cover them with the sauce, then reheat in tightly covered dish for 10 to 15 minutes.

Casserole of Cooked Cold Chicken

Serves 2-3

½ lb (240 g) cold cooked chicken
Fat for frying
2 medium onions
2 medium carrots
2 rashers lean bacon
1 pt (600 ml) stock or gravy, or stock cube with water
Salt and pepper
Peas or broad beans
¼ lb (120 g) tomatoes or mushrooms (optional)

Cut remains of roast or boiled chicken from carcase, leaving any joints and adding to them scraps of meat from breast and back. Lightly fry sliced onions and carrots, and cut up bacon and place in casserole with chicken on top. Cover with 1 pint (600 ml) of stock from boiled chicken or with gravy left from roast bird. Make up quantity with water or if you have little gravy, use a stock cube. Season, cover and put in oven preheated to 350°F/180°C/Gas Mark 4. Cook for 1 hour.

After 35 minutes, add cold cooked peas or broad beans, or raw shelled ones, and sliced tomatoes or mushrooms, if liked. Cover again. After a further 25 minutes, remove from oven. Season.

If a thicker sauce is preferred, mix 1 oz (30 g) of flour with 1 tablespoon cold water, pour a little boiling stock from casserole into this, stir well, then pour into casserole, stirring gently and replace in oven for 10 minutes.

Coq au Vin

Serves 6

3-3½ lb (1½-1¾ kg) roasting chicken (or use 6 chicken joints)
Flour
2 oz (60 g) butter
¼ lb (120 g) lean bacon
12 small onions
12 button mushrooms
1 clove garlic (optional)
1 bay leaf
Sprig of thyme
1 tbsp brandy
1 pt (600 ml) dry white wine

This is a famous French recipe, served as a very good dinner all over France.

Cut the chicken into 6 portions and rub the pieces in flour. Melt the butter in a thick, deep saucepan, and fry the bacon and onions until brown. When this is done, add the mushrooms and cook for 2 more minutes. Put in the chicken and stir well, then add the garlic and herbs. When the chicken is lightly browned, pour off fat from pan, pour in the brandy and set alight. Add the wine with an equal quantity of water. Simmer gently in a cool oven, 300°F/150°C/Gas Mark 2, for 1½ hours.

Serve just as it is, or sauce may be thickened, if preferred, by pouring a little boiling sauce on to 1 oz (30 g) of flour mixed with 1 tablespoon of water and then pouring all back into sauce and stirring over heat for 3 minutes.

Brochettes of Chicken Livers

Serves 4

2-4 chicken livers per person
1 tbsp olive oil
Salt and pepper
4 rashers bacon
2 onions
4 bay leaves
8 mushrooms (optional)
2 oz (60 g) butter

Also very good with duck livers, goose livers, or turkey livers.

Halve the chicken livers and marinate them in a little olive oil, seasoned with salt and pepper. Then spike them on skewers, alternating with a small square piece of bacon, a thin slice (not ring) of raw onion, ¼ bay leaf and a piece of mushroom. Continue to fill the skewer in this order.

The brochettes may be fried in a frying pan with the butter, turning them so that they cook on all sides, or they may be grilled, also turning them.

Serve as a savoury, a skewer for each person, or as a light supper dish with boiled rice and a salad.

Serves 3
1 duck
Flour, salt and pepper
2 oz (60 g) butter or fat

Roast Duck

Place duck in roasting tin and rub over breast and legs with flour, salt and pepper. Press the butter or cooking fat in small pieces on breast, legs and body. Put in preheated oven, 400°F/200°C/Gas Mark 6. After 20 minutes, remove and prick skin over breast and thighs between leg and body with sharp-pronged fork or pointed skewer, so that you only pierce the skin, not the flesh beneath, in a dozen or so places. This lets the fat run out so that the skin is thin and crisp when done and the flesh not too greasy. Put back in oven.

After another 20 minutes, remove, lightly prick again, and if breast is getting too dark, cover with foil. After a further 20 minutes, the bird should be cooked.

It is usual in England to stuff a duck with sage and onion stuffing · and serve apple sauce separately. If liked, Walnut Stuffing or Prune Stuffing (see Chapter 10) are excellent. If you do not wish to stuff the bird, stew some whole stoned apricots or peaches in a little water with very little sugar. When the duck is removed to the serving dish and the fat poured out of the roasting tin, before starting the gravy, place the drained cooked apricots or peaches in the tin and toss them over a low heat. Lift them out with a perforated spoon or slice and arrange round the duck, 1 for each person.

Stir flour into liquid in tin and make gravy in the normal way. It will be flavoured with the fruit and the slight sharpness brings out the flavour of the duck. A tablespoon of brandy or sherry is an improvement.

Serves 3
1 duck, 3-4 lb (1½-2 kg)
6 oranges
Flour, salt and pepper
Fat
Giblets, cooked, plus their stock
1 tbsp sherry
Fresh mint

Duck with Orange Sauce

Peel and cut one orange into thick slices and place these inside duck. Cut the orange peel up finely and boil in a little water for 10 to 15 minutes. Roast duck as in previous recipe and keep hot. Take the liver from the cooked giblets and crush with the orange peel on a board or in a mortar. Work till it is a smooth paste. (If easier, you can put liver and peel through a blender.) Stir in the sherry. Pour all fat from the pan in which the duck roasted, so that only its juice is left. Pour orange and liver mixture into pan and strain in the giblet stock. Stir over a low heat for 3 minutes. Pour the sauce over the duck and serve with a salad of thinly sliced oranges sprinkled with fresh mint.

Roast Goose

Serves 6-8
1 goose
Flour, pepper and salt
Sage and onion stuffing
3 oz (90 g) cooking fat

A goose is generally stuffed with a sage and onion stuffing.

Rub the goose all over breast and thighs and legs with flour, pepper and salt. Place in roasting tray with cooking fat in pre-heated oven, 400°F/200°C/Gas Mark 6. After 30 minutes remove from oven and prick with sharp fork or skewer all over breast, thighs and between thighs and carcase where there is a lot of fat. Prick very lightly so that you only pierce the skin and not the flesh beneath. Replace in oven and remove and prick again after 1 hour. Allow in total 1½ to 2½ hours according to weight. If breast is becoming too brown, cover with foil. Serve with apple sauce or baked apples.

Casserole of Goose

Exactly as Casserole of Turkey (see page 85) but be very careful that the stock used is free from grease. For goose, omit almonds and use mushrooms and some wine. Place a sage leaf and a sprig of parsley in the casserole and remove before serving.

Braised Guinea Fowl

Serves 3-4
1 guinea fowl (need not be young)
2 medium onions
Sprig of thyme, parsley and marjoram
2 sticks celery
¼ lb (120 g) green grapes
¼ lb (120 g) mushrooms
Flour, salt and pepper
1 oz (30 g) butter, melted
½-¾ pt (300-450 ml) stock or stock and white wine
1 oz (30 g) flour for thickening

In a large, deep casserole with close-fitting lid, place the onions, cut into rings, the herbs, the celery, cut finely, the peeled and stoned grapes, and the sliced mushrooms. On this bed of vegetables place the bird, rubbed over with flour, salt and pepper, and brushed with melted butter. Put enough stock or stock and white wine just to cover the vegetables. Closely cover the casserole and put in oven at 350°F/180°C/Gas Mark 4. After 40 minutes remove lid, baste bird with stock, continue to cook for 20 minutes without lid, raising temperature to 400°F/200°C/Gas Mark 6 so that bird browns a little. Remove from oven and arrange vegetables in a ring on a flat dish with bird in the middle. Thicken sauce with the flour mixed with 1 oz (30 g) water. Stir in a little boiling stock and pour back into casserole and allow to boil for 3 minutes. Pour sauce all over bird and vegetables and serve very hot.

Serves 3-4
1 guinea fowl
2 rashers fat bacon
2 oz (60 g) butter or cooking fat

Sauce
¼ lb (120 g) green grapes
¼ pt (150 ml) giblet stock
¼ pt (150 ml) dry white wine
Cornflour or flour
Salt and pepper

Roast Guinea Fowl

Place the trussed and drawn bird in a roasting tray with 2 slices of fat bacon over the breast. Press the butter or cooking fat in pieces down on to it. Place in oven preheated to 400°F/200°C/Gas Mark 6. Cook for 35 to 50 minutes according to weight, basting every 10 minutes, as guinea fowl is inclined to be dry.

An excellent sauce for guinea fowl may be made by blanching and stoning ¼ lb (120 g) green grapes, making the gravy in the usual way for roasts, but using ¼ pint (150 ml) of giblet stock and ¼ pint (150 ml) dry white wine, then adding the grapes and letting them simmer for 2 minutes in the clear, well-seasoned gravy. Serve in a boat with ladle so that everyone may ladle out some of the grapes with the sauce.

Roast Turkey

(See Christmas Cooking, Chapter 25.)

1 turkey
½-1½ lb (240-720 g) Prune Stuffing (according to size of bird, see Chaper 10)
¼ lb (120 g) butter, melted
Flour
½-1 lb (240-480 g) good clear honey

Turkey Nero

Place the stuffed turkey on a very large sheet of foil, or 2 sheets overlapping, leaving enough foil to wrap right over the turkey. Brush bird all over with a pastry brush dipped in melted butter, turning it so that you can cover all parts. Then dredge with flour.

Pour and spread the honey all over the bird, and turn it so that it is coated everywhere. Make sure there is a smooth thick coating over breast and thighs when you have finished. Leave the surplus which has run on to the foil and make the bird into a completely sealed parcel, breast upwards. Place in baking tray and cook exactly as in recipe in Christmas Cooking (see Chapter 25). Forty minutes before the bird should be cooked, remove from the oven, take bird from tray, unwrap the foil, and pour over the honey and butter which remain on the foil. Put back in oven. When it is ready it will be almost black – for this reason and because of the dark prune stuffing inside, the dish is called 'Nero', which is Italian for black – and is extremely tender, juicy and well flavoured, as the honey and the sealed cooking keep the rather dry meat of the turkey sweet and moist.

Casserole of Turkey

Cut all the turkey meat into neat pieces and lay in ovenproof casserole. Put a layer of stoned prunes, a few almonds and sliced mushrooms, a layer of onion, cut in very fine rings, together with some carrot, also cut very thinly, then a layer of chestnuts and more turkey and so on. Sprinkle each layer with a little salt and pepper. Fill up with turkey stock and/or wine to cover. Cover tightly and place in oven at 350°F/180°C/Gas Mark 4 for 2 hours. Serve with plain boiled rice, or purée potatoes.

The casserole can be served just as it is or the gravy slightly thickened with 1 oz (30 g) flour stirred into 2 tablespoons of water.

This is a rich and delicious casserole if the prunes, nuts and mushrooms are all used.

Serves 4-6

1 ½ lb (¾ kg) cooked turkey meat
¼ lb (120 g) prunes (stoned and soaked 12 hours but not cooked)
2 oz (60 g) almonds
¼ lb (120 g) mushrooms
2 large onions
4 carrots
¼ lb (120 g) chestnuts (shelled and blanched)
Salt and pepper
1 ½ pt (900 ml) turkey stock, or 1 ¼ pt (750 ml) stock and ¼ pt (150 ml) red wine
1 oz (30 g) flour (optional)

GAME

The following are the birds and animals to which the term 'game' is applied, with the dates between which they are in season. It is now sometimes possible to buy them deep frozen at times when they are technically out of season.

Pheasant	October 1st – February 1st
Partridge	September 1st – February 1st
Grouse	August 12th – December 10th
Blackcock	August 20th – December 10th
Capercailzie, Ptarmigan, Plover, Wild Duck, Widgeon, Teal, Snipe, Woodcock	September – May
Buck Venison	June – September
Doe Venison	October – December
Hare	August – March
Quail	Any time
Pigeon	Any time

In England game used always to be eaten 'high' which means that it is 'hung' – that is hung, undrawn (once it is cleaned it will not keep), in a cool place with a draught, where flies cannot get to it (or cats). When blood drops from the beak of the birds, they are ready for eating and can be plucked easily.

Wild duck should not be hung for more than 2 days or 3 at most. Some people like pheasant hung for another day or two after blood falls from the beak, as the flavour is thought to improve.

Length of Time for Hanging Game

Pheasant Partridge	} 5-14 days. 3 days if you do not like it high
Grouse	3-14 days, but should be plucked after 3-5 days
Blackcock Capercailzie	} 7-14 days
Ptarmigan	3-14 days
Plover, Snipe, Quail, Woodcock	} Generally cooked undrawn – woodcock always. Hung 2-5 days, never longer
Wild Duck, Widgeon, Teal	1-2 days
Hares	4-7 days
Venison	7-14 days, according to weather
Wood Pigeons	Fresh

If you order a bird from your butcher or poulterer, you can ask for it 'well hung' or 'fairly fresh'. On the whole 'well hung' game is an acquired taste, and if you have not been brought up to it, you will probably prefer it fairly fresh.

In France and most other parts of the world where the same or slightly different birds occur, they are not eaten 'high' but hung only for 24 hours or so to tenderize them.

General Notes

All young game birds are best plainly roasted and served with their proper accompaniments (see table). A chart of roasting times is given according to the size and the type of meat of the different birds, but it is pointless to give a separate recipe for roasting each kind of game bird, as the same principles apply to all.

All game birds, after hanging (see above) should be drawn and trussed for the table except in the case of woodcock, snipe, quail and plover. These are often cooked without being drawn, which improves the moistness and flavour. A piece of butter or cooking fat or small piece of fat bacon (about ½ to 1 oz (15-30 g) in all cases) should be put inside any drawn bird to help retain moisture.

The birds should be placed in a roasting tray, a little flour, salt and pepper rubbed lightly into breast, legs and thighs, and small pieces of butter, cooking fat or pork or poultry dripping dotted about over the bird. About ½ oz (15 g) is right on the tiny birds, 1 oz (30 g) on a partridge or bird of that size and 2 oz (60 g) for a pheasant. Alternatively, melt the butter or fat and pour and brush it over the bird, so that it has an even coating. Butter is by far the best fat to use as it gives the right crispness and a delicious flavour to the whole outside of the bird. All game birds require frequent basting with the fat from the pan. If there is not enough, melt a little more and pour over.

A thin rasher of fat bacon may be placed over the breast of any game bird with advantage, as it prevents it from drying. It should be removed in every case when the bird is half cooked, so that the breast may brown. Game birds may be larded with a larding needle, but this is not really necessary. (For larding see 'Cooking Terms Explained'.)

Game birds are always cooked in a hot, quick oven. A crisp, brown outside is desirable, but the meat should never be over-cooked. The oven should be preheated to 375-400°F/190-200°C/ Gas Mark 5-6 for all birds except the very small woodcock, snipe, etc., where the oven should be 450-475°F/230-240°C/Gas Mark 8-9. The smaller game birds should always be served on a slice of soft toast, or lightly fried bread as the juice which runs from them gives the bread a delicious flavour.

Accompaniments for Game

Game	Preparation	Potatoes	Other vegetables	Accompaniments and sauces
Grouse Partridge Pheasant	Prepare as for Pheasant. Insert a piece of butter inside the bird, and follow instructions for pheasant	Game Chips, roast or creamed	Cauliflower, onions, celery, green beans, brussels sprouts	Green salad, fried breadcrumbs, bread sauce, thin brown gravy
Wild Duck Widgeon	Prepare as for Pheasant. Insert piece of butter. Roast ¾-1 hour	Game Chips, roast or creamed	Celery, green peas or beans, orange salad or watercress	Cherries stewed without sugar or bottled, thin gravy or orange sauce
Snipe Plover Woodcock	Do not draw before cooking. Place a slice of toast under each bird during the cooking to catch the trail. Roast 15-20 minutes	Game Chips, roast or creamed	Orange salad, green salad	Serve on the toast, fried bread-crumbs, thin gravy
Roast Venison	See instructions on page 94	Roast or boiled	Any green vegetable, carrots, onions, celery	Clear brown gravy and red-currant jelly
Roast Hare	See instructions on page 95	Baked in jackets, or roast	Carrots, onions, or any green vegetable	Stuffing, red-currant jelly, brown gravy

Recipes

In the following section on game, separate recipes applying to individual birds and to hare and venison are given, but the recipe for Salmi of Game and Casserole of Game and Game Pie apply to any bird, or a combination of birds may be used.

Gravy for Game

Giblets from bird
½-1 pt (300-600 ml) water, or
*   ½ pt (300 ml) stock*
Salt and pepper
1 tsp cornflour

This is always made in the same way. Always put the giblets from the bird on to simmer in ½-1 pint (300-600 ml) of water, with a little salt, for at least ¾ hour before the bird will be wanted. With the small undrawn birds this will, not, of course, be possible and you will want a little stock, or a stock cube, for the gravy. The livers may be put aside, if you want to make a savoury or a brochette (see page 81). Remove bird from roasting pan and keep hot. Drain off surplus fat, if any. Place pan over low heat and stir in a teaspoon of cornflour (gravy for game should be clear and for this cornflour or arrowroot must be used, but ordinary plain flour – a level dessertspoon – will make quite good cloudy gravy). Slowly add the giblet stock, pouring through a strainer – ½ pint (300 ml) should give the right consistency. Season rather highly with salt and pepper.

A glass of any red wine, or a little brandy or sherry in place of an equal quantity of stock is an improvement for all game, as it brings out the rich flavour.

Casserole of Game

Serves 3-4
1 pheasant, or 2 smaller birds
2 onions
2 carrots
Salt and pepper
Sprig of thyme, parsley,
*   marjoram*
2 oz (60 g) bacon
¼-½ pt (150-300 ml) red wine
*   and water*
¼ lb (120 g) mushrooms
1 oz (30 g) butter
1 oz (30 g) flour

Old game birds may be used for this.

Place the bird or birds whole in a deep casserole with sliced onions, carrots, salt and pepper, herbs tied together, and the bacon cut in pieces. Cover two-thirds up the bird with red wine and water. Cover the casserole tightly and cook in a 275°F/140°C/ Gas Mark 1 oven for 2 to 3 hours, adding the mushrooms 20 minutes before the birds should be cooked. Remove birds from casserole and joint, discarding skin. Lift pieces of vegetable and bacon with a perforated spoon and put them with the birds. Keep hot.

Make a roux in a saucepan with the butter into which you stir the flour and cook for 3 minutes. Then slowly stir in the liquid in which the bird has been cooked. Season rather highly. Pour back over joints of birds and serve at once very hot.

Plain boiled potatoes or rice are best served with it and cabbage or red cabbage cooked in the oven at the same time are excellent.

Salmi of Game

The birds need not be young, though they must not be old and stringy. Two wild ducks, a partridge and a pigeon, etc., may be used together if you are using birds from a shoot and want to feed 6 or 8 people. A wild duck and 1 pheasant or 2 partridges, if you are buying from a poulterer, will be enough for 4 to 6.

Roast the birds as explained at the beginning of the section. Allow only two-thirds of time. Remove from the oven and allow to cool. The roasting may be done the day before the dish is wanted. Cut up the bird into neat joints and pieces, removing all skin. Put skin and carcase and any juices which have come from the birds, in a saucepan with just enough cold water to cover and boil for 30 to 45 minutes to make a stock. Meanwhile, peel and finely slice onion and carrot and fry to a dark brown in the fat. Stir in the flour gradually and add the stock, slowly, stirring until it boils and thickens. Season with salt and pepper. Allow to simmer on a very low heat, stirring from time to time, for 10 minutes. Meanwhile grate the orange rind and stir into sauce. Arrange the pieces of the bird in a casserole. Lightly fry the mushrooms and add. Strain the sauce through a fine strainer into a clean bowl, and stir in the wine and the lemon juice. Season more if necessary and pour over the bird and mushrooms. Cook very gently, well covered, either in a 300°F/150°C/Gas Mark 2 oven, or on top of stove over very low heat, for ¾ hour to 1½ hours, or till the pieces of bird are tender and beginning to leave the bones. Serve on a flat dish with triangular croûtons of fried bread or pastry around it.

Bird or birds
1 onion
1 carrot
2 oz (60 g) butter or cooking fat
1½ oz (45 g) flour
Salt and pepper
1 orange
¼ lb (120 g) mushrooms
¼ pt (150 ml) red wine
Juice of ½ lemon

Casserole of Cooked Game

Serves 3-4

Any joints and pieces of cooked game may be stewed in stock from the carcase which has previously boiled for at least an hour. Add to this stock the pieces of bird, the finely cut onions and carrots, the cut rashers of bacon, a sprig each of parsley and thyme and a bay leaf, salt and pepper and any or all of the following which you have available: 2 or 3 tomatoes cut in quarters and added 20 minutes before casserole is cooked; ¼ lb (120 g) of peas, cooked or raw – 15 minutes; mushrooms, sliced – 10 minutes; large cooking apple, peeled and cored and cut in thick rings – 10 minutes; young marrow, diced – 15 minutes.

Remove casserole and serve at once. Gravy can be thickened with 1 oz (30 g) flour stirred into a little water to which the boiling stock is added.

An old pheasant, or 2 smaller
* birds*
Stock from the carcase
2 onions
2 carrots
2 rashers bacon
Sprig of parsley, thyme
1 bay leaf
Salt and pepper
As available;
2 or 3 tomatoes
¼ lb (120 g) peas, cooked
* or raw*
¼ lb (120 g) mushrooms
1 large cooking apple
¼ lb (120 g) marrow, diced
1 oz (30 g) flour (optional)

*Young bird or birds, ½ or 1 per
person according to size
Salt and pepper
2 oz (60 g) butter, melted
Any of the following garnishes:
  Watercress
  Bacon
  Mushrooms
  Croûtons
1 tin pâté de foie, or
  ¼ lb (120 g) smooth pâté*

Grilled or Spatchcocked Game

All small young birds, including chickens and ducks, may be cooked in this way, which is quick and delicious, but the bird must be very young.

Take a sharp, heavy knife and cut the drawn but untrussed bird right through the breast bone so that the bird can be opened out flat, the halves joined only along the back. Lay on grill, rub with salt and pepper. Brush all over on both sides with melted butter and grill 4 minutes on each side. If it begins to brown too much, turn grill down and baste with a little more butter. Serve at once, on a hot dish garnished with watercress, grilled or fried mushrooms, rashers of bacon, or croûtons of fried bread.

Two minutes before the spatchcocked bird is cooked, see that the inside is uppermost and spread both halves with the contents of a tin of pâté de foie. Grill another 2 minutes.

Serves 6
*2 partridges or 1 and another
  game bird, or 1 pheasant
1 large onion
1 oz (30 g) butter
2 rashers bacon
½ lb (240 g) veal or steak
  (optional)
Sprig of thyme
1 bay leaf
Salt and pepper
About 1 pt (600 ml) stock
2 hard-boiled eggs
¼ lb (120 g) mushrooms
  (optional)
8-10 oz (240-300 g) short or flaky
  pastry, or 1 lb (½ kg) raised pie
  pastry (see Chapter 17)*

Game Pie

Joint the bird or birds, cut up onion and fry with joints of birds in butter until bird is lightly browned. Place in a saucepan with rashers of bacon rolled up and the veal or steak cut into 1 inch (2½ cm) pieces. Add the herbs and season. Just cover with stock and simmer till tender. Allow to cool. Tip into a suitable pie dish, add hard-boiled eggs, cut in quarters, and sliced mushrooms. Add a little more stock or water to bring liquid within ½ inch (1 cm) of top of solid meat. Cover with pastry and bake in a preheated oven at 400°F/200°C/Gas Mark 6 for 25 minutes or till pastry is well browned. Then reduce heat, covering pastry with foil or paper, if necessary, and allow to cook for a further 15 minutes.

Special Roast Grouse

1 grouse per person
Strips of fatty bacon or ham
Salt and pepper
Sprig of thyme

Wrap strips of bacon or ham around the bird and season it with salt and pepper. Put a sprig of thyme inside bird and roast the bird in a 400°F/200°C/Gas Mark 6 oven for 15 to 20 minutes according to size. Grouse should be served underdone.

As the breast only is eaten, take off the legs, remove and chop the meat and mix with a little of the gravy. Save the grouse liver, fry it slightly, mix it with the chopped leg meat and gravy, and spread the whole on piece of fried bread. Place the carved breast on this and serve.

Cold roast grouse is considered a particular delicacy for luncheon or supper. It should be very underdone and a plain green salad with a French dressing should be served with it. There should be a bird for each person. Of course, a cold roast bird is not served on toast.

Roast Partridge from Normandy

1 partridge per person
¼ lb (120 g) calves' liver
2 oz (60 g) breadcrumbs
4 cooking apples
Fat bacon
Butter, melted
¼ pt (150 ml) brandy

Fry the liver with the partridge liver. Mince and mix with bread-crumbs, and fill the bird with this stuffing. Meanwhile, peel and core the apples and place them in the roasting tray with the partridge wrapped in bacon in the middle. Brush apples and bird over with melted butter. Cook for 15 minutes in preheated oven, 400°F/200°C/Gas Mark 6. Pour cooking brandy over bird and set it alight. Remove bird and apples to a hot serving dish and keep hot while you make gravy in roasting pan.

Casserole of Partridge with Cabbage

Serves 2-3
Brace of old birds
4 onions
2 rashers bacon
2 carrots
2 oz (60 g) sliced bacon
Salt and pepper
Sprinkling of chopped parsley and thyme
1 Savoy cabbage
Stock made from trimmings
Flour

Place an onion inside each bird and a rasher of bacon over each. Put them in a large casserole with sliced carrots and remaining 2 onions cut into rings, the sliced bacon, salt and pepper, and the parsley and thyme. Cut the cabbage into 4. Place this around the birds in the casserole, cover with boiling stock, and simmer gently for 2 hours. Lift cabbage carefully on to large flat dish, arranging it to leave room for birds in the middle. Thicken the stock slightly and pour over everything. Serve very hot with plain boiled potatoes.

Both cabbage and partridges benefit from being cooked together.

Serves 6-8
2 pheasants
2 oz (60 g) butter
2 shallots or 1 onion
2 rashers fat bacon
Flour

Roast Pheasant

Put 1 oz (30 g) of butter, and 1 shallot, or ½ onion, inside each bird. Wrap a piece of bacon around the breast of each and put into the roasting tray. Cover well with foil, then put into a preheated oven, 400°F/200°C/Gas Mark 6. Roast for 30 minutes. Remove the birds from the oven and uncover them. Dredge them lightly with flour, baste them well, then return them to the oven to brown for 10 minutes.

By roasting covered, you prevent the breasts from drying. If you prefer to roast them uncovered, flour lightly at the start and baste well every 10 minutes.

Serves 3-4
1 young rabbit
Herb Forcemeat (see Chapter 25)
2 rashers fatty bacon
½ lb (240 g) dripping
1 tbsp flour
½ pt (300 ml) stock or water
Salt and pepper

Roast Rabbit

Stuff the rabbit with forcemeat. Cover the back of the rabbit with rashers of fatty bacon, and cover with foil. Heat the dripping in a baking tin, put in the rabbit, place in a hot oven and bake for 1 hour. Baste well about every 10 minutes, for rabbit is dry and flavourless unless well basted. After 50 minutes baking, remove the paper and bacon and brown. Place on a hot dish.

For gravy, drain off all the fat, stir in the flour. Pour in the stock or water and season well.

Bacon rolls and redcurrant jelly are good with roast rabbit.

Serves 4-6
1 rabbit
½ lb (240 g) ham or bacon
2 medium onions
2 oz (60 g) dripping
Salt and pepper
1 pt (600 ml) stock
Sprig of thyme
1 bay leaf
½ lb (240 g) flaky or short pastry
  (see Chapter 17)

Rabbit Pie

Cut the rabbit into joints and the ham or bacon into thin slices. Cut up the onions. Melt the dripping in a saucepan, and fry the rabbit joints, ham and onions in it for 5 minutes. Sprinkle well with salt and pepper, add the stock and herbs and simmer gently for an hour.

Leave until cold. Then fill a pie dish with the meat. Add the stock, cover with pastry (frozen short pastry is very good and may be brushed over with a beaten egg before baking, which much improves the appearance), and bake in a preheated oven, 400°F/200°C/Gas Mark 6, for 20 minutes till pastry is cooked. Then reduce the heat to 350°F/180°C/Gas Mark 4. Cover pastry with foil and cook a further 15 minutes.

Casserole of Rabbit

Cut the rabbit into neat joints and the bacon into small pieces and dust with flour. Chop the onion and parsley finely. Put a layer of bacon in a casserole, then some joints of rabbit. Sprinkle with pepper and add onion and parsley. Continue the layers until everything is used. Add water to cover. Cover tightly and cook 1½ hours at 350°F/180°C/Gas Mark 4. Remove, check seasoning, thicken gravy if liked, and serve.

Serves 4
1 young rabbit
½ lb (240 g) thin rashers bacon
1 dessertsp flour
1 large onion
Parsley
Pepper
Salt to taste

Curried Rabbit

Cut the rabbit into joints, dust with flour, and fry each in fat until brown. Cut up the onions, and fry these with the apple rings, then dust in the curry powder, and some more flour. Put the rabbit into a saucepan, and cover with stock or water. Boil up, then add the onions, etc., and simmer for 1½ hours or till the meat seems quite done.

Meanwhile cook the rice and keep hot. Squeeze the lemon juice over the rabbit, and pile in the centre of the dish with a wall of boiled rice around. Pour all the vegetables and the sauce over the rabbit.

Serves 4-6
1 rabbit
Flour
2 oz (60 g) fat
1 lb (½ kg) onions
2 large apples, peeled and cut in rings
3 tsp curry powder
Stock or water
¾ lb (360 g) rice
Juice of ½ lemon

Rabbit Pudding with Mushrooms

Line a good-sized pudding basin with a suet crust (see Chapter 17), put in a layer of rabbit, finely chopped sage and onion, then a layer of mushrooms. Continue until the basin is filled, sprinkling flour between each layer. Cut the slices of bacon in thin strips and place over the top layer of meat. Then cover firmly with suet crust pressed down to join moistened edge of the crust lining the sides. Cover with greaseproof paper or foil, twisted well over edges of pudding basin and then tie up in pudding cloth, or cover with a lid or saucer. Stand bowl in steamer top and fit over large saucepan of water, or stand direct in large saucepan with water coming halfway up bowl. Cover tightly and steam for 2 to 3 hours. Look at water level and add a little more hot water when necessary, being careful not to wet the pudding.

Either stand bowl on dish with a napkin folded round it or turn pudding out – there is always a risk of a meat pudding breaking and it is safer to serve in the bowl.

Serves 6
1 or 2 young rabbits, cut in joints
¼ lb (120 g) suet crust
6 sage leaves
2 large onions
¼-½ lb (120-240 g) mushrooms
1 oz (30 g) flour
3 slices fatty bacon

Serves 6-8
*3-4 lb (1½-2 kg) venison
(preferably the haunch)
Dripping or cooking fat
1 oz (30 g) flour*

Marinade
*1 carrot, sliced
1 onion
1 bay leaf
A few peppercorns
Sprig of thyme
1 clove garlic
1 dessertsp brown sugar
½ pt (300 ml) red wine
2 tbsp vinegar*

Roast Venison (1)

Roast venison is inclined to be hard and dry, but if it is properly cooked, the flavour is very subtle.

Marinate the venison for 24 hours in the marinade (which will afterwards make the sauce).

For the marinade, boil the carrot, onion, bay leaf, peppercorns, thyme, garlic and sugar in the wine and vinegar for 10 minutes. Leave to get cold and lay venison (saddle or haunch) in the marinade in a cool larder. From time to time turn it and spoon the mixture over it.

Remove meat from marinade and roast in preheated oven, 350°F/180°C/Gas Mark 4 allowing 15 minutes to the pound (½ kg). Use plenty of dripping or cooking fat and baste frequently.

When cooked, remove from pan and keep hot. Pour off any surplus fat from pan. Work in the flour and gradually stir into it the marinade liquor, pouring through a strainer. Stir well and allow to simmer for 5 minutes. Check seasoning and serve in sauce boat.

Serves 6-8
*3-4 lb (1½-2 kg) venison
1 lb (½ kg) flour
½ pt (300 ml) water*

Roast Venison (2)

Take the piece of venison to be roasted and make a thick paste with 1 lb (½ kg) flour to a ½ pint (300 ml) of water, allowing enough to cover meat entirely. Roll out to about ½ inch (1¼ cm) thickness. Encase the joint in the paste and seal up everywhere. Place on a roasting tray in a preheated oven at 450°F/230°C/Gas Mark 8 for 10 minutes. Then reduce heat to 350°F/180°C/Gas Mark 4 and cook for 30 minutes to each pound (½ kg) of meat and 30 minutes over. No fat is needed. Make a thin, clear gravy, as in recipe for all game gravies, but using butter in which to work the flour and meat stock or a stock cube and water.

Break the crust from the venison and discard. Place the joint on a hot dish and serve at once with the gravy and redcurrant jelly.

This way of cooking venison is well worth trying as all the flavour and moisture are kept in by the crust.

Serves 6
*1 hare
2 oz (60 g) flour
Bunch of mixed herbs
2 onions
6 cloves
½ tsp black pepper
Strip of lemon peel
½ pt (150 ml) red wine
1 oz (30 g) butter
¼ pt (150 ml) port wine*

Jugged Hare

Wash hare and cut into small joints, flouring each piece. Put these into a saucepan with the herbs, onions, each stuck with 3 cloves, pepper and lemon peel. Add red wine and enough water to cover, and let it simmer until tender – about 2 hours. Take out pieces of hare, thicken the gravy with the butter and the remaining flour, and add port wine. Let this boil for 10 minutes, then strain over the hare, and serve very hot.

Redcurrant jelly and forcemeat balls should be served with this dish.

Roast Hare

Serves 6-8
1 young hare
Forcemeat
¼ lb (120 g) rashers fat bacon
½ lb (240 g) dripping
2 dessertsp flour
½ pt (300 ml) water or stock
Salt and pepper
Juice of ½ lemon
1 tbsp redcurrant jelly
¼ pt (150 ml) red wine (optional)

Only a young hare is fit for roasting. If the hare is older, have the saddle cut separately and roast only this, jugging the remainder.

Stuff the hare with forcemeat (see Chapter 25) and tie slices of fat bacon on to it. Heat the dripping in a roasting pan, put in the hare, cover with foil and put in a hot oven. Baste it well during the cooking, otherwise it will be dry. Use more dripping, if necessary. When nearly done, remove the bacon, flour the hare, baste well and cook till nicely browned. Pour off all fat from the tin and mix in a dessertspoon of flour. Add the water or stock, and season with salt and pepper. Stir while it boils gently for 5 minutes, add lemon juice, redcurrant jelly and the wine and bring to the boil. Strain and serve.

Chestnuts made into a purée or served with brussels sprouts (see Chapter 11) go very well with roast hare.

The Royal Recipe for Hare

Serves 6
1 saddle of hare
2 oz (60 g) butter

Marinade
½ pt (300 ml) dry white wine
2 carrots and 2 medium onions,
    finely sliced
1 clove garlic
1 stick celery, sliced
1 bayleaf
3 cloves
Sprigs of parsley and thyme

Sauce
1 oz (30 g) sugar
1 tbsp wine vinegar
1 oz (30 g) almonds
1 oz (30 g) raisins
1 oz (30 g) currants
2 oz (60 g) dark chocolate

(This recipe is best of all for wild boar, but it is also excellent for hare or venison.) The meat is marinated in the marinade for about 12 hours.

To make marinade stir all ingredients together. Turn the saddle of hare in the marinade several times and spoon the vegetables and liquids over it.

Melt the butter in a large saucepan, remove the hare and the vegetables from the marinade, and brown slightly in the butter. Gradually spoon the marinade liquor over it, a little every few minutes, covering it in between. Very slowly simmer for about an hour to 1¼ hours.

Meanwhile prepare the sauce. Put the sugar into a saucepan with a teaspoon of water and caramelize over heat. Add the wine vinegar and bring to the boil. When cooked, remove the hare and keep hot. Strain into the sugar/vinegar sauce the liquid in which the hare was cooked. Add the blanched and halved almonds, the raisins, the currants, and the finely grated dark, bitter chocolate. Stir for 2 minutes. This sauce is wonderful with the strong hare or venison meat, as the chocolate brings out the flavour without being really discernible. It can be served separately and the hare carved at the table or the hare may be carved in slices in the kitchen and the sauce poured over. Be careful to keep very hot. Plain rice or boiled potatoes are best with this dish and red wine, rough cider, or beer should be drunk with it, as it calls for something with a more definite taste than water.

Chart of Roasting Times

Type	Weight	°F	°C	Gas Mark	Time per pound (½ kg)	Full roasting time
Poussin or Baby Chicken	¾-1 lb (360-480 g)	375-400	190-200	5-6	—	12-15 minutes
Spring Chicken	1-1½ lb (½-¾ kg)	375-400	190-200	5-6	15 minutes	18-20 minutes
Roaster	3-4 lb (1½-2 kg)	375-400	190-200	5-6	15 minutes	1-1¼ hours
Turkey	12-25 lb (6-12 kg)	350-375	180-190	4-5	12 minutes	2½-3½ hours
Goose	8-12 lb (4-6 kg)	350-375	180-190	4-5	12 minutes	1½-2½ hours
Duck	4-5 lb (2-2½ kg)	375-400	190-200	5-6	12 minutes	50-60 minutes
Guinea Fowl	1½-2 lb (¾-1 kg)	375-400	190-200	5-6	12 minutes	35-50 minutes
Pigeon	1 lb (½ kg)	375-400	190-200	5-6	25 minutes	20-25 minutes
Rabbit	4-5 lb (2-2½ kg)	375	190	5	12 minutes	50-60 minutes
Grouse	—	375-400	190-200	5-6	—	15-20 minutes
Partridge	—	375-400	190-200	5-6	—	15-20 minutes
Pheasant	—	375-400	190-200	5-6	—	30-35 minutes
Plover	—	375-400	190-200	5-6	—	15 minutes
Snipe	—	375-400	190-200	5-6	—	15 minutes
Teal	—	375-400	190-200	5-6	—	15 minutes
Widgeon	—	375-400	190-200	5-6	—	15-18 minutes
Wild Duck	1½-2½ lb (¾-1¼ kg)	375-400	190-200	5-6	20 minutes	30-50 minutes
Woodcock	—	375-400	190-200	5-6	—	15-18 minutes
Ptarmigan	—	375-400	190-200	5-6	20 minutes	—
Hare	3-4 lb (1½-2 kg)	375-400	190-200	5-6	20 minutes	1-1½ hours*
Black cock	1½-2 lb (¾-1 kg)	375-400	190-200	5-6	15 minutes	—
Capercailzie	2½-3 lb) (1¼-1½ kg)	375-400	190-200	5-6	15-20 minutes	45-60 minutes
Venison	—	350-400	180-200	4-6	20 minutes	—

*Oven heat may need reducing after 30-40 minutes.

BEEF, LAMB, PORK AND VEAL

Buying

All good meat should be firm and elastic in texture. It should never be flabby or moist. There should not be too much fat in proportion to lean and the lean should be finely grained.

When you buy beef, the lean should be bright, deep red, intergrained with fat, with very little gristle between fat and lean. Dark-coloured, coarse-grained beef with deep yellow fat should be avoided. Very yellow fat on any meat is a sign of inferior quality.

When you buy mutton the lean should not be so red as that of beef but should have a slightly brownish tint. The lean should be firm and close in texture, and the fat should not be grained or marbled as it is in beef, but white, hard and waxy. The best mutton is plump and has small bones.

When you buy lamb it should be paler in colour than mutton and the fat very white. Bones should be moist and red at the joints.

The flesh of pork should be pinky-white, finely grained and smooth but firm to the touch. The fat should be pearly-white.

The flesh of veal should be pale pink or white and finely grained. The fat should be white.

Remember that in working with meat, raw or cooked, at the table or in the kitchen, sharp knives make all the difference.

BEEF

Cuts

Cut	Method of Cooking
Sirloin	Roast (Minute and Entrecote Steaks are cut from the sirloin).
Topside	Roasted or braised or pot roasted.
Silverside	Boiled, fresh or salted.
Fillet	Best cut of all. May be roasted or used for steaks. (Fillet steaks, Châteaubriand, Tournedos and Filets Mignons come from it.)
Rump Steak	For grilled or fried steaks or can be roasted.

Cut	Method of Cooking
Fore Ribs	Make a prime roast, on the bone or boned and rolled.
Brisket	Boiled, generally salted.
Shank and Shin	Used for stock and beef tea. Meat from bone may be minced or diced.
Aitchbone	A fairly good roasting joint.

Recipes

Steak

¼-½ lb (120-240 g) fillet or rump steak per person
Salt and freshly ground black pepper
About ½ oz (15 g) butter for each steak

A fillet steak is the tenderest and the most expensive. Allow 4-6 oz (120-180 g) per person.

A rump steak has on the whole more flavour than a fillet steak, but there is more risk that it may be a little hard or tough. Some people beat the steak to break the fibres so that it is more tender, but this is also inclined to make it dry and should not be necessary. It is best cut about ½ inch (1¼ cm) thick. Allow ¼ to ½ lb (120-240 g) per person when trimmed.

In all cases, have the grill really hot before you put the steak under or over it – under in the case of gas or electricity, usually over if you have a special charcoal grill. Rub the steaks lightly with salt and pepper, freshly ground black pepper is best. Melt the butter in a cup and brush or spoon it over the steaks on both sides. Put them on the rack of the grill and cook on each side for

3 minutes for 'rare'
4 for 'à point'
5 for 'medium'
6 for 'well done'
} if a thick fillet or rump

½ a minute less in each case if cut less than ½ inch (1¼ cm) thick.

Serve at once. Never attempt to keep grilled steak waiting as it hardens and dries very quickly. It is best, if you have visitors, to ask them how they like their steaks before starting to cook them. You can generally cook 4 at once on a grill turn and remove any that are wanted rare before the others. The rare steaks can be served immediately while the others finish cooking.

The steaks may be served with a pat of Green Butter, well chilled, placed on each just before serving. Or simply with the butter which has run from them, seasoned with salt and pepper and a squeeze of lemon juice poured over.

Tournedos Rossini

Each fillet (or tournedos) is served on a slice of lightly fried bread, cut in a round shape to exactly fit the steak. On each fillet is placed a slice of pâté de foie gras and Espagnole Sauce is served with it.

Put the tournedos in a circle on a plate and place bunches of watercress in the centre.

4-6 oz (120-180 g) steak per person
1 slice bread per steak
2 oz (60 g) pâté
Espagnole Sauce
(see Chapter 10)
Watercress

Entrecôte Béarnaise or Entrecôte Maître d'hôtel

An entrecôte is a neatly cut and trimmed piece of rump steak, which is grilled as above. For maître d'hôtel serve with Maître d'hôtel Sauce poured over it and for béarnaise serve this sauce separately.

6 oz (180 g) rump steak per person
Maître d'hôtel or Béarnaise
Sauce (see Chapter 10)

Boiling Beef

Place meat in large, deep saucepan with water to cover. Add salt and slowly bring to the boil. Remove all scum from the top. When the liquid is clear, add the prepared vegetables, the herbs, tied together, and the onions studded with cloves. Simmer for 3 hours. Remove the meat and keep it hot, and take out the vegetables and keep them hot in a little of the stock. Strain the broth, and retain some for soup, some for boiled dumplings.

½ lb (240 g) shredded cabbage may be added 30 minutes before removing the meat from the stock, or the same quantity of peas or beans.

If the liquid boils away, it should be replaced with boiling water. The beef should be served on a flat dish with the vegetables and dumplings round it. The stock should be seasoned with additional salt and pepper and strained into a sauce boat.

Serves 4-6
About 3-4 lb (1½-2 kg) joint
1 oz (30 g) salt
Any or all of following vegetables:
4 leeks
4 carrots
1 head celery
4 turnips
Sprig of thyme, parsley and a bay leaf
2 or 3 onions
4 cloves
Dumplings (see Chapter 17)

Boiled Salt Beef

This is not always available in supermarkets, but it is worth asking for a piece of beef that is slightly salted. Silverside is generally considered the best for this purpose. If you like the meat only just salted, put it to soak overnight in cold water. The next day cook exactly as fresh beef in recipe above but omit additional salt.

May be served with Parsley Sauce (see Chapter 10) if preferred to thin stock. In this case, omit the dumplings.

Serves 4-6
3 or 4 lb (1½-2 kg) salt beef
4 carrots
4 turnips
2 onions
Dumplings (see Chapter 17)

Spiced Brisket of Beef (To be served cold)

Serves 4-6
*3 to 4 lb (1½-2 kg) salted brisket
    of beef
2 carrots
1 onion
Bunch of mixed herbs
Salt, pepper, cloves
1 tsp allspice and mace*

Put the beef in a large casserole, together with the rest of the ingredients, and cover completely with water. If preferred, any cheap red wine or cider or beer may be used instead of half the water. In all cases, use the stock to make an excellent soup. Stew gently in low oven, 250-300°F/120-150°C/Gas Mark ½-2, closely covered for 4 hours. When the beef is cooked and tender, allow it to cool in the liquor overnight.

The next day, remove it, place on large plate, put another on top and a heavy weight on that and leave again till next day. Serve with salad and potatoes in their jackets. Carve in very thin slices.

Will keep several days in a refrigerator.

Boiled Tongue

Serves 8-10
*1 slightly salted or pickled ox
    tongue – ask butcher for this
2 carrots
2 onions
2 cloves
1 stick celery
2 leeks
1 bay leaf
Sprig of thyme
Sprig of parsley*

Place the tongue in cold water. Add the carrots halved lengthwise, the onions studded with cloves, the celery, leeks, bay leaf, thyme and parsley. Simmer gently, cook for 2 hours.

When cooked, peel off the skin while still hot. It will come off very easily. Remove the small bones, which should easily pull out, and trim the root tidily. May be served hot and then cold.

If it is to be eaten cold straightaway, it is best to roll the tongue into a round before boiling, skewer and tie it firmly, and after it has cooled in its liquor, press between two plates as in recipe for Spiced Brisket of Beef. It should form a good jelly.

The stock from the tongue is not so good for soup as that from the beef as it is greasy and rather tasteless.

Boiled Tripe

Wash and scrape the tripe thoroughly in several warm waters, removing all discoloured parts. Put it into a deep pan, cover with cold water, bring it almost to boiling point, then throw away water, rinse under tap and repeat process. When it comes to the boil for the third time, simmer very slowly for 6 to 8 hours. Then prepare as in following recipe, before serving.

Stewed Tripe

Serves 6-8
*½ lb (240 g) well-boiled tripe
½ oz (15 g) flour
½ oz (15 g) butter
2 tbsp milk
2 tbsp tripe liquor
2 boiled onions
Salt and pepper*

Make a white sauce with the flour, butter, milk, and tripe liquor (see recipe in Chapter 10). Cut the tripe into neat pieces about an inch (2½ cm) square and cut up the onions. Add these to the sauce, season well, and simmer very gently for about 20 minutes. Serve very hot.

Tripe in the Manner of Caen

Soak the tripe in cold water for 1 hour, changing the water three or four times. When soaked clean, cut into 2 inch (5 cm) squares, dry them with a cloth and rub them in flour. Halve the cow heels and place them in the bottom of an earthenware dish. Slice the onions, rub them in flour and cover the cow heels with a layer of them. Cover with the tripe, then make another layer of onion blended with the shredded leeks and the sliced carrots. Flavour by adding 1 bay leaf, celery, thyme, garlic, peppercorns and salt to taste. Cover with the cider. Seal tightly with greaseproof paper and the lid. Cook in a very low oven, 250°F/120°C/Gas Mark ½, for 7 to 8 hours.

This can cook all night as it does not need watching and can be served directly from the casserole. The cow heels enrich the stock, but should be removed before serving.

Serves 6-8
2 lb (1 kg) tripe
Flour
2 cow heels (may be omitted)
1 lb (½ kg) onions
2 leeks
2 carrots
1 bay leaf
1 stick celery
Sprig of thyme
2 cloves garlic
4 peppercorns
Salt
2 pt (1 l) dry cider

Beefsteak and Kidney Pudding (1)

Prepare the steak and kidney by cutting core and skin away from kidney and removing all skin, fat and gristle from steak. Cut into 1 inch (2½ cm) pieces and roll in flour, salt and pepper.

Make the pastry, turn on to floured board, and roll out to about ⅓ inch (¾ cm) in thickness, keeping the pastry round. Line a greased bowl with the pastry, pressing it well to bottom and sides, and trim off at top. Put in half of the pieces of steak and kidney, then add stock, and fill up with the rest of the meat. Knead trimmings of pastry and roll into a round. Wet the edge of the pudding; lay the round of pastry over the top and press the edges together. Cover with buttered greaseproof paper, turned in over the rim of the bowl. Then cover with a plate or lid which fits the bowl as well as possible. Stand in large saucepan with water coming a third up the sides of bowl. Bring to boil and allow to simmer for 3 hours. Refill with boiling water whenever water has boiled low. Try to keep top of pudding dry. For greater safety you can tie a pudding cloth over top of basin, plate and all. Turn the pudding out of the basin on to a hot dish and serve, or serve in basin with napkin tied round it.

Serves 6
1 lb (½ kg) stewing steak
3 sheep's kidneys, or ½ lb (240 g) ox kidney
1 dessertsp flour
1 small tsp salt
¼ tsp pepper
1 lb (½ kg) suet pastry (see Chapter 17)
½ pt (300 ml) stock or water

Serves 6
1 lb (½ kg) topside or rump steak
½ lb (240 g) ox kidney or
    4 sheep's kidneys
1 lb (½ kg) suet pastry (see
    Chapter 17)
1 oz (30 g) chopped onion
A little parsley
Salt and pepper
¼ lb (120 g) mushrooms

Steak Pudding (2)

Dice the steak finely and trim the kidneys of all fat and skin.

Make the pastry, turn on to floured board, roll it out thinly and line the inside of the pudding basin with it, allowing the pastry to overlap the sides by ½ inch (1¼ cm). Keep a little pastry in reserve for covering the pudding. Mix the onion and meat together with a little chopped parsley, salt and pepper and sliced mushrooms. Fill the basin with this mixture and add ¼ pt (150 ml) of cold water. Wet the edges of the pastry with milk or water. Cover with a layer of pastry, and seal the edges together firmly. Cook exactly as in the previous recipe.

This pudding is quite good if the kidney is omitted, for those who do not eat kidney, but the gravy is not so rich.

In either recipe, a hole may be cut in the crust before serving and if the inside seems a little dry, hot water may be poured in – it will mix with the gravy by the time the pudding is served. Or a little warm cider or sherry may be used.

Serves 6
½ a calf's head
Salt
Lemon juice
1 carrot
1 turnip
1 onion
1 stick celery
Sprig each of thyme and parsley
1 bay leaf
6 peppercorns

Brain Sauce
Calf's brains
Salt
A little lemon juice
2 oz (60 g) butter or margarine
2 oz (60 g) flour
1 pt (600 ml) stock
Pepper
Chopped parsley
Cayenne pepper

Calf's Head and Brain Sauce

Remove the brains from the head and keep them for the sauce. Wash the head thoroughly and clean it. Soak for 2 to 4 hours in salted water, changing the water two or three times. After the soaking, wash it again, then drain and rub with lemon juice.

Put the head into a saucepan and cover it with salted water. Bring to the boil and skim. Put the carrot, turnip, onion and celery in the saucepan with the herbs and peppercorns. Cover the pan with the lid, bring to the boil, then simmer gently until the head is tender and the bones can be pulled out easily – 2 to 3 hours. Remove the head from the pan (retain stock for brain sauce), drain it and remove all the bones. Cut the meat into neat pieces, place on very hot dish and serve with brain sauce poured over.

Wash the brains in salted water, then let them soak in fresh salted water for 1 to 2 hours. This can be done while the head is cooking. Rinse the brains in several changes of water, then put them in a saucepan with enough cold water to cover. Add a little salt and lemon juice. Bring to the boil, strain, and remove the skin from the brains. Put them back into the pan and simmer gently for about 15 minutes. Drain and chop them.

Melt the butter in a small pan, stir in the flour, cook for a few minutes without browning. Add the stock gradually, still stirring, until the sauce is smooth. Cook gently for about 5 minutes, then add a few drops of lemon juice, pepper, parsley, the chopped brains and a pinch of cayenne.

Goulash

Cut up meat into small pieces, removing all skin and fat. Fry the sliced onions in fat for 5 minutes in bottom of large thick saucepan, then add the diced meat.

Continue cooking for 5 minutes, then sprinkle with paprika. Stir well and add the skinned and quartered tomatoes. Simmer for 5 minutes. Add the bay leaf, chopped celery and crushed garlic, season to taste with salt and pepper and just cover with water. Simmer gently for 2 hours.

Serve with small dumplings (see Chapter 17) and cabbage. German Cabbage (see Chapter 11) is best with this.

Serves 4
1 lb (½ kg) stewing beef
½ lb (240 g) onions, sliced
Fat for frying
1 tbsp paprika
½ lb (240 g) tomatoes
1 bay leaf
1 stick celery
2 cloves garlic
Salt and pepper

Beef of Burgundy

This is a famous French recipe which is very satisfying and easy to make.

Cut the beef into ¾ inch (1¾ cm) cubes, then marinate in a large bowl covered with the wine and brandy, together with the onions, sliced carrots and celery, bay leaf, thyme, peppercorns and chopped garlic. After 3 to 4 hours (or leave overnight in the refrigerator), drain the meat, saving the marinade, rub it in flour and fry in a little fat for a few minutes until brown. Place it in a large saucepan. Fry the vegetables from the marinade until brown and add them to the meat. Fry the mushrooms for 2 minutes, then add them to the meat, together with the herbs and seasoning. Pour the marinade over the meat and add ½ pint (300 ml) of water. Simmer over a low heat for 2 hours. The gravy may be thickened, or served plain.

Serves 4
1 lb (½ kg) stewing beef
½ pt (300 ml) red wine
3 tbsp brandy (optional)
12 small onions
2 carrots
1 stick celery
1 bay leaf
Sprig of thyme
A few peppercorns
1 clove garlic (optional)
1 oz (30 g) flour
1 oz (30 g) fat
¼ lb (120 g) mushrooms, sliced
Salt and pepper

Stewed Kidney

Remove the skin and core the kidney, and cut into pieces. Peel the onion and cut into rings. Heat some dripping in a frying pan and fry the kidney gently till brown, then lift and place in saucepan. Fry onion gently till soft and add to kidney. Add water just to cover. (A cup of red wine in place of part of water is an improvement to this dish as the flavour it gives to the kidney is particularly good.) Simmer very gently for 1 hour. Pour into a bowl.

Melt the butter or margarine in saucepan and stir in the flour. When smooth stir in liquor from kidney gradually, including the pieces of kidney and onion, and keep stirring till it just comes to the boil again. Season to taste and serve at once in a shallow dish with small triangles of toast around it or pieces of crisp fried bread.

Plain rice or mashed potato should be served with this dish.

Serves 4
1 lb (½ kg) ox kidney
1 onion
Dripping
1 oz (30 g) butter or margarine
1 oz (30 g) flour
Salt and pepper

Serves 2-3

¾ lb (360 g) stewing steak or veal
  fillet (cut in very thin slices)
½ oz (15 g) flour
½ oz (15 g) dripping
1 onion, sliced
½ pt (300 ml) stock
Salt and pepper

Stuffing

2 tbsp breadcrumbs
1 tbsp chopped prepared suet
1 tsp chopped parsley
Salt and pepper
Beaten egg

Beef or Veal Olives

Make the stuffing by mixing the breadcrumbs, suet, parsley, salt and pepper in a basin, and add enough beaten egg to bind them together.

Flatten the slices of meat by banging them with a rolling pin. Trim off all fat and cut each slice into about 2 by 3 inches (5 × 7½ cm) pieces. Place a little of the stuffing in each piece, roll up, flour, and tie the roll with a piece of thread right round it. Make the dripping smoking hot in a frying pan and brown the olives in it, then lift them into a large saucepan. Fry the onion for a few seconds, add the stock and a pinch of salt and pepper; bring to the boil and pour gently over the olives. Simmer for 1½ hours. When the olives are tender, lift, remove the thread, and lay them neatly on a hot flat dish. Thicken the gravy as in recipe for Stewed Kidney and pour over.

Allow 2 olives per person or 3 or 4 if very hungry. Chopped mushrooms may be added to the stuffing and sliced mushrooms to the gravy.

Roasting Beef

Beef should always be served a little red, at least in the middle of the cut. It should never be an even brown all through. If it is, it will be dry and tasteless. Properly cooked, the beef of the British Isles is the best meat in the world. It should be carved with a very sharp knife in flat, large, thin slices. The bigger the joint, the better the roast is an old saying. Unfortunately, nowadays, beef is very expensive and families are in general small, so small joints are the rule. It is very easy to overcook and dry out a small joint and careful timing and occasional basting are important.

The main cuts for roasting are:

a Fillet
b Sirloin and Ribs
c Rump or Topside

The cooking of each should vary a little.

With roast beef, serve potatoes roasted round the joint (except in the case of fillet), Yorkshire pudding (see recipe in Chapter 16), Horseradish Sauce, freshly made, English, French or flavoured mustard.

The gravy is always improved by adding a little red wine or dry cider instead of all stock or water.

Fillet (or Undercut)

This is the best and tenderest part of the whole animal, and is very expensive indeed. It needs very little cooking. It should always be put into a hot oven, 450°F/230°C/Gas Mark 8, and cooked for 15 minutes per pound (½ kg). If it weighs more than 2 pounds (1 kg) the heat should be reduced to 400°F/200°C/Gas Mark 6 after ½ hour. Of course, the fillet can also be cut into steaks and grilled.

Place fillet in roasting tray, longways, and rub with salt and pepper. Lay the thin rashers of bacon over it. On top put about 3 oz (90 g), for 2 lb (1 kg) meat, of good dripping, or cooking fat or lard. Baste every 10 minutes if possible. Serve with gravy made as for Roast Lamb or Mutton but a little thinner.

As the cooking time is so short, it is best not to roast potatoes around this joint.

Serves 6-8
About 2 lb (1 kg) fillet of beef
Salt and pepper
2-3 thin bacon rashers
3 oz (90 g) dripping or fat

Sirloin and Ribs

These joints need a little more cooking than the fillet. They can be boned or cooked on the bone. If boned, boil the bone to make stock for gravy.

Put the joint in a roasting tin with ¼ lb (120 g) of dripping, lard or cooking fat to a 2½-3½ lb (1-2 kg) joint. Put in an oven pre-heated to 450°F/230°C/Gas Mark 8, and cook for 20 minutes. Then reduce heat to 400°F/200°C/Gas Mark 6. Allow 20 minutes cooking to the pound (½ kg) from the beginning. Baste every 15 minutes.

2½-3½ lb (1-2 kg) joint of sirloin or ribs
¼ lb (120 g) dripping or fat

Rump, Topside and Aitchbone

The aitchbone is a rather large joint for most families today. Rump and topside give excellent flavour but are apt to become hard and dry in the cooking unless you are careful. The meat is solid and close-textured and must be basted well. Allow 20 minutes to the pound (½ kg) and 20 minutes over, except in the case of an unboned sirloin or rib, in which case the extra 20 minutes will not be required.

Place meat in preheated oven at 450°F/230°C/Gas Mark 8 for 10 minutes. Then change to 400°F/200°C/Gas Mark 6 for the remainder of time. Baste every 10 minutes. Allow ¼ lb (120 g) fat to a 2½-3½ lb (1-2 kg) joint. In the case of topside, cover with a piece of foil or greaseproof paper after the first 30 minutes of cooking.

2½-3½ lb (1-2 kg) joint
¼ lb (120 g) fat

Pot Roasting Beef

Pot roasting is an excellent method of cooking meat to ensure its tenderness. It is really something between roasting and braising. You need a small joint of topside or boned rib.

Allow 1 hour instead of 45 minutes and serve with gravy as it comes from the pot or slightly thickened.

Pot Roasted Topside of Beef with Brandy Sauce or Plain Gravy

Serves 4-6

2½ lb (1¼ kg) topside of beef
1 rasher streaky bacon
2 oz (60 g) butter
1 stick celery
1 onion
1 carrot
1 leek
1 bay leaf
Sprig of thyme
1 oz (30 g) flour
½ pt (300 ml) water
¼ pt (150 ml) brandy
Salt and pepper

This is a very good main dish for a supper party. It is very simple to cook, but impressive because it is so delicious.

Take off all fat from meat and remove skin. Cover with a thin rasher of bacon and tie it up with string. Fry in 1 oz (30 g) butter until brown all over. Remove it from the pan. Place the sliced vegetables and herbs in a wide, deep casserole dish. Place the meat on top, and add the rest of the butter. Roast in hot oven, 350-400°F/180-200°C/Gas Mark 4-6, for 45 minutes to 1 hour.

Remove the joint when cooked and keep hot on a deep serving dish, arrange vegetables round it. Stir flour into casserole until smooth. Bring to the boil and stir in the water and the brandy. Boil for 3 to 4 minutes. Season to taste, adding a little more water if too thick. The gravy is excellent without brandy, if preferred.

Braising Beef

This method of cooking is always delicious, even if you suspect that your beef is tough. It is a way of cooking between roasting and stewing, and is very good for a dinner party, as the cooking can be started early, the sauce made, and the beef kept hot for ½ hour or so in a low oven in some of the extra stock. For a rich dish you need a little red wine or dry cider.

The best cuts for braising are topside or rump.

Braised Beef

Serves 4

2 lb (1 kg) topside or rump
2 oz (60 g) fat
2 oz (60 g) butter or margarine
2 oz (60 g) flour

Marinade

Salt and pepper
Vegetables as required
1 tsp herbs
½ pt (300 ml) red wine or cider

For a rich dish it is worthwhile marinating the beef first. This makes the meat more tender and impregnates it and the vegetables with the flavour of the red wine or cider and herbs in which it is soaked.

Simply place the meat in a large bowl or fairly deep dish. Rub it with salt and pepper. Place prepared vegetables on the meat and around it, and tie the herbs in a bunch and lay on the meat. (A teaspoon of mixed dried herbs may be sprinkled over it instead, if fresh are not available, but these are not so good.) Pour over it

½ pint (300 ml) of red wine or cider, or ¼ pint (150 ml) of water. Leave for at least 4 hours or overnight. From time to time spoon the liquor over the meat and vegetables and turn the meat over two or three times.

When you are ready to begin cooking, make the fat very hot in a frying pan and fry the joint, which you have removed from the marinade and allowed to drain for a few minutes (letting the liquor from it fall back into the rest of the marinade), on all sides. Fry quite fast but for a minute only on each side. This seals the juices in the meat. Place it in a large, wide casserole, on top of the vegetables from the marinade and pour the liquor over the meat. Add cold water. It should come about halfway up the joint, and there should be about 1½ to 2 pints (900 ml-1 l) in all. Place uncovered in a slow oven, 300°F/150°C/Gas Mark 2, and cook for 2 to 2½ hours, basting from time to time. If you think the top of the joint is beginning to look dry, baste well and then cover with a piece of foil or greaseproof paper laid on the meat.

About 30 minutes before it is cooked, you can, if you wish, make a thickened sauce. Melt the butter or margarine in a saucepan, stir in the flour and pour off from your meat ¾ pint (750 ml) of liquor. Skim this and stir slowly into the roux you have made. Season it to taste. Leave on the side of the stove. Heat through just before serving.

When the meat is done, place on flat serving dish with vegetables round and sauce poured all over.

Keep the remaining stock for excellent soup or gravy. If you prefer a thin gravy, omit the thickened sauce, and simply skim the liquor when you have removed the meat, season, and pour over.

Braised Sliced Beef in Beer

Serves 4
1 lb (½ kg) topside of beef
1 oz (30 g) flour
1 oz (30 g) fat
1 lb (½ kg) onions
1 stick celery
2 oz (60 g) carrots
1 pt (600 ml) pale ale
½ oz (15 g) brown sugar
1 bay leaf
Sprig of thyme
Salt and pepper

Cut the topside in slices about ¼ inch (½ cm) thick. Rub the slices in flour. Fry them in a little smoking hot fat for a few seconds until brown on both sides. Fry the sliced onions, celery and carrots very slowly over a low heat until soft and brown. Lay half the meat in a wide shallow casserole, cover with half the vegetables and repeat, ending with vegetables on top. Bring the beer and brown sugar together with the bay leaf and thyme to the boil and pour into the casserole. Season to taste and cook in a slow oven, 300°F/150°C/Gas Mark 2 until tender.

The sauce may be thickened as in previous recipe. Tomato juice, cider or wine can be used instead of beer.

Serves 4-6
1-2 ox hearts
1 oz (30g) flour
1 oz (30g) fat
2 oz (60g) onions, sliced
2 oz (60g) carrots, sliced
2 oz (60g) bacon, diced
1 bay leaf
Sprig of thyme
½ pt (300 ml) water, wine and water, or cider
Salt and pepper

Serves 4-6
1 oxtail, 2-2½ lb (1-1¼ kg) in weight
1 oz (30g) flour
1 onion
2 oz (60g) carrots
2 oz (60g) celery (optional)
1 leek, shredded
1 clove garlic (optional)
1 bay leaf
Sprig of thyme
2 cloves
2 pt (1 l) water, wine and water, or cider

Braised Ox Heart

Cut the ox heart in half from top to bottom, remove all fat and cartilages and slice it thinly across. (Your butcher will do this, if asked.) Rub the slices in flour, brown them in smoking hot fat for a few minutes, then place in casserole. Fry the onions, carrots and bacon until brown, and add them with the herbs to the slices of heart. Cover with water, wine and water, or cider, season well and cook in a slow oven, 300°F/150°C/Gas Mark 2, for 3 to 4 hours.

½ lb (240g) tomatoes, blanched and halved, and 2 oz (60g) sliced mushrooms may be added ½ hour before it is finished.

Thicken the sauce as in recipe for Braised Beef.

Braised or Stewed Oxtail

Cut the oxtail into portions at the joints. (Your butcher will do this for you.) Place these pieces on a flat dish and bake them in a very hot oven to melt the surrounding fat for 5 minutes, or fry off in large pan. Allow to cool, then rub them in flour.

Brown in a pan containing a little fat, then place in casserole. Fry the sliced onions, carrots, celery and leek until brown, and add them to the oxtail, together with the garlic, herbs and cloves. Add the water, wine and water, or cider and cook for 2 to 3 hours in slow oven, 300°F/150°C/Gas Mark 2. Thicken as above if liked.

½ lb (240g) blanched and halved tomatoes added ½ hour before the meat is ready is an improvement.

LAMB AND MUTTON

Cuts

Cut	Method of Cooking
Neck	Boiled, stewed, braised.
Shoulder	Roasted, or in stews.
Saddle, loin	Roasted, or cut into chops and fried, grilled or braised.
Best end of neck	Roasted as a joint, or cut into cutlets and grilled, fried or braised.
Leg	Roasted, braised or boiled.
Breast	Stewed, braised, or boned and stuffed and roasted.
Kidney	Grilled, stewed.
Liver	Fried, or made into casserole.
Sweetbreads	Braised or fried.
Head	Boiled.
Tongue	Boiled.
Hearts	Roasted, stewed or braised.

The more expensive cuts are:

Neck	Best end of neck
Shoulder	Leg
Saddle	Kidney
Loin	Liver.

Cheaper cuts are:

Breast	Scrag
Middle neck	Head.

Recipes

Boiled Leg of Lamb (or Mutton)

Saw the end bone off the leg and tie the leg well with string to hold shape. Place it in a large pot, cover it with water, and add the prepared vegetables and herbs. Season to taste with the salt and pepper. Bring to the boil and remove the scum carefully as it rises to the surface. Simmer for 2 to 2½ hours until cooked. Test by pricking the meat with a skewer in the thick part; if the juice comes out clear without a trace of blood, the meat is done. Boiled meat must always be fully cooked. Unlike roasts, it is better a little overdone rather than underdone.

Serves 8-10
1 leg of lamb (or mutton)
1 head of celery
1 leek
2 carrots
4 onions
2 cloves
Sprig of thyme
Sprig of parsley
1 bay leaf
½-1 oz (15-30 g) salt
Pepper

Irish Stew

Cut the meat, except the cutlets into pieces. Arrange ingredients in a saucepan in layers – a layer of onions, then of meat, then of potatoes and so on until the saucepan is full. Cover with water and season with salt and pepper. Add a bay leaf and some thyme and simmer gently for 1½ to 2 hours in a closely covered pan. The potatoes thicken the gravy. Strain off as much fat as possible and serve in a deep dish, sprinkled with chopped parsley.

You can add carrots, turnips, peas or broad beans or cut up sticks of celery, if liked. These are not traditional in the dish, but are pleasant.

Serves 4
2 lb (1 kg) neck or breast of lamb
  and 4 cutlets
2 onions, sliced
1 lb (½ kg) potatoes, sliced
Salt and pepper
1 bay leaf
Sprig of thyme
Chopped parsley

2-2½ lb (1-1¼ kg) joint
Flour, pepper and salt
¼ lb (120 g) fat
3-4 sprigs rosemary

Roast Lamb (or Mutton)

A 2-2½ lb (1-1¼ kg) joint is plenty for 4 with not much left over. For 2, the same size is best, as a smaller joint does not roast well, being inclined to dry up. You will have enough left to have cold. A 3 to 4 lb (1½-2 kg) joint roasts better still and you can use it up afterwards.

Leg Half legs are usually obtainable: the thick end of the leg is known as the fillet end and is the more economical half. This may weigh as little as 2 lb (1 kg) and is a good joint for a small family.

Shoulder Half a shoulder is also usually obtainable. This is less economical than leg because the shoulder blade makes the proportion of bone high, but it is popular because many think the flavour and texture better than that of the leg.

Put the joint you have chosen into a roasting pan. Very lightly rub the skin and the cut surfaces of the joint with flour, pepper and salt. On top of the joint put about ¼ lb (120 g) fat (dripping, or a compound cooking fat). This will melt and run over the joint while it is in the oven. If you like, and if you have some fresh rosemary, you may stick 3 or 4 small sprigs of rosemary into the skin of the joint here and there. This gives a delicious flavour and a wonderful smell. You now have three ways of cooking your joint so that it will be moist and tender. All of them are excellent.

1 Put your joint into a hot oven, preheated to 400-450°F/ 200-230°C/Gas Mark 6-8. After 10 minutes the heat must be reduced, so turn the electric oven down to 300°F/150°C at once, and turn down gas after 5 minutes to Gas Mark 2. Leave joint at this moderate temperature for remainder of cooking time. (Assuming that your joint weighed 2½ lb (1¼ kg) this should be 1 hour and 35 minutes, because for mutton we allow 30 minutes to the pound (½ kg) and 30 minutes over. For lamb, if it is young, it is wise to allow 35 minutes to the pound (½ kg) and 35 minutes over. This timing includes the fiercer and slower cooking.

2 Same timing, but cook in a medium oven, 350°F/180°C/Gas Mark 4, from beginning of cooking process. If, 10 minutes before the end, the joint does not appear as deliciously brown as you would like, turn the oven up to 400°F/200°C/Gas Mark 6, to brown and crisp outside.

3 Allow twice as long (for 2½ lb (1¼ kg) joint, therefore, 3 hours) and put into oven preheated to 275°F/140°C/Gas Mark 1. This very slow even cooking ensures that moisture is retained and may be convenient if you want to put your joint in a regulated oven and go out and leave it. You may need to increase oven heat and brown the

outside in the last 10 minutes.

If you choose your meat carefully all those methods should be equally successful. If you know that yourself, and those you are cooking for, prefer meat very underdone and red, cut the 30 minutes extra you allow off your cooking time. In England, it is customary to serve lamb much less red, that is more cooked, than it is abroad and it can be cooked through to an even brown as long as the meat is not dry.

If you like the meat a little overcooked so that it is beginning to dry and to come away from the bone, then allow 10 minutes over the first time you roast and, if this is still not enough, 20 the next. As in all cooking, the personal tastes of the family must be consulted when roasting.

You will almost certainly want to cook roast potatoes round your joint. These should be peeled, cut in halves or quarters according to size and arranged round the joint in its pan before it goes into the oven, except in the case of a 6 or 8 lb (3-4 kg) joint, when they should be put in ¾ hour later. If you think they are getting too brown and hard, you can take them out before the joint is ready and keep them hot in your warming drawer or slow oven. If you like them well done but not at all crisp, parboil them (10 minutes cooking after the water comes to the boil), drain and put round the joint ½ hour before it will be cooked.

Serve lamb with mint sauce or mint jelly.

Roast Saddle of Lamb

Serves 6-10
1 saddle of lamb
Salt and pepper
Flour
Dripping
Sprigs of rosemary (optional)

The butcher will prepare this for you in the traditional way. Rub the saddle with mixed salt and pepper, then dust it with flour and place it in a roasting tray. Cover it with a little dripping and insert sprigs of rosemary, if liked. Cook the meat in a preheated oven at 450°F/230°C/Gas Mark 8 for 20 minutes, then reduce the heat to 350°F/180°C/Gas Mark 4 and continue roasting for 20 minutes per pound (½ kg) of meat, basting it frequently. A saddle of mutton or lamb should never be overcooked. Twelve to 16 chops are contained in a saddle, and you should allow 2 or 3 chops per person. This is a large and expensive joint, not suitable for fewer than 6 people. It is not economical, but the flavour is particularly good, and it is considered a delicacy. It is best roasted exactly at the times given above, which allow for size and proportion of bone.

Roast Loin of Lamb

Serves 4
2-2½ lb (1-1¼ kg) joint
Flour, pepper and salt
¼ lb (120 g) fat
3-4 sprigs rosemary

Proceed exactly as for roast leg or shoulder. Allow 20 minutes to the pound (½ kg) as there is more bone in this joint in proportion to meat. It is best to cook this joint by methods 1 or 2 from previous recipe. It is not so suitable for slow cooking. Loin of lamb is excellent when a small roast is wanted, as the bone of the cutlets prevents the meat drying up. It is also easy to judge exactly what you want, allowing 2 cutlets per person, or 3 if hungry, and asking your butcher for a piece of loin with 6 or 7 cutlets, or whatever.

Roast Leg of Lamb the Second Time

Remainder of leg of lamb, cold
2½ lb (1¼ kg) potatoes
About ¼ lb (120 g) butter
¼ pt (150 ml) milk
Flour
Salt and pepper

If you have roasted a fairly large, whole leg of lamb, so that only a section has been carved from the middle, and if it is not overdone at all, the following method of reheating is delicious.

Peel, cut up and boil potatoes. When soft, after about 25 minutes, mash them well and stir in 1 oz (30 g) butter and the milk. Beat with a fork till smooth and add salt and pepper to taste.

Fill the gap in your leg of lamb which was made by yesterday's carving with the potato and smooth any excess potato over the surface, keeping the shape of the leg so that it looks whole again. Sprinkle the potato very lightly with flour, salt and pepper. Put the potato-covered joint in the roasting pan, dot the potato with about 3 oz (90 g) butter in small pieces and put into a preheated oven at 300°F/150°C/Gas Mark 2. After 40 minutes turn the oven up to 450°F/230°C/Gas Mark 8 and leave for 10 to 15 minutes for potato to brown and crisp. Serve at once with the rest of last night's gravy, reheated. It is particularly good with buttered carrots, peas or broad beans.

The meat is so well protected by its covering of potato and the potato so delicious, that some people consider this second serving of a leg of lamb even better than the first.

Roast Stuffed Breast of Lamb

Serves 6
2½-3 lb (1¼-1½ kg) piece of breast
¼ lb (120 g) breadcrumbs
1 tsp salt
Pinch of dry sage, thyme and parsley
1 onion
1 egg, beaten
Milk, as required
Flour
Dripping

This is a very cheap cut, though rather fatty for some tastes. Trim the rough edges and loose flap of skin which is usually attached. Scissors do this best. The stuffing may be made from the lean of these trimmings, minced and mixed with the breadcrumbs, salt, herbs and onions (also minced) and bound together with the beaten egg. If too dry, add a little milk to moisten.

If the trimmings are not enough, or you do not want to mince them, ¼ lb (120 g) sausage meat may be used instead and the stuffing made in exactly the same way.

Put the stuffing inside the flap of the breast and sew it up with a needle and coarse thread. Roast exactly as leg or shoulder. This joint with its stuffing is very good cold.

Gravy for all Lamb Roasts

Meat juices from roasting pan
2 tsp flour
¼ pt (150 ml) stock or water
Salt and pepper

Remove joint and potatoes quickly to preheated serving dish and keep hot for a few minutes. Pour all fat from the roasting pan into a bowl to keep for dripping, leaving all the brown juice from the meat. Work 2 teaspoons of flour into the remaining juice in the tin, over a low heat. Slowly add ¼ pint (150 ml) of stock of water, stirring it all the time, and working the flour mixture into it. When it boils, it should be slightly thickened and quite smooth. Season well with salt and pepper.

If very pale, add a little gravy browning. Some sherry or red wine can always be added if you have it, to enrich the flavour. If plain water is used and the gravy has not much flavour (sometimes the case when the roast has been very small) you can flavour with Marmite, Bovril or a stock cube, but the true meat flavour is the best.

Stewing Lamb (or Mutton)

The best cuts of lamb or mutton for stewing come from the shoulder, although the scrag end of the neck and part of the breast are also good. Ask your butcher for about 2 lb (1 kg) of shoulder or scrag. He will probably dice it for you if asked. The pieces should be about an inch (2½ cm) square. Remove adhering fat as far as possible.

Navarin of Lamb

Serves 4-6
2 lb (1 kg) shoulder or breast of
   lamb, or cutlets
Fat for frying
2 sticks celery
2 large onions
2 oz (60 g) carrots
1 clove garlic
½ pt (300 ml) red or white wine
1 bay leaf
Sprig of thyme
Salt and pepper
½ lb (240 g) tomatoes
½ lb (240 g) marrow (optional)
½ lb (240 g) shelled peas
   (optional)

(This is a rich stew, as served in the South of France.)

Dice the meat into ½ inch (1¼ cm) cubes, then brown in a little fat for a few minutes. Remove the meat from the pan, drain and place in a saucepan. Meanwhile brown the diced celery, onions and carrots and the crushed garlic in the remaining fat and add to the meat. Pour in the wine and add enough water to cover level, then add the bay leaf, thyme, salt and pepper, and the skinned and chopped tomatoes. Bring to the boil, skim carefully and gently simmer for 1½ hours. Add the diced marrow and peas, if liked, 10 minutes before it is cooked.

Beans may also be added to this dish, and a few mushrooms, washed and diced, improve the flavour.

The Navarin is very good served with mashed potato, plain boiled rice or spaghetti. It needs no other vegetable.

Haricot Lamb (or Mutton)

Serves 4
1 lb (½ kg) lean lamb (or mutton)
1 oz (30 g) flour
1 oz (30 g) dripping
2 medium onions
2 carrots
1 turnip
1 ½ pt (900 ml) stock or water
6 oz (180 g) haricot beans, washed and soaked overnight
Salt and pepper
Chopped mint and parsley

Cut the lamb in pieces, not too small, and rub in flour. Melt dripping in saucepan and lightly fry the floured pieces of lamb in it, with the sliced onions, carrots and turnip. When just browning add the stock or water and the beans. Season well. Simmer very slowly for about 2 hours. Serve piled on a shallow dish and sprinkled with chopped mint and parsley.

This dish is best accompanied only by a green vegetable, as the beans take the place of potatoes or rice.

Lancashire Hot-Pot

Serves 4
¾ lb (360 g) lean lamb (or mutton)
Salt and pepper
2 large onions
1 ½ lb (¾ kg) potatoes
A little butter
Boiling water or stock, as necessary

Cut meat in slices as thin as possible. (Part of the leg is best for this dish.) Put a layer in the bottom of a fairly deep casserole, season lightly with salt and pepper. Cover with a layer of sliced onion, then a layer of sliced potato, season again. Repeat layers till ingredients are used up, ending with a layer of potato. Fill up with cold water just to cover top layer. Cover with buttered foil and firm-fitting lid. Cook in an oven at 350°F/180°C/Gas Mark 4 for 2 to 2½ hours. Fifteen minutes before it is finished, remove lid and paper so that top layer of potatoes may brown. If too little gravy is left, add boiling water or stock, but not to cover top layer of potatoes.

Grilled Lamb's Kidneys

Serves 2
4 lamb's kidneys
A little flour
Salt and pepper
2 oz (60 g) butter or margarine
2 rashers bacon
2 slices bread

With a sharp knife open the kidneys a little, remove the thin skin and the white core. Lightly flour and season with salt and pepper. Brush over with melted butter or margarine.

Place a rasher of bacon on each side of kidneys on grill. Grill for 2 minutes on each side and keep hot.

For the kidneys, 3 to 4 minutes on each side should be enough. Kidneys must not be overcooked or they become rubbery and hard. Remove from grill and keep hot for a couple of minutes. Fry the trimmed slices of bread in the juice from the kidneys. Place 2 kidneys on each piece and serve at once with the bacon.

Indian Curry of Lamb

Dice the meat into ½ inch (1¼ cm) cubes and brown in the butter for a few minutes, then drain and place in a saucepan. In the same butter and frying pan, fry the sliced onions over a low heat until soft and starting to brown. Sprinkle with curry powder, stir well and add lemon juice, salt and pepper. Then add to the meat in the saucepan. Cover level with water and add the finely chopped garlic, the bay leaf and a pinch of ground ginger. Bring to the boil, then gently simmer for 1½ hours, or less if the meat is tender. Serve with plain boiled rice and mango chutney.

Serves 6
2 lb (1 kg) lamb (or mutton) from
*   shoulder or leg*
2 oz (60 g) butter
1 lb (½ kg) onions
1½ oz (45 g) good curry powder
*   or paste*
Juice of ½ lemon
Salt and pepper
1 clove garlic
1 bay leaf
Ground ginger

Lamb Chops

Allow 2 chops or cutlets per person, unless the chops are very large.

Most meat is better grilled than fried. The grill must be preheated for some time, so that it is really fierce.

Melt a little butter or margarine and pour or brush it over the chops or cutlets. Arrange them in the middle of the grill, so that all parts get the heat. Cook cutlets for 4 minutes and chops for 6 minutes. Then turn them and baste the new side with the juice from the bottom of the grill pan. Repeat grilling for same length of time and serve at once. If heat seems too fierce – if edges are blackening – turn it down or lower chops away from grill. Chops and cutlets are best served with chips, mashed or new potatoes, grilled tomatoes, mushrooms, etc.

2 chops per person
A little butter or margarine

Fried Lamb's Liver

Ask the butcher to slice the liver thinly.

Dip each slice of liver in flour and season with salt and pepper. Melt the butter or dripping in frying pan and, when hot and smoking, put in slices of liver and reduce heat, so that they fry gently for 3 minutes. Turn them and fry for another 3 minutes. Keep hot on serving dish, pour out surplus fat and fry bacon. Arrange around liver and serve at once.

The liver is improved by being sprinkled with chopped parsley. Neat slices of fried bread may be served with it, if liked, and mashed potatoes and fried tomatoes are the best accompaniments.

Serves 2-3
¾ lb (360 g) lamb's liver
Flour
Salt and pepper
2 oz (60 g) butter or dripping
4 rashers bacon

Serves 4
4 kidneys
4 cutlets
½ lb (240 g) chipolata sausages
½ lb (240 g) tomatoes
Sugar
Salt and pepper
¼ lb (120 g) mushrooms
3 oz (90 g) butter or margarine
4 rashers bacon

Mixed Grill with Lamb

This is rather expensive but very good and quick to prepare, though it must be cooked at the last minute. Serve chips or mashed potato with it and a plain green salad.

Prepare kidneys and cutlets and separate sausages. Have a large dish ready heating in warming drawer or very low oven. First cut the tomatoes in half, sprinkle with a little sugar and salt and pepper and arrange on grill with whole mushrooms with a dab of butter on each. Grill for 5 minutes. Turn and grill the other side for 3 minutes. Remove to serving dish and keep hot. Next grill chipolata sausages and bacon. Remove to serving dish and keep hot. Then grill cutlets as above and keep hot and finally grill the kidneys (see recipe on previous page). Serve at once.

Serves 4
¾ lb (360 g) lean meat from leg of
   lamb
½ lb (240 g) lamb's liver
2 onions
4 rashers streaky bacon
¼ lb (120 g) mushrooms
1 oz (30 g) melted butter

Brochette or Kebab of Lamb

For this recipe you must have 2 skewers for each person. Have your grill very hot.

Cut the lamb into 1 inch (2½ cm) cubes – you want 12 cubes for 4 people. Cut the liver into twelve 1 inch (2½ cm) cubes.

Cut the onions into quarters downwards (not in rings) and cut bacon rashers each into three. Slice mushrooms in half. On each skewer, thread first a piece of bacon, then a slice of onion, then a slice of lamb, then liver, then mushroom, and repeat three times. Brush the filled skewers with melted butter. Arrange all 8 on grill and grill for 3 minutes on each of the sides. Make sure no angle has been missed, and is still raw. Serve at once on the skewer with plain boiled rice.

PORK

Cuts

The best cuts for roasting are a loin, best end, leg and shoulder. The shoulder of pork is known as hand of pork.

Recipes

Roast Leg of Pork

1 leg of pork or part of leg
Salt and Pepper
Flour

Pork should always be well done. The meat when cooked should look white and not at all pink. Allow 30 minutes to the pound (½ kg) and 30 minutes over.

Score the rind deeply into narrow strips about ¼ inch (½ cm) wide. You must have a very sharp, pointed kitchen knife to do this. Cut right through the skin and into the fat. Rub the surface with salt and pepper and a little flour. Place the meat in roasting tray and start in a hot oven at 450°F/230°C/Gas Mark 8 for 35 minutes. Then reduce the heat to 350°F/180°C/Gas Mark 4. When cooked, the rind should be very crisp, and is known as crackling.

Serve with Sage and Onion Stuffing either inserted in a flap of the meat, which is then sewn up, or made into small balls and baked for the last 20 minutes of cooking round the joint. See Chapter 10 for this, and Apple Sauce, which should also be served with roast pork.

Galantine of Pork and Ham

2 lb (1 kg) lean pork, cooked
½ lb (240 g) cooked ham or
* gammon*
2 onions, parboiled
Salt and pepper
Mixed spices
¼ pt (150 ml) sherry
¼ pt (150 ml) good white stock
* (or made from chicken stock*
* cube)*
6 rashers bacon
2 bay leaves
A little butter

Mince the pork with the onions and season to taste with salt and pepper and a pinch of mixed spices. Add the sherry and stock. Line a medium-sized casserole with the rindless bacon rashers and bay leaves. Cover with a layer of mince. Cut the ham into strips and place them over the mince, pressing them down into it. Cover with another layer of mince, followed by ham, until used up, finishing with strips of ham. Put buttered foil over the top. Stand in a shallow baking tray and fill tray with water so that it comes one-third of the way up the casserole. Stand in a cool oven, 300°F/150°C/Gas Mark 2, and cook for 2 hours, renewing water if necessary. Remove from oven.

Place a flat plate or lid on the foil paper and stand a weight (a large tin of fruit will do) on the plate so that it is pressing on galantine. Next day turn out. Very good served with small pickled gherkins, a salad and potatoes in their jackets.

Serves 4
1 lb (½ kg) lean shoulder of pork
1 lb (½ kg) onions
1 lb (½ kg) apples
1 tbsp tomato purée
1 oz (30 g) curry paste
Ground ginger
1 pt (600 ml) apple juice or cider
Salt and pepper
1 bay leaf
Sprig of thyme

Curried Pork

Pork makes an excellent curry, either with raw meat or with the remains of the cold roast. It is much better curried than simply stewed, braised or cooked in a casserole.

Fry the sliced onions in a saucepan over a low heat until soft. Add the diced apples and meat and the tomato purée and sprinkle with curry paste and a good pinch of ground ginger. Continue cooking very slowly until the meat is brown. Cover with the apple juice or cider, season with salt and pepper, add the bay leaf and thyme, and simmer gently for 1½ hours with the lid on. Serve with boiled rice.

Serves 4
4 pork chops
2-3 oz (60-90 g) fat

Frying and Grilling Pork

Pork chops are excellent grilled or fried, but need careful cooking, as they must be well cooked right through and yet not dried up. If allowed to dry, they harden and have a woody consistency. If underdone they are glutinous and indigestible. They should be cut about ¾ inch (1¾ cm) thick and should not be too fat.

Fry in ¼ inch (½ cm) depth of good fat, turning frequently for 15 to 20 minutes. Have the fat smoking when you put them in the pan and then reduce the heat. Grill for 15 minutes, turning them four times and spooning a little of the fat from the grill pan over them each time. Again, when grilling start with the grill hot and then reduce heat. Serve with apple sauce or fried apple rings.

Hams

Ham is the hind leg of the pig preserved by curing, or pickled in brine, dried and smoked. The meat should be pink and the white fat should have a slightly pink tinge.

Gammon is taken from the sides of the hand (or foreleg) of bacon and should be mild. Bacon should have a thin, smooth rind; the flesh should stick closely to the bones and be a dark pink colour. Fat should be free from marks, and firm.

Bacon cuts A side of bacon is made up of gammon, back, collar, hock, streaky and flank. The gammon is always removed. When this is done the side of bacon is divided into two lengthwise. The first part consists of the back and collar, and includes the long back, short back and collar. The other part consists of the streaky and forehock, including the flank.

Baking a Cured Ham

Ham or part of ham
2 lb (1 kg) flour
Cloves
Golden syrup or brown treacle
Demerara sugar

This is rather more complicated than boiling your cured ham, but the results are so delicious as to be worthwhile. A piece of cushion, hand or gammon weighing not less than 2 lb (1 kg) is excellent baked like this. In this case allow 30 minutes to the pound (½ kg) for baking.

Soak your ham for 6 to 12 hours. Take it out, dry it and remove skin. Make a crust with 2 lb (1 kg) of flour and water to mix – no fat – and be sure that the dough is fairly stiff, so that it does not pull easily into holes. Cut it in two pieces. Roll out the first about ¼ inch (½ cm) thick, into an oblong longer and wider than the ham, lay the ham on it. Stick the top of the ham all over with cloves about an inch (2½ cm) apart. Then spread the ham with golden syrup or brown treacle and then sprinkle with demerara sugar. Roll out the second piece of crust and place this over the ham. Press the crust gently down and over the sticky surface and bring the bottom crust up to meet it and seal the two pieces well together, moulding with your hands so that the whole ham is enclosed. Place it on a baking tray and bake in a moderate oven, 350°F/180°C/Gas Mark 4. Do not let the crust burn, but it does not matter how brown it gets, as it is only to protect the ham. Once it has been cooking long enough, remove from the oven and leave to cool in crust. When cool break off crust and throw away. The ham should be perfectly cooked, firm yet moist and covered with a dark brown glaze from the sugar and treacle. Serve with the cloves in place.

Neat squares of fresh or tinned pineapple, well drained, can be arranged on the ham between the cloves or pineapple is enjoyable served with it.

Ham cooked in this way is also excellent served hot and if this is to be done, it should be broken from its pastry case at once, and the liquid glaze, which will run from it, spooned over. Any surplus glaze should be put in a small saucepan and, while the ham is put back in the oven to keep hot, a little cornflour (1 level dessert-spoon) stirred into the saucepan and the result diluted with red wine or cider, or half water, half pineapple juice. This sauce should then be served with the hot ham, accompanied with slices of pineapple or tomato.

Ham or part of ham
Brown sugar, golden syrup, or
   brown treacle
6 or 7 cloves
Water, wine, cider or beer
Breadcrumbs

Boiling Cured Ham

If the ham is recently cured, it should be soaked in cold water for 6 hours; if it has been cured for some months, for 24 hours. It should be realized that a piece of home-cooked ham may be bought and cooked exactly as described here for a whole ham, in a piece as small as 2 lb (1 kg). Choose a lean piece of cushion, hand or gammon, tie it well with string, and soak as for a whole ham. When cooking allow 30 minutes to the pound (½ kg). It is very good, and economical too, if you serve it first hot and then cold.

Place the ham in cold water, well covered. Bring it to the boil slowly, then simmer. Always allow it to cool in its own liquid unless you wish to serve it first hot and then cold.

It will be much better if you add ¼ lb (120 g) of any brown sugar to the water. Never add salt, of course, as the ham is salty enough after curing. Also add 6 or 7 cloves to the water. Two tablespoons of golden syrup or brown treacle is even better than brown sugar.

Better still, is to use half red wine and half water plus sugar or treacle in which to boil it; or boil it in cider or beer, always adding sweetening. By the time the ham has cooled in any of these liquids it will have a delicious, rich, sweet flavour right through.

When you remove it from the liquid, tear off the dark brown outer skin, which should come away quite easily. Trim off odd pieces with a sharp knife and sprinkle the ham all over with fine, toasted breadcrumbs. When about to serve gently shake off loose crumbs and place on a clean dish.

VEAL

Nowadays very seldom available and always expensive but very worthwhile for special occasions.

Cuts

Cut	Method of Cooking
Leg	Roasting.
Loin	(Chop and Cutlets) Roasting.
Best end of loin	
Top of leg	Frying and braising.
Fillet	
Shoulder	Roasting.
Breast	Roasting, braising.
Shin, knuckle, foot	Boiling for stock.
Tongue	Braising.
Sweetbreads	Frying or braising.
Kidneys	Braising or frying.

Recipes

Roast Veal

The thick part of the leg is the best part of veal for roasting.

Roast veal is cooked in exactly the same way as roast lamb, remembering always that it has less fat in proportion to meat and is therefore inclined to be dry. It must be frequently basted. It should be given 15 minutes rapid cooking (see Roast Lamb) and then the heat reduced so that it cooks steadily, allowing 30 minutes to the pound (½ kg) and 30 minutes over. Undercooked veal is rubbery and unpleasant in texture, so it must be well cooked. Baste every 10 minutes.

Serve with redcurrant jelly, or with a few stewed whole cherries or plums (not too sweet) or prunes stoned and stewed with lemon and no sugar.

Serves 6
2½-3 lb (1-2 kg) of leg of veal
Fat for roasting

Roast Breast of Veal (Stuffed)

Ask your butcher to bone and trim the veal for you. Take the bone and trimmings and boil for stock. Veal always makes a very good, strong, jellied stock.

Prepare the stuffing by mixing the dry ingredients and binding with the egg and milk. Spread the stuffing on flattened out meat, roll up, and sew up the roll to hold stuffing firmly. Place in a roasting tin with the dripping and roast as for previous recipe. When cooked, remove the thread, place the veal on a hot dish and pour off the fat from the roasting tin, keeping back any brown sediment. Add the flour, mix well and brown it over the fire. Add ½ pt (300 ml) of stock from bone and a pinch of salt and pepper. Bring to the boil.

For bacon rolls, take a rasher of streaky bacon for each person to be served, flatten rasher with back of knife, roll up tightly, thread each roll on skewer, close together, and place beside veal in pan ¼ hour before it will be cooked. Remove with veal, take rolls from skewer and arrange around meat.

Potatoes may be roasted around this joint and, if there is no room for bacon, the skewer may be put in a separate small tin and cooked in oven above veal for 15 minutes.

Serves 6
2-3 lb (1-1½ kg) breast of veal
2 tbsp dripping
½ oz (15 g) flour
½ pt (300 ml) veal stock
Salt and pepper
1 or 2 bacon rolls per person

Stuffing
3 oz (90 g) breadcrumbs
1½ oz (45 g) prepared suet
A little grated lemon rind
1½ tbsp chopped parsley
¼ tsp dried herbs
6 rashers bacon
Salt and pepper
1 egg, beaten
A little milk

Serves 6-8

*3 lb (1 ½ kg) leg or chump end of
　loin of veal*
1 rasher bacon
3 oz (90 g) breadcrumbs
1 oz (30 g) chopped parsley
1 tsp chopped thyme
Salt and pepper
1 onion
½ lemon
1 egg, beaten
¼ lb (120 g) dripping

Roast Veal (Stuffed)

Cut off 2 oz (60 g) of lean meat from the joint and mince with the rasher of bacon. Mix this with the breadcrumbs, herbs, seasoning, chopped onion, grated rind (yellow part only) of half a lemon, and its juice. Stir in the egg to bind.

Stuff the veal, rolling the stuffing well in and tying the meat round with string. Place in a baking tin with ¼ lb (120 g) dripping and put in a hot oven, 450°F/230°C/Gas Mark 8. After 15 minutes, reduce the heat to 350°F/180°C/Gas Mark 4, and cook for 1½ to 2 hours. Baste often.

Serve on a hot dish. Make gravy as for Lamb.

Serves 6-8

3 lb (1 ½ kg) breast of veal
Salt and pepper
4 rashers streaky bacon
1 lb (½ kg) carrots and turnips
½ lb (240 g) onions
2 tomatoes, blanched
Sprig of parsley
1 bay leaf
1 tsp flour

Pot Roasted Veal

Sprinkle the meat with salt and pepper, and lay bacon over it. Put the meat in a roasting tin in a hot oven, 450°F/230°C/Gas Mark 8, and roast for 20 minutes. Then put in an ovenproof casserole with lid.

Fry the sliced vegetables in roasting tin in the fat from the meat for 5 minutes, then put them in with the meat. Also add the blanched tomatoes, parsley and bay leaf. Stir the flour into the fat in the roasting tin and very slowly add ¾ pint (450 ml) of water, stirring well. When boiling, pour over meat, put on cover of casserole and cook for 2 hours in slow oven, 350°F/180°C/Gas Mark 4.

Lift the meat on to a flat dish, so that it can be carved and serve the vegetables and gravy in the casserole in which they cooked.

Serves 4

1 lb (½ kg) stewing veal
1 carrot
2 large onions
*Herbs – bay leaf, thyme, parsley
　(optional)*
2 cloves
Salt and pepper
½ lb (240 g) button mushrooms
2 oz (60 g) butter
1 oz (30 g) flour
2 egg yolks
¼ pt (150 ml) cream
Juice of ½ lemon

Blanquette of Veal

Place the meat in a large saucepan with sufficient cold water to cover it. Add the carrot, onions and the herbs and cloves. Season to taste and cook gently for 1½ hours. About 10 minutes before it is cooked, add mushrooms. Strain the meat, removing any skin and gristle, and keep hot. Skim as much fat as possible off the stock, discard the vegetables, except the mushrooms, and make the sauce as follows.

Melt the butter, add the flour and cook for 2 minutes over a very low heat. Gradually add 1 pint (600 ml) of the hot veal stock and allow to simmer for 10 minutes. Beat the 2 egg yolks and cream together in a bowl, then stir in ½ pint (300 ml) of the sauce. Pour the mixture back into the pan, stir in remainder of sauce and reheat, but do not allow to boil. Add the lemon juice, stirring all the time. Pour the sauce over the meat and serve very hot.

Fricassée of Veal

This is an expensive dish because the fillet is the most expensive cut. It is traditional in English and French cookery and was very popular in the eighteenth century.

Cut the meat into cubes, then put them in a saucepan with the onion stuck with the clove, the herbs and bay leaf, and salt and pepper. Cover with water. Bring to the boil, skim well, then simmer until the meat is quite tender – about 45 minutes.

Melt the butter in a saucepan, stir in the flour, and cook gently for 5 minutes, but do not allow to brown. Remove the onion and herbs from the veal. Stir a little of the stock into the flour and butter, then add to the veal and the rest of the stock. Stir for 3 minutes till smooth and creamy, then add cream. If too thick, stir in a little milk. Season well and serve very hot with rice.

Serves 4

1 lb (½ kg) veal fillet
1 onion
1 clove
Sprig of thyme, parsley and marjoram
1 bay leaf
Salt and pepper
2 oz (60 g) butter
1 level tsp flour
¼ pt (150 ml) cream
Milk, as required

Curried Veal

Trim the veal, wipe and cut into cubes. Melt the butter in a pan, and when hot fry the meat. Lift out on to a plate. Fry the onion lightly, then the apple. Add the curry paste and mix thoroughly, then add the flour. Pour the stock in gradually together with the salt. Bring to the boil, then add the lemon juice and the chutney. Return the meat to the sauce and simmer 1½ hours, stirring frequently. Serve very hot, with plenty of rice.

Serves 4

1 lb (½ kg) shoulder or leg of veal
1 oz (30 g) butter
1 tbsp chopped onion
1 tbsp chopped apple
½ oz (15 g) curry paste
2 tbsp flour
About ½ pt (300 ml) stock
½ tsp salt
A few drops lemon juice
1 tbsp chutney

Côte de Veau en Casserole

This is one of the most distinctive and delicious dishes made with veal.

Gently cook the finely chopped onions in butter in a saucepan until golden. Add wine and stock and stir. Coat cutlets in breadcrumbs and Parmesan cheese and place flat in ovenproof dish or pie dish large enough to take them without overlapping. Pour onions over them and cook in a moderate oven for 35 to 45 minutes, or until cutlets begin to come away from the bone very slightly. If the liquid should reduce too much during the cooking, make up with extra wine and stock in equal quantities. Serve in cooking dish very hot.

Best with creamed or plain boiled potatoes and green peas or a plain green salad.

Serves 4

4 veal cutlets
½ lb (240 g) onions
2 oz (60 g) butter
¼ pt (150 ml) white wine
¼ pt (150 ml) brown stock or stock from cube
Seasoned breadcrumbs
Grated Parmesan cheese

Veal Escalope in Marsala

Serves 4
4 escalopes
About 2 oz (60 g) flour
Salt, cayenne pepper
2 oz (60 g) butter or margarine
½ pt (300 ml) stock or stock cube
3 tbsp Marsala wine
1 tsp tomato purée
1 tsp paprika

Ask the butcher to cut 4 escalopes of veal, as thin as possible. These are large flat slices from the fillet and are the best part of veal. They are rather expensive but there is no waste at all.

Flatten the escalopes with gentle pressure from the back of a heavy knife. Lightly flour them and season. Fry them in butter or margarine until well browned and cooked through, then place them in a shallow dish and keep warm.

Add remaining butter to pan. Stir in 1½ oz (45 g) flour. Cook for 3 minutes. Stir in ½ pt (300 ml) any good meat stock or make up stock cube and add this. Bring slowly to boil and simmer for 3 minutes. Stir in the Marsala. (Cooking sherry can be used and makes a good sauce, but veal in Marsala sauce is traditional.) Stir in the tomato purée and the paprika. When very hot, pour over escalopes and serve at once. Very good with spaghetti.

Fried Veal Cutlet

Serves 4
4 veal cutlets
1 egg, beaten
¼ lb (120 g) breadcrumbs
¼ lb (120 g) grated cheese
    (Parmesan if possible, but
    Cheddar will do)
2 oz (60 g) butter or margarine
2 oz (60 g) olive oil

Dip the cutlets in beaten egg. Mix the breadcrumbs and grated cheese together. Dip the cutlets into this mixture and press breadcrumbs and cheese firmly down on them to coat well. Then fry on both sides in the butter or margarine and olive oil, which have been heated together. Put the cutlets in as soon as the fat is still and smoking. Fry gently for 4 minutes on each side – heat should be turned down fairly low once the fat is hot, so that the crumbs do not become too dark. Serve with bacon rolls and quarters of lemon to squeeze over.

Veal cutlets on the bone or escalopes from the fillet may also be cooked in this way.

Fried Sweetbreads of Veal

Serves 2
2 sweetbreads
Salt
Juice of 2 lemons
Flour
1 egg, beaten
¼ lb (120 g) breadcrumbs
½ oz (15 g) butter

Soak the sweetbreads in cold, salted water for 1 hour. Rinse them several times, then place them in a saucepan and cover them with cold water, and add the lemon juice and a pinch of salt. Bring to the boil and simmer gently for 10 minutes.

Wash sweetbreads under the cold tap. Carefully clean out all gristle and skin. Lay the sweetbreads between two plates with a weight on top to press them for an hour or so. This makes them more solid and easy to cut. Cut them into slices, rub them in flour and beaten egg. Roll the slices of sweetbread in breadcrumbs and fry them gently in butter until brown on both sides.

Serve with fried bacon and slices of lemon and fried mushrooms, if possible.

Wiener Schnitzel

Flour the escalopes, then dip them in beaten egg. Roll them in breadcrumbs and fry for 5 minutes on each side in the buter mixed with the olive oil. Do not allow them to become too brown.

Place on a hot serving dish and put a slice of hard-boiled egg and an anchovy fillet on each escalope.

Serves 4
4 escalopes of veal
Flour
1 egg, beaten
Breadcrumbs
1 oz (30 g) butter
1 oz (30 g) olive oil
1 hard-boiled egg
4 anchovy fillets

Veal Kidney

Trim the kidney of all fat and gristle. Cut it into thin slices, rub them in flour and fry gently in butter for 5 minutes. Keep them hot in a casserole dish.

Fry onion or shallots in the same fat until soft and lightly browned. Stir in flour. Add the wine, boil for 5 minutes, then add the stock. Simmer for 5 more minutes. Reheat the kidney in this sauce for 5 minutes, season to taste, and serve immediately with a sprinkling of chopped parsley.

Do not allow kidney to come to the boil in the sauce. Wine may be omitted or replaced with cider. Mushrooms make an excellent addition.

A veal kidney is paler in colour and more tender than ox kidney, and makes a more delicious dish.

Serves 2
1 kidney
About 1 oz (30 g) flour
1 oz (30 g) butter
1 onion or 2 shallots
¼ pt (150 ml) dry sherry or white wine
¼ pt (150 ml) stock
Salt and pepper
Chopped parsley

Dishes to Use up Cold Meat

Stewed Cooked Lamb

Dice the lamb, removing skin and fat. Peel and cut carrots and turnips into ½ inch (1¼ cm) slices. Peel and cut up onions. In a large saucepan melt the dripping. Lightly flour the cut up meat and vegetables and put all in the hot fat. Toss until slightly brown, then just cover with stock or water, season rather highly with salt and pepper and simmer very slowly for ¾ hour. After ½ hour add any other vegetables – peas or beans, if you have them, ½ lb (240 g) tomatoes, skinned and cut-up marrow, etc. Potatoes can be cooked in the stew if liked, in which case add after 15 minutes. Dumplings may be cooked in this stew or in a steamer and served with it. It is improved by a bouquet of thyme, sage and parsley.

This is a very good stew which can be cooked equally well on top of the stove or in the oven in a closely covered ovenproof casserole. It can be made richer by the addition of ¼ pint (300 ml) of any red wine to the stock.

Serves 4-5
1½ lb (¾ kg) cooked lamb
1 lb (½ kg) carrots and turnips
2 large onions
2 oz (60 g) dripping
Flour
Stock or water to cover
Salt and pepper
Any choice of vegetables (optional)
Bouquet of thyme, sage and parsley

Serves 3-4

1 lb (½ kg) cold lamb, beef, veal,
  pork, or mixture
1 ½ lb (¾ kg) potatoes
1 ½ oz (45 g) butter or margarine
½ oz (15 g) flour
¼ pt (150 ml) stock or milk
Salt and pepper
A little extra milk

Shepherd's Pie

This is a way of using up cold meat which can be very dull, but if it is properly made it can be as delicious as many much more expensive dishes. Shepherd's Pie can also be made using fresh or frozen mince. In this case, cook the mince, allow it to get cold and break and scrape away all fat. Then proceed as with minced cold meat. Cold sausage meat, cold sausages, and cold salt beef are not suitable for this dish.

Mince the meat, removing all fat, skin and gristle first. Cook the potatoes, peeled and cut in halves, till soft enough for mashing.

Melt 1 oz (30 g) butter or margarine in a saucepan and stir in the flour. To this you add, slowly stirring, ¼ pint (150 ml) meat stock or milk. When smooth and fairly thick and just on the point of boiling, stir in the mince. Stir over very low heat for 3 minutes, seasoning with salt and pepper to taste. Pour into a flat ovenproof dish and leave to get cold.

Meanwhile mash your potatoes, season and stir in ½ oz (15 g) butter or margarine, and a little milk and whisk with a fork till smooth. Set aside until the minced meat is cool enough to have solidified and formed a solid surface. If you add the potato to the hot mince it will sink into it.

When cool, spread the potato about an inch (2½ cm) thick all over the dish, working lightly with a fork. Dot with pieces of butter or cover with grated cheese, if liked. Cook in oven at 400°F/200°C/Gas Mark 6 for 30 minutes.

The dish may be prepared in the morning and left for cooking until the evening without harm. Cabbage is the best vegetable to accompany this dish.

Serves 2-3

1 lb (½ kg) cold lamb (or mutton)
1 large onion
1 oz (30 g) butter or margarine
1 tbsp flour
½ pt (300 ml) stock or water
¼ lb (120 g) mushrooms or
  tomatoes (optional but an
  improvement)
Salt and pepper

Hash

Cut the cold meat into slices free from skin and gristle. Chop the onion finely and put into a saucepan with the butter or margarine and cook over low heat for a few minutes. Stir in the flour smoothly, and gradually add the stock or water. Slice the mushrooms, or blanch and halve the tomatoes, and add. Season with salt and pepper. Simmer gently for 10 minutes, then add the slices of meat. (½ teaspoon garlic salt, 3 teaspoons tomato purée and ½ teaspoon of turmeric, make the sauce more interesting.) Keep hot long enough for the meat to heat through (10 minutes), but do not boil, or the meat will toughen. Serve on a hot dish with fingers of toast round the edge.

Minced Cooked Lamb

Prepare exactly as the mince for Shepherd's Pie, but use a little more stock or milk, so that the mince is slightly wetter in consistency.

Serve very hot in a preheated dish with a rim. Round the rim stick small triangles of toast or fried bread, alternating with halves of grilled tomatoes.

Alternatively, prepare mashed potato or boiled rice. Make a thick border of either round the hot serving dish and pour the mince in the middle.

See Shepherd's Pie

Potted Ham

Cut the onions into slices and fry them slowly in butter over a low heat until tender, but do not allow them to brown. Put them through a mincer with the ham. Add the curry powder, cayenne and paprika, stir well and add salt, if necessary. Stir in cider or wine and simmer for 30 minutes. Allow to cool. Put into mortar or pudding basin and pound well with pestle or wooden spoon. Pack into a stone or pottery jar, whatever is not needed for immediate use. Seal with melted butter and put in refrigerator, where it should keep for weeks.

Very good in sandwiches or on hot, buttered toast, or serve as an hors d'oeuvre.

1 lb (½ kg) cooked ham
1 lb (½ kg) onions
Butter
½ oz (15 g) curry powder
½ tsp cayenne pepper
1 tsp paprika
Salt
¼ pt (150 ml) cider or red wine

Ham Mousse

Blend the egg yolks with the white sauce. Reheat gently without allowing to boil, as mixture curdles easily. Season with salt and pepper and add sherry and nutmeg. Dissolve the gelatine in 1 tablespoon of hot water and stir it into the sauce. Then add the minced ham. Remove from the heat, stir well, and when cold, fold in the stiffly whipped whites of the eggs. Place in a mould and set in refrigerator. Turn out when cold.

Serves 4-6
1 lb (½ kg) lean cooked ham
2 eggs, separated
½ pt (300 ml) white sauce
Salt and pepper
¼ pt (150 ml) sherry
Nutmeg
1 oz (30 g) powdered gelatine

Ham Toasts

Beat the eggs well. Melt the butter in a thick saucepan, and add the minced ham, pepper and the beaten eggs, and stir well. Hold just off the heat and stir until there is no liquid egg visible and the consistency is solid but creamy.

Have ready 4 rounds of hot buttered toast, pile each with the ham and egg mixture, sprinkle with parsley and serve at once.

Serves 4
½ lb (240 g) cooked ham
4 eggs
1 oz (30 g) butter
Pepper
4 slices bread
1 tbsp chopped parsley

Serves 3-4

*About ¾ lb (360 g) cold cooked
    veal
1 oz (30 g) butter or margarine
1 oz (30 g) flour
¾ pt (450 ml) milk, or
    ½ pt (300 ml) milk plus
    ¼ pt (150 ml) stock
Salt and pepper
1 dessertsp chopped parsley
1 tsp lemon juice
2 tbsp cream (optional)*

Blanquette of Veal

If the joint was stuffed, the remaining stuffing may be rolled into small balls, fried quickly for 3 minutes and served round the edges of the dish of blanquette of veal.

Cut the veal into small cubes, removing skin and gristle. Melt the butter in a saucepan, stir in the flour very gradually over gentle heat until it is a smooth paste. Take the pan off the fire and add the milk, mixing well until smooth. Season and cook gently until it has boiled for 3 minutes stirring all the time. Add the veal and stir for a further 5 minutes, till meat is hot through. Stir in the chopped parsley and lemon juice. If liked, add 2 tablespoons of cream to enrich the sauce. Serve very hot with small triangular pieces of toast round dish.

Opposite: *Roast Beef (see page 99)*

Left: *Tournedos Rossini*
(see page 99)

Right: *Baked Ham*
(see page 119)

Above: *Roast Saddle of Lamb (see page 111) and Lamb Chops (see page 115)*

Fricassée of Veal (see page 123)

Braised Oxtail (see page 108) and Goulash (see page 103)

Above: *Scalloped Potatoes (see page 167)*

Opposite: *German Cabbage (see page 155), Carrots Vichy (see page 156) and Grandmother's Peas with Bacon (see page 163)*

CASSEROLES

Anything cooked in a closely covered casserole in a slow oven will be tender and digestible – the oldest hen, the toughest steak, the skinniest rabbit.

Nothing need ever be dull and flavourless. A casserole of rather dry, cooked cold meat, provided you have some good stock or use a stock cube, or some tomato purée and plenty of onions, carrots, turnips, fresh tomatoes, and whatever vegetables you have, and season it well with salt and pepper, becomes a hot, appetizing and nourishing meal.

You can cook anything in a casserole – meat, birds, most kinds of fish, fruit, root vegetables, cabbage, etc. You can therefore put a whole dinner in your oven, if you have casseroles which you have chosen to fit in together. Meat and root vegetables in a large deep casserole; cabbage to be put in later in a smaller, shallower one; potatoes to be added to the meat, or sliced and put with milk and butter in a shallow uncovered casserole on the top shelf to brown slightly; stuffed apples put in at the same time as the meat to bake for 30 minutes and then cool; or plums, gages, apricots, placed in a shallow casserole with a lot of sugar and very little water and cooked for the same length of time as the apples. Your oven heat is therefore fully used and the top of your stove never used at all.

Casserole cooking is excellent when you are entertaining, because everything can be prepared hours beforehand and served in its cooking dish so that there is no last minute preparation beyond checking the seasoning. A savoury casserole can always be made into a rich and exciting dish if a bird or some lean beef is used, and it's cooked partly in wine as well as stock or water. Mushrooms improve almost all casseroles. The addition of a few almonds, walnuts, raisins, or soaked prunes add interest, particularly to the consistency, which is important in any dish. The thickened gravy becomes a rich sauce if wine has been used.

A casserole is the best dish of all if you do not know exactly at what time you will be able to serve the meal. Almost nothing cooked as a casserole will be dried up or spoilt if it is left for an extra ½ hour, or even longer. It is much the best and safest meal to put in the oven and leave while you go out.

The variety is infinite. You can cook casseroles for 3 or 4 days running and your family will probably never realize that they have

Opposite: *Orange Salad (see page 177) and Avocado Salad (see page 175)*

had one casserole dish after another. You can cut meat or poultry in pieces and joints; you can cook them whole so that they can be carved at table; you can cut up the remains of cold meat very finely and make the gravy into a thick sauce; you can cook cutlets of any large fish by this method – cod, hake, haddock – or cook the whole fish. Fish cooked like this is delicious if you include a little onion, tomatoes or tomato purée and a few herbs. Naturally, fish will cook sooner than meat or a bird.

If you cook in a closely covered casserole, you lose none of the goodness or the flavour of what you cook. Everything has its full taste and nutritive value.

In casserole cookery, do not forget that raw meat or a bird makes its own stock and may be put in simply with water, apart from seasoning and vegetables. Cooked meat or birds must have fresh stock, or stock from a cube, if the casserole is to be worth eating.

If you are cooking by electricity, turn the oven out at least 20 minutes before the casserole should be ready. Not only does the oven retain its heat, but so does the casserole. Everything left in a casserole, with its lid in place, goes on cooking for several minutes after it is taken from the oven.

Unless you are cooking something which needs to brown slightly on top, such as scalloped potatoes, or a bird which you are braising (when you will take off the lid for the last ½ hour or so), your casserole must be closely covered with a properly fitting lid. Make sure of this when you buy. If you break a lid and have not replaced it, or if you don't think it fits tightly, cover the top of the casserole with aluminium foil, twisted round the top of the sides to fit tightly and with a lid or an old plate or saucepan lid over it.

You cannot cook a casserole in a hurry. The essence of this method of cooking is that it is done at a slow, even temperature, the solids being gently simmered in the liquids.

In this book, all the recipes for casseroles are given in the section dealing with the meat, bird, fish, vegetable or fruit concerned. A casserole in itself is a dish. It is what you put in it that defines it. Below are six suggestions for meals which can be cooked in the oven, with the times for each dish *en casserole*. Potatoes in their jackets are not, of course, cooked in this way, but they fit very well with a main casserole dish because they require the same long, slow cooking. Milk puddings are simply cereals cooked by the casserole method, using milk instead of water and leaving the dish uncovered, because milk forms a skin which acts as its own cover to the grain and is delicious to eat. This applies to scalloped and Dauphinoise potatoes also.

Menu

1
Braised Beef (2½ to 3 hours)
German Cabbage (1½ to 2 hours)
Potatoes added to meat 30 minutes before serving
Semolina Pudding (40 minutes to 1 hour)

2
Cod, Baked and Stuffed with Tomato Sauce (30 minutes)
Scalloped Potatoes (1½ hours)
Baked Apples Stuffed with Dates (20 to 30 minutes)
Rice Pudding (1½ to 2 hours)

3
Casserole of Chicken (whole or in joints) with rice added to
    casserole (2 to 2½ hours)
Braised Celery (40 minutes to 1 hour)
Scalloped Pears (40 minutes to 1 hour)

4
Cassoulet (beans soaked overnight) (2½ to 3 hours)
Potatoes in their Jackets with Cheese (1½ to 2 hours)
Scalloped Plums (30 to 40 minutes)

5
Goulash and Dumplings (2 to 2½ hours)
Braised Marrow (30 minutes)
Dried Apricots with Almonds (soaked overnight) (40 minutes to
    1 hour)

6
Casserole of Partridge with cabbage (1½ to 2 hours)
Dauphinoise Potatoes (1½ to 2 hours)
Baked Spaghetti Pudding (1½ to 2 hours)

SAUCES AND STUFFINGS

SAUCES

Sauces really set apart good cooks from those who just cook because they have to. Any dish, however plain, economical and simple, is improved by having its traditional sauce served with it. Quite a lot of dishes don't call for a special sauce apart from their own gravy, but in England many that would be improved by sauces are often served without.

Almost all sauces are quick and easy and do not go wrong if you keep certain simple principles in mind. They don't take very much time and do make all the difference to food. These are the things to remember:

A sauce is a well-flavoured, more or less thick liquid which brings out the flavour of the meat, fish or vegetable it accompanies. It should not disguise or smother it.

Most savoury sauces today are based on a thickening of flour or cornflour. The two basic sauces, of which almost all others are a variation, are white and brown sauces. In the last few years, the use of vegetable purées to replace some sauces based on a roux of butter and flour has become popular, because the amount of fat and carbohydrates is thus cut down, so that the dish is lighter, and also because a vegetable purée, well seasoned, can give a new freshness to a chicken, steak or lamb dish.

Butter melted in a saucepan into which an equal quantity of flour is stirred over the heat until the mixture is grainy-looking, but all blended smoothly together, is called a roux. For white sauce it must not be allowed to colour, for brown sauce it must. To it, you add your liquid – milk, stock, etc. – stirring all the time and adding only a little at a time. When it comes to the boil, you simmer it gently for another 5 minutes, still stirring. It's quite simple. The result, if you follow the quantities given in this section, should be perfectly smooth and just the right thickness.

If, through inattention – the only reason – you do allow your sauce to become lumpy, you can often get rid of the lumps by beating it in the pan with an electric beater or whisk. If this does not work you can put it through a strainer.

Some tepid and cold sauces, such as Hollandaise and Mayonnaise, are based on egg for their thickening and in these cases the only thing you have to fear is curdling, either because the sauce comes to the boil and the egg curdles at once; or from the too rapid addition of lemon or vinegar to a recipe which includes milk or cream. Slow addition of ingredients to one another and patient stirring over low heat, prevents this. If your sauce has curdled, put another egg yolk in a fresh bowl and slowly beat the curdled mixture into it.

Below is a list showing the sauces traditionally served with different dishes. Simple garnishes (such as cucumber with salmon, or pineapple with ham) are suggested and described with the dish in question.

Fish

Steamed or poached cod, hake, fresh haddock, etc.	*Anchovy, Egg, Parsley, Caper*
Salmon	*Hollandaise, Tartare, Green Butter*
Mackerel	*Gooseberry, Tartare, Green Butter, Anchovy Butter*
Herring	*Mustard, Maître d'hôtel, Parsley Butter*
Fried or grilled fillets of fish	*Tartare, Hollandaise, Tomato, Green Butter, Shrimp Butter, Parsley Butter*
Sole	*Mornay, Béchamel with various garnishes, Velouté, Tartare, Green Butter, Shrimp Butter*

Meat

Roast lamb	*Mint Sauce, Mint Jelly*
Roast beef	*Horseradish*
Grilled steak and chops	*Green Butter, Anchovy Butter, Horseradish Butter, Tomato, Horseradish (steak), Béarnaise (steak)*
Roast pork	*Apple*
Cutlets	*Espagnole, Reform, Green Butter*

Poultry and Game

Roast Goose	*Apple*
Roast Duck	*Apple, Orange*
Roast Turkey	*Cranberry, Bread*
Roast Chicken	*Bread*
Roast Rabbit	*Onion, Redcurrant Jelly*
Roast Hare	*Redcurrant Jelly*
Boiled Chicken	*Velouté, Egg, Parsley, Mushroom*
Cold Chicken	*Chaudfroid*

Vegetables

Cauliflower, celery, sea kale, carrots, Jerusalem artichokes	*Béchamel, Mornay, Parsley*
Globe artichokes	*Melted butter, Hollandaise*
Asparagus	*Hollandaise, melted butter*
Broccoli	*White sauce, Hollandaise*

Recipes

Brown Sauce (Basic Recipe)

1 oz (30 g) butter or good dripping
½ pt (300 ml) stock
1 oz (30 g) flour
Salt and pepper
1 tbsp cooking sherry or red wine
*   (optional)*

For the stock, any beef or lamb stock will do. If you have none, half a stock cube dissolved in ½ pint (300 ml) water will do well.

Put butter or dripping in saucepan and melt quickly, as you want it to brown. Stir in flour and allow to colour. Your roux should be quite smooth and a deep fawn colour before you start to stir in your stock. Add the stock and proceed exactly as for white sauce in previous recipe. When finished, season well. The addition of a tablespoon of cooking sherry or of a red wine improves and enriches the sauce.

White Sauce (Basic Recipe)

1 oz (30 g) butter
1 oz (30 g) flour
½ pt (300 ml) milk
½ tsp salt
Pinch of pepper

Take a small heavy saucepan, aluminium rather than enamel. Melt the butter over low heat, not allowing it to brown. Stir in the flour, being careful not to allow it to brown and stirring till the roux is absolutely smooth and no separate flour or melted butter is visible. Add the milk a very little at a time, stirring each addition in until it is smoothly taken up by the roux. If lumps seem to be forming hold the saucepan off the heat and beat with your spoon till the sauce is smooth, before adding more milk. When all the milk is taken up, add salt and pepper and simmer gently for 3 minutes, holding the saucepan just above the heat and stirring hard, so that the bottom does not scorch.

The result should be a perfect white sauce, which is good in itself and which is the foundation of many other sauces. The whole making should take you only 8 to 10 minutes.

It should not be necessary to strain or sieve the sauce. A tablespoon or two of cream, stirred in when the sauce has cooled a little, gives a rich smooth texture. Do not let it boil again after this.

For sauces where stock is to be used, the roux is made up in the same way and ¼ pint (150 ml) of milk and ¼ pint (150 ml) veal or chicken stock used.

A sauce which is to be poured or served separately in a sauceboat should be a little thinner than a sauce which is to coat or mask a dish (for example, white sauce served over cauliflower). The quantities given will produce a thick enough sauce to coat or mask. Add another 2 fl oz to ¼ pint (60-150 ml) of milk if you want the sauce to pour freely.

Anchovy Sauce

1 oz (30 g) butter or margarine
1 oz (30 g) flour
¼ pt (150 ml) milk
¼ pt (150 ml) fish stock or
*   ¼ pt (150 ml) additional milk*
1-2 tsp anchovy essence
Salt and pepper

Proceed exactly as for Béchamel Sauce (below), using half fish stock and half milk for preference, but all milk if you have no fish stock. When finally simmering, add the anchovy essence. Taste before seasoning as the essence is very salty.

If ½ pint (300 ml) of anchovy sauce is more than you want (usually enough for 5 or 6) make up with half quantities of all ingredients.

Béarnaise Sauce

1 onion or 3-4 shallots
2 tbsp tarragon vinegar
2 tbsp malt vinegar
¼ pt (150 ml) white sauce
2 egg yolks
2 oz (60 g) butter

Boil the finely chopped onion or shallots in the two vinegars for 5 minutes (vinegar should be reduced to about one-third original quantity). Remove from heat, stir in the white sauce. Then stir in the well-beaten egg yolks. Stand over very low heat or over a pan of boiling water. Do not allow to boil or eggs will curdle. Stir in the butter, a small piece at a time. Keep warm, and not too hot, by standing saucepan in a pan of hot water on the side of the stove.

Apple or Gooseberry Sauce

1 lb (½ kg) apples or
½ lb (240 g) gooseberries
Water
Strip of lemon
Sugar
½ oz (15 g) butter

Peel and core the apples and cut into thin slices. Put them into a saucepan with 1 tablespoon of water and a piece of lemon peel and stew gently until they become pulp. Sweeten to taste, but not too much, as apple sauce is better a little sharp. Put through a food mill or a sieve. Return to saucepan with the butter and heat up before serving. Can be prepared ahead and kept warm at side of stove or in warming drawer without harm. The addition of butter is optional.

For gooseberry sauce, omit the lemon peel.

The quantities given should make enough to serve cold, with cold pork or birds, after serving hot with the hot roast.

Béchamel Sauce

1 small onion or shallot
½ carrot
½ turnip
Bouquet of parsley, thyme and
*   bay leaf*
Blade of mace
6 peppercorns
1 pt (600 ml) milk
2 oz (60 g) butter
1 ½ oz (45 g) flour
Salt

Simmer vegetables, herbs and spices in the milk for 30 minutes. Make sure that the milk is not boiling away. Strain. Make a white roux by putting butter in thick saucepan, stirring in flour, and cooking very gently, stirring all the time for 3 minutes without allowing to colour. Gradually add the strained and flavoured milk, stirring constantly, and simmer very gently, always stirring, for another 5 minutes. Season with salt and serve.

Bread Sauce

1 small onion
2 cloves (optional)
½ pt (300 ml) milk
3 oz (90 g) fresh breadcrumbs
1 oz (30 g) butter or margarine
Salt and pepper

Peel the onion and push the cloves into it. Simmer gently with the milk and a tablespoon of water for 20 minutes. Remove the onion, or, if you prefer it in, remove cloves and chop and crush it well into the milk. Add the breadcrumbs. Stir well. Add butter and seasoning. Stir again, and leave on side of stove at least 5 minutes for breadcrumbs to swell. Then beat well with spoon for a minute, and if too thick add a little more milk and another nut of butter. Reheat and serve.

Caper Sauce

1 oz (30 g) butter
1 oz (30 g) flour
½ pt (300 ml) stock in which meat
*   has been simmering*
Salt and pepper
½ pt (300 ml) milk
Juice of ½ lemon
2 oz (60 g) capers
½ oz (15 g) chopped parsley
*   (optional)*

Melt the butter in a pan and add the flour. Stir, and cook the mixture for a few minutes without allowing it to colour. Add the boiling stock gradually, stirring all the time. Season to taste with salt and pepper. Add the milk and simmer for 5 minutes. Just before serving, add the lemon juice and the capers. Stir lemon juice in slowly, a few drops at a time, to avoid curdling the sauce. Add a sprinkling of chopped parsley.

Good with boiled mutton.

Chaudfroid Sauce

Make up aspic jelly according to directions on packet and while still hot add the béchamel sauce, mixing thoroughly. Bring just to the boil. Cool slightly, stir in cream and season. Use while still warm before it thickens and sets.

¼ pt (150 ml) aspic jelly (make up from packet)
½ pt (300 ml) béchamel sauce
2 tbsp thick cream
Salt and pepper

Cheese or Mornay Sauce

Stir the grated cheese (Parmesan is best, but Cheddar will do) into the finished white sauce and simmer, stirring, for 5 minutes instead of 3, in order that the cheese can melt and flavour the sauce.

½ pt (300 ml) white sauce
¼ lb (120 g) grated cheese

Cranberry Sauce

Boil the cranberries and water for 5 minutes. Put them through a food mill or rub them through a fine sieve and reheat with the sugar. Mix the cornflour with 2 tablespoons of cold water, stir in the purée of cranberries, and boil gently for 5 minutes.

½ lb (240 g) cranberries
3 oz (90 g) sugar
2 level teasp cornflour

Egg Sauce

Make white sauce. When finished, stir in chopped hard-boiled eggs and season rather highly.

½ pt (300 ml) white sauce
2 hard-boiled eggs
Salt and pepper

Hollandaise Sauce

Boil the vinegar to reduce to half its quantity (about 5 minutes). Cool slightly and stir in the beaten yolks of 3 eggs and a small piece of butter, and salt and pepper. Stir with a wooden spoon while the saucepan stands in a pan of boiling water, as sauce must thicken but must not boil. As you see it begin to thicken, add remainder of your 3 oz (90 g) of butter, which you have softened slightly by working with wooden spoon. Add it a small piece at a time, beating the sauce as you do so. When all the butter is absorbed and the sauce is thick and creamy, keep warm in its saucepan by standing in hot water until it is wanted. It should never boil at any time during its making, after the vinegar is reduced.

3 tbsp vinegar
2-3 egg yolks
3 oz (90 g) butter
Salt and pepper

Espagnole Sauce

1 rasher bacon or ham
1 oz (30 g) butter
1 small carrot
1 small onion
1 small shallot
3 mushrooms, or mushroom stalks
1 oz (30 g) flour
½ pt (300 ml) brown stock
1 tbsp tomato purée
Seasoning
Bouquet of herbs
3 tbsp sherry

Cut up bacon or ham and fry slightly in the butter. Add the vegetables, cut up fine, and fry for 5 minutes, gently. Add the flour and cook very slowly together till a golden-brown colour is obtained. Add the stock, tomato purée, seasoning, and herbs, and simmer gently for 30 minutes, stirring occasionally. Lastly, add the sherry, bring to boil again and strain finely through a food mill or sieve. Reheat and serve.

Horseradish Sauce (to serve hot)

½ pt (300 ml) white sauce
½ tsp sugar
2 tbsp grated horseradish (fresh or bottled)
1 ½ tsp vinegar
Salt and pepper
1 tbsp cream (optional)

To the finished white sauce add the sugar, then the horseradish and vinegar, stirring all the while to prevent curdling. Season. A tablespoon of cream stirred in last, much improves this delicious sauce.

Horseradish Sauce (to serve cold)

2 tbsp grated horseradish
1 tbsp vinegar
1 tsp caster sugar
Salt and pepper
¼ pt (150 ml) fairly thick or well-whipped cream

Put the grated horseradish in a bowl. Pour over vinegar. Add sugar, salt and pepper. Finally stir in cream.

Maître d'hôtel Sauce

½ pt (300 ml) béchamel sauce
1 dessertsp finely chopped parsley
Juice of ½ lemon
Salt and pepper

To the finished béchamel sauce add the parsley and cook for 3 minutes. Then stir in the lemon juice and season. See that the chopped parsley is fresh but dry.

Mushroom Sauce

¼- ½ lb (120-240 g) mushrooms, sliced but not peeled
¾ pt (450 ml) milk
1 oz (30 g) butter
1 oz (30 g) flour
Salt and pepper
2-3 tbsp white wine
2 tbsp cream (optional)

Stew the sliced mushrooms gently in the milk for 10 minutes. When tender turn into pudding basin. Melt the butter in saucepan in which they were cooking. Stir in the flour to make a roux in the usual way. When smooth stir in the mushrooms and their milk, which will be greyish-fawn in colour, adding it slowly as for white sauce. When it is all added, simmer for 3 minutes, add salt and pepper and white wine. Cool a little before adding cream, which is optional.

Mint Sauce

Put the sugar into a sauceboat and add the boiling water to dissolve sugar. Let it cool, then add the finely chopped mint. Stir and add vinegar to taste.

1 tsp sugar
1 dessertsp boiling water
2 tbsp mint
4-6 tbsp vinegar

Mustard Sauce

Stir the mustard as well as the flour into the butter for your roux. Then proceed exactly as for White Sauce.

Serves 6
1 ½ tsp dry mustard
1 oz (30 g) flour
1 ½ oz (45 g) butter
½ pt (300 ml) milk

Onion Sauce

Peel the onions and cut in quarters downwards. Stew them for 20 minutes in the milk, to which 2 tablespoons of water have been added. Pour into a bowl and in the saucepan in which they were cooked make your roux as for white sauce. Add the onions and the milk slowly, stirring well, season and simmer as for plain white sauce.

Serves 6-8
3 medium onions
¾ pt (450 ml) milk
2 oz (60 g) butter
1 ½ oz (45 g) flour
Salt and pepper

Parsley Sauce

To the finished white sauce, add the parsley, simmer for 1 minute and serve.

Serves 4-6
½ pt (300 ml) white sauce
1 ½ tbsp finely chopped parsley

Reform Sauce

Bring Espagnole sauce (see opposite page) to the boil and stir in juice of the lemon, redcurrant jelly and wine. Add about ½ teaspoon black pepper, and ¼ teaspoon cayenne.

Serves 4
½ pt (300 ml) Espagnole Sauce
1 lemon
2 tbsp redcurrant jelly
¼ pt (150 ml) red wine
About ½ tsp freshly ground black pepper
About ¼ tsp cayenne

Tartare Sauce

Mix the mustard to a paste with vinegar. Add this slowly to the mayonnaise. Stir in gherkins, onions and capers, which must be all very finely chopped.

Serves 4-6
1 tsp dry mustard
1 tsp vinegar
¼ pt (150 ml) mayonnaise
1 dessertsp each chopped pickled gherkins and onions
1 dessertsp chopped capers

Tomato Sauce (1)

Cut onion and carrot into thin slices. Cut the bacon in pieces, put all into a saucepan with the butter, and fry gently. Add the tomatoes, cut in quarters. Fry for 4 minutes. Stir in the flour and add the stock. Bring to the boil. Season with salt and pepper and sugar. Cover and simmer gently for 30 minutes, stirring occasionally. Strain finely through a food mill or sieve. Reheat and add 2 tablespoons of cream or milk.

Tomato Sauce (2)

Slice the tomatoes and stew them gently until soft. Put through a food mill or sieve, fine enough to keep pips and small bits of skin from going through. Stir into them the white sauce, bring to the boil, add cream and pinch of cayenne and serve.

Velouté Sauce

Melt butter or margarine in thick saucepan, add the flour and stir the roux as for white sauce. Gently stir in the stock and add the mushrooms and the herbs. Simmer very gently for ¼ hour. Stir well and pour through a strainer. This is a basic sauce, made like béchamel except that it is made with a white stock instead of with milk. It can also be made with fish stock.

Butters

The easiest and quickest garnishes in the world to make, and delicious. Also excellent in sandwiches.

Anchovy or Bloater Butter

Pound anchovy fillets or essence, or bloater paste, and cayenne into butter. Form it into pats or balls unless the butter is to be used for sandwiches. Chill.

Cheese Butter

To a tablespoon of creamed butter add a tablespoon of very finely grated Gruyère cheese, a little made mustard, pinch of cayenne pepper and ½ teaspoon of tomato purée. Work together as for Anchovy Butter.

Serves 3-4
1 tbsp butter
1 tbsp Gruyère cheese
Mustard
Cayenne
Tomato purée

Devilled Butter

Work everything together as for Anchovy Butter.

Serves 3-4
2 oz (60 g) butter
1 small tsp made mustard
½ tsp curry powder
½ tsp lemon juice
A little cayenne
A little paprika

Green Butter

Put butter in a bowl. Add the finely chopped spinach and herbs (the spinach leaf gives green colour). With a wooden spoon beat them until the butter is soft and the herbs evenly worked into it. Make into pats or balls to serve. Chill a little, if possible.

Serves 3-4
2 oz (60 g) butter
1 leaf spinach
3 sprigs parsley
2 sprigs mint, marjoram, thyme

Horseradish Butter

To 1 oz (30 g) of creamed butter add a teaspoon of very finely grated horseradish, season with salt, and drop in ½ teaspoon of lemon juice. Work together as for Anchovy Butter.

Serves 2
1 oz (30 g) butter
1 tsp horseradish
Salt
Lemon juice

Prawn or Shrimp Butter

Shell and chop the prawns or shrimps, then beat them into the butter with the pepper and mace. Work together as for Anchovy Butter.

Serves 3-4
1 doz prawns or 2 doz shrimps
2 oz (60 g) butter
Sprinkling of pepper
Pinch of powdered mace

Sweet Sauces

Where sauces for meat dishes are generally based on flour, those for puddings and sweets are generally based on cornflour or arrowroot which are smoother and lighter. They must, however, be brought to the boil and allowed to boil at least 3 minutes or until the sauce becomes smooth, thick and almost transparent.

Serves 4-6
½ oz (15 g) cornflour
¾ pt (450 ml) milk
1 oz (30 g) sugar
½ oz (15 g) butter or margarine

Sweet White Sauce

(For steamed or baked puddings.)

Mix the cornflour in a basin with a little of the milk to a smooth paste. Bring the rest of the milk to the boil. When boiling, pour it all at once on the cornflour, stirring vigorously. Return to saucepan (which should be heavy aluminium) and boil for 3 to 5 minutes, adding sugar and butter or margarine and stirring all the time as it is very liable to scorch.

This is a basic sweet sauce to which various flavourings may be added.

Serves 6-8
¼ lb (120 g) fresh butter or margarine
¼ lb (120 g) icing sugar
3 tbsp brandy or rum

Brandy or Rum Butter or Hard Sauce

Cream the butter and sugar with a wooden spoon until creamy and light. Beat in the brandy (or rum) until it is all absorbed. Make into pats or balls. Chill slightly and serve. May be made with half sherry and half brandy if preferred.

Serves 4-6
½ oz (15 g) cornflour
1 oz (30 g) sugar
¼ pt (150 ml) brandy

Brandy Sauce

Mix the cornflour into ½ pint (300 ml) of water. Put into a saucepan with the sugar and boil for 3 minutes, stirring all the time. Add the brandy and serve very hot.

Serves 4
¼ lb (120 g) brown sugar, or 3-4 tbsp golden syrup
½ oz (15 g) butter or margarine
½ tsp cornflour
¼ tsp vanilla

Butterscotch Sauce

Dissolve the sugar or golden syrup in ½ pint (300 ml) of water. Add the butter or margarine and boil for 5 minutes. Mix cornflour with a few drops of cold water. Stir in and simmer for 2 or 3 minutes. Add the vanilla, stirring well, and serve very hot.

Serves 4
2 oz (60 g) plain chocolate, grated, or 2 dessertsp drinking chocolate or cocoa
1 oz (30 g) cornflour
¼ pt (150 ml) milk
1 dessertsp sugar

Chocolate Sauce

If using plain chocolate, melt it with a tablespoon of water in small saucepan. Mix cornflour to a smooth paste with a little milk. Stir into melted chocolate and add remainder of milk (boiling) and sugar. Stir and simmer gently for 3 minutes. If drinking chocolate or cocoa is used, add it to the dry cornflour and mix to a paste before adding boiling milk.

See also Ice Cream, Chapter 19.

Caramel Sauce

Put the caster sugar into small saucepan with 5 tablespoons of water. Boil till a bright brown syrup is formed. Remove at once and stir into ¼ pint (150 ml) of Sweet White Sauce which you have ready and hot.

Serves 4
2 oz (60 g) caster sugar
¼ pt (150 ml) Sweet White Sauce

Golden Sauce

Thinly cut or grate the coloured part of the lemon or orange peel (do not get any pith) and put it in a saucepan with 4 tablespoons of cold water and bring to the boil. Take out the peel, stir in the golden syrup and the juice of the lemon or orange. Simmer gently for 2 or 3 minutes.

Serves 3-4
½ lemon or orange
4 tbsp golden syrup

Jam Sauce (1)

Mix all together and bring just to boil.

Serves 4
¼ lb (120 g) any jam
1 tsp lemon juice
1 tbsp water

Jam Sauce (2)

Heat the jam with 3 tablespoons of water and the lemon juice. Meanwhile, mix the cornflour with a little more water and stir it into the jam mixture. Bring all to the boil. Simmer for 3 minutes and serve.

Serves 4
¼ lb (120 g) any jam
1 tsp lemon juice
1 tsp cornflour

Lemon or Orange Sauce (1)

Stir in the grated rind and the juice of a lemon or orange and add another 1 oz (30 g) of sugar to the recipe given for Sweet White Sauce.

Serves 4-6
1 lemon or orange
1 oz (30 g) sugar
Sweet White Sauce

Lemon or Orange Sauce (2)

(This is a little richer.)
  Bring milk to the boil with the rind of the lemon or orange and the sugar. Beat the eggs and pour the hot milk over them. Return to the pan and beat well over low heat until the sauce has thickened. Add a little of the citrus juice. Strain and serve.

Serves 4-6
½ pt (300 ml) milk
Rind and juice of ½ lemon or
  orange
½ oz (15 g) sugar
2 egg yolks

Marmalade Sauce (1)

Serves 4-6
½ oz (15 g) cornflour
½ pt (300 ml) boiling water
2 tbsp marmalade
Juice of ½ lemon

Mix the cornflour with a little cold water. Add ½ pint (300 ml) boiling water, stirring all the time. Boil for 3 minutes, stirring constantly. Stir in the marmalade and the lemon juice.

Marmalade Sauce (2)

Serves 4
¼ lb (120 g) marmalade
1 dessertsp lemon or orange juice

Put the marmalade in a saucepan with a dessertspoon of lemon or orange juice. Bring to the boil, stirring all the time, and serve.

Mousseline Sauce (Sweet)

Serves 6
2 egg yolks
2 oz (60 g) sugar
2 tbsp water
1 tbsp sherry
¼ pt (150 ml) cream

Beat the egg yolks with the sugar. Stir in water and sherry. Then beat in cream and continue beating while standing the mixture in a saucepan of boiling water over low heat, until it is creamy and thick.

Rum Sauce (Thick)

Serves 6
2 tbsp rum
½ pt (300 ml) Sweet White Sauce

Add 2 tablespoons of rum to ½ pint (300 ml) of Sweet White Sauce (see page 142).

Rum Sauce (Thin)

Serves 4-6
¼ lb (120 g) sugar
3 tbsp rum
Juice of ½ lemon

Boil the sugar in ½ pt (300 ml) water for about 5 minutes to form a syrup. Add the rum and lemon juice. Stir for ½ minute. Serve hot or cold.

STUFFINGS

For Mixed Herb Forcemeat, Oyster Forcemeat, Sausage Forcemeat, Mushroom Forcemeat and Celery Stuffing, see Chapter 25.

Chestnut Stuffing

Serves 6-8
2 lb (1 kg) chestnuts
½ pt (300 ml) water
2 oz (60 g) butter
Salt and pepper
Milk, as required

Slit each chestnut and roast them for 20 minutes in a moderate oven. Then allow to cool a little and remove outer husk and brown inner skin, put in a saucepan, just cover with water and simmer till soft and floury. Be careful that they do not boil dry and scorch. Grind finely through a food mill, beat in butter and seasoning, and a little milk if too dry.

Veal Forcemeat

(For veal, chicken or fish.)

Put all the ingredients into a bowl and stir the egg well in to bind. Press together firmly and stuff veal or bird as required. For fish it is better to use margarine than suet.

¼ lb (120 g) fresh bread crumbs
2 oz (60 g) finely shredded suet or
  margarine
1 tbsp finely chopped parsley
1 tsp finely chopped thyme
Rind of ½ lemon, grated
¼ tsp salt
Pepper
1 egg, beaten

Prune Stuffing

Soak the prunes, then stew and stone them and chop roughly. Mix together the sausage meat, ground almonds and cooked onion. Season to taste with salt and pepper, adding a little sage and nutmeg. Moisten the mixture with egg and a little milk and stir prunes into it.

1 lb (½ kg) prunes
½ lb (240 g) pork sausage meat
2 oz (60 g) ground almonds
2 oz (60 g) chopped boiled onions
Salt and pepper
A little chopped sage
Pinch of grated nutmeg
1 egg
A little milk

A Rich Stuffing for Birds or Beef or Veal

Mix all the ingredients well together and stir in egg. If too dry to bind, use a little milk also.

½ lb (240 g) white breadcrumbs
1 egg
Salt and pepper
2 oz (60 g) sultanas
¼ lb (120 g) minced pork
A little chopped parsley
2 oz (60 g) chopped blanched
  almonds
Milk, as required

Sage and Onion Stuffing, for Goose, Duck and Pork

Parboil the onions and chop finely. Mix all well together and season.

2 onions
¼ lb (120 g) breadcrumbs
1½ oz (45 g) margarine or suet
1 dessertsp chopped sage
Beaten egg to bind
Salt and pepper

VEGETABLES

Vegetables, in all their forms, are one of the most important items in our diet. If they are stale when they are bought, or bought days before they are used; if they are overcooked or boiled in a great deal of water; if they are cooked and ready long before the rest of the meal and kept hot, they will be tasteless and unappetizing, and the greater part of their Vitamin C content will be destroyed.

As in all cooking, it is necessary to find the ways of serving different vegetables that you yourself prefer, but we have tried to suggest, for each vegetable, at least one way of cooking and serving which is a little out of the ordinary and in the case of some, such as potatoes, a great many. How long is it since you served, or were served with potatoes, in any other way than boiled, mashed, roast, or baked in their jackets?

Potatoes needn't be served with every main meal. Another root vegetable, some plain, well-cooked rice, plain boiled spaghetti or an extra green vegetable might well take their place from time to time.

Some vegetables are much more interesting if two or more kinds are cooked separately, but combined and served together. This does not, in general, apply to leaf vegetables, but carrots, turnips, swedes and parsnips are good in all combinations and delicious with kernels of sweetcorn added. Leeks, celery and cauliflowers (broken into florets) are good cooked with a purée of tomatoes and brussels sprouts are splendid mixed with small turnips quartered, and the whole dish sprinkled with orange zest.

We give below a table to show the basic method, with times, for boiling different types of vegetables, and also the method of preparing the raw vegetable and how to serve it, if boiled. We shall refer to this table in the recipes, given later, for different ways of serving.

Frozen vegetables are excellent, and a blessing when you are short of time. They mean that you can eat peas and beans, small young brussels sprouts, broccoli and corn all the year round. Do not deceive yourself that you can't tell them from fresh ones. They are not the same thing at all, particularly in the case of peas. But they are much better than not eating peas from September to June and the fact that there is no preparation time and no mess to clear up is a great help to someone who is busy and who has a small kitchen. Try some of the recipes which follow with frozen vegetables as well as fresh.

Boiling Vegetables

All vegetables should be boiled with the saucepan closely covered.				
Vegetable	*Preparation*	*Whether to be started in cold or boiling water*	*Time*	*Serving and general remarks*
Artichokes (Globe)	Wash well and turn upside down to drain. Trim off any surplus stalks and cut the rough tops off the bottom leaves.	Boiling. Enough to cover them. Teaspoon salt. Boil fast for 10 minutes, then gently.	35 to 40 minutes or until leaves will pull out easily.	The artichokes should be well drained and served very hot, accompanied by a Hollandaise sauce or a French dressing or simply melted butter.
Artichokes (Jerusalem)	Peel thinly, shaping them to an even size and a smooth oval shape. Wash well and keep covered with clean water till you cook them, as they discolour in the air very quickly.	Cold. Enough just to cover them. Teaspoon salt. Bring to boil and boil fast.	20 to 30 minutes or till tender.	Drain and serve with a white sauce. Reserve a little of the liquor in which the artichokes cooked and make your white sauce half with this and half with milk to increase flavour. If you do not want a sauce, simply dot with butter and sprinkle with chopped parsley before serving.
Asparagus	Wash the spears well and cut off the hard bottoms of the stalks. Tie in bundles. If the spears are long, lay in a deep baking tray or Dutch oven of boiling salted water.	Boiling salted water and simmer very gently, so that the heads are not boiled off.	20 to 30 minutes till all the green part of the stalk is tender.	Lift out the bundles of asparagus very carefully and lay on dish, all going the same way. Hold each bundle up to drain on perforated slice for a minute before laying it on dish. Serve melted butter or Hollandaise sauce with it. If to be eaten cold, serve a French dressing.
Beans, Butter (Dried) Beans, Haricot (Dried)	Wash and soak for 12 to 14 hours. Discard any that float.	After soaking, drain and simmer gently, starting from cold, in salted water till quite tender.	40 minutes to 1½ hours or till quite tender. Dried beans vary very much in the time they take to soften.	Drain and serve very hot with parsley sauce or with plenty of butter.
Beans, French	Top and tail the beans and string if necessary. Young ones don't need it. Cut or break into 3 or 4 pieces, if large.	½ pt (300 ml) to 1 lb (½ kg) boiling salted water. Boil rapidly.	15 to 20 minutes or till tender.	Drain well and serve with a few dabs of butter.

Vegetable	Preparation	Whether to be started in cold or boiling water	Time	Serving and general remarks
Beans, Runner	Top and tail and string both sides. Be careful to cut away all the strings as they quite spoil the dish if left on. Slice the beans transversely with a sharp knife as thinly as possible, or use a special cutter.	½ pt (300 ml) to 1 lb (½ kg) boiling salted water. Boil rapidly.	10 to 20 minutes; if finely cut, the beans naturally cook more quickly.	Serve well drained, with a few dabs of butter.
Beetroots	Wash and scrub the beets well, but do not break the skin.	Cold, salted water to cover. Bring to boil and boil rapidly.	30 minutes for tiny new beets. Up to 1½ hours for very large ones.	Drain, and peel off skin with the back of a knife. It comes away very easily. If small young beets, to be eaten hot, arrange in dish and pour white sauce over or melted butter.
Broad Beans	Shell and rinse in cold water.	½ pt (300 ml) to 1 lb (½ kg) boiling salted water. Boil fast.	10 to 25 minutes according to size of beans.	Drain. Serve with butter and chopped parsley or savory or with parsley sauce. If very large and old, you can skin the cooked beans, toss in butter to reheat and serve.
Broccoli	Wash well, discard hard leaves and stems and trim so that the spears are fairly even with a few small leaves.	Boiling salted water, ½ pt (300 ml) to 1 lb (½ kg). Simmer gently so that heads do not break up.	15 to 20 minutes or till stalks are tender.	Drain very carefully, not to break, and lay on a hot dish with the heads at one end, unless too small to serve in this way. Serve with melted butter or Hollandaise sauce.
Brussels Sprouts	Wash well and trim off dark or yellow leaves from outside and also cut off bottoms of stalks. Cut an incision in stalks if very hard and thick to facilitate cooking.	Boiling salted water, ½ pt (300 ml) to 1 lb (½ kg) prepared sprouts. Boil rapidly.	15 to 20 minutes till tender.	Drain carefully and serve very hot with a few dabs of butter as soon as possible after cooking.

Vegetable	Preparation	Whether to be started in cold or boiling water	Time	Serving and general remarks
Cabbage, All Large Varieties Cabbage, Spring	Cut in half and then in quarters and eighths. Cut the thick central stem from each piece. Then cut up or break into small pieces, put in a bowl of cold salted water for a few minutes in case of slugs. Drain and wash under tap.	½ pt (300 ml) to 1 lb (½ kg) boiling salted water. Boil rapidly.	10 to 15 minutes.	Drain very well, pressing out the water with a wooden spoon. Chop with a stainless knife if you want it finer.
Cabbage, Red	As for other cabbage above. Red cabbage turns a violet blue when cooked. It is better braised or baked than boiled.	Boiling salted water, 1 tablespoon vinegar, just to cover. Boil rapidly.	30 to 40 minutes.	As above, for other cabbage.
Carrots, New Carrots, Old	Wash well and remove outer skin by scrubbing, if young. If too old for this, scrape with knife. Only peel if you must. Cut out any discolourations. Cook whole, cut in half lengthways or in rings, according to size and purpose.	Boiling salted water just to cover. Boil rapidly.	15 to 20 minutes. 25 to 35 minutes.	Drain and serve with dabs of butter and chopped parsley, if liked, or toss for a minute in melted butter.
Cauliflower	Cut off bottom of stem and hard dark outer leaves. Wash well.	Boiling salted water to come about halfway up cauliflower. Best cooked flower downwards. Boil gently, so as not to break up flower.	20 to 30 minutes or till stalk is tender.	Drain well and place whole in serving dish. Serve with white sauce, parsley sauce, or with dabs of butter and sprinkle with chopped parsley.

Vegetable	Preparation	Whether to be started in cold or boiling water	Time	Serving and general remarks
Celeriac	Wash well and cut root through into 2 or 4 according to size. Make sure all earth is removed.	Boiling salted water just to cover. Boil rapidly.	15 to 20 minutes or till tender.	Serve cold or hot, as celery.
Celery	Wash very well. Divide and scrub each stem. Trim off end of root. Cut off stringy and discoloured pieces. Make sure no earth is left.	Boiling salted water just to cover. Boil rapidly.	25 to 30 minutes.	Drain very well. Serve with white sauce made with half milk and half the liquor in which the celery is cooked.
Leeks	Cut off root, remove dark outer leaves and cut off most of green from tops. Wash very well. Earth is apt to stick between leaves. Cut down centres to avoid this.	Boiling salted water just to cover. Simmer gently not to break up or steam in steamer.	15 to 20 minutes. 30 to 35 minutes if steamed.	Drain very well and serve with white sauce or with dabs of butter, and, if liked, a little grated cheese.
Marrows Baby Courgettes Zucchini	Trim off stalks if any. Wash well. Cook whole. Never peel.	½ pt (300 ml) boiling salted water to 1 lb (½ kg) baby marrows. Simmer gently.	10 minutes.	Drain well. Serve with melted butter, or with a white sauce.
Marrows, Large	Peel marrow. Cut in half length-ways and scoop out seeds. Cut each half across 3 or 4 times.	½ pt (300 ml) boiling salted water to 1 lb (½ kg) marrow.	15 minutes.	Lift out the pieces carefully so as not to break. Drain well. Serve with white sauce, parsley sauce, or butter and chopped parsley.
Onions	Peel the thin skin away and cut off root and stalk end. Rinse. Cut in quarters vertically or cook whole if small.	Cold salted water. Bring to boil and simmer gently.	If very small or cut in quarters, 15 minutes. If fairly large, 25 to 30 minutes.	Drain well. Serve with white sauce or a little butter.

Vegetable	Preparation	Whether to be started in cold or boiling water	Time	Serving and general remarks
Parsnips	Wash well and peel. Cut in halves and quarters and wash again.	Cold salted water just to cover. Bring to boil and boil rapidly.	30 to 35 minutes or till tender.	Drain and serve with dabs of butter.
Peas	Shell, unless sugar peas, which are cooked whole in the pod, the pods also being eaten.	½ pt (300 ml) boiling salted water with 1 teaspoon sugar in it and a sprig of mint. Simmer gently.	10 to 15 minutes according to age and size.	Drain. Serve with a few dabs of butter.
Potatoes – New (1)	Scrape lightly with a blunt knife, so that you do not break the smooth inner surface. Do not cut up unless very large.	Cold salted water with sprig of mint in it. Boil gently.	25 to 30 minutes.	Drain well and serve with plenty of butter and sprinkle with chopped mint if liked.
Potatoes – New (2)	Scrub the potatoes very clean but do not scrape. Put into water in their skins.	As above.	As above.	Drain and remove skins, which will come off easily. Reheat in a little butter if necessary.
Potatoes – Old	Peel as thinly as possible. Cut large ones in halves so that all are about of equal size and will take the same cooking time.	Cold salted water just to cover. Boil gently.	25 to 30 minutes.	Drain well, being careful not to break, and serve with butter and chopped parsley if liked.
Salsify Sea kale	Wash and scrub roots and trim off outside of thick root stem. Be careful to get rid of all sand and earth. Drop into cold water with lemon juice, when cleaned, to keep colour.	Boiling salted water just to cover. Boil gently not to break. Very good steamed in steamer.	20 to 35 minutes. 40 minutes if steamed.	Drain very well and serve with a good white sauce.

Vegetable	Preparation	Whether to be started in cold or boiling water	Time	Serving and general remarks
Spinach	Wash in at least 3 waters and rinse under running tap to get rid of all earth and sand. Tear stalks and thick ribs out of leaves and discard. Also discard all yellow leaves.	1 oz (30 g) butter or margarine in bottom of saucepan and ½ teaspoon salt. *No* water. The wet spinach holds enough. Turn 2 or 3 times with wooden spoon.	7 to 10 minutes.	Drain very well, pressing out all moisture. Put back in saucepan and stir in some butter, pepper and salt. Stir over fire for a moment to reheat.
Swedes (As Parsnips)				
Sweetcorn	Strip outer husk and silk from the corn cob. Trim off stalk and rinse the cob.	Boiling salted water. Boil rapidly.	8 to 20 minutes according to age of cobs.	Drain well. Serve separately melted butter.
Turnips	Wash well. If young scrub and trim off tops and roots. If older, peel.	Cold salted water just to cover. Boil rapidly.	For small new turnips, 15 minutes. Larger old ones cut – 25 to 35 minutes.	Drain and serve with plenty of butter and pepper.

Recipes

Fried Jerusalem Artichokes

1 lb (½ kg) artichokes, peeled and sliced
Juice of ½ lemon
Salt and pepper
½ pt (300 ml) coating batter 1 or 2 (see page 209)
Oil for frying

Sprinkle the slices of artichoke with lemon juice as you take them from the water in which you have washed them. Shake each slice to dry it, sprinkle with salt and pepper and drop in the coating batter till bowl is full. Do not leave the artichokes uncovered in the air as they turn colour. Lift out slices with perforated spoon, allowing batter to drain back, so that you can put in more slices. Drop each coated slice into a pan of smoking oil at least ½ inch (1¼ cm) deep, or fry in hot deep fat. Fry till golden brown.

Excellent served with a roast or grill instead of potatoes or as a light dish with bacon rolls and a green salad.

Sautéed Globe Artichoke Hearts

1 or 2 artichokes for each person
1 oz (30 g) butter

Cook as in table for boiling. When cool, remove all the leaves and the choke, retaining only the bottom or heart. Toss 1 or 2 of these in butter for each person and serve very hot with any grill or roast. Very good with chicken.

Cold Globe Artichoke Hearts

1 or 2 artichokes per person
Lettuce leaves
French dressing, or Hollandaise Sauce (see Chapter 10)

Proceed as above. Do not reheat the hearts, but serve cold on a bed of lettuce with French dressing or Hollandaise Sauce.

Jerusalem Artichoke Soufflé

Serves 3-4
1 lb (½ kg) artichokes
¼ pt (150 ml) white sauce
1 egg yolk
3 oz (90 g) grated cheese
2 oz (60 g) breadcrumbs
Sale and pepper
2 egg whites

Put the artichokes through a food mill or blender to make a purée. Stir into this ¼ pt (150 ml) white sauce, the egg yolk, 1 oz (30 g) grated cheese and the breadcrumbs. Season well and blend all together. Add the stiffly beaten egg whites, which should hold a peak. Put into buttered ovenproof dish, sprinkle with remainder of cheese and bake in a 400°F/200°C/Gas Mark 6 oven for 20 minutes, till risen a little and golden brown. Serve at once. Makes a very good supper dish, a starting course instead of soup, or a delicious and unusual accompaniment with roasts or grills, if a green salad is served as well.

Aubergine Fritters

Serves 4
2 aubergines
A little cornflour
¾ pt (450 ml) coating batter 1 (see page 209)
Oil for frying

Cut the aubergines into slices across without peeling them. Rub them with cornflour, then dip them in the batter. Deep-fry the coated aubergine slices in hot oil until golden brown. Very good with a grill or served alone with a tartare sauce.

Aubergines à l'Orientale

Serves 4
2 large aubergines
Oil
3 small tomatoes
Salt and pepper
1 clove garlic, chopped
Chopped parsley
1 tbsp breadcrumbs
A little butter

Without peeling them, cut the aubergines in half lengthwise and fry them lightly in oil. Scoop out the pulp and chop it up, together with the skinned and seeded tomatoes. Season with salt, pepper, garlic and parsley. Stir in the breadcrumbs. Fill this mixture into each aubergine skin. Place the filled aubergines in a greased ovenproof dish, dot with butter, and bake in a 350°F/180°C/Gas Mark 4 oven for 30 minutes. Serve hot or cold.

Creamed Runner or French Beans (1)

Serves 3-4
*1 lb (½ kg) prepared beans, whole
    or sliced
1 tbsp cream
½ oz (15 g) butter
Lemon juice
Salt and pepper*

Boil the beans as in table and drain them. Put back in saucepan. Stir in the cream and butter and reheat them for a minute, seasoning with a few drops of lemon juice, salt and pepper.

Creamed Runner or French Beans (2)

Serves 3-4
*1 lb (½ kg) prepared beans, whole
    or sliced
1 oz (30 g) butter
½ oz (15 g) flour
2 tbsp milk
Salt and pepper*

Boil the beans as in table. Drain, and keep warm for a minute. Melt the butter in saucepan in which they were cooked, add flour and make a white roux, stir in milk and cook for 2 minutes, so that you have a little white sauce. Lightly mix beans into this and reheat for a minute, seasoning well with salt and pepper.

Brussels Sprouts Gratinée

Serves 4
*1 lb (½ kg) brussels sprouts
3 rashers of rather fatty bacon, cut
    in small pieces
2 oz (60 g) grated cheese
1 oz (30 g) breadcrumbs
Croûtons*

The sprouts must be firm and hard, not leafy and not too large.

Boil as described in table. Drain well. Meanwhile fry the bacon, drain, reserving the fat, and keep hot in ovenproof dish. Toss the sprouts in the bacon fat for 2 minutes, so that they are lightly fried all round – do not have the fat too hot when doing this. Lift them out with fish slice or perforated spoon and add them to the chopped bacon, lightly mixing all together. Sprinkle thickly with cheese and crumbs, brown under hot grill and serve as starting course or as supper dish, with croûtons of fried bread. Also very good served with cold meat.

Brussels Sprouts with Chestnuts

Serves 4
*1 lb (½ kg) brussels sprouts
1½ oz (45 g) butter
½ lb (240 g) cooked and skinned
    chestnuts
Salt and pepper*

Boil as described in table.

Melt butter in pan and heat without allowing to brown. Toss chestnuts in it, breaking them up into pieces as they fry for 2 minutes. Add sprouts and toss with chestnuts 2 minutes more. Mix lightly together and season, turn on to a hot dish and serve.

Very good with any roast or bird and with cold ham or any cold bird.

Brussels Sprouts with Green Grapes

Serves 4

1 lb (½ kg) small firm sprouts
½ lb (240 g) green grapes
1 oz (30 g) butter

Boil the sprouts as directed in table. Meanwhile, blanch and seed the grapes. Drain the sprouts, toss in the butter for 2 minutes, lightly mix in the grapes, turn into hot serving dish and serve at once very hot.

This is delicious served in individual dishes as a hot hors d'oeuvre, with fried croûtons to eat with it. It is also a perfect vegetable to serve with any roast bird, particularly game birds, and is very good with veal in any form.

German Cabbage

Serves 4-6

1 white drumhead or
savoy cabbage
2 large cooking apples
1 large onion
2 oz (60 g) sultanas
2 oz (60 g) butter

This is best made with a white drumhead cabbage, but a hard savoy may be used. Shred the cabbage very finely. Peel, core and slice the apples finely. Peel the onion and cut into fine rings. Mix the apple and onion with the cabbage, add 2 oz (60 g) of sultanas, and place in a well-buttered ovenproof dish. Add 2 tablespoons of water, cover closely, and cook in a 300°F/150°C/Gas Mark 2 oven for 1½ to 2 hours. When the cabbage is quite tender it may be uncovered and left to crisp slightly in the oven for 10 minutes before serving.

Baked Cabbage

Serves 4

1 hard savoy cabbage
1 ½ oz (45 g) butter
¼ pt (150 ml) stock or water
Salt and pepper
1 tsp paprika (optional)

Cut the cabbage into quarters. Wash under running tap, and remove hard stalk. Butter a fairly deep ovenproof dish, place the quarters in it, and add the stock or water. Sprinkle with salt and pepper. Cover closely and cook in a 300°F/150°C/Gas Mark 2 oven for 1½ hours. Then uncover the cabbage, dot with butter, sprinkle with paprika if liked, and replace in the top of the oven to brown slightly before serving.

Baked Red Cabbage (1)

Serves 6

2 lb (1 kg) cabbage
2 tbsp vinegar
¼ pt (150 ml) red wine
2 apples, cored and diced
2 oz (60 g) sultanas
2 onions, diced
1 rasher bacon, diced
1 bay leaf
Sprig of thyme
Salt
6 peppercorns

Shred the cabbage finely, removing the stem, and marinate it in the vinegar, wine and ¼ pt (150 ml) water for 2 or 3 hours or overnight. Place it in a saucepan with the liquid, together with the diced apples, sultanas, onions, bacon, bay leaf, thyme, and salt and peppercorns. Boil for 10 minutes. Then turn into ovenproof casserole, cover, and finish cooking in 300°F/150°C/Gas Mark 2 oven for 1 hour. Serve with hot ham or game or mutton or pork.

Baked Red Cabbage (2)

Serves 6
2 lb (1 kg) cabbage
2 oz (60 g) butter
Salt and pepper
½ pt (300 ml) stock

Wash the cabbage well, then chop up roughly, leaving out all the hard stem. Butter an ovenproof dish, put the cabbage in it, and sprinkle with salt and pepper. Add enough stock (use a stock cube if necessary) almost to cover the cabbage. Cover the dish closely and place in a 300°F/150°C/Gas Mark 2 oven. Cooking will take 1½ hours or so; when cooked the cabbage should have absorbed most of the liquid and be quite tender.

Mashed Carrots

Serves 6
2 lb (1 kg) carrots
1 oz (30 g) butter
Salt and pepper
1 tbsp chopped parsley

Cook carrots as in table for boiling. Grate fairly coarsely through a food mill. Reheat in 1 oz (30 g) butter, stirring in a little pepper and salt, and pile on a flat serving dish. Sprinkle with chopped parsley.

Carrots Vichy

Serves 6
2 lb (1 kg) carrots
2 oz (60 g) butter
Salt and pepper
A little sugar
2 rashers bacon, chopped
Chopped parsley

Scrape and then slice the carrots. Melt 1½ oz (45 g) butter in a saucepan and toss the sliced carrots in it for a few minutes. Cover level with water, season with salt, pepper and a little sugar, and add the chopped rashers of bacon. Simmer gently until tender for 25 minutes. The liquid should have almost evaporated. Do not drain, as what is left will have become a good sauce. Add ½ oz (15 g) of butter, stir it in, pour the whole into a hot serving dish, sprinkle with chopped parsley and serve very hot.

Fried Cauliflower

Serves 4-6
1 cauliflower, boiled as in table but for only 10 minutes, and divided into florets
½ pt (300 ml) coating batter
Oil for frying

Dip each well-drained floret into coating batter and drop into very hot deep oil, and fry for 2 minutes only till golden brown and crisp all over. If shallow-frying, have the oil really hot and at least ½ inch (1¼ cm) deep in pan. Drain the florets well.

Onions, quartered downwards and divided into leaves and dipped in the same way, are very good, mixed with the cauliflower fritters. Fry the onions for a little longer as they are raw when you start. If served with bacon and sausages and a green salad, this makes a very good luncheon or supper dish.

Cauliflower au Gratin

Cook cauliflower as in table for boiling. Drain. Divide into pieces and arrange in an ovenproof dish with quarters of hard-boiled egg. Cover with the well-seasoned white sauce. Sprinkle with a thick layer of crumbs and grated cheese. Dot with dabs of butter and brown under hot grill.

Serves 4
1 cauliflower
2 hard-boiled eggs
½ pt (300 ml) white sauce
Salt and pepper
3 oz (90 g) breadcrumbs
3 oz (90 g) grated cheese
A little butter

Braised Celery (1)

Prepare the celery as in table, but cook for only 15 minutes. Drain, but save the water. Toss the sliced onions in butter, together with the bacon, until tender. Place them in a casserole dish with the drained celery and pour over ½ pt (300 ml) of the liquid and the butter from the frying. Season with salt and pepper, cover and braise in the oven for 35 to 40 minutes.

Serves 4-6
2 heads of celery
4 onions, sliced
Butter
2 rashers bacon, finely chopped
Salt and pepper

Braised Celery (2)

Prepare the celery as in table, but do not cook. Lay it, cut in 2 inch (5 cm) sections in an ovenproof dish. Add the peeled and sliced onion, the bouquet and the salt and pepper. Pour over stock. Cover. Cook for 1 hour in a 400°F/200°C/Gas Mark 6 oven. Remove bouquet and serve without draining, as the sauce is very good.

Serves 4-6
2 heads of celery
1 onion
Bouquet garni
Salt and pepper
½ pt (300 ml) stock,
 white or brown

Celery Portugaise

Prepare and cut the celery into 1 inch (2½ cm) lengths. Melt the fat in a saucepan and add the celery, bacon, chopped onions, garlic, bay leaf and skinned, seeded and chopped tomatoes. Season with salt and pepper, and add water to cover. Cook gently on low heat, for 35 to 40 minutes until tender.

Good served with boiled or grilled ham or bacon.

Serves 4-6
2 heads of celery
1 oz (30 g) butter or lard
2 rashers bacon, chopped
2 oz (60 g) chopped onions
1 clove garlic
1 bay leaf
½ lb (240 g) tomatoes
Salt and pepper

Savoury Cucumber

Peel the cucumber and cut into 2 inch (5 cm) lengths. Put into boiling, salted water and cook until soft enough to break up. Drain well and put in a bowl. Mash with some butter, pepper and cream; dust with a little flour. Then put into small saucepan, and simmer for a few minutes. Serve on slices of fried bread, with a little chopped parsley on top and cayenne, if liked.

Serves 4-6
1 cucumber
Butter
Salt and pepper
1 tbsp cream
A little flour
Slices of fried bread
Chopped parsley
Pinch of cayenne (optional)

Cucumbers à la Crème

Serves 6
2 cucumbers
2 oz (60 g) butter
¼ pt (150 ml) thin cream
Salt and pepper
Lemon juice

Peel the cucumbers and split them lengthwise. Remove the seeds. Cut them into small pieces about 2 inches (5 cm) thick. Melt the butter and slowly fry the cucumber in it for 3 minutes. Pour in the cream and boil for 2 minutes. Season to taste with salt and pepper. Remove from heat and slowly stir in a dessertspoon of lemon juice. Pour into shallow dish and serve at once.

Do not cook cucumbers for more than 5 minutes as they should remain crisp but hot in the delicately flavoured cream. Very good with fried fish or any grilled meat, or as a starting course.

Leeks with Cheese Sauce

Serves 4-6
8 leeks
½ pt (300 ml) white sauce
2 oz (60 g) grated cheese
1 oz (30 g) butter
Breadcrumbs

Wash the leeks very carefully, removing all grit. Boil them gently until tender. When cooked, press well as they hold a good deal of water. Cut into small pieces. Make ½ pt (300 ml) of white sauce, and mix with it the grated cheese. Butter an ovenproof dish, put a layer of sauce in it, then a layer of chopped leeks, and continue until all are used. Sprinkle the top with breadcrumbs and dot with butter. Stand the dish in a tin with a little cold water in it and bake for about 10 minutes in a 450°F/230°C/Gas Mark 8 oven.

Braised Leeks (1)

Serves 6
8 leeks
2 oz (60 g) butter
Salt and pepper
2 tbsp water

Wash the leeks well, being careful to remove all grit. Cut the leeks in half lengthwise. Butter an ovenproof dish, arrange the leeks in it, season them with salt and pepper, and just moisten with the water. Dot them with butter, cover lightly and bake in a 450°F/230°C/Gas Mark 8 for 20 minutes. Uncover and allow to brown slightly for a further 5 minutes.

Braised Leeks (2)

Serves 6
8 leeks
¼ pt (150 ml) stock
1 oz (30 g) margarine
2 oz (60 g) flour

Follow the procedure as for (1), using stock instead of water, and keep the leeks covered throughout cooking. Then remove leeks from the stock and put them to keep hot. Melt margarine in a saucepan, stir in the flour, allow to cook for 3 minutes, then very slowly add the stock. Replace the leeks in the dish, pour the thickened sauce over them, and serve very hot.

Vegetable Marrow with Cheese

Peel, cut up and cook marrow as in table for boiling, but boil for only 5 minutes so that the pieces of marrow are still firm. Well butter an ovenproof dish and arrange the pieces of marrow in it. Stir half the cheese into the white sauce and pour over marrow. Sprinkle rest of cheese, breadcrumbs, salt and pepper over and dot with remaining butter and bake in a 350°F/180°C/Gas Mark 4 oven for about ½ hour.

Serves 6
1 medium vegetable marrow
2 oz (60 g) butter
2 oz (60 g) grated Parmesan cheese
½ pt (300 ml) white sauce
2 tbsp fine breadcrumbs
Salt and pepper

Marrow with Tomato Sauce

Prepare marrow as in table for boiling. Drain well. Put the pieces in an ovenproof dish, cover with tomato sauce, sprinkle with crumbs and grated cheese, brown under a hot grill, and serve.

Serves 4-6
1 vegetable marrow, about 4 lb (2 kg)
½ pt (300 ml) tomato sauce
2 oz (60 g) breadcrumbs
2 oz (60 g) grated cheese

Braised Marrow

Peel and cut up as for boiling. Well butter an ovenproof dish. Lay marrow in it. Dust with salt and pepper. Put dabs of butter on each piece of marrow. Closely cover dish with lid or foil.

Bake in a 350°F/180°C/Gas Mark 4 oven for 25 minutes. Serve in dish in which it was cooked.

Serves 4-6
1 vegetable marrow, about 4 lb (2 kg)
Salt and pepper
2 oz (60 g) butter

Vegetable Marrow Duck

Wash the marrow, cut a slice off one end, and scoop out the seeds. Parboil the onions, chop them up, add to them the sage, very finely chopped, and the breadcrumbs, and season with salt and pepper. Add the well-beaten egg and the melted butter. Fill the centre of the marrow with this, then put the end on again and tie round with string. Put the marrow on a baking tin, put the butter on top in small pieces, and bake in a 350°F/180°C/Gas Mark 4 oven till tender for about 40 minutes. Serve with white sauce or cheese or tomato sauce.

Serves 4-6
1 vegetable marrow about the size of a duck
2 large Spanish onions
6 sage leaves
¼ lb (120 g) breadcrumbs
Salt and pepper
1 egg
1 oz (30 g) melted butter
1 oz (30 g) butter

Mushrooms Provençale

Slice the mushrooms, and sauté for about 4 minutes in the butter, very gently. Add the parsley and the bacon cut in small strips and the wine. Boil 3 minutes only, to reduce the wine and give the full flavour. Turn heat low again and simmer for 5 minutes.

Can be served hot with croûtons as a separate course or with chicken, veal or cold meat.

Serves 4
1 lb (½ kg) mushrooms
2 oz (60 g) butter
1 dessertsp chopped parsley
2 rashers bacon
¼ pt (150 ml) wine, white or red

Scalloped Mushrooms

Serves 6
*1-1½ lb (½-¾ kg) mushrooms
(field mushrooms are good for
this)
2 oz (60 g) butter
Salt and pepper
6 oz (180 g) breadcrumbs*

Slice the mushrooms and arrange a layer in a very thickly-buttered ovenproof dish. Season well. Put a layer of crumbs and repeat layers alternately, ending with a layer of crumbs. Dot each crumb layer with butter, and put plenty on the top. Cook in a 350°F/180°C/Gas Mark 4 oven for 30 to 35 minutes. Make sure the mushrooms are tender, and brown top under hot grill if necessary.

Strips of cooked bacon may be added to each layer if liked and the dish served as a supper dish. Or it is very good as an accompaniment to a grill of sausages, kidneys and bacon.

Fried Mushrooms

Serves 2
*½ lb (240 g) mushrooms
2 oz (60 g) butter or margarine*

Trim stalks level with cap (and keep stalks for flavouring other dishes). Make butter or margarine hot, but not brown, in pan. Put in mushrooms flat gill-side down, not overlapping, and very gently fry for 2 minutes and turn and fry 3 minutes on cap side. Lift out and serve on toast sprinkled with salt and pepper, or fried bread, with bacon, for breakfast or supper, or alone to garnish any grill.

Grilled Mushrooms

Serves 2
*½ lb (240 g) mushrooms
2 oz (60 g) butter or margarine*

Exactly as fried, but arrange on grill rack and brush over with melted butter. Turn after 2 or 3 minutes and brush over second side with butter. Do not have grill too hot.

Mushrooms à la Crème

Serves 6
*1 lb (½ kg) mushrooms
2 oz (60 g) butter
2 oz (60 g) flour
Salt and pepper
½ pt (300 ml) milk, heated
2 tbsp cream
Croûtons*

Wash, dry and slice the mushrooms. Allow them to sauté in butter for 5 minutes. Sprinkle them with flour, stir, and cook for 2 minutes more. Season with salt and pepper, then add the milk, heated, and simmer for 3 minutes more. Stir in the cream. Reheat well and serve with croûtons of fried bread. Very good as a starting course.

Fried Onions

Serves 4-6
*1 lb (½ kg) onions
Oil or fat for frying*

Peel and cut the onions into thin rings. Fry in very hot oil or fat till transparent and golden brown, and just beginning to crisp.

Soft Fried Onions

Serves 4-6
1 lb (½ kg) onions
3 oz (90 g) butter or margarine

Peel and cut the onions into thin rings. Melt the butter in a thick pan till just liquid. Add the onions and move them about till all are coated with butter. Fry very gently, over very low heat, without allowing them to brown, until soft and transparent, about 10 to 15 minutes.

French Fried Onions in Batter

Serves 4-6
1 lb (½ kg) onions
A little flour
½ pt (300 ml) coating batter
Oil for frying

Peel and slice the onions downwards, cutting them in quarters and dividing each quarter into leaves. Rub these with flour. Dip in the coating batter and deep-fry in very hot oil till crisp and brown – about 4 minutes.

Floured Fried Onions (very crisp)

Serves 4
1 lb (½ kg) onions
2 oz (60 g) flour
Oil for frying

Peel and slice the onions and dip in flour. Shake off surplus and deep-fry in smoking hot oil for about 2 minutes.

Creamed Onions

Serves 4-6
1 lb (½ kg) onions
2 oz (60 g) butter or margarine
1 ½ oz (45 g) flour
½ pt (300 ml) hot water
¼ pt (150 ml) hot milk
Salt and pepper

Peel and slice the onions and sauté them in butter over a very low heat until tender but not coloured. Remove the onions, leaving the fat in the pan. To this fat add the flour, stir well, and add the hot water and the hot milk, bring to the boil, season to taste with salt and pepper, and add the cooked onions. Stir for a moment and serve.

Stuffed Roast Onions

1 large onion per person
Minced meat or poultry
Salt and pepper
Chopped sage or thyme, or sage and onion stuffing
2 oz (60 g) dripping or lard for roasting

Choose very large onions, preferably Spanish. Prepare as over page and parboil for 15 minutes. Drain well. Scoop out with a pointed knife a good deal of the inside. Fill the cavity with any mixture of minced meat or poultry, etc. Season it well and add a very little chopped sage or thyme, as these are good with the onion flavour. Or fill with a sage and onion stuffing (see Chapter 10) if they are to be served as a vegetable with roast pork, goose or mutton. Roast exactly as in following recipe, but as they are partly cooked, they will need only 45 minutes to 1 hour. If to be eaten as a main dish, serve with tomato sauce or a good brown gravy and plain boiled rice, and green peas or a green salad.

1 large onion per person
2 oz (60 g) dripping or butter
A little flour
A little sugar
A little salt

Roast Onions

Choose large onions, 1 for each person. Spanish onions are the best.

Peel and cut off roots and tops. Arrange in a baking tray, which has been well greased with dripping or butter. Dredge with flour, sugar, and salt. Put a piece of butter on top of each onion and bake in a 350°F/180°C/Gas Mark 4 oven for 1 to 1½ hours until soft and tender. Baste fairly frequently. If tops are becoming too dark, lay a piece of foil over the onions.

Serves 4
2 lb (1 kg) parsnips
2 oz (60 g) butter or margarine
2 tbsp single cream or milk
Salt and pepper
½ tsp dry mustard
2 oz (60 g) grated cheese
2 tbsp fine breadcrumbs

Creamed Parsnips and Cheese

Boil the parsnips until tender, then mash them until quite free from lumps. Beat into them 1 oz (30 g) of butter, 2 tablespoons of single cream or milk, a good seasoning of salt, pepper and dry mustard. Butter an ovenproof dish, line it with the mashed parsnips; then sprinkle on 1 oz (30 g) of grated cheese. Add the remainder of the parsnips and the rest of the grated cheese. Cover with fine breadcrumbs, put small pieces of butter on the top, and bake until brown, in a 350°F/180°C/Gas Mark 4 oven.

Serves 4
2 lb (900 g) peas in the shell, or
  large packet frozen peas
2 oz (60 g) butter
2 tbsp thick cream
Salt and pepper
A little chopped mint

Peas à la Creme

Shell and cook peas as in table for boiling. Drain. Put back in the hot saucepan with butter and toss for a minute. Lightly stir in cream, season and heat for a moment or two without allowing to boil. Pour into hot dish, sprinkle with fresh chopped mint and serve. Frozen peas served like this are excellent.

Serves 4
1½ lb (¾ kg) small young peas,
  or large packet frozen petits
  pois
1 oz (30 g) butter, in pieces
A few lettuce leaves, shredded
4-5 spring onions
Salt and pepper
Sugar
Parsley

Les Petits Pois à la Française

Shell and place the peas in a saucepan with the butter and toss them a little. If frozen petits pois are to be used, cook according to directions on packet. Add the shredded lettuce leaves, spring onions and sufficient water to half-cover the peas. Season lightly with salt, pepper, a sprig of parsley and a pinch of sugar. Cook gently for about 15 minutes until tender. Serve without draining, as the liquid which the peas have not absorbed has become a delicious thin sauce.

Grandmother's Peas with Bacon

Fry bacon in saucepan. Add butter and chopped onion and fry another minute. Put in peas and shake so that they are coated with the butter. Add sugar and salt. Put in lettuce leaf. Add ¼ pint (150 ml) boiling water. Cover closely and cook for 15 minutes, stirring from time to time. Add a little more water if it all absorbs. When peas are tender serve without draining, sprinkled with chopped mint and parsley. Frozen peas will cook a little more quickly than fresh.

Serves 4

1 ½ lb (¾ kg) shelled fresh or
  frozen peas
2 rashers lean bacon, cut in fine
  strips
1 oz (30 g) butter
1 medium onion or 2 shallots,
  chopped finely
1 tbsp sugar
1 tsp salt
A lettuce leaf
¼ pt (150 ml) boiling water
A little chopped mint and parsley

Farmhouse Peas

Proceed exactly as above, but add the 4 cooked chipolata sausages and 12 very small cooked new potatoes to the peas 3 or 4 minutes before the peas are cooked. Pour into warmed dish and serve with triangles of fried bread as a luncheon or supper dish.

Serves 4-6

2 lb (1 kg) peas
2 rashers lean bacon, cut in fine
  strips
1 oz (30 g) butter
1 medium onion or 2 shallots,
  chopped finely
4 chipolata sausages, cut in rings
  and fried until done
12 very small cooked new potatoes
1 tsp sugar
1 tsp salt
Little chopped mint and parsley
Fried bread triangles, to serve

Pease Pudding

Soak the peas overnight. Then put them in a saucepan with the chopped onion and enough boiling water to cover well. Boil until the peas are quite tender, then rub through a sieve or food mill, add the herbs, finely chopped, and season with salt and pepper. Can be put in a blender, but then the purée must be sieved. Melt the butter in a saucepan, add the flour and stir over gentle heat until it is a smooth paste, add the milk gradually and continue stirring until it has boiled for 5 minutes. Add this sauce to the pea purée and mix thoroughly. When it has cooked a little, allow it to cool, stir in the well-beaten yolk of an egg, and finally the white beaten to a stiff froth. Turn into a greased pie dish and bake in a 350°F/180°C/Gas Mark 4 oven for 15 minutes.

Serves 6-8

¼ lb (120 g) dried green peas
1 large onion, chopped
Sprig of parsley, thyme,
  marjoram and savory or a good
  pinch of dried sweet herbs
Salt and pepper
1 oz (30 g) butter or margarine
1 tbsp flour
¼ pt (150 ml) milk
1 egg

Mashed Potatoes

Serves 4
2 lb (1 kg) potatoes
2 oz (60 g) butter
2 tbsp milk
Salt and pepper

Boil the potatoes as given in the recipe for boiling. Drain them well, then put them back into the saucepan and mash them thoroughly with a fork or a potato masher or put them through a food mill. Add 1 oz (30 g) of butter, the milk and salt and pepper and continue mashing until the potatoes are creamy and entirely free from lumps. Put them in a dish, smooth over the top with a fork, and dot with remaining butter. Serve very hot.

Creamed Potatoes (1)

Serves 4
2 lb (1 kg) potatoes
3 oz (90 g) butter
¼ pt (150 ml) milk

Proceed exactly as for mashed potatoes, but when they have been drained, put 2 oz (60 g) butter and the milk in a saucepan and heat them. Then sieve the potatoes through a food mill into the hot milk and butter mixture. Beat them thoroughly with a wooden spoon, over the heat, until they have the consistency of whipped cream. Pile into a hot dish and dot with remaining butter.

Creamed Potatoes (2)

Serves 4
2 lb (1 kg) potatoes
3 oz (90 g) butter
¼ pt (150 ml) milk
1 egg

To make the above recipe even richer and smoother, remove the sieved mixture from the heat, allow it to cool a little, then break an egg into the centre, and beat with a wooden spoon. Dot with butter, and put either into a very hot oven, or beneath a hot grill, until the top is golden brown.

Chipped Potatoes

Serves 4
2 lb (1 kg) potatoes
Oil or dripping for frying

Peel the potatoes and cut them into strips ⅛ to ¼ inch (¼-½ cm) thick. Throw them into cold water as they are cut.

   Heat the oil or dripping in your deep-fryer to smoking point. Dry the potatoes well on a cloth, and drop them into the fat or place them in a frying basket and lower into fat. Fry for about 8 minutes or until a crisp golden brown, shaking the pan from time to time to prevent sticking.

Sauté Potatoes

Serves 4
8 boiled potatoes
3 oz (90 g) butter

Heat the butter in a frying pan until simmering. Slice the potatoes ¼ inch (½ cm) thick, put into the pan, and toss them in the hot butter until they are golden brown all over.

Potatoes Manon

Proceed as for Sauté Potatoes, but dice the potatoes to the size of sugar cubes. Put all the ingredients in the simmering butter and toss until well browned.

Serves 4
8 boiled potatoes
1 chopped onion
¼ lb (120 g) diced lean bacon
¼ lb (120 g) butter

Potatoes Rissolé

Heat the oil to smoking point. Halve or quarter the potatoes, drop them into the oil which must cover them. Fry until brown – about 3 minutes.

Serves 4
8 medium boiled potatoes
Oil for deep frying

Dauphinoise Potatoes

Peel and slice the potatoes finely and sprinkle them with salt and pepper. Take a shallow earthenware casserole, butter it well and place a thin layer of sliced potatoes in it. Sprinkle with grated cheese, then cover with another layer of potatoes sprinkled with cheese, and continue in alternate layers until the casserole is full. Mix the beaten egg with the milk and pour this mixture over the potatoes. Sprinkle with a few small pieces of butter, cover tightly, and cook in a 350°F/180°C/Gas Mark 4 oven for 40 minutes to 1 hour.

Serves 4
2 lb (1 kg) potatoes
Salt and pepper
2 oz (60 g) grated cheese
A little butter
1 egg
½ pt (300 ml) milk

Devonshire Fried Potatoes

Heat the butter or margarine until it simmers in a frying pan. Put the potato in the pan and smooth it down firmly. Fry for 5 minutes, shaking the pan occasionally to prevent sticking. Put a plate over the top, reverse the pan so that the potato comes out browned side upwards. Heat the butter again, and slide the potato back so that the other side browns for 5 minutes. Serve very hot.

Serves 4
1 lb (½ kg) cooked mashed potato
1 oz (30 g) butter or margarine

Potato Balls

Form the mashed potato into balls about the size of golf balls. Dip each ball in the beaten egg and then roll in fine dry breadcrumbs. Fry in oil or butter, turning till golden brown on all sides. Arrange on a dish as they are ready and keep hot till all are finished. Sprinkle with chopped parsley and serve with grills or fried fish or any cold meat.

Serves 3-4
1 lb (½ kg) cooked mashed potato
1 egg
3 oz (90 g) fine breadcrumbs
Oil or butter for frying
Chopped parsley

Serves 4-6
2 lb (1 kg) potatoes
2 oz (60 g) butter
¼ pt (150 ml) milk
2 eggs

Duchesse Potatoes

Proceed as for boiled potatoes. Drain and purée them through a fine sieve or food mill. Put the butter and milk into a saucepan and heat, add the potato and stir it until it is hot and creamy. Remove from the heat, add the eggs (unbeaten) and whip well with an egg-beater or wire whisk. Now butter a flat oven tray well; place the potato mixture on the tray in tablespoonfuls, or pipe it into éclair shapes. Put into a 350°F/180°C/Gas Mark 4 oven for 20 minutes or until the separate shapes are golden brown and beginning to crisp.

Serves 4
2 lb (1 kg) potatoes
½ lb (240 g) butter
Salt and pepper

Potatoes Anna

Wash and peel the potatoes, slice into thin, even slices. Butter a round mould well. Put a layer of potatoes at the bottom, placing them in evenly. Season with salt and pepper. Melt the rest of the butter and pour a little over the layer of potatoes. Then add another layer of potatoes, butter and seasoning, and continue until the mould is nearly full. Put the mould into a 450°F/230°C/Gas Mark 8 oven and bake for 1 hour. Then turn mould upside down on a plate to drain. Remove mould and the potatoes will be light brown and hold the shape of the mould.

Serves 4-6
2 lb (1 kg) potatoes
Dripping or butter
Salt and pepper

Roast Potatoes (1)

Peel the potatoes, cut them into halves, lengthways, or into quarters if they are very large. Put them into the hot fat around a roasting joint, or into a flat pan containing hot dripping and season. Roast them in a 400°°F/200C/Gas Mark 6 oven, for about 45 minutes, turning them occasionally to brown on all sides.

Serves 4
2 lb (1 kg) potatoes
Dripping or butter

Roast Potatoes (2)

Peel the potatoes, cut them as in the above recipe and parboil them for 10 minutes. Follow the same procedure in roasting them. These potatoes will be floury and soft when they are finished, brown, but not crisp. They may be roasted in as little as 25 minutes.

1 large potato per person

Potatoes in their Jackets

Scrub well and prick with a skewer to prevent bursting. Put on a shelf in a 400°F/200°C/Gas Mark 6 oven for 1 to 1½ hours.

Potatoes Gratinée

Butter an ovenproof dish. Slice the potatoes into it. Season well. Pour the milk over the potatoes, dot with pieces of butter and heat in a hot oven for 10 minutes. Cover the top with breadcrumbs and grated cheese, dot with further pieces of butter, and brown under a hot grill.

Serves 4
1 lb (½ kg) boiled potatoes
2 oz (60 g) butter
Salt and pepper
¼ pt (150 ml) milk
2 tbsp breadcrumbs
2 oz (60 g) grated cheese

Scalloped Potatoes

Peel and thinly slice potatoes. Butter a shallow ovenproof dish and fill with the neat slices and sprinkle over a little salt and pepper. Fill up with milk so that potatoes are not quite covered. Dot with plenty of butter and in 350°F/180°C/Gas Mark 4 oven bake for 40 minutes to 1 hour.

Serves 6
2 lb (1 kg) potatoes
¼ pt (150 ml) milk
2 oz (60 g) butter
Salt and pepper

Potatoes Lyonnaise

Slice the onions finely. Heat the butter, and fry the onions until they are brown and crisp. Remove onions and put them in a hot dish. Now slice the potatoes coarsely, drop them into the butter and fry until they too are brown. The potatoes take on the taste of the onion through being fried in the same butter. Drain the potatoes well and mix them with the onions in the hot dish.

Serves 2-3
8 boiled potatoes
2 medium onions
2 oz (60 g) butter

Fried Salsify

Boil the salsify until tender, drain and leave it until cold. Cut in pieces of a convenient size, dry them, then dip each piece in batter and deep-fry until golden brown.

Serves 4
1 lb (½ kg) salsify
Coating batter
Oil

Salsify au Gratin

Cook the salsify as in table for boiling. Drain well. Lay in a buttered ovenproof dish, pour the hot white sauce over. Cover with crumbs and grated cheese. Dot with dabs of butter. Brown under hot grill and serve.

Serves 4-6
1 lb (½ kg) salsify
1 oz (30 g) butter or margarine
½ pt (300 ml) white sauce
2 oz (60 g) breadcrumbs
2 oz (60 g) grated cheese

Serves 4-6
2 lb (1 kg) spinach
2 oz (60 g) butter

Spinach Purée (1)

Frozen spinach makes an excellent purée.

Boil the spinach as given in the table. Chop it, then purée it through a fine sieve or food mill. Put the butter in a saucepan, melt it, add the spinach, and stir until it is very hot.

Serves 4-6
2 lb (1 kg) spinach
2 oz (60 g) butter
2 oz (60 g) flour
¼ pt (150 ml) milk

Spinach Purée (2)

Cook the spinach as in table for boiling. When soft, push it through a fine sieve or food mill. Put the butter and flour in a saucepan, and cook together for 3 minutes. Gradually add the milk. Stir the sauce for 3 minutes. Remove from the heat, stir the white sauce into the spinach until well combined.

This recipe makes a very smooth purée.

Serves 6
3 lb (1 ½ kg) spinach
3 oz (90 g) butter, plus extra for the top
3 oz (90 g) flour
½ pt (300 ml) milk
6 oz (180 g) grated cheese
4 hard-boiled eggs

Spinach of the Côte D'Azur

This dish makes a good main course for lunch or supper, but it is also particularly good served with any kind of cold meat.

Cook the spinach as given in the table. Chop it, then purée it through a fine sieve or food mill. Make a roux of the butter and flour in a saucepan, and gradually add half of the grated cheese and then the milk, stirring well until a thick cheese sauce is formed. Stir the spinach purée into this sauce, and cook gently until it is really hot. Pour the mixture into a large ovenproof dish. Cut the hard-boiled eggs into eighths lengthways and arrange them around the edge of the spinach mixture. Cover the whole dish with the remaining grated cheese, scatter with small pieces of butter and put it under a very hot grill until the cheese has melted and become brown. Serve as soon as possible.

Serves 4
1 lb (½ kg) tomatoes
2 oz (60 g) butter
Salt and pepper
¼ lb (120 g) breadcrumbs

Tomato Charlotte

Blanch, skin and slice the tomatoes. Butter an ovenproof dish, and put a layer of tomatoes in it. Season and cover them with a thin layer of crumbs, and dot with small pieces of butter. Repeat these layers until all is used. The top layer should be of crumbs, dotted with butter. Place the dish in a 350°F/180°C/Gas Mark 4 oven for about 30 minutes or until the top is brown and crisp.

Fried Tomatoes

Fried tomatoes may either be blanched and skinned or left raw, according to taste. Cut the tomatoes in half, across, put the butter or dripping in a frying pan, and make very hot. Place the tomatoes in the pan, flat side down, for 3 minutes, then turn them to brown on the other side. Serve immediately, either on buttered toast or on slices of fried bread.

1 large tomato per person
2 oz (60 g) butter or good dripping
Buttered toast or fried bread,
  to serve

Tomatoes Gratinée

Blanch the tomatoes, skin and slice them, and place in a well-buttered ovenproof dish, sprinkle with salt, pepper and a little sugar, cover the top with breadcrumbs and sprinkle with grated cheese. Cook in a 350°F/180°C/Gas Mark 4 oven for 30 minutes then brown the top quickly under a hot grill just before serving.

Serves 4
1 lb (½ kg) tomatoes
1 oz (30 g) butter
Salt and pepper
A little sugar
2 oz (60 g) breadcrumbs
1 oz (30 g) grated cheese

Grilled Tomatoes

The tomatoes may be blanched or not. Cut them across and season, and place with the flat side upwards on the grid under a hot grill for 3 minutes, or until the tomatoes begin to brown. Turn them, to brown the other side. Serve either on toast or on fried bread.

1 tomato per person
Salt and pepper
Toast or fried bread, to serve

Stewed Tomatoes

Blanch the tomatoes, skin and cut them up roughly. Season with salt, pepper and a pinch of sugar and a sprig of thyme and a sprig of basil if available. Melt the butter in a saucepan, add the seasoned tomatoes, cover it closely, and cook over a low heat for 15 minutes, or until the tomatoes are soft and juicy. Remove herbs and sprinkle with parsley just before serving.

Serves 4
1 lb (½ kg) ripe tomatoes
Salt and pepper
Pinch of sugar
Sprig of thyme and sprig of basil
  (if available)
2 oz (60 g) butter
1 tsp chopped parsley

Turnips au Gratin

Peel the turnips and boil them for about 25 minutes or until tender. Cut them in slices and put them in a buttered dish. Make a white sauce with the butter, flour and milk (see Chapter 10). Mix the cheese with it and season well. Pour this over the turnips, cover with breadcrumbs and bake in a 375°F/190°C/Gas Mark 5 oven, until the top is brown and crisp.

Serves 4
6 medium turnips
2 oz (60 g) butter
1 oz (30 g) flour
½ pt (300 ml) milk
2 oz (60 g) grated cheese
Salt and pepper
2 tbsp breadcrumbs

Mashed Turnips

Serves 4
8 medium turnips
Salt and pepper
2 oz (60 g) butter

Peel turnips and cut them in quarters, put them in cold water with a teaspoon of salt and boil for about 25 minutes or until tender. Drain and mash them in a saucepan with the butter and a sprinkling of salt and plenty of pepper. Stir them over heat till they are really hot, and then serve.

Mixed Vegetables

Creamed Spring Vegetables

Serves 4
2 oz (60 g) butter
8 small young carrots
16 small new potatoes
16 small spring onions
Bouquet of thyme, parsley and mint
1 tbsp flour
¾ pt (450 ml) white stock (or
*   stock made up to ¾ pt (450 ml)*
*   with ¼ pt (150 ml) white wine)*
1 medium lettuce
½ lb (240 g) shelled or frozen peas
1 tsp salt
1 tsp caster sugar
1 tbsp cream

Melt the butter and toss all the vegetables, except the peas and lettuce, and the bouquet in it together. Stir in the flour very gently. Add the stock or stock and white wine. Cover and simmer for 8 minutes. Add the washed lettuce cut into strips and the peas, stir into the sauce and simmer for another 10 minutes or till the peas are tender. Remove from heat and stir in the salt, sugar and a tablespoon of cream. Pour into a warmed dish and serve as a separate course with croûtons or with chicken, sole or veal or any delicate meat or fish.

Macedoine of Vegetables

Serves 4
4 carrots
2 young turnips
¼ lb (120 g) shelled or frozen peas
¼ pt (150 ml) white sauce
Salt and pepper
1 egg yolk

Scrape the carrots, and peel the turnips, cut in ¼ inch (½ cm) cubes and cook separately in slightly salted water until tender. Boil the peas in the usual way. Make the white sauce. Season well. Mix in the vegetables, well drained, and just before serving, remove from heat and stir in the slightly beaten egg yolk. Do not allow to boil again.

Cooked sweetcorn, sweet pepper, chopped celery, or sliced mushrooms may also be added.

SALADS AND SALAD DRESSINGS

SALADS

Points About Salad Making

1 Remember that cabbage, as well as lettuce, can make a good basis for a salad, and that a plain cucumber or tomato salad makes a good change from a mixed one.

2 Many fresh fruits blend excellently with salad vegetables. Do not be afraid to mix sweet fruits with savoury vegetables.

3 Nuts, dried fruits and seeds also provide interest in salad.

4 Dressings are all important to good salad making. Try always to make your own, rather than relying on bought ones. Even a mayonnaise is quite easy to manage if the recipe is carefully followed. Remember that the object of a dressing is to bring out and enhance the flavour of the salad, not to conceal it, so be careful in your use of vinegar, garlic, onions and herbs.

5 Use herbs with your salads: they bring out flavours, and can add interest even to an ordinary lettuce. Herbs are particularly useful if a plain green salad is served with a main dish. A lettuce salad, decorated with cold cooked peas, and finely chopped mint makes an excellent accompaniment to roast chicken.

6 Never dress a salad with any acidulated dressing until just before serving. If it is added too far ahead, the fresh crispness of vegetables or fruit will be lost, and the salad will become wet and soggy. Never add salt until just before serving for the same reason.

7 All salads should be both crisp and cool, so take the trouble to dry your leafy vegetables in a cloth or shake them dry in a shaker before using them, handle them as little as possible, and do not prepare them too far in advance, and keep in a refrigerator until you are ready to use them.

8 Remember that a French dressing is good with practically any kind of salad, but try out different dressings from time to time.

Vegetables for Salad

	To prepare	To serve
Leaf Vegetables Cabbage (White Drumhead)	Remove all stalks and outer leaves cut into quarters, wash carefully under cold running water. Dry with cloth.	Either chop finely with sharp stainless knife, or shred on grater.
Cabbage (Green or Savoy)	Remove stalk and outer leaves, cut into quarters, wash under cold running tap. Dry in colander or shaker.	Cut into fine strips or chop. Do not grate or the leaves will be crushed.
Cabbage (Red)	Treat as for Savoy (will go a pale violet colour when washed and grated).	Grate or shred very finely. Red cabbage is more fibrous than savoy.
Celery	Cut the bottom off each root. Separate the stalks out from one another. Cut all the green leaves and sprouts off. Wash the stalks well, scrubbing them if necessary.	Celery is served either in whole stalks as an accompaniment to other salads, or roughly chopped and dressed as a separate salad, or shredded and mixed with other vegetables.
Chicory (Endive)	Cut the bottom off each head. Remove the outer leaves, then peel away the leaves one by one. Rinse in cold water.	The leaves are generally used whole and on their own, but they can be coarsely chopped and mixed with other vegetables.
Chinese Leaves	Cut the bottom off the stalk but leave the large central ribs of the leaves. Wash well and dry and chop finely.	Serve cold in a salad, or steam for about 8 minutes.
Lettuce	Remove all hard stalk and outer leaves. Separate into leaves, wash well in cold water. Shake in colander or salad shaker until dry.	Either tear into small pieces or use leaves whole.
Sorrel	Use only the youngest leaves; wash very well in cold water.	Mix with lettuce or cabbage. Always shred finely. Gives a sour, sharp taste to salad.
Spinach	Use only the youngest, palest leaves. Wash several times in cold water to remove all grit and dust. Dry in a shaker.	Use with cabbage or lettuce in a proportion of $\frac{1}{3}$ to $\frac{2}{3}$. Used alone the taste is often too strong.
Watercress	Do not use the leaves once they have become at all yellow. Pull leaves from hard main stalk. Wash leaves thoroughly in cold water.	May be mixed with other salads or served alone. If serving alone, make sure the leaves are not too bitter.
Root Vegetables (Raw) Carrots (New)	Remove tops and bottoms. Scrub thoroughly and rinse in cold water. N.B. Carrots must be very young for this or they will be too hard.	Raw new carrots may be served whole in a mixed salad. Otherwise grate.

	To prepare	*To serve*
Carrots (Old)	Wash the carrots well. Peel or scrape, remove top and bottom.	Raw carrots are usually served grated in a mixed salad.
Radishes	Remove tops and bottoms and wash thoroughly to remove all grit. N.B. very small radishes usually have a more peppery taste than large ones.	Serve just as they are, with a green salad, or slice roughly for a mixed one.
Spring Onions	Remove the top coarse leaves and the bottoms.	Serve whole in a mixed salad or chop roughly.
Other Vegetables (Cooked) Broad Beans	Unless they are very small and tender, broad beans should have their skins removed for salad.	Serve with a cream dressing as a separate salad, sprinkled with chopped savory, or use in a mixed green salad.
Carrots	Cut into dice or very thin slices.	Diced carrots are used in Russian salad. Sliced ones may be used with a mixed salad, or with lettuce and peas.
Cauliflower	To use up cold, cooked cauliflower, cut all the flower sprigs off the stalk.	Serve in mixed salad, or dressed separately.
Peas		Serve with lettuce and mint as an accompaniment to chicken, or use in Russian salad, or in any mixed salad.
Potatoes	Cut into dice.	Serve with mayonnaise as a potato salad or use in Russian salad.
Peppers (Green and Red)	Cook according to recipe, allow to get cold, then slice into thin strips.	Cooked peppers are good alone, with a French dressing. May also be used raw and finely chopped in a mixed green salad.
Sweetcorn	Boiled fresh corn – remove the kernels from the stalk – or tinned may be used.	Useful alone or in mayonnaise as an accompaniment to green salad.

Fruits, Nuts and Herbs for Salad

Almonds	Blanch the almonds and split them into their natural halves. Used in mixed salad.
Apples	Both cooking and eating apples are useful in salad, cooking apples being particularly good in a fairly bland salad such as lettuce and tomato. Always peel the apples and core them carefully. They may then be grated, diced or sliced thinly. N.B. Remember that if a salad containing apples is made far in advance, the apples will go brown unless covered by other ingredients or coated with dressing.
Avocado	Cut in halves and remove stone. Serve filled, or empty, with French or cream dressing.
Chestnuts	Score with a sharp knife point and boil until the shells are easily removable and they are soft. Quarter them and use in green winter salad. They are especially good in any salad of cabbage.
Cucumber (Ridge or Hothouse)	Cut the top and bottom off the cucumber. Peel thinly or leave the skin on, according to taste. Rinse in cold water. May be sliced thinly or cut into chunks. Serve either separately or as part of a mixed salad.
Dates	Stone and use in mixed salads.
Grapefruit	Skin, remove pips and serve in sections, removing the membranous skin of each section.
Melon	Remove rind and pips from a slice or two. Dice and add to a mixed salad.
Olives (Green or Black)	Stone and add whole or chopped. When stuffed, simply add as they are.
Oranges	Skin, remove all white pith, slice very thinly, remove pips.
Pineapple	Fresh pineapple should be peeled, cut in slices about ¼ inch (½ cm) thick and the core removed. Then fill the centre with cream cheese and serve with other salad vegetables or cut into wedges. Canned pineapple may be used, but is not as delicious.
Pistachio nuts	Shell and use whole in mixed salad, or chop and sprinkle over.
Prunes	Soaked, stoned and chopped, they are particularly good in any salad accompanied by cream cheese.
Sultanas	Soak for a few minutes and use in mixed salad.
Tomatoes	Tomatoes may be blanched for salad or served with skins. Either quarter them vertically or slice horizontally with a saw knife. Use in mixed salad or alone.
Walnuts	Shell the walnuts. Use in halves in mixed salad, or roughly chopped and sprinkled on top.
Herbs	Fresh, not dried, herbs improve, by adding to and bringing out the flavour of, most salads. Some, such as Sage, are too strong, but Parsley, Basil, Mint, Chervil, Thyme (very little), Savory, Lemon Thyme and Chives are all delicious if finely chopped. Basil is particularly good with tomato.

Avocado Salad

Scoop the pulp out of the avocados and mash it. Blanch the tomato, peel and chop it finely, add it to the mixture with the chopped sweet pepper. Blend this well with the French dressing. Wash and dry the lettuce, line the serving dish with it, and put the avocado mixture on top. Or serve in individual dishes garnished with wedges of avocado and tomato and a sprig of French parsley. Serve chilled if possible.

Serves 4
2 avocados
1 tomato
1 sweet pepper
French dressing
1 lettuce

Cream Cheese and Fruit Salad

Wash and dry the lettuce, and arrange the leaves round a dish. Peel and finely slice the orange and grapefruit or pineapple slices, arrange them in alternating slices inside the lettuce, dress with French dressing and pile the cream cheese in the centre. Serve very cold.

Serves 4
¼ lb (120 g) cream cheese
1 cabbage lettuce
1 juicy orange
1 grapefruit or 3 or 4 tinned pineapple slices
French dressing

Cream Cheese and Lettuce Salad

Wash and dry a lettuce and pull each leaf apart. Arrange the leaves round a bowl and toss them with French dressing. Chop the olives very finely and beat them into the cream cheese, at the same time adding a seasoning of salt, pepper and mustard. Pat the seasoned cheese into balls and pile them in the centre of the lettuce.

Serves 4
¼ lb (120 g) soft cream cheese
1 cabbage lettuce
French dressing
8 olives
Salt and pepper
A little mustard

Celery Rémoulade

Peel, slice thinly and shred or grate the celery or celeriac. Mix it with 2 tablespoons of lemon juice to keep it white. Place the mustard, sugar, salt and pepper in a basin, and whisk vigorously while adding the olive oil. When the sauce begins to thicken add the egg yolk and continue whisking. Finally, mix in the cream and vinegar. Stir this into the celery, and allow it to stand for 1 hour before serving.

Serves 6
1 lb (½ kg) celery or celeriac
Lemon juice
2 tbsp mustard
1 tsp sugar
Salt and pepper
¼ pt (150 ml) olive oil
1 egg yolk
2 tbsp cream
Few drops wine or tarragon vinegar

Cream Cheese and Pineapple Salad

Serves 4
¼ lb (120 g) cream cheese
3 slices tinned or fresh pineapple
Lettuce or watercress
2 oz (60 g) raisins
1 oz (30 g) shelled nuts
2 tbsp mayonnaise

Edge a salad bowl with lettuce or watercress. Cut the slices of pineapple into sections to make them easy to serve, put them together again in the centre of the dish. Pat the cream cheese into balls and put them in the centres of the pineapple slices. Stone the raisins, if necessary, and blanch and chop the nuts. Mix the mayonnaise with them. Pour this on the salad and serve.

Chicken Salad or Chicken Mayonnaise

Serves 3-4
½ lb (240 g) cooked chicken
1 cabbage lettuce
¼ lb (120 g) cooked green peas
French dressing or mayonnaise
1 tbsp finely chopped mint

Chicken salad may be made either with slices of the white meat, or with any part of the bird finely chopped.

Slice, or chop the chicken finely. Wash and dry the lettuce, shred it and mix with the peas. Make a layer of this mixture around the serving bowl, and dress with French dressing, or mix the mayonnaise with the chopped chicken. Arrange the chicken in the middle of the salad, sprinkle the whole with chopped mint, and serve.

Cucumber Salad

Serves 4-6
1 large cucumber
2-3 tbsp cream
Juice of 1 lemon
Salt and pepper
Chopped parsley

Peel the cucumber and cut it into about 1 inch (2½ cm) square chunks. Plunge into boiling water for 1 minute, allow to cool, and when cold add the cream and lemon juice. Season with salt and pepper. Mix well then sprinkle liberally with chopped parsley.

Egg Mayonnaise

Serves 4
4 hard-boiled eggs
3 tbsp mayonnaise
Heart of a lettuce
2 tomatoes cut into 8 slices
Chopped parsley
2 oranges, separated into
  segments

Make the mayonnaise. Cut the shelled hard-boiled eggs in halves, and place on young lettuce leaves. Pour the mayonnaise over the eggs or serve separately. Decorate with tomato slices, chopped parsley and orange segments.

Macedoine Salad

Serves 4
¼ lb (120 g) each, boiled carrots
  and turnips
½ lb (240 g) cooked new potatoes
¼ lb (120 g) cooked green peas
Cream Salad Dressing

This is an excellent way of using up cold boiled vegetables. Cut the carrots, turnips and potatoes into small cubes. Mix them with the peas, toss in dressing and serve on a bed of lettuce. A mayonnaise may be used instead of cream dressing if preferred.

Salad Niçoise

Wash, dry and finely shred the lettuce. Blanch, skin and chop the tomatoes, peel and chop the eggs. Mix these together in a bowl with the lettuce. Stone the olives and place them, alternating with anchovy fillets, around the edge. Crush the clove of garlic into the dressing, pour it over the salad, put the tuna fish in the centre, sprinkle with a little chopped thyme and serve.

Serves 4
1 lettuce
4 tomatoes
2 hard-boiled eggs
¼ lb (120 g) black olives
¼ lb (120 g) tinned anchovy
*   fillets, drained*
1 clove garlic
French dressing
1 large tin tuna fish
Thyme

Orange Salad

Peel the oranges, being careful to remove all the pith. Cut them into very thin slices and remove all the pips. Put the oranges in a basin and toss them with the French dressing. Wash and dry the lettuce and the watercress. Arrange them around the serving bowl. Put the oranges into the middle just before serving.

Serves 4
3 oranges
2 tbsp French dressing
1 small lettuce
Bunch of watercress

Potato Salad (1)

Dice the peeled, cooked potatoes neatly, while they are still very slightly warm, and lightly fold into the mayonnaise. Sprinkle with parsley or mixed herbs before serving.

Serves 4
1 lb (½ kg) boiled potatoes
¼ pt (150 ml) mayonnaise
Parsley or mixed herbs

Potato Salad (2)

Boil the potatoes (the waxy kind are best) and leave until cold. Wash and dry the lettuce. Peel and slice the cucumber. Arrange lettuce leaves round a bowl, then rows of sliced cucumber. Cut the potatoes into small dice, mix with mayonnaise, salt and pepper, and the finely chopped herbs. Pile this in the centre of the salad bowl and serve.

Serves 4
1 lb (½ kg) new potatoes
1 lettuce
1 small cucumber
Mayonnaise
Salt and pepper
2 tarragon leaves
1 leaf lemon thyme
Small sprig of parsley

Russian Salad

Cut the carrots, turnip and potatoes into small cubes. The French beans should be cut into diamond-shaped pieces. Put all the vegetables into a bowl, handling as little as possible and season. Pour the mayonnaise over them and stir gently. Serve piled into a dish and sprinkled with chopped parsley.

Serves 4
6 young cooked carrots or 1 large
*   old one*
1 boiled turnip
2 young boiled potatoes
A few cooked French beans
¼ lb (120 g) cooked green peas
Salt and pepper
¼ pt (150 ml) mayonnaise
Chopped parsley

Tomato Salad with Herbs

Serves 4
1 lb (½ kg) firm tomatoes
2 tbsp French dressing
1 tsp sugar
1 tsp each of chopped basil, thyme
*   and parsley*

The tomatoes for this salad may be blanched and skinned or left raw, according to taste. Slice the tomatoes as thinly as possible with a sharp serrated knife. Arrange them in overlapping rows in the serving dish and pour the dressing over them. Sprinkle lightly with sugar. Mix together the herbs and sprinkle them over the salad just before serving. Although the herbs may be omitted from this salad they have a particular part to play in bringing out the flavour. Basil is the best of all herbs with tomatoes.

SALAD DRESSINGS

Always have the best olive oil for making salad dressings. Try always to use wine vinegar such as Orléans vinegar, as the bitter taste of malt vinegar does not blend well in a dressing.

Basic French Dressing

Salt and pepper
¼ tsp mustard (optional)
1 dessertsp wine vinegar
3 tbsp oil

Place the salt, pepper, and mustard if used, in a bowl. Add the vinegar, then the oil, and whisk well. Pour this over the salad, and mix it well to distribute the dressing evenly throughout.

Cream Cheese Dressing

3 oz (90 g) cream cheese
1 oz (30 g) chopped shallots
1 oz (30 g) chopped parsley
2 tbsp French dressing

Mash and cream with a fork the cream cheese. Add the chopped shallots and the chopped parsley. Dilute with 2 tablespoons of French dressing.

Fresh Cream Dressing

1 tbsp cream
¼ pt (150 ml) French dressing

Add 1 tablespoon of fresh cream to ¼ pt (150 ml) of French dressing.

Garlic Dressing

1 clove garlic
2 tbsp French dressing

Pound the clove of garlic and add it to 2 tablespoons of French dressing. Alternatively, the salad bowl may simply be rubbed with a garlic clove and the salad dressed with ordinary French dressing; the garlic flavour will then be far less marked.

Mayonnaise

Good pinch of salt
½ tsp powdered mustard
Sprinkling of pepper
1 egg yolk
About ¼ pt (150 ml) olive oil
1 dessertsp wine vinegar

The secret of making a good mayonnaise is patience. If the oil is added too fast to the other ingredients, no amount of whisking will force it to blend with the vinegar and make the desired thick creamy mixture. However, it can be made very quickly in an electric blender using a whole egg.

Put the salt, mustard and pepper into a perfectly cold basin, then add the egg yolk unbeaten. Stir with a wooden spoon to mix. Next add the oil, drop by drop and beat with a rotary egg whisk continually. Continue the process until the mixture begins to thicken, then add a few drops of vinegar. Drop in more oil, alternating with the vinegar until all is used, and the mayonnaise has the consistency of thick whipped cream.

To ensure success, make sure all the ingredients are at room temperature.

Piquant Salad Dressing

3 tbsp mayonnaise
1 desssertsp mustard
1 tbsp gherkins
12 capers
½ tsp chopped parsley
½ tsp anchovy essence

To the mayonnaise add a dessertspoon of made up mustard (make it with vinegar, not water), a teaspoon of finely chopped pickled gherkins and 12 capers finely chopped, ½ teaspoon of chopped parsley and ½ teaspoon of anchovy essence.

Thousand Island Dressing

3 tbsp mayonnaise
2 tbsp tomato juice
1 tbsp tomato purée
½ tbsp sugar
2 chillies or good pinch of cayenne pepper

Gently simmer about 2 tablespoons of tomato juice with 1 tablespoon of tomato purée. Add ½ tablespoon sugar and 2 whole chilli peppers (or a good pinch of cayenne pepper). Cook for 5 minutes, then strain and allow it to cool, and when cold add it to the mayonnaise.

SUPPER AND TELEVISION DISHES

SUPPER DISHES

What is a supper dish, as opposed to any other kind of dish? Or rather, what kind of dish is specially suitable for supper? We are assuming here that a supper dish is one which is designed for a pleasantly informal meal. It is important that not too much time be spent on preparation. In fact, the main dish could be prepared some hours before, or very quickly in the last few minutes.

A supper dish ought to be fairly substantial and pleasantly savoury. It can be either hot or cold, but on the whole it is more interesting to have a hot dish for supper unless it is essential to leave the meal ready while you go out, or unless the weather is very hot.

A supper dish should not need soup or hors d'œuvre served before it – those are appropriate for dinner, a more formal meal. Supper should be complete in itself, perhaps with a salad, and should not need a separate vegetable. It should be followed by fresh fruit or cheese, when it is not a cheese dish, and perhaps a cup of coffee.

Most of the supper dishes given here are a little out of the ordinary. Of course, any grill, most simple fish dishes, etc., are exactly right for supper. Among the recipes which follow, however, we hope you will find, on any particular occasion, at least one which might be a change or fun to make.

TELEVISION DISHES

Television has been borne very much in mind in this whole section. If you have just come home, it is very pleasant to have a hot and tempting supper while watching something which interests you. It is much less pleasant if you have to miss something which interests you as well as the family, because, knowing how hungry your family are, you have had to go out into the kitchen to spend time cooking.

For the perfect television supper dish, you want something that can be prepared beforehand and that can sit ready and waiting in a cool oven or warming drawer from a little before 6 pm until 6-30 pm or so; or else which can wait ready in the larder or refrigerator until you slip out between programmes and put it in the oven where you can leave it to cook itself until exactly the time you want it. If you have a microwave oven, frozen prepared dishes can be heated in minutes. Cold dishes of course present no difficulties.

If you are going to prepare a hot dish to eat while you are watching, cook it in individual ovenproof dishes. Stand the small hot dish on a large plate, which need not be hot, and on which you have previously arranged salad on one side, if you are serving it, or chutney or any accompaniment. This might be butter in a neat pat, crusty French bread or a roll or crackers or crispbread, a piece of cheese and an apple, banana or whatever else you wish to serve. Cover the plates with a clean cloth which is very slightly damp, so that the bread and salad will not wilt or dry. They will keep perfectly fresh like this for several hours and you will have nothing to do but put the small hot dish into the space you have left for it. Each person will then need only a plate on his or her lap. Knife and fork for each person can be wrapped in a paper napkin and left ready also. Salt and pepper, ready-mixed, can be put on the side of the large plate.

The following are a few suggestions for dishes which can be prepared at any time of day and kept hot, but which are not included under supper and television dishes as they are given in other sections:

Hot
Steak and Kidney Pie. Make
 individual pies, if possible, in
 any small ovenproof dishes.
 A meat pie can be reheated or
 kept hot without spoiling the
 crust.
Fish Pie
Kedgeree
Stews, Casseroles (see poultry
 and game section, and meat
 section)
Baked Haddock
Cold
Eggs in Jelly
Chicken Chaudfroid
Chicken in Aspic

Of course, any omelette or other egg dish makes a quick supper dish. With salad served on a separate plate, there can be no better meal. Recipes are given in the chapter on Eggs. Below are a few recipes which are rather more substantial than most omelettes and egg dishes and which are a little out of the ordinary.

Omelette Paysanne

Serves 2

2 rashers bacon, finely cut
1 onion or 6 or 7 spring onions,
* finely chopped*

1 large potato, peeled and cut in   *chopped as fine as parsley and*
* cubes*   * mixed with it*
1 dessertsp chopped parsley   *4 eggs*
1 dessertsp sorrel or spinach,   *Salt and pepper*

Fry bacon, onion and potato together, till just soft and brown. Add parsley and sorrel or spinach. Beat the eggs well and then stir in all the other ingredients. Cook as in basic recipe for Omelettes, Chapter 14, spooning out ingredients so that they are evenly distributed in each omelette.

Savoy Omelette

Serves 2

4 eggs
2 tbsp cream
1 oz (30 g) Gruyère or Cheddar
* cheese*
Salt and pepper
½ oz (15 g) butter
2 parboiled potatoes
Chopped parsley

Beat the eggs and cream together and add the grated cheese. Season with salt and pepper. Melt the butter in the frying pan, and when hot add the diced, parboiled potatoes. Sprinkle with chopped parsley and fry for a minute. Pour egg and cheese mixture over and stir well with a fork. Fold and turn out on to dish.

Haddock Omelette

Serves 2

1 fillet smoked haddock
2 oz (60 g) Gruyère or Cheddar
* cheese*
4 eggs
Pepper
Salt (optional)

Cook and skin fillet of haddock, and flake. Grate the cheese, mix with the eggs and haddock, add pepper, but little, if any, salt, as the fish and cheese are already salty. Beat well and cook as in basic omelette recipe.

Substantial Potato Omelette

Serves 2

1 oz (30 g) butter or bacon fat
1 onion, finely chopped
2 slices bread, white or brown, cut
* in small cubes*
2 rashers bacon
½ lb (240 g) parboiled potatoes
4 eggs
Salt and pepper
Chopped parsley (optional)

Heat 1 oz (30 g) butter or some bacon fat until smoking hot in a thick pan. First fry the onion for a minute or two till golden, but not dark brown. Lift out with perforated spoon and keep hot on a plate while you fry the bread cubes till crisp and golden in the same way. Add them to the onion, and fry the bacon. Add this to the onion and bread, put a little more fat in the pan, if necessary, and put in the potatoes. Fry for a minute, then mix all the other ingredients into them, stirring them gently in pan. Pour in the well-beaten eggs, stir, season and cook for 2 minutes. Hold pan under hot grill to firm and set the top and turn out on to a hot dish. Do not attempt to fold. Sprinkle with chopped parsley.

Spanish Omelette

Fry the potatoes, cut in very small cubes, in the butter with the chopped tomatoes, onions and green pepper. When all are cooked add your beaten egg mixture to the very hot pan, and season. Turn over and cook both sides instead of folding like an ordinary omelette, as the vegetables make it very solid.

You can add chopped mixed herbs or chopped parsley, or a few mushrooms. It is good served with cheese or tomato sauce.

Serves 4
½ lb (240 g) potatoes, boiled in
  skins and then peeled
1 oz (30 g) butter
½ lb (240 g) tomatoes, blanched,
  skinned and quartered
½ lb (240 g) onions, finely
  chopped
1 green pepper, seeded and finely
  chopped
7 eggs
Salt and pepper

Surprise Tomatoes

Wash and then cut a slice off the top of each tomato and scoop out the inside (keep it for purée, soup or sauce). Be careful not to break the skin anywhere. Sprinkle the inside of the tomato with salt and pepper. Break an egg into each, top with a sprinkling of parsley, the mushrooms or shrimps, and 2 or 3 dabs of butter on each egg. Stand the tomatoes in a well-buttered ovenproof dish and bake for 15 minutes at 350°F/180°C/Gas Mark 4. Spoon butter and juice from the dish over the tomatoes at least 3 times during cooking, and add a little more butter if necessary. The eggs should be soft and the tomatoes just wrinkled when served.

1 large firm tomato per person
Salt and pepper
1 egg per person
A little parsley
2 oz (60 g) mushrooms, finely
  chopped, or 2 oz (60 g) shrimps
  thoroughly defrosted, if
  necessary
2 oz (60 g) butter

Pipérade

Fry the peppers slowly in a little olive oil. When they are beginning to soften, add the tomatoes. Season with salt and pepper and a clove of garlic, well crushed. Let the mixture simmer a few minutes till it is soft, like a purée. Break in, one by one, 4 eggs. Do not beat them first, but break up each as it goes in and stir it in quickly, stirring the mixture with a fork all the time. Stir till the eggs are cooked, when the mixture should look like a creamy purée, the eggs and vegetables all amalgamated.

Best served in individual small bowls, with a hot sausage and a piece of crusty French bread and butter for each person.

Serves 4
4 green peppers, seeded and cut in
  strips
Olive oil
4 large tomatoes, blanched,
  skinned and quartered
Salt and pepper
1 clove garlic
4 eggs

Mushroom Circles

Fry mushrooms in butter gently, until tender. Keep hot. Butter the bread on one side and spread mustard thinly over butter. Fry it on plain side only in the pan in which mushrooms were cooked, so that the bottom is crisp and the mustard and butter on the soft top have soaked in a little. Place mushrooms on each piece of bread and serve very hot.

2 fairly large flat mushrooms per
  person
3 oz (90 g) butter
2 thick slices bread per person, cut
  into rounds to fit each
  mushroom approximately
A little Dijon-style mustard

Cheese and Potato Savoury

Serves 3-4
¾ pt (450 ml) milk
Salt and pepper
1 oz (30 g) butter
2 lb (1 kg) potatoes
1 dessertsp chopped parsley
3 oz (90 g) grated cheese

Boil the milk with the salt, pepper, and butter. Cut the peeled potatoes in slices about ⅛ inch (¼ cm) thick. Place in a casserole. Pour over the boiling seasoned milk. Bake at 300°F/150°C/Gas Mark 2 for 1 hour. Five minutes before serving lightly stir in the parsley and sprinkle grated cheese over. Put back for 5 minutes so that cheese is just melting when you serve the dish.

Fondue

Serves 4
6 eggs, separated
1 oz (30 g) butter, softened
2 oz (60 g) Gruyère cheese
Salt and pepper
¼ pt (150 ml) white wine

This is a traditional dish of Switzerland and parts of France. It is very rich and good and may be made in several different ways, according to the district from which the recipe is taken. The following one is simple and very delicious.

Whisk the whites of eggs till fairly stiff, beat in the yolks, then beat in the soft butter in very small pieces, and then the grated Gruyère cheese. Season well, using freshly ground black pepper if possible. Stir over boiling water till it is as thick as very good cream and quite smooth. Cool a little and stir in the wine. Serve quickly very hot, either poured over pieces of toast or, better still, in a bowl into which each person dips a fresh crust of French bread, or strips of toast or crisp crackers. Or serve in individual heated cocotte dishes with bread or fingers of toast, so that each person may dip into his own.

Italian Macaroni

Serves 2
½ lb (240 g) macaroni, cooked
½ pt (300 ml) of any stock you have, or make up some from a stock cube
2 oz (60 g) Gruyère cheese, grated
About 2 oz (60 g) butter
2 oz (60 g) Parmesan cheese, grated

Put the cooked macaroni in a pan with the stock and simmer until it has absorbed the liquid. Stir in the Gruyère cheese over a very low heat. At the last minute, add the butter and stir well. Remove from the heat and shake thoroughly to mix and melt the cheese and butter. Turn on to a hot dish and sprinkle with the Parmesan cheese. Can be kept hot in cool oven or warming drawer and grated cheese added just before serving.

Macaroni Provençale

Serves 2
½ lb (240 g) macaroni, cooked
2 oz (60 g) butter or margarine
1 clove garlic, crushed
4 cooked sausages, cut in rings
¼ pt (150 ml) tomato sauce
Grated cheese

Melt the butter and fry the garlic and sausage slices. Add the prepared tomato sauce (see Chapter 10), stir well. When quite hot, stir in the cooked macaroni and simmer for a few minutes till hot throughout. Serve with grated cheese sprinkled over. May be kept hot.

Spaghetti Bolognese

Serves 4-6

1 lb (½ kg) spaghetti
2 small onions, finely sliced
A little olive oil
1 lb (½ kg) fresh minced beef
1 clove garlic
Bouquet garni
1 tbsp tomato purée
Salt and pepper
½ pt (300 ml) stock or half red
*   wine and half stock*
1 oz (30 g) butter
Grated Parmesan cheese

Sauté the onions in the olive oil so that they are soft but not brown. Stir in minced beef. Add crushed garlic, bouquet garni, tomato purée and seasoning and pour in stock and wine, stirring well. Simmer very gently, covered, for 45 minutes, making up the liquid if necessary as it cooks. Meanwhile put spaghetti into a very large saucepan of boiling salted water (it must be long spaghetti, unbroken). Boil for 15 minutes or until tender yet firm to the bite. Stir from time to time. Drain very well on to large shallow dish, which you have buttered. Put a little more butter in dabs on the spaghetti. Pour the meat just as it is into the centre and serve at once with grated Parmesan cheese.

Spaghetti with Tomato and Cheese

Serves 4-6

1 lb (½ kg) spaghetti
Butter
1 pt (600 ml) tomato sauce
Grated cheese

Cook the spaghetti as above, and serve with lots of butter, a pint (600 ml) of a good tomato sauce (see Chapter 10) and plenty of finely grated cheese.

Spaghetti al Burro

Serves 4-6

1 lb (½ kg) spaghetti
¼ lb (120 g) butter
¼ lb (120 g) Parmesan cheese,
*   grated*

Spaghetti is almost best served like this, that is, simply cooked as for Bolognese (see above), drained and returned to pan in which you have melted ¼ lb (120 g) butter, without allowing it to colour. Toss the spaghetti in this for a minute and then pour just as it is, with all the butter, on to a hot dish. Serve with grated Parmesan cheese.

Ravioli

Serves 4-6

1 lb (½ kg) ravioli
Salt
Butter
Tomato or Espagnole Sauce, or
*   grated Parmesan cheese*

Drop the ravioli into boiling salted water and boil gently for 15 minutes. Drain thoroughly and serve with plenty of butter. A good tomato sauce or Espagnole Sauce (see Chapter 10), or grated Parmesan cheese may simply be served separately.

Ham Croûtes

Serves 4

8 circles of bread, 2 in (5 cm)
*   across and ¼ in (½ cm) thick*
3 oz (90 g) butter, melted
2 oz (60 g) grated cheese
4 circles ham cut the same size as
*   the bread*
A little paprika
8 sprigs watercress

Dip the bread in the melted butter and toss it in the grated cheese. Place a round of ham between 2 pieces of bread. Grill on both sides until brown and crisp. Sprinkle with paprika and serve very hot, garnished with the watercress.

Serves 8

*1 lb (½ kg) haricot beans, soaked
    overnight
2 medium onions, sliced
1 clove garlic, crushed
2 or 3 rashers bacon, or a ham
    bone
¼ pt (150 ml) red wine
1 tbsp soft brown sugar
2 or 3 cloves
A pinch of ground cinnamon
3 or 4 peppercorns
1 tbsp tomato purée
Bouquet of thyme and marjoram
1½-2 lb (¾-1 kg) lean lamb or
    pork, partly cooked or at least
    not overcooked
8 frankfurter sausages, cut in bite-
    size pieces
4 rashers fat bacon*

Cassoulet

Cook the soaked beans in an ovenproof casserole in a 250°F/130°C/ Gas Mark ½ oven for 2 hours with the onions, garlic and the bacon or ham bone, wine, brown sugar, the cloves, a pinch of cinnamon, the peppercorns, tomato purée, a bouquet of thyme and marjoram and water to cover. Roast the meat in a baking tin for 1 hour in the same oven. Then remove from oven, take off all fat and skin and cut the meat into 2 inch (5 cm) pieces. Then take out the casserole and remove the bone. Pour out three-quarters of the beans and put a layer of sausage, bacon rashers and meat, replace one-third of beans, put another layer of meat, sausage, and bacon, another layer of beans, the rest of the meat and the rest of the beans. Return to oven, raise heat a little and cook 30 to 45 minutes more without a lid, so that the top makes a sort of bean crust.

This makes a large casserole, very rich and delicious for those who like beans. It is excellent for a supper party as it can be made the day before and reheated slowly without harm. It is designed to be eaten with fresh crusty bread, and should be served with red wine.

Serves 4

*8 soft roes
Flour, salt and pepper
1 oz (30 g) butter
4 slices of bread
Anchovy Butter or extra butter for
    spreading
Chopped parsley
Lemon juice, or 1 tsp capers*

Herring Roes on Toast

Coat the soft roes in seasoned flour and fry in the butter until the roes are lightly brown and crisp on the outside. Toast the bread and spread with Anchovy Butter (see Chapter 10) or extra butter. Put the roes on the toast and sprinkle with chopped parsley and a little lemon juice or with chopped capers.

*1 hard-boiled egg per person
Butter
Anchovies or anchovy essence
Salt and pepper
Chopped parsley
Lettuce or watercress*

Anchovy Eggs

Cut the eggs in halves. Remove the yolks and pound them with a little butter, anchovy fillets or essence to taste, pepper and very little salt as the anchovies are salty, so that they make a smooth paste. Cut a small piece off the bottom of each half of the whites so that they will stand. Fill with the paste, piling it up. Sprinkle with chopped parsley. Serve on a bed of lettuce or watercress.

Stuffed Tomatoes or Green Peppers

Serves 4-6
4-6 large green peppers or large
  firm tomatoes
Breadcrumbs
A little butter or margarine

Stuffing
¼ lb (120 g) minced cooked beef,
  ham, chicken or a mixture
2 oz (60 g) mushrooms, chopped
  and cooked

¼ lb (120 g) breadcrumbs
1 dessertsp finely chopped onion
1 oz (30 g) currants, well washed
A little tomato purée
Salt, pepper, paprika

Cut off the tops of the peppers or tomatoes. Remove all seeds. Parboil the peppers for 3 to 4 minutes in boiling water. Take out and drain thoroughly. The tomatoes can be used raw.

Mix all stuffing ingredients well together with a little tomato purée. Season well.

Stuff the peppers, being very careful not to break them. Place in a buttered dish with just enough water to cover the bottom. Sprinkle the stuffing with breadcrumbs and dot with butter. Bake at 375°F/190°C Gas Mark 5 for 15 to 20 minutes. Stuff tomatoes in exactly the same way, but allow 20 to 25 minutes cooking time. Can be kept hot.

Ratatouille

Serves 4
½ pt (300 ml) olive oil
2 medium onions
2 cloves garlic, crushed
8 tomatoes, blanched and skinned
2 red or green peppers
3 aubergines, peeled, de-seeded
  and quartered
6 courgettes, or 1 vegetable
  marrow
Salt and pepper
Thyme, parsley and a bay leaf

Ratatouille is the richest and most delicious summer vegetable dish of the south of France. It is very highly flavoured, but it is designed for eating in hot weather and is excellent for supper in August and September when the vegetables needed are cheap in England. Really to enjoy it, you should drink a heavy red wine or dry cider with it and serve a lot of fresh, crusty bread. After it you need nothing but a little cheese and fruit.

If you do not want to use aubergines, you can use a little extra courgette or vegetable marrow or 2 large cucumbers, peeled and quartered. If you use courgettes do not peel them. If you use a marrow, peel and remove pips and cut into pieces about 1 inch (2½ cm) wide and 2 inches (5 cm) long.

Put most of the oil into a saucepan and add the sliced onions. Allow them to colour slightly, then add the garlic cloves. Stir for 3 minutes, then add the seeded and diced tomatoes and peppers. Fry the quartered aubergines and courgettes or marrow gently in the rest of the oil in a different saucepan, drain them, then add them to the first saucepan. Season with salt, pepper and the thyme, parsley and bay leaf tied together. Allow to simmer, covered, for 30 minutes, then remove the herbs before serving.

Stuffed Marrow Rings

Serves 4-6
1 small vegetable marrow
Salt
2 heaped tbsp grated cheese
Butter for greasing

Stuffing
2 oz (60 g) butter
1 onion, finely chopped
*2 oz (60 g) mushrooms, finely
    chopped*
*2 tomatoes, blanched peeled and
    chopped*
*¼ lb (120 g) cooked rice or
    breadcrumbs*
Salt and pepper
1 dessertsp chopped parsley

Peel marrow, and cut into 8 rings. Remove seeds by cutting out centre. Put the slices in a steamer, sprinkle with salt and steam over boiling water for barely 10 minutes. Drain the rings well and arrange in a buttered ovenproof dish or individual dishes. Pile the stuffing into the centre of each ring, sprinkle with cheese and put under the grill for a few minutes to brown. May be kept hot for ½ hour or so in cool oven or warming drawer.

This is a good vegetarian filling, but any minced meat, chicken or game mixture is very good.

Melt butter in saucepan. Stir in onion, mushrooms, tomatoes and sauté till just cooked. Add rice or breadcrumbs, salt and pepper, and parsley. Mix well.

Cauliflower Cheese

Serves 4-6
1 firm cauliflower
Boiling, salted water
¾ pt (450 ml) cheese sauce
1 oz (30 g) grated cheese
2 oz (60 g) fine breadcrumbs
About 1 oz (30 g) butter

Put cauliflower into enough boiling salted water to come about halfway up the vegetable. Put on lid and cook 20 to 30 minutes according to size. It should be tender but still firm. Meanwhile, make your cheese sauce (see Chapter 10). Butter an ovenproof dish or individual dishes and arrange cauliflower, broken carefully into florets. Pour over hot cheese sauce. Sprinkle with grated cheese and top with fine breadcrumbs. Dot with pieces of butter. Brown under hot grill and serve. Will keep hot for 30 minutes or so in cool oven or warming drawer, but must not boil.

Risotto

Serves 4
½ lb (240 g) rice
2 oz (60 g) butter
2 large onions, finely chopped
*¾ lb (360 g) tomatoes, blanched
    and skinned*
½ clove garlic, crushed
*2-3 green peppers, chopped
    (optional)*
Salt and pepper
1 dessertsp chopped parsley
1 bay leaf

Boil the rice and when cooked, pour in a sieve and run cold water over it to separate the grains. Melt the butter in a saucepan, lightly fry the onions in it, but be careful not to let them brown. Add cut up tomatoes and the rest of the ingredients, except the rice. Fry very gently for 5 minutes. Then remove bay leaf, stir in the rice, reheat, stirring well all together.

This risotto will be delicious just like this, served very hot with plenty of grated cheese. You can, if you want it a little grander, add ¼ lb (120 g) diced cooked chicken or ham or any lean cooked meat and/or 2 oz (60 g) sliced, sautéed mushrooms and/or 2 oz (60 g) blanched, fried almonds, split but not chopped or ½ pint (300 ml) cooked and shelled prawns or shrimps. Can be kept hot.

Quiche Lorraine

Serves 4

½ lb (240 g) short pastry (see Chapter 17), or use frozen
4 rashers bacon
2 eggs
½ pt (300 ml) milk
Salt and pepper
Cayenne pepper

Line an 8 inch (20 cm) sandwich tin with the pastry. Fry the bacon lightly, then arrange it on the pastry. Beat the eggs into the milk, season well and pour this mixture over the bacon, sprinkle with a little cayenne and bake in a 400°F/200°C/Gas Mark 6 oven for 25 to 30 minutes.

This can be made the day before and warmed up, if liked. It is particularly good if served with a salad.

Vegetable Pie

Serves 6

2 oz (60 g) butter or margarine
1 lb (½ kg) potatoes, sliced
2 shallots or 1 onion, sliced
1 carrot, sliced
½ a small cabbage
2 tomatoes, roughly chopped
Salt and pepper
½ pt (300 ml) stock
½ lb (240 g) short pastry (see Chapter 17), or use frozen

Grease an ovenproof pie dish with some of the butter or margarine, line it with sliced potato, then some sliced shallots or onion, carrot, small pieces of cabbage and tomato, sprinkle salt and pepper on each layer, and repeat until the dish is full. Pour in the stock, dot the remainder of the butter over the top layer and bake in oven for ¾ hour at 400°F/200°C/Gas Mark 6. Remove and allow to cool until just warm, then put on pastry, and bake 20 minutes at same temperature.

Peas, broad beans, mushrooms, 1 or 2 turnips, or any vegetables you like, are good in this.

Cold Meat Loaf

Serves 6

1 average-sized loaf white, day-old bread
¾ lb (360 g) Pâté Maison or 1 lb (½ kg) Pork Galantine (see Chapter 5)
2 oz (60 g) butter
1 tbsp chopped parsley
Salt and pepper

Cut one end from loaf and, with a very sharp knife, cut out all the inside crumb, without breaking or piercing crust. Make half the crumb into fine breadcrumbs and work, together with plenty of salt and pepper and the parsley, into the pâté or galantine. Butter the inside of the loaf fairly thickly on all the inside walls (the back may be difficult to butter, and may be left plain). Mould the filling with your hand into a shape that will roughly fill the loaf and press it in. Press down with spoon, so that it is closely packed. If it does not quite fill the loaf, cut off the empty part neatly and replace crust. Tie in place with string like a parcel. Leave for an hour or two in a cool place with pressure on top and also against sides. Loaf tins will do. To serve, remove string and cut in ½ inch (1¼ cm) slices for each person – a delicious and unusual form of sandwich.

Onion Tart

Serves 4

Short pastry (see Chapter 17), or use frozen
1 pt (600 ml) Creamed Onions (see Chapter 11)
2 egg yolks
Anchovy fillets
Grated cheese

Line an 8 inch (20 cm) flan tin with short pastry, and bake it blind. Fill it with the onions blended with the 2 egg yolks. Arrange a lattice-work design with anchovy fillets on top. Sprinkle with grated cheese and bake for 15 minutes in a hot oven at 400°F/200°C/Gas Mark 6

1 oz (30 g) butter
¼ pt (150 ml) water
3 oz (90 g) flour, sifted
3 egg yolks
Salt and pepper
Cayenne pepper
*2 oz (60 g) Parmesan or Gruyère
   cheese, grated*
2 egg whites
Oil for deep-frying

Cheese Aigrettes

Put the butter and water into a saucepan and bring to the boil. Shake the flour quickly into the water when boiling. Allow to cool a little and stir for 2 minutes, remove from heat, add the egg yolks, beating them in one by one. Add seasoning, cayenne, and cheese, then fold in the stiffly whisked egg whites. Drop the mixture by teaspoonfuls into very deep hot fat, and fry till golden brown. They will take about 6 minutes to cook. Drain on paper and serve at once.

Cheese
Slice of bread, crust removed
Salt and pepper
Mustard (optional)

Toasted Cheese

Cheddar, Gruyère, Cheshire are all suitable.

Cut a slice about ⅛ inch (¼ cm) thick to fit a piece of bread from which you have removed the crust. Toast the bread on both sides if you like it very crisp, on one side only if you like it softer. Lay the cheese on and toast it for a moment, then turn cheese before it becomes melted too much and toast it well – say 1½ minutes. Remove and sprinkle with very little salt and pepper and serve at once. If liked, spread thinly with mustard before serving.

1 large potato per person
*½ oz (15 g) butter per person, plus
   extra for dotting*
*1 oz (30 g) grated cheese, or 1 oz
   (30 g) lean ham per person,
   finely chopped*
Finely chopped parsley
Salt and pepper
Breadcrumbs
Extra grated cheese

Stuffed Baked Potatoes

Scrub the potatoes well, but do not peel. Make a little hole in each to let out the air. Bake them on middle shelf at 400°F/200°C/Gas Mark 6, for about 1 hour or till soft when pressed.

Take them out and allow to cool enough to handle. Cut in half lengthways and scoop out all the inside into a bowl without breaking the skins. Mash the potato in bowl and add the butter, and either the grated cheese or finely chopped lean ham, plus a teaspoon of finely chopped parsley. Mix well and season. Replace in halved potato skins and smooth tops over. Sprinkle with breadcrumbs and grated cheese and dot with butter. Bake for 10 minutes to reheat and brown tops under hot grill. Serve with green salad and French dressing. Can be kept hot or reheated 10 minutes or so before they are wanted.

As Welsh Rarebit
1 egg per portion

Buck Rarebit

As Welsh Rarebit, but with 1 poached egg placed on each portion.

Welsh Rarebit

Serves 2

¼ lb (120 g) cheese
1 oz (30 g) butter
Mustard (optional)
Salt and pepper
2 slices bread, toasted
1 egg yolk, if necessary
1 tbsp beer (optional)

Grate the cheese – Gruyère, Parmesan, Cheddar or a mixture. Melt the butter in a small thick saucepan, stir in the cheese with a teaspoon of mustard, if liked, and seasoning. Stir over gentle heat until the cheese melts. This mixture may be spread on hot toast and toasted under grill as it is; or you may stir in an egg yolk to bind, if the butter and cheese have separated at all, and then spread and grill. If liked, you may also stir in a tablespoon of beer before grilling. Serve very hot.

Mock Crab

Serves 2

2 oz (60 g) grated cheese
2 oz (60 g) butter
Pinch of cayenne pepper
Pinch of paprika
½ tsp anchovy essence, or 1 tsp
   anchovy paste
Salt
Lemon juice (optional)
Slices of bread, toasted

Work the grated cheese into the butter. Cream well and then stir in a pinch of cayenne, a pinch of paprika, ½ teaspoon of anchovy essence or a teaspoon of anchovy paste. Season with salt, if necessary, and a little lemon juice, if liked. Spread on fresh toast and serve cold, or put under hot grill for 2 minutes only.

EGGS

Boiling Eggs

Eggs should be rolled gently from a spoon into boiling water, after you have made sure that there is no crack in the shells. From the time the water, cooled by the cold eggs, comes to the boil again, they should cook for 8 to 10 minutes, if you want them hard-boiled. If you leave them longer the whites harden. Plunge them in cold water the moment they are taken out of the boiling water, as this makes it easy to peel them.

Soft-boiled eggs are cooked in the same way.

For very soft and lightly boiled	3 minutes
Lightly boiled	4 minutes
Soft with white set	5 minutes
Beginning to harden	5½ to 6 minutes according to taste

An egg timer is very useful.

Stuffed Eggs with Anchovies (Hot)

1 or 2 eggs per person
1 anchovy fillet per egg
1 shallot
Pepper
Rounds of fried bread
1½ oz (45 g) butter
Tomato Sauce (Chapter 10)

Hard-boil the eggs, then cut in half, crossways. Remove yolks and cream them with ½ to 1 oz (15-30 g) butter, 4 to 6 fillets of anchovies, the very finely chopped shallot. Season with pepper but no salt, as the anchovies are salty. Heat the mixture for 2 or 3 minutes in a small thick saucepan, stirring. Arrange a small round of crisp fried bread for each egg in a flat ovenproof dish. Put egg white (from which you have cut a slice so that it stands firmly) on each. Fill with the hot mixture. Put a piece of butter on each egg and heat for 3 minutes in a hot oven, 400°F/200°C/Gas Mark 6. Remove and serve with tomato sauce.

Green Stuffed Eggs (Cold)

1 or 2 hard-boiled eggs per person
½ oz (15 g) Green Butter per egg
*   (see Chapter 10)*
Salt and pepper

Cream the egg yolks with the Green Butter, season well and stuff egg whites with the mixture, piling it well up. Serve on bed of salad.

Stuffed Eggs with Ham (Cold)

1 or 2 hard-boiled eggs per person
1 tbsp minced ham for every 2 eggs
½ oz (15 g) butter
Seasoning

The minced lean ham is creamed with the yolks and a little butter and seasoning. Stuff with this mixture.

Stuffed Eggs with Mushrooms (Hot)

1 or 2 hard-boiled eggs per person
1 mushroom per egg
2 oz (60 g) butter,
Salt and pepper
Toast or fried bread

Sauté the chopped mushrooms. Cream the egg yolks with 1 oz (30 g) butter and the cooked mushrooms, season with salt and pepper, fill the eggs and place on small rounds of buttered toast or fried bread. Put a piece of butter on each and heat as for Stuffed Eggs with Anchovies.

Curried Eggs (Hot)

Serves 1-2
4 eggs
1 small onion
1 small apple
½ oz (15 g) butter
1 tsp flour
2 tsp curry paste
½ pt (300 ml) stock
1 tsp lemon juice
Pinch of cayenne and paprika
1 dessertsp chutney
Plain boiled rice

Hard-boil the eggs and keep warm. Fry the onion and apple, cut up finely, in the butter. When soft, stir in the flour and the curry paste. Cook for a minute. Stir in stock and lemon juice. Add cayenne, paprika and chutney and stir well. Cut the eggs in half. Arrange in a warmed serving dish with a border of plain boiled rice. Pour the curry over the eggs and serve.

A few prawns added to the eggs are very good.

Eggs in Cheese Sauce (Hot)

1 or 2 eggs per person
½ pt (300 ml) cheese sauce
1 oz (30 g) grated cheese
1 oz (30 g) breadcrumbs

Hard-boil the eggs. Cut them across and arrange in an ovenproof dish (cut the bottoms so that they stand firmly). Have ready about ½ pint (300 ml) cheese sauce. Pour over eggs. Sprinkle top with grated cheese and breadcrumbs and heat in oven as for Stuffed Eggs with Anchovies. If you want the top to brown a little more, place dish under hot grill for a minute before serving.

Jellied Eggs with Asparagus Tips

1 or 2 hard-boiled eggs per person
About 6 asparagus tips per egg
*About ½ pt (300 ml) aspic or any
savoury jelly*

Pour a little liquid jelly into a small mould (a little larger than a cocotte is best) for each person. Then put in your egg. Arrange cooked asparagus tips around and over the egg. Fill up with jelly. Chill and allow to set. Serve very cold turned out on a bed of lettuce.

Eggs
Aspic jelly or stock and gelatine
*   (1 tbsp per egg)*
1 tbsp finely chopped parsley

Eggs in Jelly

Eggs in jelly are usually soft-boiled and shelled. Simply boil the eggs for 4 minutes. Remove, hold under cold tap, gently crack the shell and peel very carefully. You may, of course, use hard-boiled eggs if you prefer, or you can use poached soft eggs.

The jelly may be aspic or you may simply use a good stock, veal or chicken or beef which jells of its own accord or which you set with ½ oz (15 g) of gelatine to ½ pint (300 ml) stock. In all cases, see that the jelly is well seasoned. Except in the case of the aspic, a little lemon juice is generally an improvement.

Put the eggs in small individual dishes and pour the jelly over them as soon as they are cold. Put in the refrigerator to set for at least 2 hours. Sprinkle with parsley just before serving. Brown bread and butter goes very well with this dish.

1 or 2 eggs per person
About 2 oz (60 g) lean cooked ham
About ¼ lb (120 g) green peas
*   (frozen are excellent)*
About ½ pt (300 ml) aspic or
*   savoury jelly*

Jellied Eggs with Ham and Green Peas

Make as for Jellied Eggs with Asparagus Tips, using the lean of cooked ham cut into tiny strips and the cooked green peas instead of the asparagus.

For each person
1 egg
1 very large firm tomato
½ pt (300 ml) savoury jelly
Watercress

Eggs in Jelly in Tomatoes

Have a very large tomato for each person. Carefully blanch it, cut off top, remove inside and pour in a little jelly. Put in your egg. Fill up with jelly and allow it to run over tomato, so that the outside is glazed with jelly. Put into refrigerator to set and leave at least 2 hours. Serve the tomatoes on a bed of watercress.

Poaching Eggs

Fill a saucepan with 2 pints (1 l) of water, put in a little salt and a tablespoon of vinegar, bring to the boil. Break the eggs, one by one, in a cup and drop them carefully, also one by one, into the water at the place where it's boiling the most. Move the saucepan a little aside and cook for 3 to 4 minutes, keeping the water just boiling, but not enough to move the eggs about and break up the whites. Lift out with a perforated slice or spoon and allow to drain for a moment, before serving on hot buttered toast or according to recipe.

Absolutely fresh eggs set into shape much better than eggs which are a few days old, when the white always tends to drift and break up.

If you use an egg poacher, put the water on to boil in the pan, and put a dab of butter in each of the small egg pans. As soon as the water is boiling, break your eggs carefully into the melted butter, turn down heat so that the water underneath boils gently and steam eggs for 3 to 4 minutes. Remove small pans and slip eggs on to toast. Eggs cooked like this are much dryer than eggs cooked in the boiling water and so there is no risk of the toast on which you serve them becoming soggy.

Poached Eggs with Spinach

First make a good purée of spinach, about ¼ pint (150 ml) per person. Stir in the butter and cream and bring almost to the boil. Season lightly. Put it in a flat serving dish with a poached egg for each person on top.

1 egg per person, poached
¼ pt (150 ml) spinach purée per person
2 oz (60 g) butter to 1 pt (600 ml) of above
A little cream
Salt and pepper

Poached Eggs with Sweetcorn

Cook the corn as explained in table on page 152 (tinned or frozen corn may be used). Stir the corn into the white sauce. Season highly. Place in flat serving dish and dot with small pieces of butter. Keep hot while you poach your eggs. Arrange 1 egg for each person on the bed of corn. Grilled tomatoes arranged round the edge of the dish improve the appearance and the flavour.

Serves 4
4 eggs
½ lb (240 g) sweetcorn
¼ pt (150 ml) white sauce (see Chapter 10)
Salt and pepper
Butter
Tomatoes for garnish

Scrambling Eggs

Scrambled eggs must be cooked very slowly and must be stirred all the time they are cooking. They should be held just off the heat towards the end and it should be remembered that while they are in the hot saucepan, they continue to cook and thicken, so remove them from the heat ½ minute before they are quite set and start to serve them. You must have a small heavy saucepan in which to cook them, so that the egg mixture is about 1½ inches (3¾ cm) deep at a minimum and is in no danger of drying and sticking at the bottom.

Allow 1 or 2 eggs per person. Melt 1 oz (30 g) of butter gently in your saucepan, not allowing it to boil or colour. Meanwhile beat the eggs so that yolks and whites are amalgamated, but not foamy. Season with salt and pepper and stir them into the butter. Stir above the gentle heat until just thickened and creamy. Serve at once. Scrambled eggs cannot wait. You can, if you like, add a dessertspoon of milk per egg when you are beating the eggs but this makes the finished result firmer and less creamy and delicious.

Scrambled Eggs with Dried Haddock

Allow about a tablespoon of cooked and flaked, dried haddock per person. Heat it in a little milk, drain, and stir into the scrambled eggs, just as they begin to thicken. Serve on toast with a sprinkling of red pepper or in individual dishes surrounded by croûtons of fried bread.

Scrambled Eggs with Kipper Fillets

As above, using kipper fillets instead of haddock.

Scrambled Eggs with Ham

As above, using minced cooked ham and 1 teaspoon of finely chopped parsley.

Scrambled Eggs with Fines Herbes

Stir one dessertspoon of mixed and finely chopped chives or spring onions, parsley, marjoram, thyme, tarragon – any, or all of these – into 4 eggs just before they are finished.

Scrambled Eggs with Asparagus

Tips of cooked small asparagus, fresh, frozen or tinned, are suitable for this. Stir into scrambled egg. Serve with toast cut into interesting shapes.

Scrambled Eggs with Chicken Livers

Lightly fry and cut into small pieces 1 or 2 chicken livers and stir into eggs just before they are cooked.

Scrambled Eggs with Cheese

Stir 2 oz (60 g) Gruyère, Parmesan or Cheddar cheese into 4 eggs just before they are cooked.

Scrambled Eggs with Mushrooms

Stir 2 oz (60 g) of chopped and sautéed mushrooms into 4 eggs just before they are cooked.

Baking Eggs

Eggs Sur le Plat or Eggs au Miroir

1 or 2 eggs per person
1 oz (30 g) butter
Salt and pepper

In a large shallow ovenproof dish, melt the butter over a very low heat. Break in 1 or 2 eggs per person, or alternatively use individual dishes and serve 1 or 2 eggs in each. Sprinkle a little salt and pepper on each egg and spoon a little of the melted butter over the yolks. Place dishes on low heat for 1½ minutes, then finish under hot grill (or on top shelf of oven) for another 2 minutes or until whites are just set. They should form a thin film over the yolk which looks like a mirror. The eggs should not stick to the dish or show any sign of browning or crisping. Eggs cooked like this are really much better than fried.

Eggs Sur le Plat with Beurre Noir

1 or 2 eggs per person
1½ oz (45 g) butter
A little vinegar or lemon juice
Salt and pepper

Cook the butter quickly in a flat ovenproof dish, earthenware or enamel, until it is black, before breaking the eggs into the dish. Add, 2 minutes before serving, a few drops of vinegar or lemon juice, salt and pepper.

Eggs Sur le Plat Florentine

Serves 4
1 egg per person
½ pt (300 ml) spinach purée
¼ pt (150 ml) white sauce
  (see Chapter 10)
4 small, thin slices ham or bacon.

Make a purée of spinach and stir it into the white sauce. Then add a slice of cooked ham per person, cut in dice, or a rasher of cooked bacon, diced. Keep it hot. Butter a large shallow ovenproof dish, put the purée into it and flatten to make a bed, break the eggs carefully on to this and cook them as above.

Eggs Sur le Plat with Bacon

For each person
1 or 2 eggs
1 small rasher bacon
½ oz (15 g) butter

Cook a few thin, small pieces of bacon in a flat ovenproof dish with a small piece of butter. When cooked break your eggs over them. Finish cooking as above.

1 or 2 eggs per person
1 oz (30 g) butter
Salt and pepper

Eggs en Cocotte

You want 1 or 2 small cocotte dishes (or ramekins) for each person. Stand them in a baking tray with about ½ inch (1¼ cm) of hot water in it. Put a small dab of butter in each dish. Stand the whole tray in a fairly hot oven, 375°F/190°C/Gas Mark 5, for 2 minutes. Take out and break 1 egg into each cocotte dish. Sprinkle lightly with salt and pepper. Put a small dab of butter on each yolk and return to the oven. Leave for 4 minutes and then look to see if whites are set to your taste. If not, leave another minute or two and look again. Serve at once. Eggs should be eaten straight from the cocottes with a teaspoon.

1 or 2 eggs per person
1 oz (30 g) butter
Salt and pepper
2 oz (60 g) cream
Fresh herbs

Eggs en Cocotte à La Crème

Proceed as in previous recipe but remove eggs after they have been in the oven 3 minutes, and put a dessertspoon of cream over each. Replace in oven for 3 minutes more. Remove and serve at once. Very delicious just as they are, but may be subtly flavoured by sprinkling a pinch of fresh, and very finely chopped, tarragon, parsley, or mint and parsley, over them, when you finally take them from the oven.

Omelettes

People tell you that to make a good omelette you should:
Beat egg yolks and whites separately. Add water. Add milk. Add cream. Beat eggs whole but very foamy. Hardly beat them at all.

You can, in fact, do any or all of these things and you will still make a good omelette provided that you have a thick, heavy pan and that you make it really extremely hot.

Take 3 or 4 eggs for 2 people (7 or 8 for 4 people). Break them into a bowl and beat them till whites and yolks are well amalgamated and foaming a little. Season with salt and pepper. Just grease the pan with butter or margarine – it should be smoking hot and the pan should look moist with the fat, not running with it. Pour in the beaten, seasoned eggs and work them away from the edges with a palette knife, spatula or fork. Shake the pan and gather the omelette in towards the centre a little. In 2 minutes it is done. Fold it with a shake of the pan or with your palette knife and serve on a hot plate at once.

1   If you like your omelettes really wet inside, cook only 1½ minutes and do not beat eggs too much.

2   If you like them dryish, beat fairly well and cook a little more before folding.

3   If you like them foamy and light, beat very well and cook 2 minutes.

4   A 2-egg omelette is done in 2 minutes, a 3-egg in 3 to 4 minutes, and so on. Do not try to cook more than a 6-egg omelette in one pan. If you want more than this, make 2.

You must be quick. If you are slow in cooking (i.e. pan is not hot) or folding and serving, the omelette will be hard and leathery and more like a badly-made pancake than an omelette.

Some savoury omelettes have the flavouring ingredients mixed into the egg yolks before the white is added. In others the filling, hot and seasoned, is put on to the cooked egg mixture just before you fold it over.

Asparagus Omelette

Cook the asparagus tips in butter and add to basic omelette recipe just before folding over.

2 eggs per person
8-12 asparagus tips per person
Butter
Salt and pepper

Omelette Chasseur

Cut the mushrooms, onion or shallots, and the chicken or duck livers into small pieces and add a little chopped garlic, if liked. Fry gently in butter. Stir in the chopped parsley, add about 1 tablespoon sherry and stir all together. Make your omelette as in basic recipe and lightly spread the hot mixture over it, keeping back the juice. Fold over and serve on a hot dish with juice poured over outside.

Serves 4
7 or 8 eggs
¼ lb (120 g) mushrooms
1 medium onion, or 3 shallots
2 chicken or duck livers
Garlic (optional)
Butter
1 tsp chopped parsley
1 tbsp sherry

Cheese Omelette

Add 2 oz (60 g) grated cheese to 4 eggs and beat well. Proceed as in basic recipe.

Serves 2
4 eggs
2 oz (60 g) grated cheese
Salt and pepper
Butter

Cheese Omelette Soufflé

Beat whites and yolks separately. Add grated cheese to yolks and season well. Lightly fold whites into yolks and proceed as above, except that you should not fold it. Either turn it over and cook second side for ½ minute or hold pan for ½ minute under grill.

Serves 2
4 eggs, separated
2 oz (60 g) grated cheese
Salt and pepper
Butter

Eggs
Onion
Butter
Salt and pepper

Onion Omelette

Cut an onion into very thin rings, brown gently and then add to omelette before folding.

Serves 2
4 eggs
2 or 3 potatoes
Butter
Salt and pepper
Parsley
Spring onion

Potato Omelette

Cut 2 or 3 potatoes in cubes, fry them in butter till cooked, add salt and pepper and a little parsley and spring onion chopped together. Put this in a bowl, pour the beaten eggs over the mixture and make omelette as in basic recipe, stirring as you pour into pan so that potato cubes are evenly distributed in omelette mixture.

Serves 2
4 eggs
Parsley
Chives
Tarragon, thyme or marjoram
Salt and pepper
Butter

Fines Herbes Omelette

Finely chop parsley, chives, a little tarragon, thyme or marjoram, mix together and stir into omelette mixture before beating and cooking. One tablespoon of finely chopped herbs is enough for 4 eggs.

Eggs
Mushrooms
Butter
Salt and pepper

Mushroom Omelette

Cut the mushrooms in thin slices, cook them slowly in butter, and add them to the omelette mixture.

Eggs
Lean ham
Salt and pepper
Parsley
Butter

Ham Omelette

Cut some lean ham into matchstick slices and add to the omelette mixture with a teaspoon of chopped parsley.

Serves 3-4
6 eggs
1 lb (1/2 kg) cleaned and chopped
(or large pkt frozen) spinach
1 oz (30 g) butter
1 tbsp cream
Salt and pepper
Nutmeg
Grated cheese
1/2 oz (15 g) chopped parsley

Omelette Florentine

Cook the spinach in a saucepan with the butter for 8-10 minutes, turning it from time to time. Stir in the cream. Season to taste with salt and pepper and nutmeg.

Beat the eggs and, when the omelette is made, fill it with the spinach mixture. Serve with grated cheese and chopped parsley.

Kidney Omelette

Serves 2
4 eggs
2 lamb's kidneys
1 oz (30 g) butter
Flour
Salt and pepper

Skin and trim the kidneys. Cut into small pieces and fry them in a little butter for 3 minutes. Sprinkle with a little flour, stir again, cook for another minute. Make the omelette as usual, and lightly spread the kidney mixture into it just before folding.

Jam Omelette (1) Soufflé

Serves 2-3
4 egg yolks
1 oz (30 g) sugar
6 egg whites
Salt
1 oz (30 g) butter
Jam

Beat egg yolks and sugar together. Whisk the egg whites with a pinch of salt until quite stiff and holding a peak. Stir them lightly into the yolks. Melt the butter in an omelette pan, and when very hot pour in the mixture. Allow to cook for 3 minutes, then finish cooking by holding pan under hot grill for another 2 minutes until risen and turning golden. Turn the cooked omelette on to sugared paper, and spread it lightly with heated jam before folding in half by folding the paper. Pull the paper out, and serve very hot.

Jam Omelette (2)

Eggs
Caster sugar
Butter
Jam

Prepare the eggs as for an ordinary omelette, but without salt and adding a teaspoon of caster sugar. Just before folding the omelette in the pan put in a layer of whatever jam you like. Fold in the usual way and put the omelette into an ovenproof dish. Sprinkle with caster sugar and glaze it quickly under a hot grill.

Fresh Raspberry or Strawberry Omelette

Serves 2-3
4 egg yolks
¼ lb (120 g) raspberries or
*   strawberries*
3 oz (90 g) caster sugar
6 egg whites
Pinch of salt
Butter

Crush raspberries or small strawberries, very lightly with the sugar. Make a soufflé omelette as in Jam Omelette (1). Lay fruit in it before finishing under grill. Quickly sprinkle a little caster sugar over fruit and omelette and hold 2 minutes under hot grill. Serve at once, without folding. Thin cream is good with this.

Rum Omelette

Eggs
Caster sugar
Butter
Rum

Prepare your eggs in the ordinary way and add caster sugar, beating them well. Put in the pan a little more butter than for an ordinary omelette. Fold it as usual, sprinkle with sugar and glaze for a minute under hot grill. Warm some rum, pour it over the omelette and light it. Carry flaming to the table.

SOUFFLÉS

Many housewives are afraid to attempt soufflés in case they do not puff up, or 'go flat' and become tough and leathery. This is a great pity, as soufflés are really extremely quick and easy to make and are light and delicious to eat. They make an excellent starter for a cold meal, a good main lunch or supper dish, or an exciting hot sweet. There are, however, certain rules you must remember and stick to.

1 You must allow at least 1 egg per person and 1 over. Two whole eggs plus 1 extra white serves 2 people, 4 whole eggs plus 1 extra white serves 4 people and 6 whole eggs plus 2 extra whites serves 6 people. A soufflé larger than this is really better made as 2, as, if it is very big, you cannot avoid the sides and top being overcooked before the centre is risen and set.

2 Your oven must be preheated and really hot, 450°F/230°C/Gas Mark 8. The soufflé should be placed level in the centre of the oven.

3 The soufflé will sink, never to rise so well again, if you open the oven door wide very quickly, so that a draught reaches it, or bang the oven door when you close it, or if you snatch it from the oven into the cold air. Move it gently and move everything gently around it. Carefully open the oven door a little to look at it. If you think it well risen, cracking on top and probably done, touch it very lightly with a couple of fingers. If the top crust feels almost firm and not floating, it is ready. Take it out smoothly and gently and carry it quickly to table, where – this is absolutely necessary – those who are to eat it are already sitting. Serve at once on hot plates. The diners must wait for the soufflé, never the soufflé for the diners.

4 You cannot judge the time for a soufflé to be cooked absolutely accurately to the nearest minute, because consistencies vary a little and so does oven heat. On the whole, however:

2 whole eggs plus 1 white   –   5-10 minutes
4 whole eggs plus 1 white   –   12-15 minutes
6 whole eggs plus 2 whites   –   18-20 minutes

5 A soufflé must be cooked in a deep dish (about 4-5 inches, (10-12½ cm) which should be straight-sided and ovenproof. Proper soufflé dishes, of which you can buy a set for the different sizes you want to make, are best of all, but you can of course use any ovenproof casserole of more or less this shape, or even a deep cake tin, which you have lined with greaseproof paper or foil.

Savoury Soufflés

The basis for all savoury soufflés is a white sauce (see Chapter 10), not too thick, into which you stir first your flavouring – cheese, mushroom, fish, shellfish, etc. – and then your well-seasoned egg yolks. Beat the egg yolks well into the sauce, then stir the mixture for 2 or 3 minutes, holding the pan just off the heat or standing it in a tray of boiling water on the heat, or using a double-boiler. Allow to cool to blood heat before folding in the egg whites, whipped absolutely dry and stiff so that they hold a peak. Butter your soufflé dish well and pour the mixture in, making sure that the whites and yolk mixture are evenly mixed. Do not fill the dish more than three-quarters full. Put soufflé at once into preheated oven. See cooking temperature and times on opposite page.

Cheese

Mix the grated cheese into the prepared white sauce. Stir well over a gentle heat until the cheese has all melted, then proceed as above.

Serves 3-4
4 whole eggs and 1 extra white
¼ pt (150 ml) white sauce
2 oz (60 g) grated cheese (Gruyère, Parmesan or Cheddar)
Salt and pepper

Spinach

Mix the spinach purée (see Chapter 11) into the prepared white sauce. Stir until well amalgamated, then proceed as above.

Serves 3-4
4 whole eggs and 1 extra white
¼ pt (150 ml) white sauce
¼ pt (150 ml) spinach purée
Salt and pepper

Mushroom

Chop mushrooms finely, and stew them for 5 minutes in the milk. Melt the butter and stir in the flour. Cook for 2 minutes. Stir in mushrooms and milk. Cook 3 minutes more. Season well and proceed as above.

Serves 4
4 whole eggs and 1 extra white
½ lb (240 g) mushrooms
½ pt (300 ml) milk
1 oz (30 g) butter
1 oz (30 g) flour
Salt and pepper

Serves 4
4 whole eggs and 1 extra white
¼ lb (120 g) sole or haddock,
*   cooked, flaked and pounded*
¼ pt (150 ml) white sauce
Salt and pepper

Fish

Stir the fish into the white sauce, season well. Mix all together well and proceed as above.

Serves 4
4 whole eggs and 1 extra white
¼ lb (120 g) lean ham, minced
¼ pt (150 ml) thin white sauce
Salt and pepper

Ham

For the best flavour, take the ham from a piece you have baked yourself. Mix well into the white sauce, then proceed as above.

Serves 4
4 whole eggs and 1 extra white
¼ lb (120 g) lean ham, minced
¼ pt (150 ml) tomato sauce
*   (see Chapter 10)*
1 dessertsp chopped parsley
*   (optional)*
Salt and pepper

Ham and Tomato

Prepare the tomato sauce (remember not to add too much salt as ham is already salty), add the minced ham and chopped parsley, if liked, then proceed as above.

Sweet Soufflés

A sweet soufflé is based on a crème pâtissière (see Chapter 19), to which you add your egg yolks and whites. If you have not time to make this, you can make a very good sweet soufflé based on a sweet white sauce (a cornflour mixture, see Chapter 10), to which you add your flavouring or into which you mix a fruit purée, then your yolks and stiffly whipped whites. Chocolate soufflé does not need any basis other than the chocolate. We give alternative recipes below.

Serves 3-4
4 whole eggs plus 1 extra white
2 oz (60 g) cocoa
2 oz (60 g) caster sugar

Chocolate Soufflé (1)

Stir cocoa, sugar and about 2 tablespoons water over heat till melted. It should be thick and dark. Stir in the beaten yolks while hot, but not boiling, or they will curdle. Stir well. Allow to cool. Fold in the stiffly whipped whites. Put in greased soufflé dish and cook as explained at the beginning of this section.

Chocolate Soufflé (2)

Melt the chocolate in a little water. Stir in the beaten yolks. Allow to cool a little and add stiffly whipped whites and proceed as explained at the beginning of this section.

Serves 3-4
4 eggs and 1 extra white
¼ lb (120 g) slab chocolate, plain or bitter

Chestnut Soufflé

Add the egg yolks to the chestnut purée. Stir well and flavour with vanilla, brandy or rum. Fold in the stiffly beaten egg whites, and fill a buttered and sugared soufflé mould with this mixture and cook as explained at the beginning of this section.

Serves 4
4 egg yolks
½ pt (300 ml) chestnut purée (tinned will do)
Vanilla
1 tbsp brandy or rum
5 egg whites
A little butter
A little sugar

Coffee Soufflé

Stir coffee and coffee essence well into cream or sauce. Add egg yolks and whipped whites and proceed as explained at the beginning of this section.

Serves 4-6
4 egg yolks
5 egg whites
2 tbsp very strong black coffee
1 dessertsp coffee essence
½ pt (300 ml) Crème Pâtissière (see Chapter 19), or Sweet White Sauce

Raspberry, Lemon or Orange Soufflé

Mix the cold fruit purée or juice with the cold cream or sauce. Blend well. Add yolks and cook for 3 minutes with pan standing in boiling water, stirring all the time. Allow to cool before adding stiffly beaten whites. Then proceed as explained at the beginning of this section.

Serves 4
4 egg yolks
5 egg whites
¼ pt (150 ml) raspberry purée, or 2 tbsp lemon or orange juice plus 1 tsp rind grated very finely
¼ pt (150 ml) Crème Pâtissière (see Chapter 19) or Sweet White Sauce (see Chapter 10)

PANCAKES AND BATTERS

General Notes

A batter is a mixture of flour, milk or milk and water, and generally egg. These must be well beaten in order to incorporate air into the mixture. When the mixture becomes hot, the air in it expands and so lightens the consistency of the mixture. Always therefore, beat any batter mixture very well. It is easiest to use an electric or a rotary beater, but if you use a fork or a wire whisk, remember that you are trying to let air into the mixture, encouraging tiny air bubbles to form, in fact, and beat with a lifting movement. It is not necessary to mix a batter some hours before it is needed and then allow it to stand in a cool place, as old-fashioned cooks used to advise. It will not hurt it to do so, but it will not improve it either. If you do mix it ahead, leave it in a cool place and, preferably, give it a last beating just as you are going to use it. A batter mixture should be as cold as possible and then be quickly cooked. For this reason a batter is always dropped into hot fat, for frying or baking, and, if baked, is cooked in a quick oven.

There are two types of batters: thick or coating batters, and thin batters for pancakes.

You do not need baking powder – plain flour should be used. Self-raising flour is unnecessary, but will not harm the result if you prefer to use it or have no other in the house.

Pancakes must be cooked in a really heavy pan, which is just greased not running, in fat that is smoking hot. Butter is best, as it gives the outside of the pancakes a delicious flavour. Cooking oil is also good as it makes the pancakes very crisp.

Very thin, crisp pancakes can be made about half an hour before they are wanted and stacked, one on top of another, to keep hot, uncovered, in a very low oven or warming drawer. The very hot greased pan should be tipped about when pouring in the batter so there is the thinnest possible unbroken coating.

Larger pancakes can be filled with a savoury mixture such as smoked haddock or finely chopped chicken in a béchamel sauce. Very small ones can be filled with a teaspoonful of lumpfish roe and served with soured cream in imitation of one of the most famous of all Russian dishes, Blinis, made with beluga caviar, which is the highest quality and the most expensive in the world.

PANCAKES

Pancake Batter, Basic Recipe (1)

¼ lb (120 g) flour
Pinch of salt
2 eggs
½ oz (15 g) butter, just melted
½ pt (300 ml) milk

The inclusion of melted butter in this recipe gives a delicious flavour and added crispness to the pancakes. You can make the batter with 1 egg but it is better with 2.

Put the flour in a large bowl with the salt, make a well in the centre and break in the eggs. Add the butter and mix well together. Slowly stir in the cold milk. Beat well until of a smooth consistency, about the thickness of thin cream. Grease a heavy pan with fat, and when hot pour 2 tablespoons of the mixture into the centre of the pan, tilting it to ensure that the liquid covers the whole pan surface. When cooked on one side, toss and brown the other side. If you can't toss the pancake over or are afraid to try, simply slip a palette knife or spatula under it and turn it, this is just as good. The results are not in any way improved by tossing.

When cooked on both sides (about ½ minute a side) roll it up with palette knife, place on a hot dish and either serve at once or keep hot for a few minutes. Pancakes keep hot quite well for a short time and, if the batter has been well mixed, do not become leathery, but they are at their very best served straight from the pan to the plate of the diner.

Traditionally, sweet pancakes are served rolled with fine sugar and quarters of lemon to squeeze over them. They are also good with jam, marmalade, golden syrup or honey.

Pancake Batter, Basic Recipe (2)

¼ lb (120 g) flour
¼ tsp salt
1 egg
½ pt (300 ml) milk

This is a plainer recipe than the one above but makes very good pancakes, which are not quite so buttery in taste.

Sieve the flour and salt into a basin. Make a hole in the centre of the flour and drop in the egg. Add just enough milk to incorporate all the flour. Beat until the mixture is smooth. Add the remainder of the milk gradually, beating all the time and continuing to beat until air bubbles have formed on top of the mixture. Use at once, or, if you prefer to leave the mixture for a while, beat it again just before using.

Apple Pancakes

Serves 4
Pancake batter as basic recipe 1
or 2
¼ pt (150 ml) apple purée
A few raisins
A little sugar

Make the pancakes according to either basic recipe. Have ready the apple purée, which should be hot, fairly thick and dry, well-sweetened and contain some raisins. When the pancake is turned, place a dessertspoon of the apple mixture in the centre, fold the pancake over this, sprinkle with sugar, and lift on to hot dish with palette knife.

*Pancake batter as basic recipe 1
  or 2
½ banana per pancake
Caster sugar
Little butter*

Banana Pancakes

For each pancake, fry the ½ banana, split lengthwise and rolled in caster sugar, in a little butter, for only a minute, till just beginning to soften. Keep hot while you make the pancakes according to either basic recipe. When the second side is cooked, place each piece of banana near the side from which you will fold, and roll pancake as usual with banana in centre.

*Pancake batter as basic recipe
  1 or 2
Mincemeat
Chopped almonds (optional)*

Christmas Pancakes

Use either basic recipe. Spread lightly with mincemeat and add a few chopped almonds, if liked. Roll and serve.

*Pancake batter as basic recipe
  1 or 2
1 orange
Caster sugar*

Orange Pancakes

Use either basic recipe 1 or 2 and add the grated zest of the orange to the flour before beating. Proceed as in recipe. The zest flavours the whole of the batter. Serve with orange quarters and caster sugar.

*Pancake batter as basic recipe 1
Brandy Butter (see Chapter 10)*

Winter Pancakes

Use basic recipe 1. Spread the cooked side of the pancake with brandy butter. Spread it very lightly. Roll the pancake as usual and serve at once, before the brandy butter completely melts and runs out.

*Pancake batter as basic recipe 1
2 oz (60 g) butter
Zest of lemon and orange
Caster sugar
1 tbsp brandy*

Crêpes Suzettes

Make 4 very thin pancakes from basic recipe 1 (basic recipe 2 is not rich enough for this). Then cream the butter with the zest of a lemon and an orange and melt in a small, heavy pan. Reheat the cooked, warm pancakes in it one at a time, turning each on both sides. Sprinkle with caster sugar. Fold over in half and then fold again. Place the finished pancakes on a hot dish. Pour the brandy over them, set it alight and serve immediately. The flavour is very rich and delicious.

Opposite: *Eggs en Cocotte (see page 198) and Scrambled Eggs with Asparagus (see page 196)*

Spanish Omelette (see page 183) and Stuffed Baked Potatoes (see page 190)

Fondue (see page 184)

Left: *Cheese Soufflé*
(see page 203)

Left: *Lemon Meringue Pie*
(see page 221)

Opposite: *Crêpes Suzettes*
(see page 208), *Banana*
Pancakes (see page 208)
and Pineapple Fritters
(see page 210)

Above: *Bread (see page 248)*

Opposite: *Pork Pie (see page 223), Sausage Rolls (see page 221) and Cornish Pasty (see page 222)*

BATTER DISHES

Coating batters are used for dipping fillets of fish, or of meat, or minced mixtures which are to be fried in a coating batter. It is best of all to deep-fry batter-coated food in oil, although they can be shallow-fried. These batters are used for all fritters.

Coating Batter, Basic Recipe (1)

¼ lb (120 g) flour
Pinch of salt
1 egg
¼ pt (150 ml) milk
½ oz (15 g) butter

Mix the flour and salt and sift them into a bowl. Add the egg and, if necessary, a little of the milk and beat until smooth. Stir in the butter after having made it liquid, and continue beating while you add the milk gradually. Beat until smooth and covered with air bubbles. If the mixture is correct in texture it should coat the beater when you lift it out.

Coating Batter, Basic Recipe (2)

¼ lb (120 g) flour
Pinch of salt
1 egg
2 tbsp milk
2 tbsp water

Mix as for previous recipe. This is a plainer batter, without butter and using only half milk, but it gives good results.

Coating Batter, Basic Recipe (3)

¼ lb (120 g) flour
Pinch of salt
1 egg yolk
1 oz (30 g) butter
2 tbsp warm water
2 egg whites

Sieve the flour and salt into a basin containing the egg yolk. Add the melted butter and warm water and beat until a smooth paste is obtained. Beat the mixture very well indeed and allow to get perfectly cold. Just before using, stir in the whisked egg whites.

This gives a crisp casing which stands away from the filling and is very fluffy. It is best cooked in oil, which must be really hot.

Apple Fritters

Coating batter as basic recipe 1, 2
or 3
2 or 3 cooking apples
Caster sugar
Lemon juice
Oil for frying

Use any of the recipes for coating batters. Peel and core the apples and cut into rings. Sprinkle with caster sugar and squeeze lemon juice over. Leave a few minutes. Drain and dip in the batter, so that each ring is well coated all over. Deep-fry for about 3 minutes. Lift out with perforated slice or spoon and drain well on sugared greaseproof paper. Transfer to hot dish and serve. If you must fry in shallow oil make sure it is really hot and at least ¼ inch (½ cm) deep all over pan. Cook fritters for 2 minutes on one side, then turn and cook for 2 minutes on the other.

Opposite: *Home-made Crumpets (see page 254) and Chelsea Buns (see page 252)*

*Coating batter as basic recipe 1, 2
   or 3
2 bananas per person
Sugar
Lemon juice
Oil for frying*

Banana Fritters

Cut each banana in half longways and then each half into 2 or 3 pieces according to size. Proceed exactly as for Apple Fritters.

*Coating batter as basic recipe 1, 2
   or 3
2 apricots per person
Sugar
A little brandy or lemon juice
Oil for frying*

Fresh Apricot Fritters

Halve and stone the apricots, which should be fresh and not too ripe. Sprinkle with sugar and brandy or lemon juice. Leave a few minutes. Drain. Coat each half and proceed as for Apple Fritters.

*Coating batter as basic recipe 1, 2
   or 3
4 dried apricots per person
Oil for frying*

Dried Apricot Fritters

Soak and stew the apricots, drain well and coat with batter. Proceed as for Apple Fritters.

*Coating batter as basic recipe 1, 2
   or 3
1 pineapple ring for each person
A little Kirsch
Caster sugar
Oil for frying*

Pineapple Fritters

Quarter section of a ring of fresh or canned pineapple for each fritter. If you have some Kirsch, sprinkle them with a little, as well as with caster sugar, as it much improves the flavour. Coat with the batter and proceed as for Apple Fritters.

*Coating batter as basic recipe 1, 2
   or 3
1 sausage per person
Bacon
Mushrooms or tomatoes*

Sausage Fritters

Cut a cold, cooked sausage in half longways for each fritter. Coat in batter and fry – deep or shallow – for 3 or 4 minutes, turning once. Drain well and serve with rashers of bacon and mushrooms or tomatoes.

Serves 4-6
*1 lb (½ kg) sausages
2 tbsp dripping
Yorkshire Pudding batter*

Toad-in-the-Hole

Fry the sausages which you have first cut into halves, by twisting the skins in the middle and cutting. Place the cooked sausage halves in a tin of hot fat and pour the batter gently round them, so that they are not pushed out of position. Use Yorkshire Pudding recipe mixture. Cook for 25 to 30 minutes at 450°F/230°C/Gas Mark 8. Serve at once. Tomato sauce is good with this.

Yorkshire Pudding

6 oz (180 g) flour
Pinch of salt
2 eggs
1 pt (600 ml) milk
2 tbsp dripping

Mix exactly as for pancake or coating batter.

Pour off some of the dripping from roasting beef into a baking tin (Yorkshire pudding is better cooked in a tin than in a glass or earthenware dish) – about 2 tablespoons of dripping is enough. Make smoking hot in oven, remove tin and quickly pour in the batter all at once. Immediately put in oven on a low shelf, below the joint, so that it gets bottom heat to start with; the oven should be 400-450°F/200-230°C/Gas Mark 6-8. After 10 minutes, quickly change it to a higher shelf (above the joint). Do not allow it to chill and sink while you do this. Cook another 10 to 15 minutes and serve.

If you prefer, you can cook it entirely above the joint at the top of the oven but the bottom does not, in this case, get the traditional crisp consistency. Traditionally, Yorkshire pudding used to be cooked under the joint, when roasted on a spit or jack before the fire. You can still do this, if you put the beef on a stand in a roasting tray, pour in the batter and remove the beef, which should be ready 10 minutes before batter is done, so that it can rise and brown on top.

PASTRY

Pastry was very important to our ancestors. In great households, it enclosed a huge pie filled with meat or birds and delicacies such as veal kidneys, sweetbreads, coxcombs, artichoke bottoms, mushrooms and almonds to set off the main ingredients. In poorer households, the pastry was made with coarser flour and less fat and the meat and vegetables were enclosed in a pastry which a farm hand or fisherman could conveniently carry with him wrapped in a cloth.

In the Middle Ages, pies were not absolutely divided into sweet or savoury. A meat pie might have sliced pears or apples included and rose-water or orange flour water poured in and a sweet pie might have minced beef and other ingredients which we think of as savoury included.

Things to Remember

1 Always make pastry in a cool place; use cool utensils and very cold water, except in the case of choux and raised pie pastry.

2 The richness of the pastry depends on the fat content. Too little fat will make it dry and crumbly, too much will make it oily and hard to handle.

3 The quantity of water used is of great importance. Too much will make the pastry hard and leathery. Too little will make it crumbly and incapable of holding its shape. Add water gradually, and mix each spoonful completely in before adding more.

4 Note the required oven temperature carefully, and preheat the oven to this level. Pastry baked in too slow an oven will sink, and will be heavy and tough. If the oven is too hot it will brown on the outside, while still remaining soggy inside.

5 The less the dough is handled, the lighter the result will be.

6 Always roll pastry lightly. If force is used the paste will be heavy. If rolling is difficult, leave the dough to rest in a cool place, when it will regain its natural elasticity. (Frozen short and puff pastry are available from most supermarkets and are very good if you are short of time.)

7 All pies with lids, sausage rolls, etc., are much improved in appearance by being brushed over with beaten egg yolk. This was always done in the Middle Ages – the great time for huge pies – and was called 'gilding'.

Pastry Making

Short Pastry

These quantities will make a large pie and a flan or some tarts.

Mix the flour and the salt, and pass through a sieve to remove any lumps. Then rub in the fats lightly with the tips of the fingers and continue until the mixture looks like fine breadcrumbs and there is no dry flour left in the basin. Add very cold water very gradually, until you have a fairly soft dough. The dough should be soft enough to roll easily, but it must not be sticky at all – wet pastry means that it will be hard. Roll out on a floured board.

It should be baked in an oven preheated to 400°F/200°C/Gas Mark 6.

This pastry will keep for a few days if it is wrapped in grease-proof paper and left in a cool place. It will keep for a week in a refrigerator but will then be too hard to work and must be left for several hours at room temperature to soften again. ½ lb (240 g) of flour makes enough pastry for a pie, tart or flan for 4.

1 lb (½ kg) flour
Good pinch of salt
¼ lb (120 g) lard or cooking fat
¼ lb (120 g) butter or margarine
Very cold water to mix.

Short Sweet Pastry

These quantities will make a large flan.

Mix the flour and the salt and sift them into a basin. Rub in the fat, and add the sugar. Now stir in the well-beaten egg, and add enough cold water to form a rather stiff dough. Roll out and bake in oven preheated to about 400°F/200°C/Gas Mark 6.

This pastry can be flavoured in any way you wish. A ¼ teaspoon of grated lemon or orange rind added to the dry ingredients makes a delicious pastry for a lemon curd or a marmalade tart.

½ lb (240 g) flour
Pinch of salt
¼ lb (120 g) butter or margarine
3 oz (90 g) caster sugar
1 egg
Cold water to mix

Flaky Pastry

Sieve the flour and salt into a bowl. Rub into it 1 oz (30 g) of butter and add the lemon juice. Add the (iced) water slowly, stirring all the time until a smooth paste is formed. Roll the dough out lightly on a floured board, then dab it with small pieces of butter using a knife blade. Sprinkle with a pinch of flour. Fold the pastry towards you and pinch the edges so that it forms an envelope. Roll again, rolling away from the joined edge and towards the fold so that the air is not forced out. Dab with butter again. Repeat 3 times until all the butter has been used and you have an oblong shape about ½ inch (1¼ cm) thick. Roll out as required and bake in oven at 400°F/200°C/Gas Mark 6. A pastry crust will take 15 to 20 minutes. This pastry may be used in place of the Raised Pie Pastry recipe, or for canapés or cheese straws.

½ lb (240 g) self-raising flour
½ tsp salt
6 oz (180 g) butter or margarine
1 tsp lemon juice
¼ pt (150 ml) water
(iced if possible)

½ lb (240 g) self-raising flour
½ tsp salt
¼ lb (120 g) butter or margarine
About 3 tbsp very cold water

Rough Puff Pastry

Sift together the flour and salt. Cut the butter or margarine into the flour in small pieces no bigger than marbles. Do not rub the fat in. Mix to a stiff dough with cold water. Roll the dough out on a floured board to an oblong shape about ½ inch (1¼ cm) thick. Fold the pastry by bringing the side edges into the middle, and then the bottom and top edges to the middle. Press the edges together so that an envelope is formed, keeping the air inside. Leave the pastry to rest in a very cold place for 10 minutes, and then repeat the folding and rolling process. Rest again in a cold place, then roll out. Bake in oven at 400°F/200°C/Gas Mark 6.

This pastry is useful for meat pies or sausages rolls when puff pastry takes too much time. It should be used as quickly as possible after making.

2 oz (60 g) cooking fat
½ pt (300 ml) milk
10 oz (300 g) plain flour
½ tsp salt

Raised Pie Pastry

Put the fat and milk into a saucepan and bring to the boil. Sieve the flour and salt into a bowl and make a well in the centre. Into this well pour the hot milk mixture, and stir until a solid lump is formed. Place this on a floured board and knead with the hands until all cracks have disappeared and the paste is smooth and pliable. Roll out while still warm.

This pastry is used for all meat and game pies. When the pie is to be used cold, as in pork pies, the pie tin should be lined about ¼ inch (½ cm) thick, then filled with the uncooked mixture, and the pastry lid well pressed against the lining. A small hole is made in the top for testing the meat and for the addition of extra gravy after cooking. It should be baked in oven at about 375°F/190°C/Gas Mark 5.

When the pastry is cooked, the pie should be moved to the lowest shelf of the oven, the heat reduced to 300°F/150°C/Gas Mark 2 and left until the meat is tender when tested with a skewer.

½ lb (240 g) self-raising flour
Pinch of salt
6 oz (180 g) butter or margarine
Milk to mix

Milk Pastry

Mix the flour and the salt and sift it. Rub in ¼ lb (120 g) of fat lightly with the tips of the fingers, until it is evenly distributed. Then add just enough cold milk to form a rather stiff dough, sprinkle the remainder of the fat with a little flour and roll it out to a very thin sheet. Roll out the dough and put the fat on it, sprinkle with a little flour, fold over and roll out. Then bake at once in oven at about 475°F/240°C/Gas Mark 9.

This pastry is both simple to make and very rich. It may be used in place of the more difficult puff pastry and is particularly good for flans which are to be eaten cold, since it retains its crispness without becoming hard.

Puff Pastry

¾ lb (360 g) plain flour
½ tsp salt
½ lb (240 g) butter or margarine
Very cold water to mix

This pastry must be made in a cool place, with cold utensils, and should be handled as little as possible.

Sieve the flour and the salt into a basin. Now cut the butter or margarine into thin slices; a ½ lb (240 g) piece of fat should be cut into 8 slices. Fluff up the flour in the basin with an egg whisk or fork, so that it does not lie heavily. Put each piece of butter into it in turn and coat it well with the flour. Lightly flour a pastry board and roll out each slice of butter or margarine quite thinly; place them on a cold plate in a pile as you do them. Next form the flour in the bowl into light dough with very cold water. Use a knife for mixing, and add the water very gradually. Be very careful not to put in too much, the paste must be soft enough to roll easily, but it must not be at all sticky. You will probably find you have to use your hands to form the paste into a ball, but do not handle it more than you need. Roll out the dough *as thinly as possible*, then cover the centre of the dough with the rolled out butter – this should use 4 of the slices – leaving an equal space of uncovered pastry on either side. Fold over the plain pastry on the right side so that it covers the butter, and place the remaining 4 slices of butter on the piece of pastry you have folded over, and cover it by folding the plain piece of pastry over from the left side. Now roll it out, rolling away from you. Use the rolling pin lightly, giving short rapid rolls, and always rolling forward, not backward. Never roll right off the pastry – stop before you get to the edge. This is important, as the object is to keep the air in the paste, and if you roll off the edge you naturally push it out. Leave the pastry for 10 minutes in a cool place. The pastry is now a long oblong shape. Cut it in half, put one half aside on a cold plate, and fold and roll the rest of the pastry in the same way as you did before – folding from either side to centre, and then rolling out to an oblong shape. Repeat the process of folding and rolling, then put it aside and do the same with the other half. Leave for 10 minutes. Then put it on top of the other pastry on the board and cut through the centre, making two halves again. Roll each piece out thinly, fold and roll out once more, and it is ready. Bake in oven, 450-475°F/230-240°C/Gas Mark 8-9.

This will keep for a few days if wrapped in greaseproof paper and kept cool. Puff pastry is used for vol-au-vents, mince pies and all fancy dishes where a very light pastry is needed. It is troublesome to make, but no other pastry can quite replace it for party dishes.

1 lb (½ kg) self-raising flour
Good pinch of salt
Good tsp baking powder
6 oz (180 g) shredded suet
Cold water to mix

Suet Pastry

This is generally used for roll puddings and boiled puddings of many kinds, also for dumplings and steak and kidney pudding.

Mix together the flour, salt and baking powder, and sift them. Stir in the suet and mix well. Add gradually enough cold water to form a dough that is sufficiently soft to roll easily, but not in the least sticky. Roll out on a floured board and use at once.

½ lb (240 g) self-raising flour
Pinch of salt
1 tsp baking powder
3 oz (90 g) shredded suet
Cold water to mix

Dumplings

Make up as in recipe above. Form into small balls with the hands. Flour the dumplings. These may either be arranged in a steamer with ½ inch (1¼ cm) between them and cooked with the lid tightly on for 20 minutes, or they may be dropped directly into the boiling soup or stock in which they are to be served, and cooked for 10 minutes.

½ pt (300 ml) water
3 oz (90 g) butter
1 tsp sugar
¼ lb (120 g) plain flour
3 eggs

Choux Pastry

Bring the water, butter, and sugar to the boil in a heavy saucepan. Stir in the flour, reduce the heat, and stir until a solid mass is formed which leaves the sides of the pan. Add the unbeaten eggs one at a time, stirring well. The mixture should be the consistency of a thick smooth batter. Bake in oven about 375°F/190°C/Gas Mark 5.

This pastry is used for éclairs, cream buns and rich savoury patties. The paste is piped on to a baking tray and rises to form crisp shapes almost hollow inside, which are split open, in the case of éclairs, and filled with whipped cream, and the tops iced with Chocolate Icing (see page 280).

½ tsp mixed salt and pepper
½ lb (240 g) self-raising flour
6 oz (180 g) butter or margarine
Cold water to mix
2 oz (60 g) grated cheese
(Parmesan if possible.)

Cheese Pastry

Mix the salt and pepper with the flour, and rub in the fat with the finger tips until the mixture looks like fine breadcrumbs. Add enough cold water to make a stiff paste. Roll out on a floured board, sprinkle with cheese, fold over, and repeat the process. Bake in oven at 450°F/230°C/Gas Mark 8.

Use for savoury tarts, flans or patties.

Recipes

Apple Pie

Serves 4-6
½ lb (240 g) short pastry
1 ½ lb (¾ kg) cooking apples
1 tbsp cold water
3 oz (90 g) sugar
1 tsp grated lemon rind (optional)
Caster sugar

Peel, core and slice the apples, and put them in a pie dish moistened with the water, and sprinkled with the sugar and lemon rind. Make sure the top layer of apple is not sugared, as, if the pastry touches the sugar, it will be soggy. Place a pie funnel or an egg cup in the middle to support the crust. Roll out the pastry. Cut an oval a little larger than the pie dish. Cut off a strip ½ inch (1¼ cm) wide, dampen the edges of the pie dish and cover with the strip. Moisten the strip and place the pastry lid over it. Do not stretch the pastry. Pinch the edges firmly to the dish, and decorate with a fork. If no pie funnel is being used, slit the pastry with the point of a knife in two places in the middle, so that the steam can escape while it is baking. This should be baked in oven at about 400°F/200°C/Gas Mark 6. Dredge with caster sugar before serving.

If the pastry is cooked before the fruit is soft when tested with a knife through the slits in the pastry, move to lowest shelf and continue cooking. If the pastry still browns too fast, cover with foil.

Blackberry and Apple Pie

Serves 4-6
½ lb (240 g) short pastry
1 lb (½ kg) apples
½ lb (240 g) blackberries
1 tbsp cold water
3 oz (90 g) sugar
1 tsp grated lemon rind (optional)
Caster sugar

Follow exactly the same method as for Apple Pie, but substitute ½ lb (240 g) blackberries for ½ lb (240 g) of the apples. Remove the blackberry stalks and wash them well before mixing them with the apple slices.

Rhubarb Pie

Serves 4-6
½ lb (240 g) short pastry
2 lb (1 kg) rhubarb
1 tbsp water
6 oz (180 g) sugar
Caster sugar

Remove the ends of the rhubarb stalks, wash the stalks and cut into 1 inch (2½ cm) lengths, then put rhubarb in the moistened pie dish with the sugar between two layers of fruit, before proceeding as for Apple Pie. Bake in oven at 400°F/200°C/Gas Mark 6.

Gooseberry Pie

Serves 4-6
½ lb (240 g) short pastry
1 ½ lb (¾ kg) gooseberries
1 tbsp water
¼ lb (120 g) sugar (more if fruit is
*   very green)*
Caster sugar

Top and tail the fruit and wash it well. Then put it in the moistened pie dish with the sugar between two layers of fruit. Proceed as for Apple Pie, and bake in oven at 400°F/200°C/Gas Mark 6.

Serves 4-6
½ lb (240 g) short pastry or rough puff pastry
2 lb (1 kg) plums (these need not be quite ripe)
1 tbsp cold water
¼ lb (120 g) caster sugar (less if plums are sweet)

Plum or Greengage Pie

Wash the plums well, then halve them and remove the stones. Moisten the pie dish, then put in the plums, with the sugar between two layers of fruit. Proceed as for Apple Pie. Bake in oven at 400°F/200°C/Gas Mark 6.

Serves 4
½ lb (240 g) short pastry or rough puff pastry
Any jam or marmalade

Jam Tart

Roll out the pastry, and line a tin or ovenproof dish with pastry about ⅛ inch (¼ cm) thick. Moisten the edges of the pastry and fix it firmly to the tin with thin strips of pastry pressed around it. Spread the bottom with jam. This should not come more than a third of the way up the side of the tart, or it will boil during cooking and overflow. Further strips of pastry may be floured and twisted and placed across the tart as cross-bars, if liked. Bake at 450°F/230°C/Gas Mark 8 until the pastry is golden brown and crisp to the touch. May be served hot or cold.

½ lb (240 g) short or rough puff pastry
Jam, lemon curd, marmalade or jelly for filling

Small Jam Tarts

Roll pastry out to ⅛ inch (¼ cm) thickness. Have ready a sheet of 12 and a sheet of 6 bun tins, plus a cutter slightly larger than the circumference of each. A tumbler can be used or a round tin lid if you have no cutter at hand. Cut out circles and press each into patty pan. Put a spoonful of the desired filling in each – not more than enough to fill the tart a third full as the filling liquefies when cooked and will overflow so that you cannot get the tarts out. Put into hot oven, about 450°F/230°C/Gas Mark 8, and bake 10 minutes or until edges of pastry show golden brown and crisp.

If preferred, you can bake the cases 'blind', that is empty, with a dried bean in each to keep the bottom from rising. Then fill when cold. If you want lids, cut with a size smaller cutter and fit on, after moistening edges with milk.

Serves 4
½ lb (240 g) short pastry
About 1 oz (30 g) fine breadcrumbs
Golden syrup
1 oz (30 g) butter or margarine

Treacle Tart

Line a tin in the same way as for Jam Tart. Sprinkle half the breadcrumbs on to the pastry, then add a layer of syrup, top with the remaining breadcrumbs. This mixture should only half fill the tart. Dot with small pieces of butter or margarine. Bake at 450°F/230°C/Gas Mark 8 until the pastry is golden brown. Serve either hot or cold.

Bakewell Tart

Line a pie dish with a thin layer of short pastry and spread the jam at the bottom. Cream together the butter and sugar, add the unbeaten egg and beat to a smooth mixture, adding the lemon juice during the beating. Sift the flour and stir gradually into the egg mixture. Spread this over the jam in the pie dish and bake at 450°F/230°C/Gas Mark 8 for about ½ hour until the cake surface is firm and spongy.

Serves 4
½ lb (240 g) short pastry
2 tbsp strawberry jam
2 oz (60 g) butter
2 oz (60 g) caster sugar
1 egg
1 tsp lemon juice
2 oz (60 g) self-raising flour

Custard Tart

Line a tin with pastry, and flute the edges with a knife. Put a piece of foil in the centre, with a few haricot beans or crusts to weigh it down and prevent the pastry rising. Bake blind in a hot oven, 400°F/200°C/Gas Mark 6, for 10 minutes. Take the pastry case out of oven, remove foil and spread a thin layer of any kind of red jam on the bottom. Warm the milk. Beat the eggs and sugar together in a bowl. Pour the warmed milk slowly on to the egg mixture, stirring carefully while pouring. Pour this into the partially-cooked pastry, sprinkle the butter cut into little pieces over the top and grate a little nutmeg over it, if you wish. Turn the oven down to 300°F/150°C/Gas Mark 2, put the tart back on to the middle shelf and bake until the custard is set to the consistency of blanc-mange.

This tart is particularly good served with cream, which has been whipped firm, piped around the edges.

Serves 4
½ lb (240 g) short pastry
1 tbsp of red jam
¾ pt (450 ml) milk
2 eggs
3 oz (90 g) sugar
1 oz (30 g) butter
Nutmeg to taste (optional)

Apple Tart

Peel and core the apples, and cut them into thin slices. Line a tin with pastry, putting a strip round the edges as in Jam Tart. Lay the slices of apple on the pastry, so that they overlap and no space can be seen between them. Sprinkle with sugar, being careful not to touch the pastry at the sides, or it will become soggy. Scatter with the raisins (or sultanas). Dot with pieces of butter or margarine and bake in oven at 400°F/200°C/Gas Mark 6. If you want a closed tart, cover the fruit with a pastry lid. Serve hot or cold.

The sultanas may be omitted if a simple tart is preferred, or they may be replaced by 3 tablespoons of melted redcurrant jelly or strawberry jam, poured over the apples before baking.

Serves 4
½ lb (240 g) short sweet pastry (ordinary shortcrust may be used)
1 lb (½ kg) cooking apples
2 oz (60 g) demerara sugar
2 oz (60 g) stoned raisins or sultanas which have been soaked in water for a few minutes
1 oz (30 g) butter or margarine

Flans

Flans can be made with many different fruits, both fresh and tinned. Fresh fruits which are suitable include plums, apricots, cherries, greengages, strawberries and raspberries. Any fairly dry tinned fruit will do. Cherries, apricots and peaches are particularly good. Avoid the squashy tinned fruits such as raspberries or loganberries since they make too much juice, which will make the pastry soggy.

Fresh Fruit Recipe

½ lb (240 g) short sweet pastry
1 lb (½ kg) fresh fruit
2 oz (60 g) sugar
1 tsp cornflour

Skin and stone the fruit and stew it very gently with the sugar (more if the fruit is sour). Add 2 tablespoons of water. Line a flan tin with short sweet pastry. Cover the centre with greaseproof paper and weigh it down with bread crusts or dried beans. Bake this pastry case in a hot oven, 400°F/200°C/Gas Mark 6, for 10 minutes. Meanwhile remove the fruit from the heat, strain off the juice, and heat in a saucepan. Put the cornflour in a bowl, mix it with a tablespoon of cold water and, when the juice boils, add the cornflour mixture to it. Boil for 10 minutes and then allow to cool. It should now be thick and syrupy. Remove the pastry from the oven and allow it to cool. When the pastry case is almost cold, arrange the fruit in it. Pour the syrup over the fruit, and allow it to get really cold, so that the syrup will be almost set. Serve with cream.

Fruit Flan with Meringue

For the Meringue
2 egg whites
¼ lb (120 g) caster sugar

A top of crisp meringue may be added to any fruit flan. When the thickened syrup has been poured over the flan, place 2 egg whites in a bowl, and whip them until they are stiff enough to hold a peaked shape when dropped off the whisk. Gently fold in the caster sugar. Put this meringue on top of the flan, spreading it into attractive peaked shapes. Put into a very cool oven, 225°C/110°C/Gas Mark ¼. Leave until the meringue is golden brown and crisp to the touch. Serve hot, as the meringue may lose its crispness if allowed to get cold.

Lemon Meringue Pie

Line a flan tin with the pastry. Line the centre with foil, weigh it down with crusts or dried beans, and bake in a hot oven, 400°F/200°C/Gas Mark 6, for 10 minutes.

For the filling use a double saucepan, or a basin or saucepan which will fit into a large one containing boiling water. Put the sugar into the small saucepan or basin. Grate the rind of the lemon into it, then squeeze the juice into it. Stir the egg yolks slightly, and add them with the butter. Keep the basin or small saucepan in gently boiling water until the mixture thickens. Stir continually. This curd is ready when it has the consistency of thick cream. Allow the lemon curd to cool. Then pour it into the pastry case, filling it not more than three-quarters full.

To make the meringue, whip the egg whites until they are stiff enough to hold a peaked shape when dropped from the whisk. Gently fold in the caster sugar. Spread the meringue on top of the lemon pie, and place in a very cool oven 225°F/110°C/Gas Mark ¼, for about 1 hour. Serve hot.

Serves 4
½ lb (240 g) short sweet pastry or
  short pastry
¼ lb (120 g) caster sugar
1 lemon
2 egg yolks
1 oz (30 g) melted butter

For the Meringue
2 egg whites
¼ lb (120 g) caster sugar

Meat Pies

Sausage Rolls

Roll out pastry and cut into a long strip 4 inches (10 cm) wide. Season the sausage meat and work it into a long roll and lay this longways on the strip of pastry. Damp the edge of the strip and fold it over sausage meat, and press firmly. Then cut the long roll into even lengths for sausage rolls, say 2 inches (5 cm) long. Cut 3 slashes on top of each and brush with egg. Bake 20 to 30 minutes in a hot oven, about 400°F/200°C/Gas Mark 6. Brush each roll over with a pastry brush dipped in the beaten egg yolk before baking. If you are using separate sausages, lay them along in the same way as the sausage meat, but be careful to divide at the ends of each sausage. It is best to divide sausages or chipolatas in half, by working, and twisting the skins and then cutting.

6 oz (180 g) flaky or rough puff
  pastry
¾ lb (360 g) sausage meat
Salt and pepper
Egg yolk for glazing

Pigeon Pie

Cut the pigeons each into 6 pieces, cut the steak up into thin slices and the bacon into strips. Put into pie dish in layers, seasoning each layer and adding the eggs cut into quarters. Cover with the stock. Put on pastry as described for Apple Pie and decorate with a rose and leaves. Brush over with beaten egg. Bake in a hot oven at 450°F/230°C/Gas Mark 8 until the pastry is cooked (about 20 minutes). Then cover with foil and reduce heat to 300°F/150°C/Gas Mark 2 and cook a further hour.

Serves 4-6
1 lb (½ kg) puff, rough puff or
  flaky pastry
2 pigeons
½ lb (240 g) rump steak
2 rashers lean bacon
Seasoning
2 hard-boiled eggs
¾ pt (450 ml) stock
1 egg yolk

1 lb (½ kg) puff pastry
Any mixture of ham, chicken,
*   mushrooms, egg, fish, lobster,*
*   prawns, etc.*
½ pt (300 ml) Béchamel Sauce or
*   Velouté Sauce (see Chapter 10)*
1 egg yolk

Vol-au-vents and Patties

Always use puff pastry for vol-au-vents. 1 lb (½ kg) pastry will make 12-16. The cases should be cut from the rolled-out pastry using a 2 inch (5 cm) diameter round cutter. Dip the cutter in almost boiling water before stamping out each round. Place on a water-moistened baking tray, upside down from the way you cut them. Leave 20 minutes in a cool place after cutting out. Then put in preheated oven at 475°F/240°C/Gas Mark 9 for about 10-15 minutes. Cut out tops as soon as they come from oven and remove some of the inside. Fill with any mixture of diced ham, chicken, mushrooms, egg, flaked fish, lobster, prawns, etc., which has been folded into a good béchamel or velouté sauce. Brush each over with beaten egg yolk. Put the tops on and reheat very gently to serve.

Serves 6
1 lb (½ kg) rough puff pastry
2 lb (1 kg) scrag end of lamb (or
*   mutton)*
½ lb (240 g) onions
1 lb (½ kg) turnips
1 dessertsp chopped parsley
½ oz (15 g) butter
½ oz (15 g) flour
Salt and pepper
1 egg yolk

Lamb and Turnip Pie

Stew the lamb (or mutton) with the onions, cut in quarters, and the sliced turnips for 2 hours in water – just enough to cover. Remove from heat and allow to cool. Cut up the lamb, removing very carefully all skin, fat and gristle. Put it with the onion and turnip in a large pie dish and sprinkle with parsley. Slightly thicken the stock by making a roux of the butter and the flour and stirring in stock in usual way. Season. Pour this over the meat, but do not put on pastry till it stops steaming. Put on pastry as described for Apple Pie, but do not cut a slit. Make a pastry rose with 3 leaves to decorate, if you wish and brush with beaten egg. Bake in hot oven, about 400°F/200°C/Gas Mark 6, for 25 minutes. Then cover pastry with foil and reduce heat slightly and cook a further 10 minutes to make sure the inside is properly heated.

1 lb (½ kg) flour
½ lb (240 g) butter or margarine
Salt and pepper
4 medium potatoes
2 onions
½ lb (240 g) steak
A little stock

Cornish Pasty

Sieve the flour, rub in the fat, add the salt and pepper and mix into a stiff dough with a little cold water. Divide into 4 and roll each piece out thinly into a round. Season the chopped potatoes and onions and the sliced meat. Mix together, place a generous layer on one half of each piece of pastry, and put 2 teaspoons of stock on the meat mixture. Fold over the other half and pinch together. Bake in a moderate oven for 45 minutes at about 350°F/180°C/Gas Mark 4. Then reduce heat to 250°C/120°C/Gas Mark ½ and cook another 30 minutes in order that the steak may become tender.

Pork Pie

Serves 6-8
1 ½ lb (¾ kg) raised pie pastry
3 lb (1 ½ kg) lean pork on the bone
1 onion
Bouquet garni
Salt and pepper
Egg yolk for glazing

Cut all the lean meat from the bones and roughly dice it. Then boil the bones with the onion and bouquet garni for 2 hours in about ¼ pint (150 ml) of water in order to make a stock which will jell. Line a mould or tin about ¼ inch (½ cm) thick with the pastry. (If you prefer, you can 'raise' the pie without a tin or mould, moulding it by hand to the required height and shape and tying 3 layers of greaseproof paper round it to keep the shape.) Fill it with the diced meat, packing it firmly in layers and seasoning each layer. When full, pour in ¼ pint (150 ml) of the seasoned and strained, cooled bone stock. Keep the rest and pour in when the pie is baked but still hot, through a hole in the lid. Put on lid. Brush over with beaten egg yolk and bake in a moderate oven, 375°F/190°C/Gas Mark 5 for 1½ hours. Remove. Add stock and leave overnight to set.

Steak and Kidney Pie

Serves 4-5
½ lb (240 g) rough puff or flaky pastry
1 lb (½ kg) rump steak
6 oz (180 g) kidney
1 oz (30 g) flour
Salt and pepper
½ pt (300 ml) stock

Wipe the steak and cut into thin slices or neat pieces. Clean the kidney and cut into small pieces. If the steak is sliced, wrap each slice round some pieces of kidney. Toss the meat and the kidney in the seasoned flour. Pack neatly into a 1 pint (600 ml) pie dish. Pour the stock over the meat. Roll out the pastry to ⅛ inch (¼ cm) thickness, cover the pie as for Apple Pie, but do not cut a slit. Decorate with a pastry rose and 3 leaves, then bake in the centre of an oven preheated to 450°F/230°C/Gas Mark 8 for 10 minutes. Reduce to 350°F/180°C/Gas Mark 4 for a further 2 to 2½ hours, or until the meat is tender. After an hour's cooking, cover the pie with foil to prevent pastry getting too brown.

Mushrooms or oysters can be added to the meat, if available.

Veal and Ham Pie

Serves 8
1 lb (½ kg) rough puff or flaky pastry
1 lb (½ kg) fillet of veal
¼ lb (120 g) ham or gammon – must be home cooked
1 onion
2 cloves
1 tsp chopped parsley
½ tsp herbs
A little grated lemon rind
Salt and pepper
2 hard-boiled eggs
1 egg yolk

Stew the veal for 40 minutes in enough cold water to cover, with the onion stuck with 2 cloves. When cold, cut into thin slices, put parsley, herbs, lemon rind and salt and pepper on each slice and roll up. Pack the rolls in a pie dish, with the ham and hard-boiled eggs, cut into slices. Reduce the stock from the veal, season and pour it into the pie dish. Roll out the pastry and cover as for Apple Pie. Decorate with a rose and 3 leaves, brush over with a beaten egg yolk and bake in an oven preheated to 400°F/200°C/Gas Mark 6 for 30 minutes, or until pastry is golden and crisp. Cover with foil move to a lower shelf, and leave for a further 10 minutes to ensure that the inside is really hot.

HOT PUDDINGS

Hot Soufflés and Sweet Omelettes are given under 'Eggs'. Pancakes, Batters and Fritters are given under 'Pancakes and Batters'.

Recipes

Apple Crisp

Serves 4
4 medium cooking apples
2 oz (60 g) margarine
¼ lb (120 g) brown sugar
¼ lb (120 g) flour

Grease a baking dish and three-quarters fill with sliced, cored apples. Rub the margarine into the sugar and flour until the mixture is like fine breadcrumbs. Spread it over the apples. Bake in a hot oven, 400°F/200°C/Gas Mark 6, for 10 minutes, then reduce the heat and bake until the apples are soft and the top nicely browned. May be served hot or well chilled with cream.

Apple Charlotte

Serves 4-6
2 lb (1 kg) cooking apples
3 oz (90 g) butter
Bread
1 lemon
¼ lb (120 g) brown sugar

Melt 2 oz (60 g) butter, dip in it slices of bread to line an ovenproof dish and strips for the sides. Peel, core and slice the apples. Stew them with the rind of the lemon and 2 oz (60 g) of sugar until they form a thick purée. Remove lemon rind. Pour the purée on to the bread lining. Top with further bread slices. Sprinkle with remaining brown sugar, and dot with the rest of the butter. Bake for 30 minutes in oven at 400°F/200°C/Gas Mark 6 until brown and crisp.

Apricot Rice

Serves 4-6
¼ lb (120 g) apricots (stewed fresh, or dried, or tinned)
¼ lb (120 g) boiled rice
2 eggs
2 oz (60 g) brown sugar
¾ pt (450 ml) milk

Place the apricots in the bottom of a greased ovenproof dish. Cover with the rice. Beat the eggs till light, then add the brown sugar. Scald the milk and cool a little then stir in the egg mixture by degrees. Pour over the rice. Stand dish in a pan of hot water. Bake in a 350°F/180°C/Gas Mark 4 for about 30 minutes or until the rice is set in the egg custard.

This is good made in the same way with pears.

Apple Betty

Mix butter with breadcrumbs. Grate rind of lemon and mix with caster sugar, nutmeg and cinnamon. Cover the bottom of a greased ovenproof dish with a quarter of the crumbs then with half the apples. Sprinkle with the sugar and spice mixture, then with another quarter of the crumbs. Add remainder of the apples, then the rest of the sugar and spice mixture. Pour in water and juice from lemon. Cover with remainder of the crumbs. Bake in a 350°F/180°C/Gas Mark 4 oven for 40 minutes. If not brown enough, put under grill.

Serves 4
1½ lb (¾ kg) cooking apples, peeled, cored and sliced
2 tbsp melted butter
2 oz (60 g) breadcrumbs
1 lemon
2 oz (60 g) caster sugar
¼ tsp grated nutmeg (optional)
¼ tsp ground cinnamon (optional)
2 tbsp water

Bread Pudding

Pour milk over the breadcrumbs, and stand for ½ hour. Stir in fruit, sugar, butter, eggs beaten with a pinch of salt, and vanilla essence. Pour into a greased pie dish. Place small dabs of butter over the top. Place in a baking tin containing an inch (2½ cm) of hot water. Bake in a 300-325°F/150-160°C/Gas Mark 2-3 oven for 30 minutes till set in centre and golden brown on top.

Serves 4
1 pt (600 ml) milk
¼ lb (120 g) breadcrumbs
2 oz (60 g) currants
2 oz (60 g) raisins or sultanas
2 tbsp caster sugar
1 tbsp melted butter
2 eggs
Salt
1 tsp vanilla essence
Extra butter

Bread and Butter Pudding

Cut some thin slices from a sandwich loaf, butter each slice on one side and cut it diagonally, removing the crust. Soak the dried fruit in warm water, then spread some of it on the bottom of a greased pie dish. Put a layer of bread and butter on it. Sprinkle a few currants and sultanas, then put another layer of bread and butter, and so on until the dish is full. Take care not to press the bread down. Mix the sugar and eggs with a whisk in a basin and gradually add the cold milk. Add a few drops of vanilla essence and pour the egg mixture into the dish, pouring in a little at a time to allow the bread to absorb the custard. Sprinkle the top with sugar and dot with pieces of butter. Place the pie dish in a tray with an inch (2½ cm) of water and bake in a 350°F/180°C/Gas Mark 4 oven for 35 minutes. It should be crisp and golden brown on top.

Serves 4
8 thin slices of bread
2½ oz (75 g) butter
¼ lb (120 g) currants and sultanas
2 oz (60 g) caster sugar
2 eggs
½ pt (300 ml) cold milk
Vanilla essence

Serves 4

1 pt (600 ml) milk
1½ dessertsp cocoa, or 2 dessertsp
drinking chocolate
2 oz (60 g) sugar
2 egg yolks
6 oz (180 g) breadcrumbs
Strip of lemon rind
Jam

For the Meringue

2 egg whites
2 oz (60 g) caster sugar

Chocolate Queen Pudding

Boil the milk and add the cocoa or drinking chocolate to it while it is still boiling. Mix the sugar and egg yolks in a basin and gradually add the milk. Pour this over the breadcrumbs and leave to soak for 10 minutes, then add the lemon rind. Grease a pie dish, pour the mixture into it and bake in a 350°F/180°C/Gas Mark 4 oven for about 30 minutes until set. Remove from oven, place a layer of jam on top.

For the meringue, whip the egg whites with an electric beater or whisk until they hold a peak, then fold in sugar and smooth lightly over top of pudding. Sprinkle the meringue with sugar and bake in a very cool oven for 30 minutes, until pale brown and crisp.

Serves 6

1 oz (30 g) candied peel (optional)
3 oz (90 g) shredded suet
2 oz (60 g) currants or other dried
fruit
¼ lb (120 g) breadcrumbs
2 oz (60 g) self-raising flour
2 oz (60 g) sugar
Pinch of salt
1 tsp grated nutmeg
2 eggs
1 tbsp milk

College Pudding – Baked, Individual Puddings

Grease 6 cups or cocotte moulds well. Shred the peel (if used). Mix the shredded suet, fruit, breadcrumbs, flour, sugar, salt and peel together. Add the nutmeg, beat the eggs and stir them into the mixture. Add the milk and pour the mixture into the cups. Bake in the oven at 350°F/180°C/Gas Mark 4 for about 20 minutes to ½ hour, standing the cups in a baking tray containing an inch (2½ cm) or so of water. When ready, turn out and serve with Hard Sauce, or Sweet White Sauce (see Chapter 10).

Serves 4

1 pt (600 ml) milk
Strip of lemon rind
Pinch of salt
¼ lb (120 g) breadcrumbs
2 oz (60 g) butter
¼ lb (120 g) sugar
2 eggs, separated
2 tbsp jam (preferably strawberry)

Queen of Puddings

Put the milk into a saucepan, add the lemon rind and the salt, and bring to the boil. Remove the rind. Put the breadcrumbs, butter and half the sugar into a bowl and pour the boiling milk over them. Cover the bowl and leave to stand for about 10 minutes. Beat up the egg yolks and add them to the bread mixture. Pour the mixture into an ovenproof dish and bake in a 350°F/180°C/Gas Mark 4 oven for 20 minutes. When baked, spread the jam over the top. Whip up the egg whites and fold in the remaining sugar. Pile on top of the pudding. Brown lightly in the oven for a few more minutes.

Sponge Pudding

Grease a pint (600 ml) basin, then put a thick layer of marmalade, jam or syrup at the bottom. Beat butter and sugar to a cream. Sift the flour and stir into the mixture alternately with the beaten eggs and milk. Beat well for a moment or two, then turn into the prepared basin, cover with foil and steam for 1 hour.

Serves 4
Marmalade, apricot jam or
*   golden syrup*
2 oz (60 g) butter
2 oz (60 g) caster sugar
¼ lb (120 g) self-raising flour
2 eggs, beaten
4 tbsp milk

Light Cherry Pudding

Put the cherries in a greased pudding bowl and sprinkle with the sugar. Sift flour and salt into a basin. Make a hole in the centre of flour and gradually beat in egg, milk and melted butter. When a smooth batter is formed, pour over the cherries. Cover with foil and steam for 1 hour. Serve with Hard Sauce (see Chapter 10).

Serves 4
½ lb (240 g) stoned cherries
3 oz (90 g) sugar
¼ lb (120 g) self-raising flour
¼ tsp salt
1 egg
3 tbsp milk
1 tbsp melted butter

Coconut Pudding

Cream the fat and sugar. Add flour, egg yolks, milk, coconut and vanilla, or other flavouring, to taste. Beat the egg whites till stiff and stir them into the mixture. Turn into a greased mould, cover with foil and steam for 2 hours. Turn out, pour melted red jam over it and sprinkle all over with more desiccated coconut. Serve extra Jam Sauce (see Chapter 10).

Serves 4
¼ lb (120 g) butter or margarine
¼ lb (120 g) sugar
¼ lb (120 g) self-raising flour
2 eggs, separated
¼ pt (150 ml) milk
2 tbsp desiccated coconut
Vanilla essence
Red jam

Hot Cabinet Pudding

Cut the sponge cakes and crumble lightly. Whisk the eggs with the sugar. Heat the milk slowly. Add the hot milk and the vanilla essence to the eggs and sugar. Pour gently over the cake. Cover and leave to soak until quite cold. Grease a plain mould. Decorate with pieces of cherry and angelica. Pour the soaked mixture into this. Steam gently until firm, about ¾ hour. Turn out of the tin and pour the syrup or honey around it.

Serves 2-3
3 sponge cakes, or 6 cabinet
*   fingers*
2 eggs
1 oz (30 g) sugar
½ pt (300 ml) milk
Vanilla essence
Glacé cherries and angelica
¼ pt (150 ml) fruit syrup or honey

Castle Puddings

Serves 4

2 oz (60 g) butter
2 oz (60 g) sugar
1 egg
3 oz (90 g) flour
½ tsp baking powder
1 tbsp milk
Lemon juice

Grease 4 cups or dariole moulds. Cream butter and sugar, add egg and beat well. Fold in the sifted flour and baking powder, then add the milk and some lemon juice. Half fill each mould with the mixture and bake for 10 minutes at 400°F/200°C/Gas Mark 6. Turn out and serve with Jam Sauce (see Chapter 10).

Saucer or French Pancakes

Serves 4

2 oz (60 g) butter
2 oz (60 g) caster sugar
1 egg
3 oz (90 g) flour
A little milk
2 oz (60 g) jam

Cream butter and sugar. Stir in well-beaten egg, add sifted flour and beat well. Add a little milk till of a dropping consistency. Grease well 4 old saucers or scallop shells. Put a tablespoon of jam in the bottom of each. Pour in the mixture and bake 7 minutes in oven at 450°F/230°C/Gas Mark 8. Turn out and serve at once.

Milk Puddings

Milk puddings are the simplest puddings of all to make but many people dislike them because they were served too often in old-fashioned nursery menus and were often badly made, being stodgy or lumpy and watery. The proportion of cereal to milk must be right and the pudding must be cooked slowly so that it becomes rich and creamy. People who think they will never eat milk puddings now that they are grown-up are often surprised and pleased by a well-made rice pudding.

Milk Puddings with Whole Grains

Serves 4

1½ oz (45 g) rice, sago or tapioca
*   (large or small)*
1 oz (30 g) sugar
Grated lemon rind or vanilla
*   essence (optional)*
1 pt (600 ml) milk

Put the cereal in a pie dish, with the sugar. Grease the pie dish with butter, if liked, as this enriches the pudding slightly; it is not, however, necessary. Also add a little grated lemon rind or vanilla, if you wish. Pour on the milk. Bake in an oven at 250-300°F/120-150°C/Gas Mark ½-2. After 10 minutes, stir with a wooden spoon to prevent the cream rising to the top. Stir again 10 minutes later. Then leave till rice has been in the oven 2 hours in total and sago or tapioca about 1½ hours. If you must have the oven a little hotter, stand the pudding in a tray of water.

Rice Pudding

Serves 4
1 ½ oz (45 g) rice
1 pt (600 ml) milk
1 oz (30 g) sugar
2 eggs
1 tsp vanilla essence

(A richer pudding.)
   Boil rice in milk with sugar and cook over very low heat, preferably in a double saucepan till rice is tender. Allow to cool. Stir in well-beaten eggs and vanilla essence. Pour everthing into a buttered pie dish and bake for 1 hour at 250°F/120°C/Gas Mark ½.

Macaroni or Spaghetti Pudding

Serves 4
2 oz (60 g) macaroni
1 pt (600 ml) milk
1 egg
2 oz (60 g) sugar

Break the macaroni into short pieces. Bring 1 pint (600 ml) water to the boil in a pan. Add the macaroni to the boiling water and cook, uncovered, for 20 minutes, stirring occasionally – or use quick macaroni and cook according to directions. Drain. Place the macaroni in a buttered pie dish, beat milk, egg and sugar together and pour over. Bake in slow oven for 35 minutes at 300°F/150°C/Gas Mark 2. The pudding is still good if the egg is omitted.

Semolina Pudding

Serves 4
1 pt (600 ml) milk
1 ½ oz (45 g) semolina
½-1 oz (15-30 g) sugar
Nutmeg
1 egg, separated

Bring the milk to the boil, sprinkle in the semolina and cook until it thickens, stirring all the time. Remove from the heat, and add the sugar and a little grated nutmeg. Stir in beaten egg yolk, blending well. Beat egg white stiffly and fold in. Place in buttered pie dish and bake for 30 minutes in oven at 350°F/180°C/Gas Mark 4.

Ground Rice Pudding

Serves 4
1 pt (600 ml) milk
1 ½ oz (45 g) ground rice
1 dessertsp sugar
1 egg, separated

Heat the milk slowly. Just before boiling, sprinkle in the ground rice. Stir until boiling then simmer for 10 minutes, stirring frequently and carefully. Be careful to avoid lumps forming or rice sticking to bottom of saucepan. Remove from the heat, then add the sugar and leave to cool. Add egg yolk to the ground rice, mixing well, then add stiffly beaten white. Pour into a greased pie dish and bake in a 350°F/180°C/Gas Mark 4 oven for about 20 to 30 minutes. Serve immediately, as it will be deliciously fluffy when removed from the oven.

Chocolate Cornflour Pudding

Serves 4
1½ oz (45 g) cornflour
1 level tbsp cocoa
1 pt (600 ml) milk
1-2 oz (30-60 g) sugar
½ tbsp vanilla essence

Blend the cornflour and cocoa with a little of the cold milk. Put the rest on to heat and, when boiling, pour over the blended mixture, stirring well. Rinse saucepan with cold water and return mixture to pan. Bring to the boil, stirring all the time, cook gently until it thickens. Add sugar and vanilla, and pour into greased 1½ pint (900 ml) pie dish and bake in oven at 400°F/200°C/Gas Mark 6 for 20 minutes.

Steamed Suet Puddings

In all the following recipes prepared shredded suet is used, though they can of course be made with butcher's suet, which you chop very finely and evenly.

Fruit Hat

Serves 4-6
¾ lb (360 g) self-raising flour
Good pinch salt
3-4 oz (90-120 g) chopped suet
1-1¼ lb (½- ¾ kg) cooking apples, plums, apricots, cherries, rhubarb, etc.
2-4 oz (60-120 g) sugar
About 4 tbsp cold water

Sieve the flour and salt into bowl, add suet and mix to a firm dough with cold water. Grease a 1½ pint (900 ml) pudding basin and divide the dough, leaving a quarter for the top. Put the rest into the basin, mould quickly and evenly round the sides of the basin, drawing it well up to the top.

Fill with fruit, prepared as for stewing, and sugar, add the water, roll the remaining dough into a round the size of the top of the pudding. Damp the edges and fit on to pudding. Cover with foil, tie cloth over, stand in a large saucepan of water coming half-way up the bowl and steam 1½ to 2 hours. Turn out and serve.

Jam or Treacle Roly-Poly Pudding

Serves 4-6
¾ lb (360 g) self-raising flour
¼ lb (120 g) finely chopped suet
Pinch of salt
Red jam or golden syrup

Put the flour into a basin, add to it the suet and salt. Mix it with a little cold water, roll it out and wet the edges. Spread it with jam, leaving 1 inch (2½ cm) all round and roll it up in the form of a bolster. Scald and flour a cloth and sew or tie the pudding securely in it. Drop into large saucepan of rapidly boiling water and boil for 2 hours. Do not allow the pudding to go off the boil, or it will be soggy and heavy. If water is boiling away, add more boiling water. Lift pudding on to a dish, unwrap cloth quickly, being careful not to break it and let the jam run out, and serve at once with more jam or Jam Sauce (see Chapter 10). For treacle roly-poly use golden syrup to replace jam.

Plain Suet Pudding

Serves 4
½ lb (240 g) flour
Pinch of salt
1 tsp baking powder
3 oz (90 g) suet
Cold water to mix

Sift flour, salt and baking powder. Add suet and just enough cold water to make a stiff paste. Dip a pudding cloth into boiling water, wring it out and flour it well. Put the paste into the cloth, roll it up and leave enough room for the pudding to swell. Tie up the ends very securely and plunge it into a pan full of fast-boiling water and boil for 2 hours, being careful not to let water go off the boil and replacing with boiling water if there is danger of the pudding boiling dry.

Traditionally served with butter and brown sugar, but also good with jam, treacle, marmalade, or Hard Sauce (see Chapter 10).

Sultana or Raisin Pudding

Serves 4
3 oz (90 g) self-raising flour
2 oz (60 g) sugar
½ level tsp baking powder
3 oz (90 g) fresh breadcrumbs
3 oz (90 g) chopped suet
2 oz (60 g) sultanas or raisins
1 egg
2 tbsp milk
Grated rind of ½ lemon

Sieve flour, sugar and baking powder, then stir in breadcrumbs, suet, and fruit. Mix with beaten egg and milk and add lemon. Pour into greased 1 pint (600 ml) basin and cover with foil. Steam for 1½ hours.

For a steamed jam pudding, use the same mixture without the fruit. Put 2 tablespoons of jam in the greased basin, and pour pudding mixture on top of it. Turn out when cooked and serve with Jam Sauce (see Chapter 10).

Ginger Pudding

Serves 4
3 oz (90 g) plain flour
1 level tsp bicarbonate of soda
Pinch of salt
2 level tsp ground ginger
2-3 oz (60-90 g) suet
3 oz (90 g) fresh breadcrumbs
1 egg
2 tbsp milk
2 tbsp golden syrup

Sieve the flour, soda, salt and ground ginger. Add the suet and the breadcrumbs and mix to a soft consistency with the beaten egg, milk and syrup. Turn into a greased 1 pint (600 ml) basin, cover with foil and a pudding cloth and steam 1¼ to 1½ hours. Serve with Sweet White Sauce (see Chapter 10) to which chopped preserved ginger or a little ginger syrup has been added.

Apple Dumplings (Steamed)

1 large cooking apple per person
1 lb (½ kg) suet pastry
*   (see Chapter 17)*
½ oz (15 g) sugar per apple

Cut the pastry into rounds about ⅛ inch (¼ cm) thick and the size of a tea plate. Peel and core apples, being careful not to break. Place each apple on a round of pastry. Fill middle of apple with sugar. Draw up the edges of the pastry, wet them and press on to the apple. Wrap each one in foil, stand in a steamer or colander, cover closely and steam for 2 hours.

Serves 4

6 oz (180 g) flour
2 oz (60 g) suet
Pinch of salt
1 oz (30 g) sugar
*2-3 oz (60-90 g) currants or
   raisins*
¼ tsp mixed spice
Lemon peel
Milk

Serves 4

2 oz (60 g) breadcrumbs
¼ lb (120 g) self-raising flour
3 oz (90 g) suet
*1½ oz (45 g) sugar (preferably
   brown)*
1 egg
*2 tbsp golden syrup, plus extra for
   serving*
About ¼ pt (150 ml) milk
1 tbsp lemon juice

Spotted Dick

Mix together the flour, suet, salt, sugar, currants or raisins, mixed spice, and a grating of lemon peel. Moisten with a little milk to a stiff dough, place in a well-greased pudding basin and steam for 1½ hours.

Treacle Pudding

Put all the dry ingredients in a bowl. Mix well together. Beat the egg and add the syrup. Pour the mixture into the middle of the dry ingredients and beat it in gradually, adding enough of the milk to make a dropping consistency. Grease a pudding basin and pour the mixture into it. Cover with foil and a pudding cloth. Put into a pan with boiling water rising about halfway up the basin. Steam, for 2 hours. Turn out and serve with warmed golden syrup, to which the lemon juice has been added.

COLD SWEETS

Creams

All the recipes for creams and mousses tend to be extravagant in their use of cream and eggs – unavoidably, since that is what they are. They are delicious, rich, party sweets, intended for occasions and not suitable for everyday.

Bavarian Cream

Serves 4-6
¾ oz (22 g) gelatine
2 large or 3 small eggs
2 oz (60 g) sugar
1 pt (600 ml) milk
1-2 tsp vanilla or almond essence

Dissolve the gelatine in 2 tablespoons of water. Separate whites from the yolks of the eggs. Beat yolks with sugar, stir in milk, and add vanilla or almond essence, which you have boiled and allowed to cool a little. Return to saucepan and stir till custard thickens, holding it just off heat. Allow to cool a little and stir in gelatine. Cool till tepid and whisk in egg whites which have already been beaten stiffly till they hold a peak. Put into a mould and leave till cold and set. When turned out the jelly will have risen to the top and the egg cream will remain at the base.

Crème Brûlée

Serves 6
½ lb (240 g) caster sugar
6 egg yolks
½ pt (300 ml) cream
6 oz (180 g) demerara sugar

Perhaps the best cold sweet of all. A speciality of Trinity College, Cambridge and a favourite of Edward VII.

Beat caster sugar into egg yolks, fold in cream, stir over a saucepan of boiling water, or in a double saucepan, until it thickens and begins to coat on spoon. Pour into a wide flat dish and stand in a baking tin of water in oven preheated to 350°F/180°C/Gas Mark 4 till it is set. Remove and allow to cool. Sprinkle top thickly with the demerara sugar. Place under preheated grill to caramelize sugar. It is as well to fill grill tray with cold water or ice cubes to protect cream from heat. As soon as sugar begins to bubble and form a toffee crust, remove. When tapped with a spoon the top should crack crisply. Allow to cool and chill before serving.

Serves 4
¼ lb (120 g) bitter chocolate
3 eggs, separated
Salt
3 tbsp brandy
A little whipped cream

Negrita

An extravagant sweet for chocolate lovers.

Melt the chocolate in a basin over a saucepan half-filled with boiling water. When the chocolate has melted add the egg yolks and a pinch of salt, and whisk well over the heat until it thickens like custard. Flavour with the brandy. Allow to cool then fold in the stiffly beaten egg whites. Serve in individual glasses with whipped cream on top. May be flavoured with rum instead of brandy.

Serves 4-6
3 eggs
3 oz (90 g) caster sugar
Vanilla esence
½ pt (300 ml) milk
Chopped blanched almonds

Chantilly
½ pt (300 ml) cream
2 oz (60 g) caster sugar
Almond or orange essence, or
*   brandy or any liqueur*

Double Cream

This is a sweet for a party.

Mix the eggs and sugar together with a whisk and add the vanilla and the cold milk gradually. Sprinkle a ring mould, with a hollow centre, with chopped blanched almonds and fill it with the mixture. Place the mould in a baking tray and bake at 300°F/150°C/Gas Mark 2 for 40 minutes or till set. Chill in refrigerator for several hours.

When cold, turn out and fill centre with Chantilly for which you whisk cream stiff, stir in caster sugar and flavour with a few drops of almond or orange essence, brandy or any liqueur.

Serves 6
2 eggs
2 extra yolks
¼ lb (120 g) sugar
1 pt (600 ml) boiled milk
A few drops of vanilla, or
*   1 dessertsp of coffee essence, or*
*   1 oz (30 g) melted chocolate*

The Little Pots of Cream

Beat eggs and yolks together with sugar. Pour in warm, but not hot, boiled milk. Flavour with a few drops of vanilla essence or a dessertspoon of coffee essence or 1 oz (30 g) melted plain chocolate, stirred well in. Pour into cocotte dishes or individual moulds. Place these in baking tray with hot water coming halfway up the little pots and bake in oven at 350°F/180°C/Gas Mark 4 for 20 to 30 minutes till they are just set. Allow to cool and chill. Do not turn out. Decorate with whipped cream, cherries, almonds, angelica, etc., if liked.

Serves 6-8
3 egg yolks
3 oz (90 g) caster sugar
1 oz (30 g) cornflour
¾ pt (450 ml) milk
2 egg whites

Crème Pâtissière

Cream the egg yolks with half the sugar and stir in cornflour and ¼ pint (150 ml) milk. Scald the rest of the milk and pour at once on to the egg mixture, stirring all the time. Return to pan and bring slowly to the boil, always stirring. It is best to do this in a double saucepan or over another saucepan of boiling water. Cook for 3 minutes, stirring. When quite cold, whip egg whites and remaining sugar and beat into the custard. Can be made without the egg whites, if preferred.

Crème Caramel

Serves 4
4 tbsp sugar
2 tbsp water

For the custard
¾ pt (450 ml) milk
1 oz (30 g) sugar
3 eggs

Make the caramel by putting the sugar and water into a small saucepan and heating over a low heat. Stir all the time to dissolve the sugar. Bring to the boil, then without stirring, simmer until it turns a rich brown. Pour into 4 individual moulds. Swish them around until the sides are well coated.

Make the custard by heating the milk in a saucepan. Put the sugar into a basin and add the eggs. Beat together. Pour the hot milk on to them gradually. When ready pour at once from the pan into the caramel-coated cups. Place moulds in baking tray of hot water and cook in oven at 350°F/180°C/Gas Mark 4 till set. Chill and turn out to serve.

Charlotte Russe

Serves 6
¼ lb (120 g) sponge fingers
Pistachios, almonds or walnuts
½ oz (15 g) gelatine
1 oz (30 g) sugar
½ pt (300 ml) cream
Vanilla essence

Line a straight-sided round dish with the sponge fingers (casino fingers are best). Sprinkle chopped nuts thickly over the bottom. Melt the gelatine in 2 tablespoons of water, and stir over the heat until it is thoroughly dissolved. Remove from the heat and add sugar. Whip the cream stiffly, flavour it with a few drops of vanilla essence and stir it into the gelatine mixture. Stir until nearly set, then carefully pour into the lined mould. Allow to set, chill and then turn out.

Decorate with a little plain, whipped cream and crystallized cherries and angelica.

Chocolate Mousse

Serves 8-10
½ lb (240 g) chocolate (must be plain, dessert chocolate or bitter chocolate)
8 eggs

So rich that each serving should only consist of about 1 tablespoon of mousse.

Put chocolate to melt in double saucepan or over hot water, separate yolks and whites of eggs, beat the yolks thoroughly. Allow melted chocolate to cool, meanwhile beat the whites until they will hold a peak when dropped from the whisk. Now pour the warm chocolate slowly on to the egg yolks, stirring well all the time. Beat over a saucepan of boiling water until the mixture thickens. Allow to cool. If very thick stir in 2 tablespoons water. Then add this mixture slowly to the beaten egg whites, beating it in thoroughly so that the whites and the chocolate mixture are well mixed. Pour the mixture into the serving dish or individual dishes and place in refrigerator to set. This is best made the day before serving, but must be made at least 6 hours in advance. Serve topped with whipped cream and flaked chocolate.

Serves 6-8
8 large oranges
8 eggs
¼ lb (120 g) caster sugar

Orange Mousse

Separate yolks and whites of eggs. Beat yolks thoroughly. Squeeze oranges and grate finely the yellow part of 4 rinds. Put with these the juice and sugar and heat, stirring until sugar is dissolved. Allow to cool. Now pour the mixture on to the egg yolks, beat well and stir over a saucepan of boiling water till the mixture thickens. Allow to cool to blood heat. Meanwhile, beat the egg whites until they will hold a peak when dropped from the whisk. Add the orange mixture to the egg whites slowly, and fold in, disturbing the whites as little as possible but making sure that the whites and the orange are mixed right through. Pour the mixture into the serving dish, and place in refrigerator for several hours.

Serves 6-8
2 lemons
6 oz (180 g) caster sugar
3 tbsp brandy
3 tbsp sherry
1 pt (600 ml) cream

Syllabub

A traditional Old English recipe.

Grate the rind of the lemons, or slice it off very finely, with as little of the white as possible. Leave it to soak in the juice of the lemons for 2 or 3 hours. Strain it over the sugar, stir in brandy and sherry and pour in cream. Beat till stiff with an electric beater. It should just hold its form when piled up. Pile it into tall glasses and chill. It tastes better if it is made the day, or at least some hours, before it is wanted.

Serves 4-6
1 pt (600 ml) milk
3 oz (90 g) semolina, or 2 oz (60 g) sago, or 3 ½ oz (105 g) ground rice, or 2 oz (60 g) rice
1-2 oz (30-60 g) caster sugar
Flavouring

Semolina, Sago or Rice Mould (Basic Recipe)

Bring milk to the boil and sprinkle in the cereal. Boil for 20 to 30 minutes in a double saucepan or in a basin standing in a saucepan of water, except for ground rice and semolina, which need only 10 minutes. Stir well at the beginning and from time to time as mixture thickens. When thick and well cooked, add the caster sugar, according to taste, and flavouring in essence form. If you wish to make the dish with chocolate or coffee (apart from essence), simply add ½ pint (300 ml) of very strong strained black coffee or ½ pint (300 ml) strong cocoa or drinking chocolate, to ½ pint (300 ml) of milk and use this mixture instead of all milk. Rinse a mould or basin with cold water and turn mixture into it. Leave to set in refrigerator. Gently pull away from sides of basin with fingers before placing dish over mould and reversing to turn out.

Cornflour Mould (Basic Recipe)

Serves 4-6
1 pt (600 ml) milk
1 ½ oz (45 g) cornflour, or ½ oz
(15 g) arrowroot
2 oz (60 g) caster sugar
Vanilla or almond essence

Boil ¾ pint (450 ml) milk and stir the cornflour, or arrowroot, and sugar with the other ¼ pint (150 ml) of cold milk. Pour the boiling milk gradually on to the prepared mixture, stirring all the time. Return to heat, bring to the boil and cook for 5 minutes, still stirring. On removing from the heat, add flavouring to taste and pour it into previously moistened moulds. Allow to set and when cold turn out on to a dish.

This is a basic recipe. You may use 2 oz (60 g) of cornflour and an extra ¼ pint (150 ml) of liquid and make it up with coffee, chocolate, fruit juice, etc.

Meringues

3 egg whites
6 oz (180 g) caster sugar
Pinch of salt
A little butter

Put the egg whites into a bowl and beat, using electric beater, until the egg whites are stiff enough to hold a peak or to remain in the bowl when reversed. Fold in the sugar, a spoonful at a time, together with the salt, disturbing the mixture as little as possible. Pipe or place in small spoonfuls on a flat, well-buttered baking tin. Cook at 250°F/120°C/Gas Mark ½ for 2 to 2½ hours, or until crisp and a pale biscuit colour. No attempt to remove the meringues from the tin should be made until they are perfectly cold. They are best served sandwiched with plain, whipped cream but are also a good accompaniment to any fruit cream or fool. This makes about 24 halves.

Trifle

Serves 4
¾ pt (450 ml) custard
½ lb (240 g) sponge cake or cakes
(can be stale)
Jam (preferably strawberry)
¼ pt (150 ml) sherry or fruit juice,
or cider, or jam thinned with
water and lemon juice
½ pt (300 ml) cream

Make the custard and leave to cool slightly. Slice the sponge cakes thinly and spread with jam. Arrange the slices in a glass dish, then soak with the sherry or whatever you have chosen. Cover with the custard. Allow to get quite cold.

Whip the cream stiffly and pipe, or heap it neatly, on the top. Decorate with crystallized cherries, violets, angelica, almonds, crystallized fruit, etc.

Fruit Trifle

This is made exactly as in the above recipe except that jam, sherry, etc., are not required. The cut up and well-sweetened stewed or canned fruit is placed between layers of sponge cake and the juice used to soak it.

Jellies

If you are using a packet jelly, simply follow directions. You can use fruit juice instead of part of the water required, or all fruit juice. And you can set any kind of stewed fruit, sliced banana, etc., in the jelly. Remember that your liquid should be strongly flavoured and well-sweetened.

If you want a jellied sweet of more than one colour, make up separate pints (600 ml) of jelly in different colours. Leave in separate containers, but pour half of one into the mould or individual glasses you are going to use. Allow to set in refrigerator or stand in cold water – do not do this to the remaining jellies as you want them to set as slowly as possible. As soon as the first layer is solid – it need not be quite firm – pour a layer of the next colour on to it. Repeat process till all the jelly is in the serving mould.

When turning out a jelly, run hot (not boiling) water over the outside of the mould, then put dish over top of mould, reverse, and shake gently before lifting mould off.

Jelly Trifle

Serves 4-6

1 pt (600 ml) fruit jelly (packet or gelatine and fruit juice)
6 sponge cakes
Some stewed or fresh fruit, if available
1 pt (600 ml) custard

Make exactly as in recipe for Trifle. Use the hot jelly instead of jam, sherry or fruit juice, placing any fruit between the layers of sponge cake. Leave to set in refrigerator, with custard cooling separately, before pouring custard over the jellied surface.

Jelly Whip

Serves 4

1 pt (600 ml) pkt fruit jelly
Cream (optional)

Make a pint (600 ml) of fruit jelly and allow to begin to set. While still setting, break it up with a fork, then whip with electric beater or continue with fork till light and fluffy. Leave in cool place to finish setting or chill in refrigerator. A little cream can be whipped into it, if liked.

Fruit Snow

Serves 4-6

1 pt (600 ml) apple, plum, apricot, raspberry, or any other fresh fruit, or canned fruit, purée
Sugar
Lemon juice (optional)
1 pt (600 ml) jelly, or 1 oz (30 g) powdered gelatine
2 egg whites

Cook and sieve the fruit, or sieve direct if canned, using half juice, half solid fruit. Sieve through a wire sieve and sweeten. Add a little lemon juice, if liked. Make up jelly using purée instead of water or juice. Allow to cool and almost set. When half set, fold in the stiffly-whisked egg whites. Fold and beat till the whole is light and frothy. Leave to cool and set in refrigerator. This is best served in the dish in which it was set, decorated with whipped cream, glacé cherries, etc.

'Hedgehog' Prune Jelly with Almonds

Soak the stoned prunes overnight, then stew with a little sugar and a piece of lemon peel. Arrange the prunes, cut in halves, in a pint (600 ml) mould. Strain the juice and bring almost to the boil and make up a packet of lemon jelly or stir into the juice 1 oz (30 g) of powdered gelatine. As soon as gelatine is dissolved, pour over prunes in mould and allow to set firmly. The prunes should almost fill the mould, so that not much clear jelly is left above them. Chill. Turn out on to dish and stick all over with almonds, blanched and halved longways. Surround with whipped cream.

Serves 6
1 lb (½ kg) prunes
Sugar
Lemon peel
1 lemon jelly, or 1 oz (30 g)
  gelatine
¼ lb (120 g) almonds
Whipped cream

Wine Jelly

Port or claret are generally used for a wine jelly.

  Follow the basic recipe for making jelly with powdered gelatine, using 1 pint (600 ml) of wine in place of water. Pour the wine through a strainer. Sweeten to taste. Colour with a little cochineal if the colour is dull.

Serves 4
1 pint (600 ml) wine or claret
1 oz (30 g) powdered gelatine
A little sugar

Milk Jelly

Soak lemon peel in the milk. Bring to boiling point and strain the milk on to the gelatine and sugar, stirring until the gelatine is dissolved. Keep in basin, stirring from time to time until the mixture is of the consistency of cream. Pour into wetted mould and turn out when set. Unless the milk jelly is allowed to thicken partly before being poured into mould it will separate.

Serves 4
Piece of lemon peel
1 pt (600 ml) milk
¾ oz (22 g) powdered gelatine
1 ½ oz (45 g) caster sugar

Fresh Fruit Salad

Almost everyone, child or grown-up, likes fresh fruit salad, and so many combinations of fruits may be used according to the season, that no definite recipe need be given. You can, of course, use as many varieties of fruit as you have available, or you may combine only 2 or 3 varieties, as the French usually do, choosing flavours which enhance each other. The following are all particularly good together:

  Strawberries with thin slices of orange
  Banana and fresh pineapple
  Raspberries with a few redcurrants or redcurrant juice
  Peaches and grapes.

  Blackcurrants are not good in fruit salad, as if raw, their skins are too tough and, if stewed, their strong flavour is apt to overcome all the other fruit used.

  Remember, if you are using rather hard fruits and have not enough juice, you can squeeze oranges and pour the juice over or melt 2 oz (60 g) of sugar in ¼ pint (150 ml) of water, allow to cool and pour over some time before serving, if possible, so that the flavour of the fruit is taken up by the syrup. A proportion of wine, however little, or a little brandy or a liqueur, such as Kirsch or Maraschino, much improve fruit salad. If the salad seems sweet and insipid, add lemon juice.

Canned or cooked dried fruit, or stewed fresh fruit can be used in combination with raw fruit and provide plenty of juice. Frozen fruits are excellent. A few blanched almonds, walnuts, dates, dried figs, or slices of crystallized fruit all make a fruit salad more interesting, as they give variety to the texture. Banana is good in fruit salad for the same reason.

A good fruit salad should not be too wet and mushy. The pieces of fruit should retain their flavour and texture and the juice should be clear and not thick and cloudy.

Fruit salad should always be served slightly chilled. Prepare 2 or 3 hours before it is wanted, if possible, and leave with sugar over the fruit to draw out the juice.

Fruit should be prepared as follows:
(always use a stainless steel or silver knife when preparing fruit because acid stains steel)

Apples	Peel and slice finely
Bananas	Peel and slice (keep covered with syrup or fruit juice)
Red or white currants	Strip from stalks with fork
Ripe gooseberries	Top and tail
Grapes	Remove seeds and skin, if you wish
Oranges, grapefruit, etc.	Peel, remove white pith and pips, slice thinly across
Blackberries Raspberries Strawberries	Stem and wash
Stone fruit	Halve to remove stones and slice again, if you wish.

Melon Cup

Serves 8
*Any really ripe melon
    (a canteloupe is best of all)*
1 lb (½ kg) white grapes
2 bananas
2 ripe peaches
½ lb (240 g) greengages
2 oz (60 g) caster sugar
*¼ pt (150 ml) white wine, or
    3 tbsp Kirsch or Maraschino*

Cut the top off the melon at the stalk end. Carefully insert a spoon and scoop out all the pips, holding the melon cut end downwards so that they pour out. When all the pips are cleared, very gently scoop out all the melon flesh into a bowl, being very careful not to break the skin. Cut all the melon flesh into cubes about ½ inch (1¼ cm) square. Stone the grapes and peel, if you wish. Peel and slice the bananas and the peaches, and stone and quarter the greengages. Very lightly mix together with the caster sugar and the wine or liqueur. Using a silver spoon, spoon back into melon, replace slice which you cut off. Pile any surplus fruit in a glass bowl and keep. Chill both melon and extra fruit thoroughly.

Stand melon on a flat dish or a bed of washed vine or lettuce leaves and sprigs of mint. Serve fruit from the melon. When finished take dish out and refill melon with the surplus fruit you have in bowl.

The whole dish is fragrant and cool, all the fruit being green or pale yellow. Cubes of ice may be placed round the melon among the green leaves if liked.

Summer Pudding

Serves 4-6)
8-9 slices of bread
*1 lb (½ kg) fresh raspberries and
    redcurrants, or blackcurrants,
    or loganberries*
*Sugar to sweeten (about ½ lb
    (240 g))*

The bread should be stale and should be cut about ½ inch (1¼ cm) thick. Line the bottom and sides of a 1½ pint (900 ml) pudding bowl with bread. Fit it together so that the bowl is closely lined, with no gaps. Very lightly mix the raspberries with the stalked redcurrants and plenty of sugar. Put in a layer of fruit and press down slightly, sprinkle thickly with sugar. Put another layer of fruit and more sugar, till the bowl is almost full. Press down and fit a slice of bread over the top, filling any gaps with small pieces cut to fit. Stand in refrigerator with a weight on it and leave several hours. It should turn out perfectly and all the bread should have become the colour of the fruit and be soaked in the juice. Serve with cream or chilled custard and caster sugar. The outside can be stuck all over with blanched almonds if you want to dress it up.

Cooked Fruit Dishes

Almost any fruit except strawberries, melons, bananas, oranges, lemons and grapefruit may be stewed. Fruit can be cooked just as well in a casserole in the oven as on top of the stove, according to which is most convenient. There are only a few things to remember. No fruit is good cooked to a mush. If you want a fruit purée, the fruit should be stewed and then put through a sieve or blender so that it is really smooth. Therefore, prepare your fruit keeping it whole or in halves, but always cored or stoned (no one likes finding plum or cherry stones served up to him) and then cook it *slowly* –

no fast boiling – with just enough water to prevent it from drying and sticking, and plenty of sugar. In this way you get delicious, soft pieces of fruit in a rich strongly-flavoured syrup and not a watery, flavourless mush.

Most stone fruits are improved by the addition of a strip or two of lemon peel (yellow part only) and to cook them with a little wine or rough cider instead of all water makes a change.

An excellent plan is to make a syrup of 2 oz (60 g) of sugar to each ½ pint (300 ml) of water, and pour this over the fruit, which you have previously arranged in the casserole or saucepan in which you wish to cook it. Then simmer very slowly in this syrup. The fruit will become quite soft but will retain its shape and the syrup will take on its flavour.

Never stew overripe fruit. Slightly underripe fruit is best for stewing. Times cannot be given as they vary not only with the different types of fruit but according to their ripeness. For very hard pears, to be stewed in the oven, you must allow 2 or 3 hours. Apples and stone fruits usually require 20 to 30 minutes and prunes only 10 to 15 minutes.

Always cover the fruit closely while it is stewing. If you are cooking it in the oven, the temperature should be about 350°F/ 180°C/Gas Mark 4. Several kinds of stewed fruit may be cooked together with advantage.

Dried Fruit (Hot or Cold)

Prunes
Figs
Apricots
Peaches
Apple rings
Little sugar
Slivers of lemon or orange peel

These can all be bought dried and are good value when fresh fruit is dear and scarce. All must be well washed, then soaked for 2 hours and stewed in the water in which they were soaked, else part of their flavour is lost. Just a little sugar should be added and a sliver or two of lemon or orange peel. After soaking they are generally tender from being simmered for 15 to 20 minutes in the oven or on top.

Gooseberry Charlotte

Serves 4-6
1 lb (½ kg) gooseberries
1 lb (½ kg) caster sugar
12 sponge fingers

Top and tail the gooseberries and wash. Put them into a saucepan with the sugar. Stir until the sugar has melted, then simmer until quite soft. Put through a sieve or blender. Line a pudding basin with the sponge fingers, cutting them to fit, pour in the gooseberry purée, cover with more sponge fingers, cover with a plate, put a weight on the top and leave to chill. Turn out and serve with cream or custard.

Fruit Fools

Allow the purée and the custard to cool at least to blood heat. Remove any skin that may have formed over the custard. Mix purée and custard together, beating well with a fork or using an electric whisk. Sieve again if you like it very smooth. Pour into a glass dish and chill.

The addition of thick or thin cream improves a fruit fool out of all knowledge. Use as much as possible, reducing the amount of custard, if you have ¼ pint (150 ml) or so. A fool made entirely with thick purée and fairly thick cream is a wonderful sweet, fit for a dinner party.

Fairly acid and strongly flavoured fruits are the best for fools – gooseberries, rhubarb, strawberries, and blackberry-and-apple are the best. A strip of lemon peel improves the rhubarb and the blackberry-and-apple, if stewed with the fruit.

Serves 4
1 pt (600 ml) fruit purée made from any fresh, stewed or dried fruit
1 pt (600 ml) cornflour custard, made fairly thick according to directions on pkt
Cream

Raspberry and Strawberry Fool

For these, the fruit should not be stewed but washed and put through a sieve fine enough to hold back pips. Add about 3 oz (90 g) of sugar and if possible use all cream, as the texture is much better and the flavour wonderful. If you use custard, do not make it quite so thick as for stewed fruit purées. These raw fruit fools, being thinner, are best served in individual glasses.

Serves 4
1 pt (600 ml) fruit purée
3 oz (90 g) caster sugar
¾ pt (450 ml) cream or custard

Duchess Apples (Hot or Cold)

Blanch and cut the almonds in strips. Peel and core the apples, put them in a saucepan with the sugar and a little water, cover tightly and simmer until the apples are soft but unbroken. Cut rounds of bread, butter them and brown them in a quick oven or in a frying pan. Take out the apples and keep them hot. Reduce the apple syrup by rapid boiling until there is only about ¼ pint (150 ml). Add the apricot jam and stir until quite hot. Put an apple on each piece of bread, cover with apricot syrup and stick in the almonds.

For a cold sweet, use sponge cakes instead of the fried bread. Put them in a glass dish, place a cooked apple on each, coat with jam and stick with almonds as before.

Serves 6
1 oz (30 g) sweet almonds
6 small apples
2 oz (60 g) sugar
A little water
6 rounds of bread
Butter
2 tbsp apricot jam

Apricot Mould

Serves 4
½ lb (240 g) dried apricots
3 oz (90 g) sugar
1 oz (30 g) almonds
1 pt (600 ml) milk
¾ oz (22 g) gelatine

Soak the apricots for 12 hours in cold water. Put them in a saucepan with 2 oz (60 g) of sugar and simmer till tender. Blanch the almonds and cut them into small strips. Put the milk in a double saucepan, with the remainder of the sugar and the gelatine, and boil very gently until the gelatine has dissolved. Add half the apricots, cut small, and the almonds. Turn into a mould, and leave till set – it is best made the previous day. Strain the juice from the rest of the apricots, put it in a saucepan and boil rapidly until it is a thick syrup, pour it back over the apricots and leave until cold.

When required, turn out the mould and serve in glass dish. Pour the apricots in syrup right over it and allow them to coat it and run down and surround it.

Baked Apples (Hot or Cold)

1 large cooking apple per person
2 oz (60 g) sugar
1 oz (30 g) butter

Wash and core the apples but do not peel. Score them all round, halfway between top and stem. Place on a greased baking tray with the centres filled with sugar and a piece of butter. Sprinkle a little more sugar over. Bake in oven at 350°F/180°C/Gas Mark 4 for 20 minutes or till soft all through – time varies with kind of cooking apple.

If liked, a dessertspoon of golden syrup placed on each apple before cooking gives a good syrupy juice. The cores may be stuffed with dates or raisins, with or without nuts, and the butter placed on top and sugar sprinkled over.

Scalloped Pears (Hot or Cold)

Serves 4
6 tinned pear, or stewed pear,
    halves
Butter
Juice of ½ lemon
¼ pt (150 ml) pear syrup
1½ oz (45 g) breadcrumbs
Brown sugar
Cinnamon

Cut the pears into fingers. Arrange in the bottom of a buttered, shallow ovenproof baking dish. Pour over the lemon juice and the pear syrup. Sprinkle with breadcrumbs. Mix brown sugar and cinnamon to taste and sprinkle over crumbs. Dab with small bits of butter. Bake in a fairly hot oven at 425°F/220°C/Gas Mark 7 till the breadcrumbs are brown.

Scalloped Plums (Hot or Cold)

Serves 4
¼ lb (120 g) sponge cake crumbs
    or breadcrumbs
1 pt (600 ml) stoned, stewed
    plums, or any stewed fruit, well
    sweetened
2 tbsp butter

Grease an ovenproof dish. Put a layer of crumbs in the bottom. Cover with a layer of the stewed plums. Repeat layers till all the ingredients have been used up, reserving some crumbs for the top. Dab with butter. Bake for 30 minutes in a moderate oven at 350°F/180°C/Gas Mark 4. Serve with custard or cream.

Bought Ice Cream

Plain ice cream can be served with the following sauces: butterscotch, hot chocolate, caramel or strawberry jam (for caramel and strawberry jam see Chapter 10).

Butterscotch

½ lb (240 g) brown sugar
¼ pt (150 ml) water
1 dessertsp butter

Boil sugar and water for 10 minutes, add butter in small pieces and boil a few minutes longer until it forms a soft ball when tested in cold water. Use very hot.

Hot Chocolate Sauce

2 oz (60 g) block chocolate (plain)
¼ pt (150 ml) water
2 tbsp sugar
Vanilla
1 egg yolk

Simmer chocolate, water and sugar in a pan for about 15 minutes. Add vanilla, cool a little, stir in the beaten egg yolk, whisk and serve very hot.

Fruit Napolitaine

Serves 6-8
Ripe fruit – pears, bananas,
*   peaches, etc.*
Rum
Sugar
Large block of vanilla, coffee and
*   chocolate ice creams*
Shredded toasted almonds
Cream

Finely slice the fruit, sprinkle with rum and a little sugar, leave for an hour at least. Chill a large dish and arrange alternate slices of each kind of ice cream with a little of the mixed fruit between each. Scatter some almonds thickly over it, leave in freezer till you serve it.

Serve with whipped cream on top, added at the last minute.

Baked Alaska, or Ice en Surprise

Serves 6-8
Victoria sponge or sandwich cake
Rum
Large block vanilla ice cream

To make meringue top
3 egg whites
6 oz (180 g) caster sugar

Always a very impressive sweet. The cake can be any shape, but if you make one slightly larger than your ice cream block it is easier to manage.

Set the cake on an ovenproof dish. Sprinkle it with rum, prepare the meringue (see page 237) making sure it is really stiff. Put the hard frozen block of ice cream on the cake, and cover completely with the meringue (some people use an icing bag for this). Dust with caster sugar and put in a hot oven, 475°F/240°C/Gas Mark 9, for 2 or 3 minutes to set and colour the meringue. The plate can be stood on a tray of crushed ice while it is in the oven. Remove and serve immediately.

If you like, you can pour a tablespoon of rum over the meringue when you remove the pudding from the oven, light it quickly and serve it flambé, but everything must be done very fast.

Serves 6
3 large, good dessert pears
Vanilla flavoured syrup
Vanilla ice cream
Chocolate sauce
Shredded, browned almonds

Pears Belle Hélène

Peel the pears, cut in half, and core. Poach gently in the syrup till they are soft. They must remain whole. Cool. Place a block of ice cream on a decorative dish, arrange the pear halves on it, pour chocolate sauce over them and scatter shredded almonds on top.

Peaches or apricots can be served in the same way.

Chocolate cake
Vanilla ice cream
Chocolate sauce
Chopped nuts (optional)

Chocolate Ice Cream Cake

Bake the chocolate cake (see Chapter 22) in flat baking tin, and divide into 2 lengthwise, so the pieces will fit neatly on top of one another. Sandwich the slices together with an equal sized piece of ice cream, pour chocolate sauce over and sprinkle with chopped nuts.

N.B. Any kind of cake and flavour of ice cream can be used, and decorated with nuts, whipped cream or grated chocolate. Sponge cake and vanilla or strawberry ice cream, with whole strawberries and cream on the top, makes a most elegant party sweet.

Halves of fresh or tinned peaches
Vanilla ice cream
Strawberry or raspberry purée
Whipped cream

Peach Melba

Have ready the necessary number of glasses or cups and put a spoonful of vanilla ice cream into each. Lay half a tinned peach on the top, pour over about 2 tablespoons of fruit purée and top with whipped cream.

Pineapple
Cream
Custard
Sugar
Lemon Juice

Pineapple en Surprise

Cut off the top of a ripe pineapple and keep it, and carefully scoop out the inside without piercing the skin. Sieve the pulp or put through a blender and add to it an equal amount of cream and custard mixed with sugar to taste, and a little lemon juice. Freeze in the usual way until the right consistency is obtained. Stand the pineapple case in a glass dish, cutting the stalk end so that it stands firmly, and when it is time for serving fill up with the frozen mixture and replace the top.

Fruit and Nut Sundae

Put a spoonful of ice cream into a glass. Pour over the fruit syrup, cover with whipped cream and sprinkle with chopped nuts. Sundaes may be made in a variety of ways, by changing either the frozen mixture or the sauce that is poured around. A coffee, caramel, or chocolate sauce may be used instead of fruit syrup, and sometimes the sauce is hot. Contrast in flavour and consistency is a good thing to remember – it is easy to make a sundae too sickly sweet. Chopped nuts, or crystallized fruit or stone ginger may be used to give 'bite' to the mixture.

Ice cream
Fruit syrup
Whipped cream
Chopped nuts

BREADS, BUNS AND TEACAKES

BREAD

Plain flour can be used for bread making. Strong white flour is even better for making bread.

Yeast is a living micro-organism which needs warmth and food to make it grow. It 'lightens' the bread dough by producing bubbles of carbon dioxide (the chemicals in baking powder produce the same gas). The right warmth is just below blood heat, 80 to 83°F (26 to 28°C). If the dough is heated above 95°F (35°C), the yeast is killed, and if the temperature is below 77°F (25°C), it is dormant and gives off no carbon dioxide. When the dried yeast is mixed with sugar and warm water it begins to 'work' and give off bubbles of carbon dioxide. Then when it is mixed with the flour, and the dough placed in a warm place to 'sponge' or 'prove', the carbon dioxide makes it spongy and full of air. This takes about 30 minutes. Then the sponge is kneaded to make a smooth elastic dough, and the bread left again in a warm place for 1½ hours to double its original size. When the dough is finally put in the oven, the yeast is killed so no more carbon dioxide is produced. It is therefore important to make sure a yeast dough has been 'proved' thoroughly before baking, or the bread will be close and heavy. On the other hand, overrising can stretch and weaken the dough, so that it collapses in the oven, which again results in heavy bread. With most yeast mixtures the dough should double its size before baking. If you remember that the yeast is alive and must always be kept warm and handled gently, using it is not difficult. It should not be put in a cold mixing bowl, or mixed with cold liquid. Always warm all the things you are going to need, and use warm sugar and warm milk or water to mix into it. A third of boiling water and two-thirds of cold water mixed together, is just right. The dough must be put in a warm place to rise, not too hot, and not in a draught. The plate rack over a stove or an airing cupboard are good places, or the warming drawer of your cooker, left open.

Most of the commercial bread mixes on the market produce very good results, but work out as much more expensive than starting from the beginning.

White Bread (1)

Warm all the utensils before you begin to make the bread. Mix the flour and salt together and pass them through a fine sieve. This ensures that the flour is free from lumps, and also mixes the salt evenly with it. Put these into a mixing bowl, as the flour must be in a heap, otherwise you cannot make a hole in the centre. Now cream the yeast and sugar together. Make the water just lukewarm and add it to the yeast and sugar. Then with a wooden spoon make a hole in the centre of the flour, and pour all the liquid gently into the hole. The hole must not go to the bottom of the bowl, as there must be a layer of flour under the liquid. Now, with the spoon, stir a little of the flour from the sides into the liquid, sufficient to form it into a fairly stiff batter that will just drop from the spoon. Sprinkle a little dry flour over the batter and leave the remainder of the dry flour in a wall round it. Cover the bowl with a cloth and stand it in a warm place for the 'sponge', as it is called, to rise. This will take about 30 minutes. When the yeast has risen through the flour and is a mass of bubbles, it is ready to knead.

To do this, just mix the remainder of the flour with the batter, then turn it on to a floured board. Knead with your knuckles, lightly but firmly, turning and gathering the dough for about 10 minutes. When the dough is smooth and elastic, put it back in the bowl and cover again with the cloth. Leave it in a warm place for 1½ hours to rise. It should then have doubled its original size.

If you are baking the bread in tins, warm them but do not grease. Half fill each tin with the dough and put them in a warm place to 'prove' for a ¼ hour. Then put in a hot oven at 400°F/200°C/Gas Mark 6, and reduce the heat to a moderate 350°F/180°C/Gas Mark 4 after 10 minutes. Bake for about 45 minutes. Reduce heat a little halfway through cooking, if darkening too much.

If it is done, the loaf should sound hollow when tapped. If you like, test with a skewer, which should come out clean if cooked.

For a richer bread, use half milk and half water.

3½ lb (1¾ kg) flour
1 tbsp salt
1 oz (30 g) yeast
1 level dessertsp caster sugar
1½ pt (900 ml) water
(The flour should be best plain or strong white flour not self-raising)

White Bread (2)

Cream the yeast with a little of the sugar, and add the milk. Mix all dry ingredients. Rub in butter or cooking fat. Make a well in the centre, and add half of the fluid. Mix well. Stand in a warm place for 20 minutes. When risen add the remainder of the liquid, mix into dough and knead well. Divide into 2 baking tins. Set aside to rise in a warm atmosphere. Bake for 1 hour in a 400°F/200°C/Gas Mark 6 oven.

1 oz (30 g) yeast
1 oz (30 g) sugar
1 pt (600 ml) warm milk
2 lb (1 kg) flour
1 dessertsp salt
1 oz (30 g) butter or cooking fat

Rolls

Ingredients as above
Egg yolk or milk for glazing

When making rolls, divide the dough into small, even-sized pieces. Knead each piece lightly and shape into balls, twists, etc. Place on a greased baking sheet, score with a knife and prove for about 20 minutes in a warm place. Glaze with egg or milk and bake until the rolls sound hollow when tapped – about 15 minutes. See detailed instructions above.

Vienna Loaves

1 lb (½ kg) flour
1 tsp salt
1 ½ oz (45 g) butter
About ½ pt (300 ml) milk
½ oz (15 g) yeast
1 tsp caster sugar
1 egg, well beaten

Sieve flour and salt into a basin. Melt the butter, add the milk and make tepid. Cream yeast and sugar until liquid. Pour tepid milk over beaten egg, add to the yeast and pour into flour and make a soft, smooth dough. Beat well. Cover with a cloth and put to rise in a warm place for about 1 hour. Form into loaves, place on greased baking sheet and prove for about 15 minutes. Bake in a 450°F/230°C/Gas Mark 8 oven for 20 to 30 minutes.

Milk Loaves (Small)

¾ pt (450 ml) milk
½ oz (15 g) yeast
1 tsp caster sugar
2 eggs
1 ½ lb (¾ kg) flour
1 small tsp salt
2 oz (60 g) butter or margarine

Heat the milk until lukewarm. Cream the yeast and sugar in a basin, add the milk to it, and a well-beaten egg. Put the flour into a bowl, add the salt and mix well. Rub in the butter or margarine until evenly mixed. Pour in the yeast mixture and beat to a dough. Put it in a warm place to rise for 1¼ hours, then form the dough into little cottage loaves, horseshoes or twists. Leave them in a warm place for 10 minutes. Brush over with the other beaten egg and bake in a 425°F/220°C/Gas Mark 7 oven for 20 minutes.

Wholemeal Splits

¾ lb (360 g) wholemeal flour
¼ lb (120 g) white flour
1 tsp salt
1 heaped dessertsp sugar
½ oz (15 g) yeast
½ oz (15 g) cooking fat
½ pt (300 ml) water
1 tbsp milk

Take the wholemeal, the white flour and the salt and mix thoroughly in a basin. Make a well in the middle and into this put the sugar and the yeast. Melt the cooking fat and mix this with the tepid water to which the milk has been added, and pour over the yeast. Allow to stand till the batter rises and bubbles. Do not knead, but mix with knife or spoon to the consistency of a soft paste, adding more warm water if necessary. Dust over with flour and set in a warm place to rise well. Then turn out on to a well-floured board, and lightly roll out to less than ½ inch (1¼ cm) in thickness. Place on a warmed greased tin and set to rise once more. Bake in a 40°F/200°C/Gas Mark 6 oven for 10 minutes
When cold, cut into squares, split and butter to serve.

Wholemeal Bread

1 ¾ lb (¾ kg) wholemeal flour
1 tsp salt
½ oz (15 g) yeast
1 tsp sugar
½ pt (300 ml) water
½ pt (300 ml) milk

Put the flour and salt into a warm basin and make a well, leaving a thick layer of flour at the bottom. Put the yeast and sugar into a smaller basin, and cream them together with a spoon. Add to them the milk and water, which should be lukewarm, and add to the centre of the flour. Work in some of the flour gradually with the tips of the fingers until a batter is formed. Sprinkle a little dry flour over the top and cover the basin with a folded towel. Set the basin in a warm place for about 1 hour, or until the yeast begins to work and form bubbles on the top of the batter. Then mix in the flour from the sides of the basin and make a dough, using a little more warm milk or water if necessary. Knead for 3 or 4 minutes, and divide it into 2 or 3 small greased bread tins, half filling them with dough. Cover again with a clean cloth, and set the dough to rise in a warm place until it has doubled its original size. Then bake the loaves in a 400°F/200°C/Gas Mark 6 oven until they sound hollow when tapped on the bottom (from ¾ to 1 hour). When sufficiently cooked, turn out the bread onto a wire rack, and allow free circulation of air round it while cooling.

Soda Bread

1 lb (½ kg) flour
2 tsp cream of tartar
1 tsp bicarbonate of soda
1 tsp salt
1 tbsp sugar
½ pt (300 ml) milk

Mix all dry ingredients together with the milk to a soft dough. Knead a little. Bake on a greased tin as a flat cake or in a bread tin for ½ hour at 375°F/190°C/Gas Mark 5.

For wholemeal soda bread use equal quantities of wholemeal and white flour.

Potato Loaf

¼ lb (120 g) mashed potato
¾ lb (360 g) flour
2 tsp cream of tartar
1 tsp bicarbonate of soda
1 tsp salt
¼ pt (150 ml) milk

Make exactly as for soda bread, but use ¼ lb (120 g) sieved mashed potato and ¾ lb (360 g) flour and omit sugar. Mix potato and flour well in together.

Quick Rolls

½ lb (240 g) flour
2 tsp baking powder
Pinch of salt
½ pt (300 ml) milk

Put flour, baking powder, and salt in basin, pour in milk gradually, and mix into firm dough. Divide into small rolls and brush over the tops with milk. Prick rolls with a fork and place them on a greased baking tin. Bake for 10 minutes in a 450°F/230°C/Gas Mark 8 oven.

BUNS

Chelsea Buns (1)

¾ lb (360 g) flour
Pinch of salt
4-5 oz (120-150 g) currants and
  sultanas
2 oz (60 g) sugar
1 oz (30 g) yeast
¼ pt (150 ml) warm milk and
  water
1½ oz (45 g) margarine or
  cooking fat
1 egg
A little melted fat
Sugar or golden syrup to glaze

Sieve together the flour and salt, and put to warm. Mix the currants and sultanas with 2 teaspoons of sugar. Cream the yeast with ½ teaspoon sugar and add 2 tablespoons of the milk and water, stirring well. Add this to one-third of the flour and set to sponge. Rub the fat into the rest of the flour and add the remaining sugar and gradually beat in the egg and the rest of the liquid. Next mix in the sponged mixture. Beat all thoroughly and put in a warm place to rise. When double its size knead lightly on a floured board and then roll into an oblong strip. Brush over with melted fat and sprinkle evenly over it the fruit and sugar mixture. Roll up and cut into 12 even-sized slices. Place lightly on a greased tin, cut side down. Allow to prove for 25 minutes, then bake in a 400°F/200°C/Gas Mark 6 oven for 15 to 20 minutes. Glaze with sugar and water or with melted golden syrup.

Chelsea Buns (2)

1 lb (½ kg) flour
½ oz (15 g) yeast
3½ oz (105 g) caster sugar
½ pt (300 ml) milk
¼ lb (120 g) margarine or lard
3 oz (90 g) currants
1 egg, beaten
2 tsp mixed spice
3 oz (90 g) sultanas
Melted butter

Sift the flour, and cream the yeast with a dessertspoon of the sugar. Make the milk lukewarm and melt the margarine or lard in it. Mix the currants with the flour in a basin, add the creamed yeast and the milk mixture to the beaten egg and pour this into a well in the centre of the flour. Mix all to a dough, and let it stand in a warm place for 2 hours. Then roll it out on a board, sprinkle with spice and sultanas, and roll it up as you would a jam roll. Cut it across in slices, and pack them in a greased square baking tin with the cut side up. Pack them rather closely together, and leave them in a warm place for 1 hour. Then bake in a 425°F/220°C/Gas Mark 7 oven for 20 minutes. Directly the buns are baked, brush them over with melted butter mixed with the rest of the sugar.

Christmas Loaf

1 lb (½ kg) flour
½ tsp salt
½ oz (15 g) yeast
2½ tbsp warm milk and water
2½ oz (75 g) butter
½ lb (240 g) sugar
½ lb (240 g) currants
½ lb (240 g) raisins
1 oz (30 g) mixed peel
1 tsp mixed spice

Sieve the flour and salt together. Mix the yeast with a very little of the warm milk and water. Rub the fat into the flour, make a well in the centre, pour in the yeast and allow to sponge for 20 minutes. Add the rest of the ingredients, beat very thoroughly until a soft dough is obtained. Grease and warm 3 loaf tins and half fill with the dough. Put to rise in a warm place until the dough comes to the top of the tins (about 1½ hours), then bake in a 375°F/190°C/Gas Mark 5 oven for ¾ hour. Turn out and cool on a rack. Can be iced with royal or transparent icing.

Doughnuts – Jam

Mix the yeast to a smooth paste with a little of the milk, and gradually stir in the remaining milk and water. Place ¼ lb (120 g) of the flour in a warmed bowl, gradually add the milk and water mixture, and stir in. Whisk or beat well, cover with a cloth, and leave in a warm place for about 45 minutes, until well risen, with bubbles appearing. Sieve the remainder of the flour and salt together, and rub in the butter. Stir in the sugar. Make a well in the centre of the flour, and pour in the yeast mixture, and the slightly beaten egg. Mix well, cover with a cloth, and again leave in a warm place for ½ hour. Press the dough down with the knuckles until it is reduced to its original size, and again cover and leave in a warm place for a further ½ hour. Turn out on to a floured board, shape into a round or roll, and divide into 12 or 16 equal portions, according to the size required. Form each portion into a ball, flatten out, place about a teaspoon of jam in the centre, brush halfway round the edge with a little milk, fold over and press the edges securely together so that the jam cannot ooze out, then place on a floured baking sheet and set aside in a warm place for a further 20 minutes to prove.

Have ready the smoking hot oil. Drop in as many doughnuts as the pan will hold conveniently, and cook for 5 to 7 minutes. When one side of each doughnut is cooked, it will, if the correct mixture has been used, turn over to the other side automatically without being touched. When cooked, lift out, drain on kitchen paper, and roll in sugar and cinnamon.

½ oz (15 g) yeast
2 tbsp warm milk
2 tbsp water
10 oz (300 g) flour
¼ tsp salt
1 oz (30 g) butter
1 oz (30 g) sugar
1 egg
Jam
Oil for deep-frying
Sugar and cinnamon to coat

Hot Cross Buns

Cream the yeast and teaspoon of sugar until liquid and add the milk. Sprinkle a little flour on top, cover, and put in a warm place for about 15 minutes to begin rising. Sift the rest of the flour into a warm bowl, with the salt. Rub in the lard. Add the sugar, spice and fruit, and then the yeast mixture. If necessary, add more milk to make a soft dough. Knead well. Cover and leave to rise until double in bulk. Knead lightly, shape into buns, and place on greased trays. Cut a cross on the top of each with a sharp knife and leave to rise until double the size. Bake in a 425°F/220°C/Gas Mark 7 oven until they sound hollow when tapped on the bottom. While still hot brush with a light syrup of sugar and water. Sufficient for 12 to 16 buns.

½ oz (15 g) yeast
1 tsp sugar
½ pt (300 ml) warm milk
1 lb (½ kg) flour
1 tsp salt
¾ oz (22 g) lard
2½ oz (75 g) sugar
1 tsp mixed spice
2 oz (60 g) sultanas

Teacakes

Home-made Crumpets

1 tsp caster sugar
1 oz (30 g) yeast
1 pt (600 ml) milk
1 lb (½ kg) flour
Pinch of salt
2 eggs

Cream the sugar and yeast together until liquid, then add the warmed milk. Make a hole in the flour, add the salt, pour in the liquid and mix well. Add the beaten eggs and beat the batter well for 10 minutes. Put in a warm place to rise, which will take about 1 hour, then cook the crumpets either in the oven or over the heat. If in the oven, heat the baking tin and brush it over with melted dripping. Put large tablespoons of the mixture at equal distances on the greased tin, turn them once when holes have formed on the surface, cook for a further 3 or 4 minutes, butter them and serve hot.

To cook over the heat, generously grease a large frying pan and make very hot, or grease a gridiron or the top of the grill. Then drop the mixture in tablespoonfuls at equal distances on the hot surface. Turn over and brown the other side, when well risen. Grease a little more if they start to stick or burn.

Sally Lunn

1 oz (30 g) sugar
Good pinch of salt
1 lb (½ kg) flour
2 oz (60 g) butter or margarine
1 oz (30 g) yeast
1 tsp caster sugar
½ pt (300 ml) lukewarm milk
1 egg

Mix the sugar and salt with the flour and sift them. Rub in the fat until it is evenly distributed. Cream the yeast with the caster sugar, add a tablespoon of the milk to it, and let it stand in a warm place for 10 minutes. Then make a hole in the centre of the flour, and pour in the yeast. Mix a little of the flour and the yeast. Then add the well-beaten egg and mix to a soft dough with milk. Grease small round baking tins. Knead the dough for a few minutes, then take pieces of it and half fill the tins, leave them in a warm place until nearly double their original size. Then bake for 20 minutes at 425°F/220°C/Gas Mark 7. Serve with butter.

BISCUITS AND SCONES

BISCUITS

Biscuit doughs may be rich or plain, but they are much drier than bun or scone mixes. The dough should be very stiff if the biscuits are to be rolled or cut out with a cutter. Softer dough can be shaped by hand into small balls and flattened on top, and decorated with a nut or cherry before baking. Biscuit mix should be kneaded before being cut, and the biscuits should be thin. Extra crisp biscuits can be made by taking them out of the oven when half baked, letting them cool for a few minutes and then finishing baking in the usual way. The cooked biscuits *must* be kept in an airtight jar or tin, and they will become soft if stored with cakes.

Basic Recipe for Biscuit Dough

7 oz (210 g) flour
1 oz (30 g) cornflour
Pinch of salt
¼ lb (120 g) butter
¼ lb (120 g) sugar
1 egg
Milk to mix, if necessary

Sieve flour, cornflour, and salt together. Cream the butter. Beat sugar into creamed butter. Stir half of whisked egg into mixture. Work in flour mix, add remainder of egg and very little milk to make a smooth but dry dough which can be rolled out. Knead paste for a few minutes then set in a cold place for ½ to 1 hour. Roll out on a lightly floured board to about ⅛ inch (¼ cm) thick. Cut into rounds, squares, rectangles or fancy shapes – makes 30 to 40 biscuits according to size preferred. Place on very lightly greased baking sheets and bake in a 375°F/190°C/Gas Mark 5 oven for 15 to 20 minutes.

Ginger Biscuits (1)

6 oz (180 g) flour
Pinch of salt
1 tsp mixed spice
2 tsp ground ginger
1 tsp cinnamon
2 oz (60 g) butter
¼ lb (120 g) brown sugar
1 tbsp golden syrup to mix

Sieve the flour, salt, spice, ground ginger, and cinnamon together. Cream the butter and sugar, stir in the dry ingredients alternately with the golden syrup (which may be warmed very slightly in order to make the mixing easier) to make a stiffish paste. Flour a pastry board lightly. Roll out the mixture and cut into small rounds with a pastry cutter. Place on a greased baking tin and bake in a 350°F/180°C/Gas Mark 4 oven for about 15 minutes.

1 full tbsp golden syrup
1 tbsp sugar
¼ lb (120 g) butter or margarine
½ lb (240 g) flour
1 level tsp ground ginger
Pinch of salt
1 egg

Ginger Biscuits (2)

Melt the golden syrup, sugar and butter or margarine, and cool slightly. Sieve flour, ground ginger and salt into a basin. Pour over the melted mixture and the egg and mix to a stiff dough. Roll out, cut into rounds, and bake on the second shelf of a 350°F/180°C/Gas Mark 4 oven for 10 minutes.

½ lb (240 g) self-raising flour
Pinch of salt
3 oz (90 g) butter
1 oz (30 g) cooking fat
2 level tbsp honey

Honey Biscuits

Sieve flour and salt into a bowl and rub in fats. Add the honey and work into the dry ingredients with a knife, until the mixture holds together. Roll out to ⅛ inch (¼ cm) thick and cut into rounds with small scone cutter. Bake on a greased baking sheet for 15 to 20 minutes at 300°F/150°C/Gas Mark 2. Remove at once and cool on a wire rack.

½ lb (240 g) medium oatmeal
1 tbsp salt
1 oz (30 g) dripping, melted
1 tbsp golden syrup
Boiling water to mix

Oatmeal Biscuits

Put oatmeal and salt into a basin. Add melted dripping, golden syrup and enough boiling water to form mixture into a soft dough. Knead well, roll out thinly. Cut into rounds. Bake in a 350°F/180°C/Gas Mark 4 oven for 20 minutes.

¼ lb (120 g) butter
¼ lb (120 g) caster sugar
1 level tsp grated lemon rind
1 egg
½ lb (240 g) flour
½ tsp baking powder

Shrewsbury Biscuits

Cream butter and sugar, add lemon rind and beat in egg. Work in flour and baking powder. Knead lightly and roll out thinly. Prick well and cut in rounds or fingers. Place on greased baking trays and bake at 375°F/190°C/Gas Mark 5 for 15 minutes.

¼ lb (120 g) butter and cooking fat mixed
¼ lb (120 g) sugar
1 egg
½ lb (240 g) flour
1 tsp cinnamon
2-3 oz (60-90 g) currants

Easter Biscuits

Cream together the fat and sugar very thoroughly, and add the egg, well beaten, a little at a time. Sieve the flour and cinnamon and add it to the creamed mixture, together with the currants. Roll out to about ⅛ inch (¼ cm) in thickness and cut into rounds with a cutter. Place on a greased baking tin and bake in a 350°F/180°C/Gas Mark 4 oven for about 15 minutes until pale brown in colour.

Chocolate Biscuits

Sieve together the flour and cocoa. Mix and bake as for basic Biscuit Dough.

5½ oz (165 g) flour
1½ oz (45 g) cocoa
Pinch of salt
3 oz (90 g) butter
3 oz (90 g) sugar
1 egg
Milk to mix

Cheese Biscuits

Rub fat into flour, add cheese, which must be finely grated, and salt and pepper. Mix to a stiff paste with cold milk, and roll to about ⅛ inch (¼ cm) thickness. Cut into rounds or fingers, prick with a fork to prevent rising, and bake in a 425°F/220°C/Gas Mark 7 oven for 7 to 10 minutes.

¼ lb (120 g) butter
6 oz (180 g) flour
3 oz (90 g) grated cheese
Salt and pepper to taste
A little milk to mix

Almond Macaroons

Whip egg whites and salt until stiff enough to hold a peak. Fold in the ground almonds, sugar and rice or semolina. Put in little mounds or roll into balls and then flatten on rice paper or a well-greased baking tray. Place an almond on each, bake in a 300°F/150°C/Gas Mark 2 oven till crisp, about 30 to 40 minutes.

3 egg whites
Pinch of salt
6 oz (180 g) ground almonds
½ lb (240 g) caster sugar
1 tbsp ground rice or fine semolina
18 blanched almonds

Shortbread

Cream butter and sugar, till very soft, add vanilla and work in the flour, salt and semolina, which have been sieved together. Knead into a smooth ball and roll out till ¼ inch (½ cm) thick. Place on greased baking sheets; prick well. Bake at 375°F/190°C/Gas Mark 5 for 15 minutes. While still hot, dust with caster sugar.

¼ lb (120 g) butter
2 oz (60 g) caster sugar
Few drops of vanilla essence
6 oz (180 g) flour
Pinch of salt
2 oz (60 g) semolina

Scotch Shortbread (Basic)

Cream butter and sugar, till very soft. Beat in flour and salt. Roll out to 1 inch (2½ cm) thickness, or the paste can be pressed into a tin by hand if it will not roll out. Prick it well with a fork. Cook for 45 minutes at 250°F/130°C/Gas Mark ½.

2 oz (60 g) butter
1 oz (30 g) sugar
¼ lb (120 g) flour
Pinch of salt

¼ lb (120 g) butter
¼ lb (120 g) caster sugar
1 egg, separated
¼ lb (120 g) flour

Shortcake Biscuits

Cream butter and sugar. Beat in egg yolk, and sieved flour and mix to a smooth dough. Roll out a bare ¼ inch (½ cm) thick. Stamp out with a 2 inch (5 cm) cutter. Place well apart on a baking tray. Brush with lightly beaten egg white. Bake at 375°F/190°C/Gas Mark 5 for 12 minutes, or until a light brown. This makes about 30 biscuits.

SCONES

There are two main types: (1) the baked scone, cooked in the oven and (2) griddle (or girdle) scones and drop scones, which are both cooked over heat, first on one side and then on the other. Either a griddle or the hot plate of an electric cooker is needed for these. A strong thick frying pan can be used, but beware of burning. Drop scones are made from a much softer mixture, and are halfway between a pancake and a baked scone.

Scones are easy to make and there are many different kinds. They can be made from white flour, wholemeal, barley or corn-meal, or a mixture of two different kinds, and mixed into sweet milk, sour milk or, when obtainable, buttermilk. Baking powder, or cream of tartar and sodium bicarbonate are added to lighten the dough, or self-raising flour can be used. A pinch of salt should always be sifted in with the flour or meal, and sugar can be added to taste.

The handling and working of the dough has a great deal to do with the lightness of the scones. It is astonishing what different results can be obtained from the same recipe, owing to the manner in which the dough is treated. It should be handled as little as possible, and cooked at once while it is soft and pliable.

The griddle is a round sheet of thick iron, with a handle, which is heated on top of the stove. It should be put on to heat before mixing the dough. It should never be washed, but cleaned when hot by sprinkling with salt and rubbing with paper. The heat can be tested by sprinkling a little dry flour on the griddle; if too hot the flour will brown at once, but, if right, it should turn to golden brown in about 1 minute. The griddle can either be greased or floured to prevent the scones from sticking. When cooking potato or drop scones, the griddle is first greased with butter or lard and regreased between each batch.

Wholemeal Scones

Mix the flour and salt. Rub in the margarine, add the milk and water to make a stiff dough. Knead this for a few minutes. Roll out, form into scones and bake on hot tins in a good oven for about 20 minutes at 425°F/220°C/Gas Mark 7.

¾ lb (360 g) wholemeal flour
Pinch of salt
2 oz (60 g) margarine
¼ pt (150 ml) milk and water mixed

Wholemeal Date Tea-Scones

Mix together the wholemeal flour, bicarbonate of soda, cream of tartar and salt. Rub in the fat, mix in the sugar, add dates and mix. Then add sufficient buttermilk, or milk, to knead to a firm dough (slightly softer than for bread). Cut in triangles and bake about 20 minutes at 450°F/230°C/Gas Mark 8.

Delicious hot with butter.

½ lb (240 g) wholemeal flour
½ level tsp bicarbonate of soda
½ level tsp cream of tartar
½ level tsp salt
1½ oz (45 g) butter or margarine
3 tsp caster sugar
¼ lb (120 g) dates, stoned and cut into pieces the size of sultanas
Buttermilk (if obtainable) or milk

Oatmeal Scones

Beat the dripping or butter to a cream, mix in the sugar, then add the flour, oatmeal, salt and baking powder. Mix to a dough with the milk. Roll out, cut into cakes, and bake on floured tins in a moderately hot oven at 400°F/200°C/Gas Mark 6.

2 oz (60 g) dripping or butter
1 oz (30 g) sugar
2 oz (60 g) flour
¼ lb (120 g) fine oatmeal
2 oz (60 g) medium oatmeal
Good pinch of salt
1 heaped tsp baking powder
1 tbsp milk

Coarse Oatmeal Buns

Rub the cooking fat into the flour, add the oatmeal, sugar, baking powder and well-beaten egg, and enough milk to make a stiff paste, and mix well. Drop the mixture on to a greased baking tin in spoonfuls, and bake for 15 to 20 minutes at 425°F/220°C/Gas Mark 7.

3 oz (90 g) cooking fat
5 oz (150 g) flour
6 oz (180 g) coarse oatmeal
¼ lb (120 g) sugar
1 tsp baking powder
1 egg
A little milk

Dripping Teacakes

Mix together the flour, salt and baking powder. Cream the dripping as you would butter, and blend it with the flour, then add the currants, sugar and enough milk or water to make a stiff dough. Cut flat round cakes and bake in a greased tin for 20 minutes at 425°F/220°C/Gas Mark 7.

To serve, split in half and butter.

1 lb (½ kg) flour
Pinch of salt
1 small tsp baking powder
3 oz (90 g) beef dripping
2 oz (60 g) currants
1 oz (30 g) sugar
Milk or water to mix

Oatcakes

¼ lb (120 g) fine oatmeal
Pinch of salt
Pinch of bicarbonate of soda
1 tsp melted butter or bacon fat
Hot water to mix

Put the oatmeal into a basin with the salt and bicarbonate of soda. Add the melted butter or bacon fat, and make into a soft paste with hot water. Turn this onto a board sprinkled with oatmeal, and roll out very thin. Rub over with more oatmeal and cut into a large round, and then across again into·4 to 6 pieces. Slide the cakes carefully on to a hot griddle, and cook over a moderate heat until they begin to curl up. Then carefully slide on to a grill pan and put under the grill for a few minutes. Serve with butter.

Potato Scones

6 oz (180 g) cooked potatoes
6 oz (180 g) flour
Pinch of salt
2 level tsp baking powder
1 oz (30 g) butter
Milk (if necessary)

Cold cooked potatoes can be used, but it is better to cook them specially for the scones, and allow them to cool, but not get quite cold. No milk should be used with freshly-boiled potatoes.

Rub potatoes through a sieve. Sift the flour, salt and baking powder in a basin. Rub in the butter with tips of the fingers. Add the sieved potatoes and mix to a fairly soft dough, adding a little milk if necessary. Roll out very lightly to about ¾ inch (1¾ cm) thick, cut into rounds 2 inches (5 cm) in diameter and bake in a 350°F/180°C/Gas Mark 4 oven until golden brown. Serve hot with butter.

Potato Griddle Cakes

1 lb (½ kg) floury potatoes
¾ tsp salt
Flour

Boil or steam the potatoes, rub them through a sieve and mix in the salt. Turn them on to a pastry board, and when cool, knead flour into them, a spoonful at a time, till the mixture is a smooth, even dough. The quantity of flour needed will vary according to the dryness of the potatoes. The dough should be soft, but not sticky. Roll out rather thinly, cut into rounds, prick them all over with a fork to prevent them blistering and cook on a griddle, turning them when brown on one side. Split them through, butter and serve hot.

Scottish Pancakes

¾ lb (360 g) self-raising flour
½ tsp salt
1 egg
½ oz (15 g) butter
Milk to mix

Mix together the flour and salt, and sieve. Add the well-beaten egg, and the melted butter. Mix with milk to make a batter that will drop readily from the spoon, like thick cream. Drop table-spoonfuls on to a hot, greased griddle, a little distance apart, and cook for 3 to 4 minutes, then turn and cook on the other side. Serve hot or cold.

A very thick frying pan can be used instead of a griddle.

Fruit Griddle Scones

Sieve together the flour, cream of tartar and bicarbonate of soda. Then rub in the butter. Mix in the fruit and sugar. Add the egg, well beaten, and form a soft dough with the milk. Roll out, cut into scones, and cook on a hot, floured griddle, or bake for 15 minutes at 450°F/230°C/Gas Mark 8.

½ lb (240 g) flour
1 tsp cream of tartar
½ tsp bicarbonate of soda
1 oz (30 g) butter
2 oz (60 g) seedless raisins
1 dessertsp caster sugar
1 egg
¼ pt (150 ml) milk

Dripping Scones

Beat the dripping to a cream, mix with it the sugar, then add the rest of the dry ingredients. Mix to a dough with the milk. Roll out, cut into rounds, and bake on floured tins in a 450°F/230°C/Gas Mark 8 for 20 minutes.

2 oz (60 g) dripping
1 oz (30 g) sugar
¼ lb (120 g) fine oatmeal
2 oz (60 g) medium oatmeal
2 oz (60 g) flour
Good pinch of salt
1 heaped tsp baking powder
2 tbsp milk

Buttermilk Scones

Rub the fat into the flour, stir in the salt, bicarbonate of soda and cream of tartar. Mix to a soft, but not sticky, dough with the buttermilk. Roll out thinly. Cut into rounds and cook on a hot griddle that has been well floured.

½ oz (15 g) butter or margarine
½ lb (240 g) flour
Pinch of salt
½ tsp bicarbonate of soda
½ level tsp cream of tartar
¼ pt (150 ml) buttermilk

Australian Cheese Scones

Mix together the dry ingredients. Form into a dough with the milk, mix well, and cut into rounds. Bake in a 475°F/240°C/Gas Mark 9 oven for 10 to 15 minutes.

½ lb (240 g) flour, sifted
3 oz (90 g) grated cheese
2 tsp baking powder
Pinch of salt
¼ pt (150 ml) milk

CAKES

General Notes

Many people think that baking a cake demands an experienced cook. This is nonsense. Anyone who can and will follow a recipe exactly can bake an excellent cake at the first attempt.

In all baking it is essential to preheat the oven, so that it has reached the required temperature when your cake is ready to go in. This takes about 15 minutes with electricity or gas as a rule, but ovens do tend to vary and yours may take 20 minutes, so allow a little extra time until you are used to it and know the timing definitely.

The cake tin should be prepared before you start your mixing, as a mixed cake dough or batter should not be kept waiting. Grease the tin generously, using lard, butter or cooking fat.

Lining a cake tin

For large cakes, particularly if they contain fruit, the tin should be lined with paper so that the bottom and sides of the cake do not brown too much before the centre is cooked. Cut a strip of grease-proof paper long enough to reach round the tin and an inch (2½ cm) higher. Fold up ½ inch (1¼ cm) along one side and make small cuts in it. Stand the tin on another piece of paper, cut around it, then cut a circle a little smaller to fit the tin. Grease the papers and fit into the greased tin, with the snipped pieces overlapping at the bottom, and fit the circle over the side paper.

Get out everything you are going to need before you begin. Weigh the ingredients carefully.

Methods

There are four methods of combining the fat and the rest of the ingredients:

1 *Rubbing in* The flour, salt and spice are sieved into a mixing bowl, then the fat is added in small pieces. Rub the mixture

between the fingertips until it is like fine breadcrumbs, then stir in sugar, grated lemon peel, fruit, etc. Make a well in the middle of the dry mixture and add beaten egg, milk or water, or warmed syrup, or whatever liquid is used in the recipe. This is the method used for scones and plain cakes and buns.

2 *Creaming* Soften the weighed fat with a wooden spoon. It must be really soft. If you can remember to put the fat you are going to use in a warm place a little while beforehand it is a great help, but if you warm it too much and it oils, the consistency of the cake will not be good. It is almost impossible to cream fat straight from the refrigerator. Do use some butter, and for your best cakes all butter, as nothing else gives the same flavour. Add the sugar next, and beat well with spatula or spoon. Syrup or honey can be creamed with the fat too. The result must be a smooth, light and fluffy cream, and not a collection of little hard lumps of fat and gritty sugar. Then sieve the flour and salt together, and add the eggs, one at a time, and a little of the flour mixture, to the fat and sugar, and beat thoroughly. It does not matter if it appears curdled. When all the flour is added, the curdled look will disappear as you beat. Stir in some more of the liquid (milk or syrup) and more of the flour, and beat well. Then add the rest of the flour, flavouring, and fruit. Stir thoroughly. This is the method used for rich cakes.

3 *Gingerbread or batter method* This is a very simple and quick method, and useful for impatient cooks faced with hard, cold blocks of fat. Sift the dry ingredients into the mixing bowl, and add dried fruit. Melt the fat in a small saucepan, with the treacle or syrup. It should not be allowed to boil. Sometimes the sugar is added too, sometimes it is included with the dry ingredients. When the fat and syrup are melted, but *not* too hot, stir into the flour and mix to a batter. Eggs are added at the same time as the 'melt'. Mix well and bake in a cool oven. The consistency of the raw cake is wetter by this method, and the batter should pour into the tin. This is used for gingerbreads, syrup cakes and flapjacks.

4 *The sponge method* A true sponge has no fat and depends for its lightness on the air beaten in with the eggs. All the ingredients should be at room temperature or slightly warm. In cold weather it is a help to beat the eggs and sugar in a basin standing over hot water. The eggs and sugar should be whisked until they are very thick, light, airy, and the colour of salad cream. Then the sieved flour is added by folding it in with a metal spoon, carefully so that the air you have whipped in is retained. The tins should be evenly greased, preferably by brushing with melted lard, and then dusted over with a mixture of half caster sugar and half self-raising flour, well mixed. Swiss Roll tins must be papered too.

Sponges must be baked in a moderate oven, so that the mixture rises gradually and evenly. With a Swiss Roll, the oven must be hotter, as it is baked in a shallow tin. The Swiss Roll needs extra baking powder, because it must rise and set so quickly. The mixture must be spread evenly in the tin so that it will roll up easily, and the rolling must be done quickly, before it cools and stiffens too much.

Baking

Large cakes should be baked for the first hour in a moderate oven and then the heat reduced for the rest of the time. Cover the top with greased paper when it is brown enough. When the time is up, test the cake to see if it is cooked. It should have shrunk a little away from the sides of the tin. When you touch the top gently, it should feel firm and springy. Stabbing a cake with a skewer to see if it is cooked is a time-honoured, if barbaric, method. If you feel you must, use a fine steel knitting needle, which should come out shiny and clean, with no uncooked cake mixture sticking to it.

Uneven rising
1 Baking too quickly.
2 The cake being placed on one side of the oven.
3 Use of too much baking powder or other raising agent which has not been evenly absorbed into the mixture.

Sinking in the middle during or just after cooking
1 Too cool an oven.
2 Not enough flour used.
3 Moving the cake while rising and before it had firmed.
4 Not cooking long enough.

Too dry a cake
1 Too slow cooking.
2 Cooking the cake too long.
3 Making the mixture too stiff and dry.

A heavy cake
1 Too much fat.
2 Too much flour.
3 Too much liquid in the mixture.
4 Overbeating of the cake after the flour was added.

Holes in the finished cake
1 Too hot an oven.
2 Too much flour.
3 Too much bicarbonate of soda, if used.
4 Overbeating of the cake after the flour was added.

Fruit sinking to bottom of cake
1 Too much raising agent.

2 Not enough flour used.
3 Damp fruit.
4 Too much fruit.
5 Too hot an oven at the start.

The oven door should not be opened until two-thirds of the baking time has passed, and the cake should not be moved in the oven till it has set properly, or it will sink in the middle. The consistency of the raw mixture varies with the kind of cake.

1 *Stiff dough* Add just enough liquid to bind the ingredients together; for example, pastry and most biscuits.
2 *Soft dough* Add enough liquid to make a mixture which is as soft as possible without being too soft to handle easily and roll out; for example, scones.
3 *Very stiff batter consistency* Add a little more liquid than used for the soft dough. The mixture should be too sticky to handle but stiff enough to keep its shape; for example, rock cakes.
4 *Dropping batter consistency* The mixture should drop in lumps from the spoon but is too thick to pour; for example, most cake mixtures.

It is assumed that self-raising flour is used in all the recipes that follow, unless plain is specifically given.

Sponges

Hollowed top	Too much raising agent
Close, rather doughy texture; or damp streak at base	Too much liquid; or too much sugar
Overbaked outside, soft doughy centre	Too hot an oven, or cake placed too high in the oven
Baked through, but pale	Too cool an oven, or cake on too low a shelf
Sticking to sides of tin; sticky and damp when cold	Slightly underbaked; needs a little longer
Too shallow and not risen	Not whisked sufficiently; or oven too cool; or raising agent insufficient

Swiss Roll

Very crisp edges, dark over-baked appearance	Too high baking temperature, or baked too long
Wet and sticky when turned out	Too much sugar; or too much liquid; or not enough flour; or badly underbaked
Thin, and badly risen	Not whisked enough
Risen unevenly	Not spread evenly in tin
Cracks when rolling	Over or underbaking; edges not trimmed, or not rolled quickly enough, or jam cold

Recipes

10 oz (300 g) self-raising flour
5 oz (150 g) margarine or butter
5 oz (150 g) sugar
2 eggs
¼ lb (120 g) glacé cherries,
  halved
Milk to mix
Caster sugar to sprinkle on top

Cherry Cake

Line a 7-8 inch (17½-20 cm) cake tin with greaseproof paper. Sieve the flour into a mixing bowl, and rub in the margarine with the fingertips until no lumps can be felt. Add sugar, and then the well-beaten eggs. Add cherries, reserving about 6 for decorating the top of the cake, and sufficient milk to give a dropping consistency. Put into a greased cake tin and put the rest of the cherries on the top of the cake and sprinkle with a little caster sugar. Bake in a moderate oven about 375°F/190°C/Gas Mark 5 for about 1¼ hours.

½ lb (240 g) flour
1½ tsp baking powder
2 oz (60 g) margarine
2 oz (60 g) cooking fat
¼ lb (120 g) sugar
3 oz (90 g) currants
4-5 chopped dates
Grated rind of 1 orange
Few drops of vanilla essence
2 eggs
Water or milk to mix

College Cake

Line a 7 inch (17½ cm) round cake tin with greaseproof paper. Sieve together the flour and baking powder and rub in the margarine and cooking fat until no lumps remain. Add the sugar, stir in the currants, dates and grated rind. Add the vanilla essence. Mix thoroughly and add the beaten eggs. Mix to a dropping consistency with water or milk and turn into a well-greased cake tin. Bake at 375°F/190°C/Gas Mark 5 for about 1½ hours, until well risen and firm to the touch. Cool on a cake rack.

Coat with white icing if liked.

½ lb (240 g) butter
½ lb (240 g) caster sugar
4 eggs
½ lb (240 g) flour
1 tsp salt
¼ tsp mixed spice (optional)
½ lb (240 g) currants and
  sultanas
½ lb (240 g) seedless raisins
¼ lb (120 g) glacé cherries
1 tbsp brandy
Milk, if necessary
Few halved walnuts to decorate

Rich Pound Cake

Line a 9 inch (22½ cm) cake tin with greaseproof paper. Cream together the fat and sugar very thoroughly and add the beaten eggs, a little at a time. Fold in the sieved flour, salt and spice and add the fruit. Mix to a soft dropping consistency with the brandy, and milk if necessary, turn into prepared tin and place the walnuts on the top of the mixture. Bake at 275°F/140°C/Gas Mark 1 for 4 to 5 hours or until cooked. Allow to cool slightly before turning out.

Dundee Cake

Line a 9 inch (22½ cm) tin with greaseproof paper. Cream fat and sugar. Add grated rinds and juices of orange and lemon, and eggs and beat well. Mix together the dry ingredients, and fold into the mixture. Fill the tin not more than two-thirds full, make a deep depression in the centre and scatter blanched almonds, previously dipped in milk, on top. Bake 2 hours, the first hour at 350°F/180°C/Gas mark 4 and the next at 300°F/150°C/Gas Mark 2.

1 lb (½ kg) butter
6 oz (180 g) soft brown sugar
1 orange
1 lemon
5 eggs, beaten
6 oz (180 g) each currants and sultanas
¼ lb (120 g) each chopped raisins, candied pineapple and almonds
2 oz (60 g) chopped ginger
3 oz (90 g) each chopped dates and peel
1 lb (½ kg) self-raising flour
Blanched almonds, to scatter on top
Milk

Soda Cake

Prepare a 7 inch (17½ cm) cake tin with greaseproof paper. Sift the flour with the spice, rub the fat into the flour very finely until like crumbs, then stir in the sugar and fruit. Stir the vinegar into ¼ pint (150 ml) of warm milk, then add the bicarbonate of soda. As the mixture fizzes up pour at once into the dry ingredients and mix to a soft dough, adding more warm milk as required. The dough should be of a consistency that will drop easily from the mixing spoon, but slightly stiffer than a dough containing eggs. Turn the dough into a cake tin and smooth evenly on top with a spoon dipped in milk, then bake for about 1 hour at 400°F/200°C/Gas Mark 6.

¾ lb (360 g) self-raising flour
Pinch of mixed spice (optional)
¼ lb (120 g) lard or cooking fat, or a mixture of margarine and lard or cooking fat
¼ lb (120 g) soft brown sugar
½ lb (240 g) mixed dried fruit
1 tbsp vinegar
About ¼ pt (150 ml) warm milk
1 heaped tsp bicarbonate of soda

Genoa Cake

Prepare a 9 inch (22½ cm) cake tin with greaseproof paper. Chop all the fruit, as the cake is very light and it would otherwise sink. Cream the fat and sugar very thoroughly, then beat in the egg yolks and the flavourings. Sift the flour well with the ground almonds and then add to the mixture, a little at a time, alternating it with handfuls of the fruit and the whole almonds. Beat well after each addition. The baking powder should be sifted in with the last spoonful of flour. Whip the egg whites very stiffly and fold in gently. The mixture must be cooked at once in a tin which should not be more than three-quarters full.

Bake at 325°F/170°C/Gas Mark 3 for ½ hour, then 375°F/190°C/Gas Mark 5 for 1½ hours. Do not open the oven before the cake has been in for at least 1 hour. Leave in the tin until cold.

½ lb (240 g) raisins
¼ lb (120 g) currants
2 oz (60 g) glacé cherries
¼ lb (120 g) mixed peel
¼ lb (120 g) sultanas
½ lb (240 g) butter
¼ lb (120 g) caster sugar
4 eggs, separated
1 tsp almond essence
1 tsp grated orange rind
¾ lb (360 g) plain flour
¼ lb (120 g) ground almonds
1 oz (30 g) whole almonds, blanched
2 tsp baking powder

6 oz (180 g) dripping or butter
1 lb (½ kg) self-raising flour
1½ tsp baking powder
6 oz (180 g) raisins
¼ lb (120 g) currants
Rind of ½ lemon
½ lb (240 g) sugar
2 eggs
2 or 3 tbsp milk

2-3 oz (60-90 g) cooking fat or
  butter
½ lb (240 g) self-raising flour
½ tsp salt
6 oz (180 g) dried fruit
3 oz (90 g) sugar
1 tsp mixed spice
1 tbsp golden syrup
1 tbsp marmalade
¼ pt (150 ml) milk

¾ lb (360 g) self-raising flour
¼ tsp salt
½ tsp mixed spice (optional)
¼ lb (120 g) butter
¼ lb (120 g) caster sugar
2 eggs
2 tbsp golden syrup
6 oz (180 g) chopped dates
1½ oz (45 g) walnuts
¼ pt (150 ml) milk and water to
  mix, if necessary

3 oz (90 g) margarine
3 oz (90 g) caster sugar
2 eggs
1 oz (30 g) plain flour
3½ oz (105 g) cornflour
1 tsp baking powder
Flavouring
Icing sugar

Raisin Cake

Prepare a 9 inch (22½ cm) tin with greaseproof paper. Rub the fat into the sieved flour and baking powder. Add the fruit, lemon rind and sugar. Mix well together, make a well in the centre, add the well-beaten eggs and the milk gradually. The mixture should be stiff enough to hold a spoon upright. Beat well. Bake in greased, lined tin at 375°F/190°C/Gas Mark 5 for about 1½ hours.

Eggless Fruit Cake

Grease a 7 inch (17½ cm) tin. Mix the fat with the flour and salt by the rubbing-in method, adding the fruit, sugar and mixed spice next. Add the syrup and marmalade together with the milk, mixing all to a rather stiff consistency. Bake at 375°F/190°C/Gas Mark 5 for about 1 hour.

Date and Walnut Cake

Sieve flour, salt and spice together. Cream butter and sugar. Add eggs, syrup, and then the sieved flour mixture by degrees. Finally add the dates and nuts and mix well, adding milk and water if necessary. Bake in a shallow 9 inch (22½ cm) baking tin for 1¼ hours at 350°F/180°C/Gas Mark 4.

Sand Cake

Cream together the fat and sugar. Beat in the eggs a little at a time. Sieve together the flour, cornflour and baking powder, and stir lightly into the creamed mixture. Add flavouring if liked. Put the mixture into a greased 8×4 inch (20×10 cm) square or oblong tin and bake for about 1 hour at 350°F/180°C/Gas Mark 4. Turn carefully on to a cake rack and allow to cool. When cold dredge with icing sugar.

American Shortcake

Put the margarine and sugar into a basin and beat them well with a wooden spoon until they are of a light and creamy consistency. Add the eggs and beat again. Sieve together the flour, and salt and add them to the mixture alternately with the milk, mixing as lightly as possible. Bake in 2 greased 7 inch (17½ cm) sandwich cake tins for about 30 minutes at 375°F/190°C/Gas Mark 5. When ready, put the cakes together with crushed fresh berries or other filling.

¼ lb (120 g) margarine
¼ lb (120 g) caster sugar
2 eggs
6 oz (180 g) self-raising flour
1 tsp salt
About 2 tbsp milk

Victoria Sandwich

Cream together the butter and sugar until very light and creamy. Beat the eggs and add them a little at a time to the creamed mixture. Sieve the flour and fold very lightly into the mixture, together with a little milk to give a soft dropping consistency. Turn into 2 well-greased 7 inch (17½ cm) sandwich tins and bake at 375°F/190°C/Gas Mark 5 for 25 to 30 minutes, until well risen, golden brown and firm to the touch. Cool on a cake rack, and when cold, sandwich together with jam or other filling. Dust lightly with icing sugar. This may be flavoured with lemon or orange peel to give a different cake.

¼ lb (120 g) butter
¼ lb (120 g) sugar
2 eggs
¼ lb (120 g) flour
A little milk
Jam or other filling
Icing sugar

Rich Chocolate Cake

Cream the butter and sugar together and beat in the syrup and vanilla. Add the eggs and beat again. Sift in the dry ingredients, except the soda which is dissolved in the milk, and stir into the creamed mixture with extra milk, if necessary to make a soft consistency. Spread evenly in well-greased 6 inch (15 cm) sandwich tins and bake at 350°F/180°C/Gas Mark 4 for 25 to 30 minutes. Leave the cake in the tin to cool for a few minutes before turning out. Fill with Chocolate Butter Cream (see page 280).

2 oz (60 g) butter
2 oz (60 g) sugar
1 level tbsp golden syrup
A few drops of vanilla essence
2 eggs
6 oz (180 g) plain flour
1 level tsp baking powder
2 level tbsp cocoa
¼ level tsp salt
1 level tsp bicarbonate of soda
¼ pt (150 ml) milk

Chocolate Cake to Keep Well

Prepare a 7-8 inch (17½-20 cm) cake tin. Cream butter and sugar and add the beaten eggs. Add ground almonds, vanilla and chocolate which has been melted in a basin over hot water. Sift in flour and salt and mix well. Bake for 1¼ hours at 350°F/180°C/Gas Mark 4. The oil in the chocolate, and the almonds, helps to keep this cake moist.

¼ lb (120 g) butter
¼ lb (120 g) caster sugar
2 eggs
2 oz (60 g) ground almonds
1 tsp vanilla essence
2 oz (60 g) grated chocolate
6 oz (180 g) self-raising flour
Pinch of salt

½ lb (240 g) self-raising flour
4 tbsp sugar
2 tbsp cocoa
1 tbsp golden syrup
14 tbsp hot water
½ tsp bicarbonate of soda
3 oz (90 g) cooking fat, melted

Mrs Instone's Chocolate Cake (Eggless)

Mix the flour, sugar and cocoa. Mix the syrup and the hot water, and stir into the flour. Add the bicarbonate of soda and stir it in, and then the melted cooking fat. Mix well and pour into 2 greased 7 inch (17½ cm) sandwich tins, and bake at 400°F/200°C/Gas Mark 6 for 30 minutes. Sandwich together with Chocolate Butter Cream (see page 280), and ice with Glacé Icing made with chocolate (see page 279) for a special occasion.

3½ oz (105 g) butter
3½ oz (105 g) caster sugar
½ tsp coffee essence or powdered instant coffee
2 eggs
5 oz (150 g) self-raising flour
1½ tsp baking powder

Special Coffee Cake

Cream butter and sugar till very light and fluffy. Add coffee essence, beat eggs well and add alternately with the sifted flour. Add the baking powder at the end. Bake in two 7 inch (17½ cm) sandwich tins lined with paper for 15 to 20 minutes at 325°F/170°C/Gas Mark 3. When cold, sandwich together with Coffee Butter Cream (see page 280), and either fork more butter cream on the top or decorate with nuts, or ice with Glacé Icing made with coffee (see page 279).

3 oz (90 g) butter
10 oz (300 g) self-raising flour
3 oz (90 g) soft brown sugar
Pinch of salt
2 tbsp coffee essence or 1 tbsp powdered instant coffee
2 eggs
2 tbsp warmed golden syrup
A little milk

Plain Coffee Cake

Line a 7 inch (17½ cm) cake tin. Rub the butter into the flour. Add sugar, salt and essence or powdered coffee. Add eggs, syrup and milk. Bake for 1 hour at 350°F/180°C/Gas Mark 4. If liked, split and fill with Coffee Butter Cream (see page 280).

6 oz (180 g) butter
6 oz (180 g) sugar
Rind of ½ lemon, grated
4 eggs
9 oz (270 g) flour

A Good Rich Birthday Cake

Line a 9-10 inch (22½-25 cm) tin. Put the butter into a basin, sieve the sugar on top, and beat these together with a wooden spoon until of a soft creamy consistency. Add the grated lemon rind, 1 egg, and a little of the flour, which has been sifted. Beat well for a few minutes. Then add the second egg and a little more flour, and so on, repeating the process until all the flour and eggs have been added. Beat all well together, lifting the mixture up in the spoon, in order to introduce air. Pour the mixture into the tin and bake at 350°F/180°C/Gas Mark 4 for about 1½ hours, or until the cake is well risen and feels firm to the touch. Turn out, and cool on a wire stand. Can be split when cold and filled with butter cream icing.

Seed Cake

½ lb (240 g) flour
Pinch of salt
1 tsp baking powder
¼ lb (120 g) margarine
¼ lb (120 g) sugar
1 oz (30 g) caraway seeds
2 eggs
3-4 tbsp milk

Very popular in the eighteenth century, but rarely made today as the flavour of caraway seeds is not so popular.

Thoroughly grease and flour a 5 inch (12½ cm) cake tin. Sieve the flour, salt and baking powder into a basin. Rub in the fat with the tips of the fingers until it resembles fine breadcrumbs. Add the sugar and caraway seeds and mix well. Make a well in the centre, stir in the beaten eggs and just sufficient milk to mix. Put into the prepared tin and bake at 400°F/200°C/Gas Mark 6 for 25 minutes or till firm to the touch.

Rich Madeira Cake

½ lb (240 g) butter
½ lb (240 g) sugar
4 eggs
½ lb (240 g) flour
1 tbsp baking powder
Pinch of salt
Grated rind of 1 lemon
1 tbsp lukewarm milk

Line a 7 inch (17½ cm) cake tin. Cream the butter and the sugar very well. Add the beaten eggs gradually. Sift the flour three times and add gradually with the baking powder and salt added. Put in the lemon rind. Work in the warm milk and bake for 1½ hours at 325°F/170°C/Gas Mark 3.

Ground Rice Cake

6 oz (180 g) cooking fat or butter
  or margarine
6 oz (180 g) sugar
3 eggs
5 oz (150 g) self-raising flour
3 oz (90 g) ground rice
Pinch of salt
Milk to mix

Line a 6-7 inch (15-17½ cm) cake tin. This cake has a delicious, slightly rough texture. Mix and bake as for Madeira Cake, adding the ground rice with the flour. Grated orange or lemon or grapefruit rind can be added if liked, or almond essence. Bake at 350°F/180°C/Gas Mark 4 for 1½ hours.

Orange Cake

½ lb (240 g) self-raising flour
Pinch of salt
¼ lb (120 g) margarine or butter
¼ lb (120 g) sugar
1 orange
2 eggs

Sieve the flour and salt together. Rub in the fat very lightly, using the tips of the fingers, until the mixture resembles breadcrumbs. Add the sugar and grated rind of the orange, then beat the eggs and add to the dry ingredients, together with enough juice to make a soft dough. Place the mixture in the prepared 7 inch (17½ cm) tin, and bake at 375°F/190°C/Gas Mark 5 for 1 to 1½ hours.

¼ lb (120 g) butter
¼ lb (120 g) caster sugar
2 eggs
2 oz (60 g) chopped walnuts
¼ lb (120 g) plain flour
2 oz (60 g) cocoa powder
1 tsp baking powder
Pinch of salt
Water to mix
Coffee Butter Cream
Glacé Icing made with coffee
A few walnuts, halved

Walnut Cake

Prepare a 7-8 inch (17½-20 cm) cake tin. Thoroughly cream together the butter and sugar, gradually add the beaten eggs. Add the nuts and sieve together the flour, cocoa, baking powder, and the salt and fold into the creamed mixture, adding sufficient water to give a dropping consistency. Bake at 375°F/190°C/Gas Mark 5 for 1 hour. Split and spread with Coffee Butter Cream (see page 280). Coat with Glacé Icing made with coffee (see page 279) and decorate with the walnuts.

¼ lb (120 g) shelled walnuts
½ lb (240 g) glacé pineapple
¾ lb (360 g) flour
½ lb (240 g) butter
½ lb (240 g) caster sugar
5 eggs
A little milk

Rich Pineapple and Walnut Cake

Line a 9 inch (22½ cm) cake tin. Chop the walnuts, but not finely. Cut the glacé pineapple into small pieces, and sieve the flour. Cream the butter, add the sugar, then the beaten eggs, and beat thoroughly. When the mixture has been well beaten, stir in the flour very lightly. Mix carefully, adding a little milk if necessary to bring it to the right consistency. Add the prepared walnuts and pineapple and bake at 300°F/150°C/Gas 2 for 1½ to 2 hours, until cooked. This cake may either be left plain or decorated with a coating of glacé icing, and pieces of thickly cut glacé pineapple on the top.

1½ lb (¾ kg) flour
½ lb (240 g) caster sugar
1 tsp cinnamon
1 tsp ginger
1 tsp bicarbonate of soda
Pinch of salt
½ lb (240 g) butter or margarine
6 oz (180 g) candied orange peel
1 orange
½ lb (240 g) golden syrup or
  treacle
3 eggs
Little milk or water, if necessary

Orange Gingerbread

Grease well a 9 inch (22½ cm) square tin. Sieve all the dry ingredients into a large basin, and rub in the fat with the tips of the fingers until it has the consistency of breadcrumbs. Add the orange peel cut in fine shreds along with the grated rind of the fresh orange and make a well in the centre. Warm syrup and pour in with the well-beaten eggs and the strained juice of the orange. Mix gradually from the centre outwards, until all the ingredients are thoroughly blended. The addition of a little milk or water may be necessary if the eggs are small, but the mixture should be of a consistency that will just drop from the spoon. Beat well for a few minutes, then pour the mixture into the well-greased tin, filling it no more than three-quarters full. Bake the gingerbread at 325°F/170°C/Gas Mark 3 for 1 hour or longer, until it is well risen and feels firm to the touch. Turn out on a wire rack and leave until quite cool. This will keep well if stored in a covered container.

Opposite: *Scottish Pancakes (see page 260)*

Above: *Queen of Puddings
(see page 226) and
Bread and Butter Pudding
(see page 225)*

Left: *Fruit (Apple) Hat
(see page 230)*

Opposite: *Fresh Fruit Salad
(see page 239) and
Chocolate Mousse (see page 235)*

Above: *Easter Biscuits
(see page 256) and Ginger
Biscuits (see page 256)*

Left: *Raisin Cake
(see page 268)*

Opposite: *Flapjacks (see
page 277) and Coffee
Kisses (see page 276)*

Above: *Green Tomato Chutney (see page 296) and Gooseberry Chutney (see page 297)*

Opposite: *Roast Turkey (see page 302)*

Old-fashioned Gingerbread

Grease a square 10 inch (25 cm) baking tin well and dust with flour. Sieve together flour, ground ginger, cinnamon and salt. Chop and add the dates. Put the treacle or syrup and margarine together in a pan over gentle heat, allow to melt and leave to cool slightly. Meanwhile beat together the egg and sugar. Add the melted fat and syrup to the flour alternately with the beaten egg and sugar. Lastly add the dissolved bicarbonate of soda and mix well to a soft consistency, adding a little water if necessary. Pour into the prepared tin and bake at 325°F/170°C/Gas Mark 3 for 1½ to 2 hours. Cool on a cake rack.

10 oz (300 g) flour
1 tsp ground ginger
½ tsp ground cinnamon
Pinch of salt
¼ lb (120 g) dates, chopped
5 oz (150 g) treacle or golden syrup
3 oz (90 g) margarine
1 egg
¼ lb (120 g) soft brown sugar
¾ tsp bicarbonate of soda, dissolved in 3 tsp of milk

Gingerbread

Grease a square 7 inch (17½ cm) sandwich tin thoroughly. Mix the flour, salt and spices together. Chop the peel and the dates and add them to the flour. Melt the fat, sugar and syrup with the milk and water in a saucepan, taking care not to boil them. Stir the warm liquid into the flour mixture and mix very thoroughly. Lastly, add the bicarbonate of soda dissolved in a little water. Pour into the greased tin, decorate with nuts or peel, and bake at 300°F/150°C/Gas Mark 2 for 1½ hours. If possible, keep a few days before cutting, as this will improve the flavour.

½ lb (240 g) flour
½ tsp salt
½ tsp cinnamon
1 tsp ginger
1 oz (30 g) candied peel
1 oz (30 g) dates
3 oz (90 g) margarine
2 oz (60 g) soft brown sugar
2 tbsp golden syrup
1 tbsp milk and water
1 tsp bicarbonate of soda
A few whole nuts or candied peel

Ginger Cake

Line a shallow 8 × 4 inch (20 × 10 cm) oblong tin. Cream the lard or margarine and sugar together, add the treacle and sour milk, then the bicarbonate of soda dissolved in the boiling water. Sift together the ginger, salt and flour and beat them into the mixture. Put in tin and bake at 325°F/170°C/Gas Mark 3 for 40 minutes.

6 oz (180 g) lard or margarine
½ lb (240 g) sugar
4 tbsp black treacle
¼ pt (150 ml) sour milk
1 tsp bicarbonate of soda
1 tbsp boiling water
2 tsp ground ginger
Pinch of salt
1 lb (½ kg) flour

Simple Sponge

Line a 6 inch (15 cm) tin. Break the eggs into a large bowl, add the sieved sugar, and whisk until the mixture is thick and creamy. Now add the sieved flour and fold in lightly with the whisk. Pour into the tin and bake at 375°F/190°C/Gas Mark 5 for the first 10 minutes, lowered to 350°F/180°C/Gas Mark 4 for 15 to 20 minutes. Invert the tin and leave to cool on a wire tray. Ease cake out gently, running a knife blade round the sides.

3 eggs
3 oz (90 g) sugar
3 oz (90 g) flour

Opposite: *Christmas Cake (see page 307), Mince Pies (see page 307) and Brandy Butter (see page 142)*

3 large eggs
¼ lb (120 g) caster sugar
3 oz (90 g) butter
2½ oz (75 g) flour
½ oz (15 g) cornflour

Genoese Sponge

Whisk the eggs and sugar in a basin over a saucepan of boiling water for about 20 minutes. Melt the butter and allow to become lukewarm. Add to the eggs with the sieved flour and cornflour, folding in very lightly. Pour into a 6-7 inch (15-17½ cm) baking tin lined with greased paper. Bake at 375°F/190°C/Gas Mark 5 for about 45 minutes.

This can be baked in an oblong tin or used for little cakes.

3 eggs
3 oz (90 g) sugar
3 oz (90 g) plain flour
1 tsp baking powder
2-3 tbsp hot water
Jam

Swiss Roll

Grease and line a shallow baking tin about 8×9 inches (20× 22½ cm). Put the eggs into a bowl with the sugar and 2 oz (60 g) of the flour, and whisk over boiling water. Continue whisking until the mixture is light and spongy and thick; this will take about 20 minutes. Remove from the heat and fold in the sieved flour and baking powder, adding hot water to keep the mixture slack enough. Put at once into the tin and bake in the top of a hot oven at 475°F/240°C/Gas Mark 9 for about 8-12 minutes, or until well risen, brown and firm to the touch. Turn upside down on a piece of sugared greaseproof paper and carefully strip off the paper lining. Trim off the crisp edges and spread with warm jam. Very carefully roll up.

Chocolate Log

Make Swiss Roll from previous recipe, spread with Chocolate Butter Cream (see page 280), mark with a fork to look like bark, dust with icing sugar and put a robin and some holly leaves on the top.

¼ lb (120 g) butter
¼ lb (120 g) caster sugar
½ tsp almond essence
¼ lb (120 g) flour
2 oz (60 g) cornflour
1 tsp baking powder
4 or 5 egg whites

Silver Cake

This is a good cake to make when there are whites of eggs left over from other cooking.

Grease an 8×4 inch (20×10 cm) cake tin and dust it with mixed sugar and flour. Put the butter into a warm basin with the sugar and almond essence, and beat them together with a wooden spoon to a soft, creamy consistency. Sieve the flour, cornflour, and baking powder, and add them alternately with the whites of eggs, which have been beaten to a stiff froth. Mix very lightly. Half fill the tin with the mixture, and bake at 350°F/180°C/Gas Mark 4 until well risen and firm to the touch, about 45 minutes.

Angel Food Cake

½ lb (240 g) caster sugar
¼ lb (120 g) flour
Pinch of salt
10 egg whites
1 tbsp mixed lemon juice and
    water
1 tsp vanilla essence
1 tsp cream of tartar

Grease a deep round 8 inch (20 cm) cake tin and sprinkle with mixed flour and sugar. Sift the sugar and flour. Add a quarter of the sugar to the flour with the salt and resift 3 times, holding the sieve high to incorporate as much air as possible. Beat the egg whites with the lemon juice and water and vanilla essence until frothy, then add cream of tartar and beat until stiff and fine in grain. Do not overbeat egg whites or they will become leathery. Beat in the remaining sugar, a tablespoon at a time, then gradually fold in the sifted flour and sugar very gently. Pour in the mixture, filling the tin not more than three-quarters full. Bake on middle shelf for ½ hour at 300°F/150°C/Gas Mark 2, then increase heat slightly for another ½ hour, covering top with paper to avoid browning. Leave in tin until cold.

Queen Cakes

3 oz (90 g) butter or margarine
3 oz (90 g) sugar
2 eggs
2 oz (60 g) currants or sultanas
Few drops of vanilla essence
5 oz (150 g) flour
1 tsp baking powder
1-2 tbsp milk to mix

Cream together the butter or margarine and sugar, and add the beaten eggs, a little at a time, beating all the time. Add the fruit and vanilla essence. Lightly fold in the sieved flour and baking powder and mix to a soft dropping consistency with the milk. Half fill some well-greased tins and bake at 350°F/180°C/Gas Mark 4 for about 15 minutes or until well risen, golden brown and firm to the touch.

Small Brown Bettys

2 oz (60 g) butter
3 oz (90 g) sugar
2 tsp golden syrup, warmed
1 egg
¼ lb (120 g) flour
1 tsp ground ginger

Beat the butter and sugar to a cream, and add melted syrup, then the beaten egg, and beat well. Add the flour and ginger gradually. Half fill well-greased patty tins and bake at 350°F/180°C/Gas Mark 4 for 15 to 20 minutes.

Raspberry Buns

¼ lb (120 g) butter or margarine
1 lb (½ kg) self-raising flour
3½ oz (105 g) caster sugar
Pinch of salt
1 egg
Raspberry jam
3 tbsp milk

Rub fat into flour. Add 3 oz (90 g) of the sugar, salt and well-beaten egg. Mix to a soft dough and turn on to a well-floured board, knead lightly till smooth. Roll out lightly and cut into 3 inch (7½ cm) rounds. Put a little jam in the middle, close up the edges and make into small balls. Place on a greased baking sheet and make a cross on the top of each with the back of a knife. Brush with milk, dredge with remaining caster sugar, and bake at 400°F/200°C/Gas Mark 6 for 20 minutes.

3 oz (90 g) margarine or butter
6 oz (180 g) self-raising flour
2 oz (60 g) caster sugar
1 egg yolk
1 tsp coffee essence, or powdered
    instant coffee and a little water
Coffee Butter Cream
Icing sugar for dredging

1 lb (½ kg) self-raising flour
¼ tsp salt
6 oz (180 g) margarine or butter,
    or cooking fat
¼ pt (150 ml) milk, plus extra for
    glazing
2 eggs
3 oz (90 g) sultanas
3 oz (90 g) sugar
Golden syrup, warmed, for
    glazing

½ lb (240 g) plain flour
Good pinch of salt
1 tsp baking powder
2 oz (60 g) margarine or butter
2 oz (60 g) caster sugar
2 oz (60 g) sultanas
1 oz (30 g) candied mixed peel
½ tsp grated lemon rind
1 egg
Milk to mix
1 egg beaten with a little sugar for
    glazing

1 egg
Its weight in shell in margarine or
    butter
Its weight in shell in sugar
Its weight in shell in self-raising
    flour
Pinch of salt

Coffee Kisses

Rub the fat into the flour, add the sugar. Mix to a stiff paste with the egg yolk and coffee. With your hand roll the mixture into balls the size of a small walnut and put these well apart on a greased baking sheet. Bake at 350°F/180°C/Gas Mark 4 for about 15 minutes. When cold, put two together with Coffee Butter Cream (see page 280), and dredge with icing sugar.

Chelsea Buns (without yeast)

Sieve together the flour and salt. Rub in the fat. Add milk to beaten eggs, make a hole in the centre of the flour and pour in. Mix to a smooth dough. Turn out on to a floured board and knead a little. Shape into an oblong and roll out into a long strip about ¼ inch (½ cm) thick. Sprinkle the fruit and sugar evenly over the surface, saving about a dessertspoon of the sugar to sprinkle on the tops of the buns before baking. Roll up firmly like a Swiss roll and cut into pieces about 1 inch (2½ cm) wide. Place on a greased baking sheet with the cut side up, and packed closely together to keep shape. Brush with a little milk and sprinkle with the remainder of the sugar. Bake for 15 minutes at 400°F/200°C/Gas Mark 6. When cool, break the separate buns apart and brush over with warmed golden syrup.

For recipe using yeast, see previous chapter.

Morning Buns

Mix together the flour, salt, and baking powder, rub in the margarine or butter, and add the sugar, sultanas, peel and lemon rind. Mix all these dry ingredients well together, then beat in the well-whisked egg and enough milk to form a light dough. Shape into small buns, brush over with beaten egg mixed with a little sugar and bake at 400°F/200°C/Gas Mark 6 for 15 to 20 minutes.

Madeleines

These are the standard small, plain cakes of France.

Grease small patty pans (in France long shell-shaped ones are used). Cream fat and sugar, add egg alternately with the flour and salt. Half fill the tins with the mixture, and bake for 10 to 15 minutes at 400°F/200C/Gas Mark 6. Allow to cool for 10 minutes and then turn out onto a wire rack. Makes about 12.

Rock Cakes

Rub fat into flour, add sugar, salt, grated rind and fruit, and mix with eggs and milk. It should be stiff enough to stay in little rocky heaps on a greased baking tin. Bake for 15 minutes at 400°F/200°C/ Gas Mark 6. Ginger and chopped dates is a delicious variation.

3 oz (90 g) butter or margarine
½ lb (240 g) self-raising flour
3 oz (90 g) sugar
Pinch of salt
Grated orange or lemon rind
*3 oz (90 g) mixed currants and
    sultanas*
2 eggs
Milk to mix

Doughnuts (without yeast)

Sieve the flour, salt and baking powder into a bowl and rub in the fat. Add the sugar and mix to a stiff paste with the well-beaten eggs and milk. Roll out to ¼ inch (½ cm) in thickness, cut into rings. Use large cutter and cut out centres with a smaller one. Roll out leftover centres to cut second batch. Fry to a golden brown in deep and very hot fat. Drain, then lightly roll on sugared paper. (For recipe with yeast see previous chapter).

1 lb (½ kg) plain flour
1 tsp salt
2 tsp baking powder
2 oz (60 g) cooking fat
2 oz (60 g) sugar
2 eggs
⅓-½ pt (200-300 ml) milk
Fat for deep-frying
Caster sugar for coating

Flapjacks

Cream fat and sugar, add golden syrup or treacle, and work in the oats, sprinkled with salt and ground ginger. When well blended, turn into a greased 8 inch (20 cm) sandwich tin. Flatten and spread mixture evenly with palette knife. Bake at 400°F/200°C/Gas Mark 6 for 15 to 20 minutes. While still warm, mark into sections and break apart when cold. If the mixture has set too hard to mark, replace in warm oven for a minute, then cut through.

3 oz (90 g) margarine or butter
*3 oz (90 g) white or soft brown
    sugar*
1 tbsp golden syrup or treacle
¼ lb (120 g) flaked oats
Pinch of salt
½ level tsp ground ginger

Yorkshire Parkin

Mix all the first 5 ingredients together. Warm the treacle and butter together and dissolve the bicarbonate of soda in the slightly warm milk and mix all well together. Grease a flat tin and bake at 325°F/170°C/Gas Mark 3 for ¾ hour or until it is just firm to the touch. Cut in squares when cold.

½ lb (240 g) medium oatmeal
¼ lb (120 g) flour
½ tbsp sugar
Pinch of ground ginger
Pinch of salt
9 oz (270 g) treacle
3 oz (90 g) butter
½ tsp bicarbonate of soda
3 tbsp lukewarm milk

Date Slices

Rub fat into flour, add everything else, mix well to a soft dough, lightly spread in baking tin and bake for 25 minutes at 350°F/ 180°C/Gas Mark 4. Cut in slices when cold.

1 oz (30 g) butter or margarine
3 oz (90 g) self-raising flour
5 oz (150 g) chopped dates
¼ lb (120 g) sugar
1 egg, beaten
A little milk

¼ lb (120 g) golden syrup
¼ lb (120 g) margarine or butter
3 oz (90 g) caster sugar
3 ½ oz (105 g) flour
Whipped cream for serving

Brandy Snaps

Melt the syrup, fat and sugar together, remove from the heat, stir in the flour gradually and mix well together. Drop the mixture on to a baking sheet by teaspoonfuls. Give plenty of room for the mixture to run. Bake at 400°F/200°C/Gas Mark 6 for 3 to 4 minutes, until brown. Take off with a knife and, when beginning to get crisp, roll up. If they get too crisp to roll up, put back in the oven for a minute and try again.

Brandy snaps should be filled with whipped cream.

6 oz (180 g) plain flour
Good pinch of salt
1 heaped tsp baking powder
¼ lb (120 g) shelled nuts –
*   walnuts, blanched almonds, or*
*   hazelnuts*
1 egg
3 oz (90 g) sugar
3 tbsp milk

Nut Buns

Mix the flour, salt and baking powder, and sieve them. Chop the nuts finely. Break the egg into a basin and beat it well. Stir in the sugar, then the milk and add the flour mixture gradually. Stir well all the time and be very careful to keep the mixture smooth. Beat in the nuts. Half fill greased patty pans with the mixture and bake for 15 minutes at 400°F/200°C/Gas Mark 6.

These can be served plain or they are also very good cut in halves and buttered.

½ lb (240 g) flour
6 oz (180 g) caster sugar
½ tsp baking powder
Grated rind of 1 orange
Pinch of salt
¼ lb (120 g) butter or margarine
1 egg

Orange Buns

Mix together the flour, sugar, baking powder, grated orange rind, and a pinch of salt. Melt the butter and stir it in. Add the well-beaten egg and mix thoroughly. Form into little balls, place them on a well-greased baking tin, with space between them as they will spread. Bake for 15 to 20 minutes in a moderate oven at 325°F/170°C/Gas Mark 3.

Very good iced with Glacé Icing made with orange (page 279).

Icings and Fillings

Icing a cake is a pleasant, creative and festive job. If possible, plenty of time should be allowed, so that the icing syringe, the different funnel ends and the consistency of the icing, can all be tried out before you start on the cake. Your cake will look much better if you work out a design before starting and roughly measure the distances between rosettes or loops of icing and the spacing of your lettering.

Remember that for butter creams and fillings, salted butter will spoil the flavour. Slightly salted is fairly satisfactory but unsalted is well worth buying specially. Butter gives a much better flavour and consistency than margarine.

To smooth over icing that is inclined to dry out, have a tall jug of boiling water standing near you with two stainless steel table knives or palette knives standing up in it, blades down. Use them alternately to smooth the icing so that the one you use is always very hot. Shake the surplus water from the knife as you take it from the jug.

Uncooked Icing

For a 6-7 in (15-17½ cm) cake
¼ lb (120 g) icing sugar
Few drops of lemon juice
1 tbsp water
Colouring, if desired

This is the quickest of all icings to make. Sieve the icing sugar into a bowl, stir in the lemon juice, then add the water a few drops at a time, until the mixture is just thick enough to coat the back of a spoon. Lastly add any colouring and beat well.

Glacé Icing

For a 6-7 in (15-17½ cm) cake
¼ lb (120 g) icing sugar
1 tbsp water
1 tsp lemon juice

A soft icing to be put directly on the cake. It can be flavoured with coffee essence, grated chocolate, almond essence, orange juice, etc., instead of lemon juice.

Sieve the icing sugar into a saucepan in which you have already put the water and lemon juice. Stir it over a low heat, holding it just above the heat, until the sugar is melted and the temperature is just above blood heat. Pour it over the cake and allow it to run down the sides, smoothing it with a hot knife.

Royal Icing

For a 9-10 in (22½-25 cm) cake
1 lb (½ kg) icing sugar
1 dessertsp lemon juice
2 egg whites

This is the icing to use for the final coating and for piped decorations. Sieve the icing sugar, making sure that it is quite free from lumps and lying slightly fluffed in the bowl. Stir in the lemon juice. Whip the egg whites to a medium stiffness, not until they will stand in peaks. Stir in gently, and then beat with a wooden spoon till you have a perfectly smooth, very white cream. If there is any delay before using, cover the bowl with a damp tea towel tightly stretched across the top to prevent air entering and hardening the icing. If icing seems too thin, more sugar may be beaten in. The icing may be put in a bowl and colouring beaten into it.

Fondant Icing

For a 6-7 in (15-17½ cm) cake
3 tbsp water
6 oz (180 g) caster sugar
¼ tsp cream of tartar
1 egg white

You need a sugar thermometer for this kind of icing.

Put the water in a saucepan, rinsing it up the sides. Add sugar and cream of tartar and dissolve over low heat. When dissolved, bring to boiling point, 240°F (115°C), and boil without stirring for 3 minutes or until a thread forms from a spoon, 255-260°F (124-127°C). Leave to cool slightly and beat the egg white stiffly. Pour the sugar syrup in a thin, slow stream over the egg white. Beat until it starts to thicken. Pour quickly over cake.

For a 9-10 in (22½-25 cm) cake
*3 oz (90 g) plain or bitter
   chocolate, grated
1½ tbsp water
1 tsp unsalted butter
A few drops vanilla essence
½ lb (240 g) icing sugar*

Chocolate Icing

Put the chocolate, water and butter into a saucepan and melt together until smooth, then allow to cool a little. Add the vanilla and sifted icing sugar and beat well. If the icing gets cold, place in a saucepan of warm water and beat again until smooth and of a coating consistency. Spread over cake with a hot, wet knife.

For a 9-10 in (22½-25 cm) cake
*6 oz (180 g) sugar
2 tbsp boiling water
1 dessertsp golden syrup
1 tsp lemon juice
2 egg whites*

Boiled Frosting

This icing is very good, but is much easier to make if you have a sugar thermometer.

Boil sugar, water, syrup and lemon together to 240°F (115°C) or until a ball forms when dropped in cold water. Do not stir while boiling or it will crystallize. Beat egg whites until stiff, then pour over them the boiling syrup in a thin, slow stream, beating all the time. Continue beating for 7 to 8 minutes, or until cool and easy to spread.

For a 6-7 in (15-17½ cm) cake
*3 oz (90 g) butter or margarine
6 oz (180 g) icing sugar, sieved
1 tsp coffee essence, or 2 tsp cocoa
   or chocolate powder*

Chocolate or Coffee Butter Cream Filling

Cream the butter or margarine, adding the sugar greadually. Beat till smooth and creamy, then add the flavouring.

Chopped nuts or cherries may be stirred into the filling for variety.

For a 6-7 in (15-17½ cm) cake
*1½ oz (45 g) plain chocolate
3 oz (90 g) unsalted butter
6 oz (180 g) icing sugar*

Rich Chocolate Butter Cream

Melt chocolate in a tablespoon of water, over low heat and cool a little. Cream butter with sieved icing sugar and when creamy, beat in the soft chocolate. Can be used as a filling or on top of cake.

For a 6-7 in (15-17½ cm) cake
*¼ lb (120 g) soft brown sugar
2 oz (60 g) unsalted butter
1 tsp coffee essence
1 tbsp golden syrup
1 tbsp milk*

Fudge Filling

Bring all the ingredients slowly to the boil and stir all the time while gently simmering for 10 minutes. Remove from heat and allow to cool for 10 minutes. Then beat until thick and creamy. When quite cold use to fill cake.

Excellent when chopped nuts are added.

JAM MAKING

Jams and Jellies

Before you start, see that you have plenty of jars of the sizes you prefer and that they are really clean and dry. Also that you have the necessary covers. Remember:

1 Always have your clean, dry jars hot. Either fill with boiling water and drain them on a dish rack or stand them in your oven warming drawer or put them in your oven at its lowest temperature until warm to the touch.

2 Each jar must have a fitting waxed circle pressed gently on to the jam and, over it, an air-excluding cover which fits over the top of the jar securely with a rubber band.

When you make jam, you are trying to prevent fermentation and mildew. These develop if the jam gets moist and air can get to it, and if it is very acid. Therefore by boiling with plenty of sugar, you remove moisture and acid, producing a sugar syrup which is sterilized by the boiling.

However, your jam must set or jell. A combination of pectin, acid and sugar produces this. All fruits contain pectin, but some more and some less. Fruits with plenty of pectin set well with plenty of sugar, but those with less do not. You cannot, however, use too little sugar or the jam will be too acid and will not keep for that reason. Therefore, follow quantities in recipes exactly, and use perfectly ripe or just underripe fruit. All overripe fruit contains less pectin.

With fruits that have a low pectin content, you make up for this in one of three ways:

1 Various pectin preparations can be bought and added according to directions.

2 Low pectin-content fruits may be mixed with others which have a high content; such as strawberry and gooseberry, blackberry and apple, etc.

3 A small quantity of juice or syrup from a fruit which has a very high pectin content may be added to your main jam fruit. Redcurrant is usually chosen because it does not spoil the colour of jams and does not alter the flavour, except to give it a little sharpness. In very sweet jams, such as strawberry and raspberry, this is an advantage. Three recipes are given using redcurrant syrup in the following section.

Blackcurrants are a special case. The skins are tough, so for jam it is best to boil them for some time before adding the sugar. Also, they are so rich in pectin that they can take 1¼ lb (600 g) of sugar to 1 lb (½ kg) of fruit and still set readily and firmly. All other fruits only take ¾-1 lb (360 g-½ kg) of sugar to each 1 lb (½ kg) of fruit, as you will see from the following recipes.

Lemon juice also helps fruits weak in pectin to set.

Fruits with a high pectin content, which set easily and firmly:

Apples	Gooseberries	Raspberries
Currants	Plums	Gages
Apricots		

Fruits with a low pectin content, which need help with setting:

Cherries	Strawberries	Blackberries

Hard fruits, such as plums, greengages, apricots and apples are boiled with a small quantity of water until soft before the sugar is added. Berries do not need extra water and are only brought to the boil, before adding sugar.

Preserving Pan

You can of course make jam in a large, thick saucepan. However, if you are going to make jam regularly, a preserving pan is much better than a saucepan. The wider, shallower shape distributes the heat better and more quickly. The fruit and sugar should leave not less than 2 to 3 inches (5-7½ cm) above it to the top of the pan to allow for rapid boiling. If you have an old copper preserving pan, be sure that the inside tinning is not worn through and that there is no sign of verdigris. Modern preserving pans are generally made of aluminium. In any case, rinse well before using.

Skimming

Almost all fruit forms a scum when being boiled with sugar. This can be lightly and carefully skimmed off into saucers and eaten immediately it is cold, when it is liquid underneath and fluffy on top. It will not keep, but is delicious and a great pleasure to children. It does, on the other hand, waste some of the jam, and all the scum need not be removed as a little does not affect appearance or keeping quality when the jam is put into jars.

Testing for Setting

The best way is the simplest. Stir the jam. Take a small spoonful from the centre of the pan and drop on a cold plate or saucer. Leave for a minute or two in a cool place while you continue stirring the jam over the heat – or if you are almost sure the jam is done, move it to side of the stove and wait, so that it will not overcook. If the jam on the saucer has skinned over and does not run freely when you tip the saucer, it is done. If it remains shiny and unskinned and runs freely, go on boiling, and test again after another 3 to 5 minutes.

Recipes

Apricot Jam (Fresh Fruit)

6 lb (3 kg) apricots
5 lb (2 ½ kg) sugar
1 ½ pt (900 ml) water
¼-½ lb (120-240 g) almonds
 (optional)

Cut the apricots in halves, and remove the stones. Break a few of the stones by hitting lightly with a hammer, remove the kernels and reserve. Put the sugar and water in a preserving pan, and stir over gentle heat until the sugar has dissolved. Boil quickly for 10 minutes, then add the fruit and boil until it sets when tested. Add a few of the kernels when the jam is nearly done. Turn into hot dry jars, seal and tie down. Add ¼ to ½ lb (120-240 g) almonds, blanched and halved, if liked, with the kernels.

Apricot Jam (Dried Fruit)

2 lb (1 kg) dried apricots
8 pt (4 l) water
2 oz (60 g) almonds
2 lemons
7 lb (3 ½ kg) sugar

Boil the water and leave it until cold. Wash the apricots well, put them in a bowl with the cold water and leave until next day. Blanch the almonds and cut them in halves. Grate the rind of the lemons and reserve. Put the apricots in a preserving pan with the water in which they were soaked, and boil gently until tender. Then add the grated lemon rind, the strained juice of the lemons and the sugar. Boil gently until it sets when tested. Add the almonds, stir and pour into hot dry jars, seal and tie down.

Damson Jam

4 lb (2 kg) ripe damsons
3 tbsp vinegar
4 lb (2 kg) sugar
¼ pt (150 ml) water

Put the vinegar, sugar and water into pan, and boil until the sugar dissolves; then put in the fruit and boil for 10 minutes. Pour into hot dry jars, seal and tie down.

Blackcurrant Jam

To every 1½ lb (¾ kg) blackcurrants
1 pt (600 ml) water
3 lb (1½ kg) sugar

Stalk and cut brown ends off fruit. Boil fruit and water together for 20 minutes, then add the sugar and boil for 5 minutes. Test. Put into hot dry jars, seal and tie down at once if it sets, or boil another 5 minutes and test again.

Blackberry and Apple Jam

3½ lb (1¾ kg) apples (windfalls will do)
2 lb (1 kg) blackberries
4 lb (2 kg) sugar

Peel, core and cut apples into thin slices and put in preserving pan with ½ pint (300 ml) of water. Let them simmer until tender; then add blackberries and boil together for 5 minutes before adding sugar. Bring to the boil and boil well for 25 to 30 minutes. Test and, if ready, pour into hot dry jars, seal and tie down.

Greengage Jam

4 lb (2 kg) greengages
1 pt (600 ml) water
4 lb (2 kg) sugar

Wash the greengages, and cut in half to remove the stones. Split some of the stones and remove kernels. Put them together with the fruit into a pan with the water. Bring to the boil, and simmer until the greengages are tender. This should take about 30 minutes. Add sugar, stirring until dissolved, and bring again to the boil. Boil rapidly for 15 minutes, then test. When ready, pour into hot dry jars, seal and tie down.

Green Gooseberry Jam

6 lb (3 kg) unripe gooseberries
3 pt (1½ l) water
9 lb (4½ kg) sugar

The fruit for this jam should be quite large but unripe.

Top and tail the gooseberries. Put the sugar in a preserving pan with 3 pints (1½ l) of cold water and bring to the boil. Boil quickly for ½ hour. Add the fruit, bring again to the boil, skim and boil steadily until it sets when tested, about ½ hour. Pour into hot dry jars, seal and tie down.

Red or Yellow Plum Jam

6 lb (3 kg) plums
½ pt (300 ml) water
5 lb (2½ kg) sugar

The plums must not be fully ripe. They should be hard and firm but beginning to turn colour. Victoria or egg plums are suitable, or greengages.

Remove the stalks. Cut the plums in halves and remove the stones. Then put the fruit in a preserving pan with the water and boil gently until they are tender. Meanwhile, warm the sugar in a low oven and add it when the fruit is tender and stir until it has dissolved. Then boil until the preserve sets when tested. Pour into hot dry jars, seal and tie down.

Raspberry Jam

4 lb (2 kg) raspberries
1 tbsp water
3½ lb (1¾ kg) sugar

Hull the berries, and put them into a preserving pan with a tablespoon of water to moisten them, place over gentle heat and cook slowly until the fruit is quite soft. Then add the warmed sugar, bring to the boil quickly and then boil fast for 8 minutes only – if overboiled the pectin is destroyed and it will not set. Pour into hot dry jars, seal and tie down.

Unboiled Raspberry Jam

4 lb (2 kg) raspberries, hulled
5 lb (2½ kg) sugar (must be caster)

Place the raspberries in a large dish and put into a 400°F/200°C/ Gas Mark 6 oven. Then place the sugar in another large dish and put that also into the oven. When they are very hot (not boiling), beat the fruit thoroughly, in a large bowl, then gradually add the hot sugar, beating well together until the sugar is dissolved. Then put at once into hot dry jars, seal and tie down.

This jam will keep any length of time, and has the full flavour of the fresh fruit. It should be a light coral-red in colour.

Strawberry Jam

Small, firm strawberries or wild strawberries or alpine strawberries, hulled
Sugar

Put equal weight of sugar and berries into an earthenware bowl. Stir gently, so as not to bruise the berries, until they are coated with sugar. Put aside for 24 hours. Pour off sugary juice that has come from berries. Place over medium heat and bring to the boil. Boil gently for 3 to 4 minutes. Remove from heat. Skim. Place berries in small hot jars. Replace syrup over heat and boil gently until spoon is thickly coated. Fill up hot dry jars of berries, seal and tie down. Though it may not set, this is the best strawberry jam in the world.

Damson Cheese

Ripe damsons
1 lb (½ kg) sugar to each 1 pint (600 ml) of pulp

Put some sound ripe fruit into a casserole, cover it, and bake in a 250°F/120°C/Gas Mark ½ oven until the damsons are tender. Then drain off the juice, skin and stone the cooled fruit and beat with a wooden spoon to form a smooth pulp. Add 1 lb (450 g) sugar to each pint (600 ml) of this pulp. Boil together, in thick pan, stirring furiously as it is apt to stick, for 10 minutes, then test for setting, and boil again if necessary. This makes a very firm cheese of a rich dark red, which can be cut in slices, and is excellent with all cold meats.

2 lemons
½ lb (240 g) sugar
5 oz (150 g) butter
2 eggs

Lemon Cheese

Peel the lemons as thinly as possible, and squeeze out the juice. Put both the rind and the juice in a saucepan with the sugar and butter and dissolve very slowly. Beat up the eggs, then stir the lemon, etc., into them. Strain, return to the pan, and stir over a low heat until the mixture comes to the boil and is thick and creamy. It is best to use a double saucepan or to stir in a bowl standing over the saucepan of simmering water. Pour into a hot, dry jar, seal and tie down. This makes a rich, delicious lemon cheese which keeps well.

2 lemons
1 oz (30 g) butter
½ lb (240 g) sugar
2 eggs

Lemon Curd

Put the grated rind and juice of lemons, butter and sugar either into a double saucepan, or a basin or stone jam jar, and stand in a saucepan half full of boiling water. While this is getting hot, beat the eggs. Stir into other ingredients and cook till thick. This takes about ½ hour. Never let the mixture boil. Pour into a hot dry, jar, seal and tie down.

Marmalades

An electric food processor slices the fruit evenly at the thickness required and, of course, does it in a moment compared with the ½ hour or so that it takes to do it by hand.

8 seville oranges
2 large sweet oranges
2 lemons
10 pt (5 l) water
10 lb (5 kg) preserving sugar

A Good Ordinary Marmalade

Cut all the fruit across into halves, and squeeze out the juice. Put the pips in a jug with a pint (600 ml) of cold water and leave until the following day. Add the juice to the water. Meanwhile, cut the half fruit cases in pieces and put them twice through a mincing machine, using the finest plate, or a food processor. Put the fruit with the juice and the remaining water and leave to soak for 24 hours. Then turn it into a preserving pan, strain in the water from the pips. Bring to the boil and boil gently for 2 hours. Add sugar and boil until the marmalade sets when tested, after about 30 minutes. Pour into hot dry jars, seal and tie down.

Thick Coarse-Cut Marmalade

1 lb (½ kg) Seville oranges, or 2 good-sized Seville oranges and 1 sweet one
2 pt (1 l) of water
2 lb (1 kg) demerara sugar
1 tsp lemon juice

Wash oranges, put whole into a pan with the water. Put on lid and simmer gently until oranges are so soft that a spoon will squash them easily. Remove fruit from pan, cut up into chunks. Save all pips, return these to liquid in the pan and simmer gently for 10 minutes. Strain off pips, then return liquid, fruit, sugar and lemon juice to preserving pan. Stir over a gentle heat until sugar has quite dissolved, then boil rapidly until it sets when tested – probably 15 minutes.

When marmalade is ready, allow to cool. Stir briskly to distribute peel, then pour into hot dry jars, seal and tie down.

Jellied Marmalade

8 Seville oranges
2 sweet oranges
2 lemons
3 pt (1 ½ l) water
About 4 lb (2 kg) sugar

Use 1 sweet orange and 1 lemon to every 4 Seville oranges. Allow roughly 1 pint (600 ml) of water to every pound (½ kg) of fruit.

Grate off only the rind of the fruit. Remove all the white pith. Slice the pulp and put it into a preserving pan with the water. Boil for ½ hour. Stir occasionally. Strain through a hair sieve or clean scalded muslin. Measure the liquid, and allow 1 lb (½ kg) of sugar to each pint (600 ml). Put the juice and sugar into a pan. Add the grated rinds of fruit. Stir until the sugar has dissolved. Boil fast from 10 to 15 minutes or until the mixture jellies when tested. Keep skimmed. You will have a quite clear jelly with tiny flecks of golden rind in it. Pour into hot dry jars, seal and tie down.

Mixed Marmalade

8 sweet oranges
2 large grapefruit
2 lemons
10 pt (5 l) water
7 lb (3 ½ kg) sugar

Remove the juice and pips from the fruit. Put the fruit through the mincer or food processor and soak it with the juice and water for 48 hours. Tie up pips in muslin and add to the mixture.

After soaking, boil until the fruit is tender (about 2 hours). Remove the bag of pips and add the sugar; boil fast until marmalade sets. Pour into hot dry jars, seal and tie down.

Grapefruit Marmalade

3 lb (1 ½ kg) grapefruit
1 pt (600 ml) boiling water
2 small lemons
3 ½ pt (2 ¼ l) cold water
7 ½ lb (3 ¾ kg) sugar

Slice the grapefruit finely, place the lemon and grapefruit pips in 1 pint (600 ml) of boiling water, and soak. Grate the rind from the lemons and peel away the pith. Add the grated rind and the inside of the lemons, finely chopped, to the grapefruit, and cover with the cold water. Stand for about 24 hours. Place in the preserving pan with the water strained from the pips and simmer for ½ hour. Be very careful not to let it boil. Then add the sugar and bring to the boil. Boil rapidly for about 1 hour, or until it sets when tested. Pour into hot dry jars. Seal and tie down when cold.

12 large lemons
1 pt (600 ml) water to every 1 lb
(½ kg) fruit
1 lb (½ kg) sugar to every 1 lb
(½ kg) fruit

Lemon Marmalade

Wash the lemons and put them in a preserving pan with enough water to cover them well, and boil them gently until they are quite tender. Let them cool, then take out the lemons and cut them in the thinnest possible slices, removing all the pips, or take out all the pips and put the fruit through a mincer or food processor. Put the sliced lemons in the preserving pan with a pint (600 ml) of the water in which the lemons were boiled and 1 lb (½ kg) of sugar to every pound (½ kg) of fruit.

If the water in which the lemons were boiled is not sufficient, make up with plain water. Boil gently until the marmalade sets when tested (about 1 hour). Pour into hot dry jars, seal and tie down.

Jelly Making

Unless you use extra pectin – either bought or prepared from redcurrant syrup as described earlier – you must have a fruit with a high pectin content to make jelly or you will only succeed in producing a runny syrup.

Apple	Redcurrant	Blackcurrant
Gooseberry	Raspberry	Blackberry (with Apple)

are the best and easiest jellies to make.

You wash your fruit and add water to come a third of the way up the quantity of fruit when it is in the pan. You need not top and tail gooseberries nor stalk currants for jelly. Simmer gently (without sugar) until the fruit is quite soft and there is as much liquid as possible. Then pour into your jelly bag.

If you do not want to buy a proper jelly bag you must buy about 3 yards (1 metre) of butter muslin. Turn a stool or a chair upside down – if a chair, rest the seat on another. Tie the muslin folded in four thicknesses to each leg with string, so that it hangs in a loose bag between the legs. Put a large bowl underneath. Pour the fruit into the muslin and leave to drip several hours or overnight. Press gently on fruit with a wooden spoon occasionally. When nothing but dryish pulp is left in the bag throw the pulp away. You can wash out the muslin or bag and use it again.

Measure the juice in a jug marked with liquid measures. To each pint (600 ml) of juice add 1 lb (½ kg) of sugar (except in recipes which call for more) in preserving pan. Bring to the boil and boil quickly for 10 to 20 minutes, testing for setting on cold saucer from time to time. As soon as it sets, pour it into hot dry jars, but do not cover until it is cool.

If, by unfortunate chance, you find that when cool, your jelly is not as firm as you would like, you can stand the jars in hot water and heat gently, until the jelly pours out freely, tip it back in the preserving pan and bring to the boil again and boil a further 5 minutes and test. (If you boil too much, however, the sugar may crystallize.) This reboiling is not advisable and should never be necessary if instructions are carefully followed, but things do go wrong for everyone sometimes and it is worth knowing about second chances.

Apple Jelly

Small windfall apples
1 lb (½ kg) sugar to each pint (600 ml) of juice
Lemons or cloves

Small windfall apples will do for this jelly. Put apples in preserving pan, and barely cover with water. Boil till pulpy. Then strain all night through a jelly bag. To every pint (600 ml) of juice add 1 lb (½ kg) preserving sugar. About ½ hour of rapid boiling is necessary. Test on cold plate to see if it sets readily. Pour into hot dry jars. When cool, seal and tie down.

Flavour with juice and rind of 1 lemon to every 2 lb (1 kg) of pulp or 2 cloves to every pint (600 ml) of juice. Add together with the sugar and remove cloves or rind while testing to see if it sets.

Blackcurrant Jelly

4 lb (2 kg) ripe blackcurrants
1½ pt (900 ml) water
Sugar

Wash fruit. Put into preserving pan, add water and simmer till soft. Stir well. Strain through jelly bag and allow to drip overnight.

Measure, and to each pint (600 ml) allow 1 lb (½ kg) sugar. Heat juice, dissolve sugar in it, and boil rapidly until the syrup sets when tested. Skim if liked and quickly pour into hot, dry jars. When cool, seal and tie down.

Bramble Jelly

6 lb (3 kg) blackberries (or more)
2 lemons
1 lb (½ kg) preserving sugar to each pint (600 ml) juice

Put fruit into a preserving pan and cover with water. Add rind cut thin from 2 lemons. Bring to the boil, and then simmer very slowly until all the juice is extracted from the fruit; strain through a jelly bag. Next day, put the juice in the pan, add strained juice of 2 lemons and 1 lb (½ kg) of sugar to each pint (600 ml) of juice and boil rapidly for 30 minutes, or until it jells when tested. Put into hot dry jars. When cool, seal and tie down.

Gooseberry Jelly

8 lb (4 kg) fully grown but unripe gooseberries
¼ pt (150 ml) water
¾ lb (360 g) sugar to every pint (600 ml) juice

Wash the gooseberries and put them wet into a preserving pan, add a ¼ pint (150 ml) of water and simmer until they are quite soft. They will need stirring at first to prevent burning. Put the fruit in a jelly bag and leave until the juice has ceased to drip.

Measure the juice, put it into a preserving pan with ¾ lb (360 g) of sugar to every pint (600 ml) and boil rather quickly until it sets when tested. Pour into hot dry jars. When cool, seal and tie down.

4 lb (2 kg) ripe fruit
1 ½ pt (900 ml) water
1 ¼ lb (600 g) to each pint
*   (600 ml) juice*

Redcurrant Jelly

Wash fruit and simmer in water in preserving pan for about
½ hour, or till fruit is quite soft. Strain through jelly bag, leaving
overnight.

To each pint (600 ml) of juice add 1¼ lb (600 g) sugar. Bring to
the boil and boil for 3 minutes only. Skim and pour into hot, dry
jars as quickly as possible. When cool, seal and tie down.

This is a very well-flavoured, firm jelly. Good with mutton.

4 lb (2 kg) cooking apples
12 good sprigs mints
1 lb (½ kg) preserving sugar to
*   every 1 pint (600 ml) juice*

Mint Jelly (from Apples)

Wash the apples, and cut them in small pieces, but do not peel or
core them. Put them in preserving pan with enough water to cover
and simmer until they are quite soft. Do not stir them. When soft,
turn into jelly bag and leave until they have ceased to drip. Then
put the juice into a stewpan. Bruise the mint and add it, stalks as
well as leaves. Simmer for 10 minutes and then remove the mint.
Strain the juice, measure it, and put it into a preserving pan with
the sugar and boil until it sets when tested. Remove scum, pour
into small, hot dry jars. When cold, seal and tie down.

3-3 ½ lb (1 ½-1 ¾ kg)
*   redcurrants*

Redcurrant Juice

To make ½ pint (300 ml) of redcurrant juice.

Stalk about 3 lb (1½ kg) of very ripe redcurrants into a 2 lb (1 kg)
glass preserving jar, by pulling berries off stems with a fork. Stand
full jar in warm water, bring water to boil and let it boil round it.
Pour off juice from currants from time to time through fine strainer
or muslin, until there is about ½ pint (300 ml).

6 lb (3 kg) Morello cherries
½ pt (300 ml) Redcurrant Juice
6 lb (3 kg) sugar

Cherry Jam

Cherries have a low pectin content and cherry jam is very difficult
to set without the redcurrant juice which is very high in pectin and
improves colour and flavour. Wash the cherries, if necessary, and
remove the stalks. Put them in a preserving pan with a little water
and cook gently until they are quite soft. Turn into a bowl and
leave until cold. Then take out the stones, crack about 3 dozen of
them and blanch the kernels. Put the redcurrant juice in a preserving pan with the sugar and stir over gentle heat until sugar has
dissolved, bring to the boil, then add the cherries and boil until it
sets when tested. Add the kernels when the mixture is almost set.
Pour into hot dry jars, seal and tie down.

Raspberry Jam

6 lb (3 kg) raspberries, hulled
½ pt (300 ml) Reducurrant Juice
5 lb (2 ½ kg) preserving sugar

When making raspberry jam you will find, if you add redcurrant juice in the above proportion, you will have not only a better flavoured but a better coloured jam. Put the raspberries in a preserving pan with the redcurrant juice, bring slowly to the boil and boil for 5 minutes. Add the sugar, stir until it has dissolved, then boil until it sets when tested. Pour into hot dry jars, seal and tie down.

Whole Fruit Strawberry Jam

4 lb (2 kg) strawberries (use the smallest berries)
½ pt (300 ml) Redcurrant juice
4 lb (2 kg) sugar

Hull strawberries. Put juice into preserving pan with sugar and stir over low heat until sugar is dissolved. Simmer gently for 5 minutes. Add strawberries, a handful at a time, scattering them in, so that they do not form a mass. Boil gently till juice jellies when tested. Pour into hot dry jars distributing the whole berries among the jars, seal and tie down.

PICKLES AND CHUTNEYS

General Notes

The principle behind all pickling is that the meat, vegetables, or fruit concerned are preserved in brine or vinegar, seasoned and spiced.

A general recipe for a pickle suitable for most vegetables, using vinegar, is given below:

For pickling in brine only, ¼ lb (120 g) salt is dissolved in 1 pint (600 ml) of water.

Pickles are best put up in wide-mouthed jars – any clean, dry jars are suitable – so that the vegetables can be easily got out with a fork. They must be carefully sealed exactly in the same way as jam.

Chutneys are really a form of savoury jam made with fruits cooked with vinegar and spices. Keep in clean, dry, heatproof jars.

Bottled sauces are usually made in much the same way as chutneys, but are strained so that they are smooth.

All pickles and chutneys are very easy to make at home and, if you have a garden, are a particularly good way of using up surplus vegetables.

You will find that some of the recipes which follow call for ingredients which you probably do not usually have on your shelves. Some of them can be more easily obtained from a chemist than a supermarket. They are not always essential in the recipes in which they occur, but it is a pity to omit them, as they are put in to improve flavour and keeping quality. These special ingredients are listed below, so that you can check whether any of them occur in the recipe you are going to make.

Special pickling ingredients:

Allspice	Chillies – dried	Thyme (fresh or dried)
Cayenne Pepper	Nutmeg	Parsley (fresh or dried)
Cloves	Paprika	Mint (fresh or dried)
Mace	Peppercorns	Sage (fresh or dried)
Turmeric	Coriander seeds	Oil of Cloves
Ginger root	Bay leaves	Acetic acid
Stick Cinnamon	(fresh or dried)	

You will almost certainly also need, but you will probably already have on your shelves:

Vinegar – you will need	Pepper	Raisins
2 pt (1 l) at least	Sugar	Garlic
Curry Powder	Dry mustard	Cloves
Salt		

PICKLES

Pickling Vinegar

Boil everything together for 4 or 5 minutes. Strain through fine strainer. Vegetables may be boiled in this or, if they are wanted uncooked, it may be poured over them after they are prepared and packed into jars. This latter is called a 'hard' pickle.

2 pt (1 l) good malt vinegar
2 tsp whole peppercorns
½ tsp allspice
Piece of ginger root, crushed
Blade of mace
½ tsp cayenne pepper
1 tsp salt

Pickled Beetroot

Slice cold cooked beetroot into rounds ¼ inch (½ cm) thick. Pack into clean, dry bottles, cover with cold spiced vinegar. Seal securely and do not use for at least a week.

Cold boiled beetroot
Pickling vinegar (above)

Cauliflower Pickle (Clear)

Wash and thoroughly drain the white part of the cauliflowers, and divide it into tiny sprigs. Spread them on a dish, sprinkle the salt over, cover with another dish and leave for 24 hours, then drain thoroughly. Put them into clean, dry, heatproof jars, cover well with pickling vinegar. When cold, seal and tie down.

For the pickling vinegar, peel and chop the shallot, chop the chilli, put them in a pan with the vinegar, peppercorns, allspice and the well-bruised ginger. Bring to the boil, simmer for 15 minutes, then strain and use.

Keep the cauliflower pickle for some weeks before using.

1 large or 2 small cauliflowers
1 large tbsp salt
1 shallot
1 dried chilli
2 pt (1 l) vinegar
8 peppercorns
½ tsp allspice
1 inch (2 ½ cm) root ginger

Pickled Onions (Whole)

Peel the onions, put the salt and peppercorns in a pan with the vinegar and bring slowly to the boil; remove the scum as it rises. Put in the onions and simmer for 5 minutes. Pack them into clean, dry, heatproof jars and cover with vinegar. When cold, seal and tie down.

2 lb (1 kg) small onions
2 tsp salt
1 oz (30 g) whole white peppercorns
2 pt (1 l) distilled white vinegar

Pickled Onions (Sliced)

4 lb (2 kg) large onions
4 pt (2 l) vinegar
6 oz (180 g) mixed whole spices
1 dessertsp salt

Peel the onions, and slice them thinly. Pack them into clean, dry heatproof jars. Put the spices, salt and vinegar into a pan and boil for 5 minutes. Cover the onions with this mixture. When they are cold, seal and tie down. Must be absolutely airtight.

Vegetable Marrow Pickle (Thick)

1 vegetable marrow 14-18 in (35-45 cm) long
1 large tbsp salt
12 shallots
½ oz (15 g) dry mustard
½ oz (15 g) ground ginger
1 large tsp turmeric
3 pt (1½ l) malt vinegar
4 dried chillies
6 oz (180 g) demerara sugar
8 cloves

Peel the marrow and remove the seeds and weigh 4 lb (2 kg) of the pulp. Cut it into cubes, put them on a deep dish, sprinkle with salt, cover with another dish and leave until next day. Then drain it well. Peel and chop the shallots. Mix the mustard, ginger and turmeric together, then add enough vinegar to make a thin paste. Put it into a saucepan with the chillies, sugar, shallots, cloves and the remaining vinegar. Bring to the boil, then boil gently for 10 minutes. Add the marrow and boil until it is quite tender. Put into clean, dry, heatproof jars. When cold, seal and tie down.

Mixed Pickles (Thin)

Cauliflower
French beans or scarlet runners
Small onions or shallots
Vegetable marrow, de-seeded
Gherkins
Cucumber
1 oz (30 g) salt
For every 2 pt (1 l) vinegar:
 1 oz (30 g) allspice
 1 oz (30 g) root ginger
 ½ oz (15 g) peppercorns
 1 dried chilli

Use only white part of cauliflower, divided into small florets. String and cut up beans. Peel onions or shallots, and cut marrow, gherkins and cucumber into cubes. Put the prepared vegetables into a pan of boiling water with salt in the proportion of a dessertspoon to 2 pints (1 l) of water and simmer for 3 to 4 minutes. Drain well and spread them out to dry. When quite dry, pack them into clean, dry, heatproof jars and cover well with hot pickling vinegar. Cover and seal the jars as soon as the vinegar is cold.

To prepare the vinegar, put it in a pan with the spices and boil gently for 20 minutes. Strain and then use.

Thick Mixed Pickles or Piccalilli

Cauliflower
French beans or scarlet runners
Small onions or shallots
Cucumber
Vegetable marrow
Gherkins
Salt
For every 2 pt (1 l) vinegar allow:
 ½ oz (15 g) turmeric
 1 oz (30 g) dry mustard
 2 oz (60 g) caster sugar
 ½ oz (15 g) whole mixed spices
 1 tbsp cornflour

Prepare the vegetables as in the previous recipe. Spread them on dishes and sprinkle with salt – about 1 oz (30 g) to 2 pints (1 l) of vegetables. Leave until next day, then drain well, put them into a pan with the vinegar mixed with the turmeric and mustard, the sugar, and the spices tied in a muslin bag. Boil gently for 10 minutes. Mix the cornflour with a little cold vinegar and add. Stir while it boils 5 minutes longer. Remove the bag of spices and bottle as in the previous recipe.

Pickled Pears

Peel and halve pears, placing each one immediately in cold water to keep them from discolouring. Boil the rest of the ingredients together for 2 minutes, add the pears, cover and boil until tender. Transfer into clean, dry, heatproof jars, seal and tie down, when cold.

Delicious with hot and cold roasts.

7 lb (3 ½ kg) firm pears
3 ½ lb (1 ¾ kg) lump sugar
1 large lemon
½ pt (300 ml) white vinegar
½ oz (15 g) root ginger, bruised
A few cloves

Sweet Pickled Plums

Prick the plums with a fork, and put them in an earthenware mixing bowl. Boil the vinegar with the sugar, cloves, cayenne and cinnamon, let it cool and when only just warm, pour it over the plums. Leave them for 3 days, reboiling the vinegar each day and pouring it back on the plums when warm. On the 5th day, bring the plums to the boil in the vinegar and boil for 2 minutes. Turn into clean, dry, heatproof jars. When cold, seal and tie down then store in a cool, dry place.

8 lb (4 kg) plums
2 pt (1 l) vinegar
2 lb (1 kg) sugar
12 cloves
Small pinch of cayenne pepper
Small piece of stick cinnamon

Sweet Tomato Pickle

Remove any stalks from the tomatoes, wipe them and cut them in quarters. Peel and slice the onions, bruise the ginger and put it with the peppercorns in a little muslin bag. Chop the chillies. Put the sliced tomatoes and onions in a mixing bowl, mix the chillies with them and sprinkle salt over them. Leave until next day. Then drain off the liquid. Put the tomatoes, onions and chillies in a preserving pan with the bag of spices, pepper and sugar. Cover with vinegar. Bring to the boil and simmer until soft and brown. Take out the bag of spices. Turn into clean, dry, heatproof jars. When cold, seal and tie down.

6 lb (3 kg) green tomatoes
2 lb (1 kg) onions
1 in (2 ½ cm) root ginger
8 peppercorns
½ oz (15 g) dried chillies
Salt
½ tsp pepper
2 lb (1 kg) demerara sugar
Vinegar to cover

CHUTNEYS

Apple Chutney

Peel, core and chop the apples, add the onions, sugar and sultanas or dates (chopped finely). Sprinkle with a tablespoon of salt, and a pinch of cayenne pepper. Cover with a pint (600 ml) of vinegar, and simmer gently for 2 hours, stirring frequently. Put into clean, dry, heatproof jars. When cold, seal and tie down.

4 lb (2 kg) apples (windfalls are
* suitable)*
2 lb (1 kg) onions
½ lb (240 g) sugar
½ lb (240 g) sultanas or dates
Salt
Cayenne pepper
1 pt (600 ml) vinegar

3 lb (1½ kg) sharp cooking apples
3 shallots
¼ lb (120 g) dates
¼ lb (120 g) sultanas
½ lb (240 g) raisins
1 tsp salt
¼ tsp cayenne pepper
2 tsp dry mustard
½ oz (15 g) ground ginger
1 pt (600 ml) vinegar

Madras Chutney

Peel and core the apples, and cut them into quarters or eighths if very large. Peel and chop the shallots, stone and chop the dates. Mix all these ingredients with the sultanas, raisins, salt, cayenne pepper, mustard and ginger, put them in a preserving pan, pour the vinegar over and boil gently until the mixture is quite thick. Stir occasionally, then put into clean, dry, heatproof jars and, when cold, seal and tie down.

This is a true Indian recipe and is very good with curry.

2 lb (1 kg) green tomatoes
2 lb (1 kg) green apples
1 lb (½ kg) shallots
3 cloves garlic
1 lb (½ kg) demerara sugar
½ lb (240 g) sultanas
6 dried red chillies, seeded and
  chopped
1 pt (600 ml) vinegar
1 in (2½ cm) root ginger, whole

Green Tomato Chutney

Quarter the tomatoes. Peel and core the apples, and cut them in pieces; peel the shallots and garlic. Mix these ingredients together and put them through a mincer or food processor. Put the mixture into a preserving pan, add the sugar, sultanas, chillies, vinegar, and the ginger tied in a little bag of muslin. Bring slowly to the boil, then simmer until thick and soft. Remove the ginger, squeeze out as much juice as possible. Put into clean, dry, heatproof jars. When cold, seal and tie down.

A 4 lb (2 kg) vegetable marrow
Salt
½ lb (240 g) pickling onions
6 cloves
1½ lb (¾ kg) sugar
½ oz (15 g) ground turmeric
9 dried chillies
1½ oz (45 g) ground ginger
1½ oz (45 g) dry mustard
2 pt (1 l) vinegar

Marrow Chutney

Cut the unpeeled marrow into ½ inch (1¼ cm) squares, lay on a dish and sprinkle with salt, leaving overnight. Drain. Boil the other ingredients for 10 minutes, then add the marrow and boil for ½ hour, or until tender, and put into clean, dry, heatproof jars. When cold, seal and tie down.

4 lb (2 kg) small tomatoes
6 oz (180 g) salt
½ lb (240 g) small onions
1 large head of celery
1 tsp pepper
2 tsp dry mustard
2 tsp ground cinnamon
2 tsp ground allspice
½ lb (240 g) demerara sugar
2 pt (1 l) vinegar

A Very Good Soft Tomato Chutney

Cut the tomatoes in small pieces. Mix the salt with them, and leave for 24 hours. Then drain them. Put the tomatoes in a preserving pan with the onions, peeled and chopped. Remove the outer leaves and root from the celery, and add the heart, finely chopped. Add the spices and sugar and mix well. Pour in the vinegar. Simmer until the vegetables are quite soft, then turn into clean, dry, heatproof jars. When cold, seal and tie down.

Ripe Tomato Chutney

8 lb (4 kg) ripe tomatoes
1 lb (½ kg) onions
1 pt (600 ml) vinegar
6 oz (180 g) sugar
3 oz (90 g) salt
½ oz (15 g) cloves
About ¾ tsp cayenne pepper
About ¾ tsp ground ginger

Cover tomatoes and onions with water and boil for 2 hours, then beat through a sieve until nothing remains but the seeds, skin, etc. Return to pan, add the vinegar and sugar, salt, cloves, cayenne and ginger, boil for ½ hour or until thick. Pour into clean, dry heatproof bottles. When cold, seal and tie down. This is excellent with fish, or with meat dishes.

Gooseberry Chutney

1 ½ lb (¾ kg) green gooseberries
½ pt (300 ml) vinegar
¼ lb (120 g) chopped onion
½ oz (15 g) salt

1 tsp ground nutmeg and allspice
   mixed together
3 oz (90 g) stoned raisins
5 oz (150 g) demerara sugar

½ oz (15 g) dry mustard
Pinch of cayenne pepper
Pinch of ground ginger

Wash, top and tail gooseberries, and put them in a pan with ½ pint (300 ml) of vinegar and the onion. Bring to boil and cook till tender (20 minutes). Add remainder of ingredients. Boil 5 minutes. Put into clean, dry, heatproof jars. When cold, seal and tie down.

Apple and Tomato Chutney

1 lb (½ kg) apples, peeled, cored
   and cut small
1 lb (½ kg) onions, chopped
1 lb (½ kg) ripe tomatoes,
   blanched, skinned and sliced

½ pt (300 ml) vinegar
1 tsp salt
½ lb (240 g) very dark brown soft
   sugar
¼ lb (120 g) sultanas

½ oz (15 g) mixed pickling spice,
   tied in muslin (taken out after)

Mix all ingredients well and simmer for about 2 hours. Put into clean, dry, heatproof jars. When cold, seal and tie down.

Beetroot Chutney

2 pt (1 l) cooked beetroot, finely
   chopped
2 pt (1 l) chopped, raw cabbage
3 oz (90 g) horseradish grated

½ lb (240 g) sugar
Pinch of cayenne
½ tsp white pepper
1 tbsp dry mustard

1 tsp salt
1 pt (600 ml) vinegar

Mix the ingredients well together and cook for ½ hour. Put into clean, dry, heatproof jars. When cold, seal and tie down.

1 lb (½ kg) dates
3 lb (1½ kg) apples, peeled, cored
and chopped
2 pt (1 l) vinegar
1 lb (½ kg) onions
2 oz (60 g) ground ginger
Pinch of Cayenne pepper
A few cloves
1 lb (½ kg) sugar

Sweet Chutney

Simmer everything together for 2 hours. Pour into clean, dry bottles, seal and tie down.

This is a recipe for those who like a very sweet chutney indeed.

Bottled Sauces

3 lb (1½ kg) cranberries
½ pt (300 ml) water
1 lb (½ kg) preserving sugar to
each pint (600 ml) of prepared
fruit

Cranberry Sauce

Put the fruit and the water into a preserving pan and simmer until soft. Then rub through a sieve. Measure the pulp and to every pint (600 ml) add 1 lb (½ kg) of sugar. Boil gently until it sets when tested and store in small jars.

This can be heated and served hot as a sauce or cold as a jelly. Particularly good with turkey at Christmas or with any game.

6 lb (3 kg) green tomatoes
6 large onions
1 handful salt
½ lb (240 g) soft brown sugar
2 tsp cayenne pepper (optional)
¾ tsp ground white pepper
¾ tsp dry mustard
Vinegar to cover
In a muslin, bag:
1 tsp ground cloves
1 tsp dried chillies
1 tsp ground ginger

Governor's Sauce

Wash and cut tomatoes, peel onions and cut in slices, sprinkle over them the salt. Mix all together and let stand all night. In the morning drain off the water and put fruit in preserving pan (not copper) with the rest of the ingredients and boil until soft. Remove muslin bag. Pour into clean, dry, heatproof jars. When cold, cover and seal.

The best sauce in the world for all cold meats.

Fresh mint
Vinegar

Mint Sauce (1)

Wash the mint, then dip in hot water. Remove the stalks and chop the leaves finely. Fill wide-necked jars three-quarters full with the chopped mint and then fill with vinegar. Cork securely and seal. Keep in a dry place. Add sugar to taste when required. Should keep indefinitely.

Mint Sauce (2)

Boil vinegar and sugar together, withdraw from heat and add chopped mint. Bottle when cold in glass-stoppered bottles. When required for use, add more vinegar, as the sauce should be quite thick and sweet when made. This sauce will keep for a year.

½ pt (300 ml) vinegar
6 oz (180 g) sugar
3 tbsp finely chopped fresh mint

Tomato Catsup

Peel the onions and slice them, slice the tomatoes, put them into a pan, add the vinegar, and simmer until quite soft. Then rub all through a fine wire sieve or put through a food mill at the finest mesh. Return the purée to the pan, add the sugar, salt and pepper, cayenne, if liked, and the spices tied in a muslin bag. Simmer gently for 30 minutes, stirring. When cool, remove the bag of spices. Turn the catsup into clean, warm, dry jars. When cold cover and seal.

1 lb (½ kg) Spanish onions
6 lb (3 kg) tomatoes
1 pt (600 ml) vinegar
½ lb (240 g) caster sugar
1 oz (30 g) salt
¼ tsp pepper
A little cayenne pepper (optional)
1 dessertsp cloves
1 dessertsp allspice

Tomato Sauce

The tomatoes should be red, but not overripe. Remove the stalks, wipe the tomatoes with a cloth and cut them in small pieces. Peel and chop the onions and garlic, chop the chillies. Put the tomatoes, chillies, onions, sugar, salt and garlic in a preserving pan and boil gently for 2½ hours. Rub through a sieve or put through a food processor and strain and leave until cool. Then stir in the oil of cloves and acetic acid. Mix well and pour into clean, dry bottles, cover and seal. Keeps very well.

8 lb (4 kg) tomatoes
¼ lb (120 g) onions
2 cloves garlic
3 dried chillies
6 oz (180 g) sugar
3 oz (90 g) salt
12 drops oil of cloves
1½ oz (45 g) acetic acid

CHRISTMAS COOKING

Timetable

October 1st-December 15th
Mincemeat and Christmas pudding may be made whenever convenient, but they are much better stored for a few weeks, so try to make them by December 1st. In an emergency you can make them even as late as Christmas Eve and they will still be good, but less rich in flavour and consistency.

For Christmas pudding, you mix ingredients one morning and let them stand overnight and then boil the puddings the next day for 6 to 8 hours, so you need 2 days when you are mostly at home.

December 21st-24th
Any time in these days, you can finish icing and decorate the Christmas cake.

December 23rd
Prepare all ingredients for stuffings for bird.

December 24th
Stuff and sew up turkey. Make pastry, fill and bake mince pies. Prepare vegetables for next day.
Make brandy butter and store in refrigerator or cool larder.
Boil piece of ham or bacon (see page 120) to eat with cold turkey on Boxing Day.

December 25th

For Christmas dinner at 1 pm

16 lb (8 kg) bird	9.00 am	Preheat oven to 350°F/180°C/ Gas Mark 4.
	9.30 am	Put in bird.
10-12 lb (5-6 kg) bird	10.00 am	Preheat oven as above.
	10.30 am	Put in bird. Put pudding on to reboil.
	11.30 am	Put prepared potatoes in to roast
	12.00 noon	Lay table and set out dessert, etc.

12.15 pm	Put vegetables on to boil.
12.30 pm	Turn off oven and leave bird to keep hot. Cover breast to prevent further browning. Make gravy and dish up vegetables at leisure.
12.50 pm	Put everything to keep hot, comb your hair and redo your face, and drink your sherry or cocktail, before serving at 1 pm.

For Christmas Dinner at 8 pm

16 lb (8 kg) bird	4.00 pm	Preheat oven as above.
	4.30 pm	Put in bird.
10-12 lb (5-6 kg) bird	5.00 pm	Preheat oven as above.
	5.30 pm	Put in bird. Put on pudding to reboil
	6.30 pm	Put prepared potatoes on to roast. A quiet half hour in which to change and have your sherry or cocktail.
	7.00 pm	Lay table and set out dessert, etc.
	7.15 pm	Put vegetables on.
	7.30 pm	Turn off oven. Make gravy and dish up vegetables at leisure.
	7.50 pm	Put all to keep hot, tidy yourself and drink your final before-dinner drink.

The Bird or Joint

The following are all traditional to serve on Christmas Day:

Turkey	Too large for 2 or 3. A small bird, 8 to 10 lb (4-5 kg), is suitable for 4 to 6.
Large Cockerel or Capon	Very good for 2 to 4.
Goose	Many people prefer this to turkey as it is less dry. Those who like white meat generally like turkey and those who like dark prefer goose. Children generally prefer turkey.

| Roast Beef | This was the traditional Christmas fare up to the nineteenth century, nowadays it is much more expensive than turkey. Get as large a joint as you can possibly use, as a large roast of beef is so much better than a small one. Christmas beef tends to be rather fat. |

Not traditional, but very good for the small family:

Duck	One for 2 or 4. A pair for 4 to 6.
Pheasant	One for 2. A brace for 3 or 4.
Partridge	You really want one each.
Veal	A large roast.

There is nothing wrong with a roast of lamb (or mutton), but it is not traditional and does not seem quite right at Christmas, when lamb is not really at its best.

Turkey and Stuffings

Turkey is inclined to be dry, so it must be well and richly stuffed, so that the fat from the stuffing works through from inside. It must also be well basted and covered with fat bacon and greaseproof paper or foil.

Make sure that the size of the bird you choose will go into your oven. Most ovens easily take a 15 to 16 lb (7½ to 8 kg) bird, if you want one so large. Larger birds can, of course, have the legs removed and cooked separately.

Make your stufffings on Christmas Eve – the dry mixture can be got ready the day before that if more convenient – and get the turkey stuffed and sewn up, ready in your biggest tray for the oven. A hen turkey has more meat to the amount of bone than a turkey cock.

Two kinds of stuffing, or even three are good. Put them in from the back in the order you prefer and press them well forward into the breast, moulding it into a good shape. Sew up with needle and thread the loose skin underneath, so that the stuffing is held firmly in place. For chestnut stuffing – best of all with turkey – see Sauces and Stuffings, Chapter 10. Use any two or three others, taking the mushroom and oyster as alternatives.

When the turkey is stuffed and sewn, place it on a large baking tray. Put 2 rashers of fat bacon over the breast. Spread ¼ lb (120 g) softened butter or cooking fat fairly thickly all over the rest of it and cover it with foil.

On Christmas Day, allow 15 minutes to the pound (½ kg), so that a 10 lb (5 kg) bird will take 2½ hours. A 16 lb (8 kg) bird will probably be ready in about 3 hours rather than its full 4 hours, and should be tested with a skewer after this time. Preheat oven to 350°F/180°C/Gas Mark 4 and keep it at this low temperature until ¾ of an hour before the bird should be done, basting every

30 minutes, and using more fat if necessary. Three-quarters of an hour before serving, turn the oven up to 450°F/230°C/Gas Mark 8, remove paper and bacon rashers, baste well and allow the breast to brown to a rich mahogany.

Sausages may be served with a turkey, and bread sauce is a usual accompaniment. Cranberry sauce is also excellent (see Bottled Sauces).

The traditional vegetables are brussels sprouts and celery and roast potatoes, but with frozen vegetables available, a much greater choice is open to you. In America, bread sauce is not usually served and creamed onion (or onion sauce) almost always is. If there is no room round the turkey for roast potatoes and not enough space in the oven to cook them in a separate tray, creamed potatoes with plenty of butter and milk are excellent.

Recipes

Mixed Herb Forcemeat

Mix together the breadcrumbs and suet. Add the ham or bacon, finely chopped, the herbs, parsley, salt and pepper. Bind with the well-beaten eggs.

½ lb (240 g) fresh breadcrumbs
3 oz (90 g) shredded suet
2 oz (60 g) lean ham or bacon
4 tsp finely chopped fresh mixed herbs – marjoram, thyme, sage, bay leaf, or 2 tsp mixed dried herbs
1 dessertsp chopped parsley
Salt and pepper
2 eggs

Oyster Forcemeat

Mix the breadcrumbs with the suet, add the liquor from the oysters, a good sprinkling of salt and pepper, the cream and the oysters cut in small pieces. Mix well with the beaten eggs. Stir in a double saucepan over boiling water for 5 minutes. Leave until cold, then use.

¼ lb (120 g) fresh breadcrumbs
1 oz (30 g) finely chopped suet
1 small tin oysters
Salt and pepper
2 tbsp cream
2 eggs

Sausage Forcemeat

Remove the skins from the sausages. Mix thoroughly with the other dry ingredients, moisten with the stock and use.

1 lb (½ kg) pork sausages, or 1 lb (½ kg) pork sausage meat
2 tbsp fine breadcrumbs
1 tsp finely chopped fresh herbs, or good pinch of dried herbs
1 tbsp stock or gravy

Mushroom Forcemeat

¼ lb (120 g) fresh breadcrumbs
1 tsp finely grated onion
Sprig of thyme or marjoram,
    chopped, or pinch of dried herbs

Sprig of parsley, chopped
¼ lb (120 g) mushrooms, coarsely
    chopped
¼ lb (120 g) fatty bacon

Salt and pepper
2 eggs
2 oz (60 g) butter, melted and
    cooled

Mix the first 7 ingredients together and stir in the well-beaten eggs and the melted but cooled butter. Beat well with a fork and insert into bird.

Celery or Walnut Stuffing

½ lb (240 g) finely chopped celery
    heart, or 1 lb (½ kg) shelled
    walnuts, chopped

¼ lb (120 g) shredded suet
1 tbsp chopped parsley
Grated rind of ½ lemon
½ lb (240 g) fresh breadcrumbs

2 oz (60 g) ham
Good pinch of dried mixed herbs
Salt and pepper
2 eggs

Mix all the dry ingredients together and blend with the well-beaten eggs.

Christmas Pudding (1)

¾ lb (360 g) shredded suet
½ lb (240 g) prunes, stoned
½ lb (240 g) mixed peel, cut in
    strips
½ lb (240 g) small raisins

½ lb (240 g) sultanas
½ lb (240 g) currants
½ lb (240 g) flour, sifted
½ lb (240 g) sugar
½ lb (240 g) brown breadcrumbs
¼ lb (120 g) dates, chopped
1 tsp mixed spice

½ tsp nutmeg, freshly grated
½ tsp salt
¼ lb (120 g) glacé cherries
4 eggs
¼ pt (150 ml) milk
Juice of ½ lemon
¼ pt (150 ml) brandy

This is a very old recipe which makes a most excellent pudding. The quantities given make 1 large and 2 small puddings.

Mix the dry ingredients, stir in the eggs, beaten to a froth, and the milk, lemon juice and brandy. Stand for 12 hours in a cool place, then turn into buttered pudding basins. Boil for 6 hours and cool, then for 2 hours before serving.

For boiling, cover the basins with foil and then tie each one with a cloth. Stand in a fish kettle or bath or separately in large saucepans, so that the water comes halfway up each bowl. Add more boiling water from time to time.

Christmas Pudding (2)

1½ lb (¾ kg) raisins	*Rind of 1 large lemon*	*½ lb (240 g) dark sugar*
1½ lb (¾ kg) currants	*¼ lb (120 g) candied mixed peel*	*8 eggs*
1 lb (½ kg) suet	*¼ lb (120 g) almonds, blanched*	*¼ pt (150 ml) brandy*
1½ lb (¾ kg) breadcrumbs	*A little mixed spice*	*½ pt (300 ml) milk*

Stone the raisins if necessary, wash and pick the currants, chop the suet very finely, and mix them with breadcrumbs. Add the grated rind, the candied peel cut into shreds, the blanched almonds, chopped, and the mixed spice and sugar. When all are thoroughly blended, stir in the well-beaten eggs, brandy, and milk. Put into pudding basins as for previous recipe and boil for 6 hours.

Christmas Pudding (3)

¼ lb (120 g) raisins	*3 oz (90 g) flour*	*1 tsp grated lemon rind*
2 oz (60 g) mixed peel	*¼ tsp salt*	*¼ lb (120 g) currants*
2 oz (60 g) blanched almonds	*1½ tsp mixed spice*	*3 eggs*
¼ lb (120 g) suet	*½ tsp ground ginger*	*¼ pt (150 ml) milk mixed with*
6 oz (180 g) soft brown sugar	*½ tsp cinnamon*	*whisky or ale or stout*
¼ lb (120 g) fresh breadcrumbs	*A little grated nutmeg*	

Stone the raisins if necessary and chop. Chop suet, peel, and nuts. Mix all dry ingredients, then stir in eggs and liquid. (Use 1 tablespoon of whisky or 2 tablespoons of ale or stout and make up to ¼ pint (150 ml) with milk.) Turn into greased 1½ pint (900 ml) pudding basin and cover with foil and a pudding cloth, which should be securely tied. Put the pudding in fast boiling water and cook for 5-6 hours. Add fresh boiling water several times during cooking. When reheating, steam for 2 hours.

Brandy or Rum Butter (see Chapter 10)

Mincemeat

All mincemeat, if it is to be made at home, should be prepared at least a fortnight before Christmas, and to make it in November is better still. Mincemeat keeps almost indefinitely and some people prefer it when it has been kept from the year before. If you have some from last year, you will probably find that it has become a little dry and crumbly-looking. In this case, turn it into a bowl and mix it briskly with a little brandy, which will restore the consistency and improve the flavour. Failing brandy, use cooking sherry or lemon juice.

Mincemeat (1)

½ lb (240 g) currants
1 lb (½ kg) raisins
¼ lb (120 g) sultanas

Rind and juice of ½ lemon
1 lb (½ kg) cooking apples
½ lb (240 g) marmalade
½ lb (240 g) suet
½ tsp mixed spice

¼ lb (120 g) candied peel
½ lb (240 g) demerara sugar
¼ tsp ground nutmeg
Good pinch of ground ginger
2 tbsp brandy

Stalk currants if necessary and wash all the dried fruit. Grate the rind of ½ lemon. Peel, core and slice apples, put all through mincer. When minced, stir all the ingredients together thoroughly, add lemon juice and brandy, stir again, fill into sterilized jars and tie down so that they are airtight. Keep in a dry, cool place.

A ½ teaspoon of brandy put over the top of mincemeat in each jar before they are covered improves it greatly.

Mincemeat – Without Brandy (2)

1 lb (½ kg) apples
6 oz (180 g) raisins
½ tsp mixed spice

½ tsp ground cinnamon
½ tsp ground mace
Rind and juice of ½ lemon
6 oz (180 g) suet

¼ lb (120 g) caster sugar
2 oz (60 g) blanched almonds,
chopped
½ lb (240 g) currants

Peel, core and cut up apples, and stone the raisins, if necessary. Mix the spices together and grate in lemon rind. Mix all the dry ingredients thoroughly, then add the lemon juice. When well mixed, put into jars, cover and store in a cool, dry place.

Mincemeat (3)

1 lb (½ kg) suet	*1 tsp ground nutmeg*	*Juice and rind of ½ lemon*
1 lb (½ kg) apples	*1 tsp ground ginger*	*3 tbsp brandy*
1 lb (½ kg) raisins	*¼ lb (120 g) soft brown sugar*	*3 tbsp white wine*
¼ lb (120 g) candied mixed peel	*1 tsp ground allspice*	
1 lb (½ kg) currants	*1 tsp salt*	

Mince suet, peeled, cored and cut up apples, raisins, stoned if necessary, and candied peel. Stir all together, and then stir in the washed currants, stalked if necessary, the nutmeg, ginger, brown sugar, allspice, salt, lemon juice and grated rind, and the brandy and wine. Put into jars, make airtight and store.

Mince Pies

1 lb (½ kg) pastry (short or flaky)
Mincemeat
Milk
A little caster sugar

Line 24 bun tins with pastry and fill generously with mincemeat, cover with pastry, damping the edges with cold water and pressing them together. Brush over with milk, sprinkle with caster sugar and bake in a hot oven at 450°F/230°C/Gas Mark 8 for about 10 minutes.

Cakes

Christmas cakes are better if made about the beginning of December and kept in a tin until a few days before Christmas when they may be iced and decorated.

Christmas Cake (1)

2 oz (60 g) almonds	*½ lb (240 g) self-raising flour*	*6 oz (180 g) soft brown sugar*
6 oz (180 g) raisins	*1 tsp mixed spice*	*3 eggs*
6 oz (180 g) currants	*¾ tsp ground ginger*	*3 tbsp milk*
¼ lb (120 g) sultanas	*¾ tsp ground cinnamon*	*3 dessertsp rum, sherry or whisky*
2 oz (60 g) mixed peel	*½ tsp salt*	
2 oz (60 g) glacé cherries	*6 oz (180 g) butter*	

These quantities are for a 7-9 inch (17½-22½ cm) cake tin.

Prepare tin by lining with greased greaseproof paper. Blanch and chop the almonds, prepare fruit, chop peel, and cut cherries in half. Sieve the flour, spices and salt together. Beat the butter and sugar to a cream and beat in the eggs. Mix dry ingredients with the fruit and stir in egg mixture, moistening with milk and rum or sherry or whisky. Turn into prepared tin and hollow out the centre slightly. Place on the second level from the bottom of the oven. Bake at 325°F/170°C/Gas Mark 3 for 2½ hours. Leave in the tin until cold.

1 lb (½ kg) unsalted butter
10 eggs
1 lb (½ kg) soft brown sugar
1 ½ tsp mixed spice
½ lb (240 g) almonds
1 lb (½ kg) flour
1 lb (½ kg) currants
1 lb (½ kg) sultanas
1 lb (½ kg) raisins
½ lb (240 g) glacé cherries
½ lb (240 g) candied mixed peel

¾ lb (360 g) butter
¾ lb (360 g) sugar
6 eggs
1 lb (½ kg) self-raising flour
1 tsp bicarbonate of soda
½ lb (240 g) currants
½ lb (240 g) raisins
½ lb (240 g) sultanas
¼ lb (120 g) chopped walnuts
½ lb (240 g) ground almonds
1 tsp salt
½ lb (240 g) mixed peel
½ lb (240 g) preserved ginger
1 tbsp golden syrup
1 lb (½ kg) blackcurrant jam
3 tbsp rum or whisky

Christmas Cake (2)

Line an 11-12 inch (27½-30 cm) tin well with greaseproof paper. Beat the butter to a cream, and stir into it the eggs, well beaten with the sugar, then add the spice and the almonds chopped very finely. Stir in the flour, add the currants and sultanas washed and dried, the raisins and cherries, chopped up, and the candied peel cut into pieces. As each ingredient is added, the mixture must be beaten. Bake for 3 hours at 300°F/150°C/Gas Mark 2.

Dark Fruit Cake for Christmas (3)

Line an 11-12 inch (27½-30 cm) tin well with greaseproof paper. Cream butter and sugar, beat in eggs one at a time, then add flour sifted with a teaspoon of bicarbonate of soda. Add the cleaned fruit and nuts, the ground almonds and a teaspoon of salt, the peel, ginger and syrup, and lastly the jam. Put a double thickness of greased paper in the tin and bake in the middle of the oven for 1 hour at 325°F/170°C/Gas Mark 3, then 2 hours at 300°F/150°C/Gas Mark 2.

When placing mixture in tin, scoop out a big hollow from the middle, almost down to bottom of tin, to allow centre to cook. When the cake is done, (test by running a metal skewer into it near the middle; if it is clean and does not stick when it comes out, the cake is done), pour the rum or whisky over the top when it comes from the oven and cover with a cloth until it is cold. This is an excellent cake and keeps indefinitely. Only remove from tin when cold.

Icing

For Glacé Icing and Royal Icing for finishing the Christmas cake and for notes on decorating with an icing syringe, see section on Icings.

If you want a snow scene on your Christmas cake, with figures and small trees, you can roughen the white royal icing into even peaks with a fork. If it is to be conventionally decorated with lettering, apply it as smoothly as possible with a hot, wet knife.

Almond Icing

½ lb (240 g) ground almonds
½ lb (240 g) icing or caster sugar
1 egg
1 tsp lemon juice
1 dessertsp water
Apricot jam

This is enough for an 8-9 inch (20-22½ cm) cake.

Not everyone likes this icing, but it can be omitted and replaced by a layer of glacé icing.

If you use caster sugar, the slightly rough texture of the ground almonds is enhanced. If you use icing sugar the paste is smoother.

Sieve almonds and sugar together into a mixing bowl. Stir in the beaten egg and lemon juice and water. Dust pastry board with icing sugar and knead the almond paste on it till it is smooth and coagulated. Roll out about a ¼ inch (½ cm) thick. Brush the cake over with warm apricot jam. Fit almond paste over and press gently onto cake, being careful not to break. Cut away surplus from bottom edges of cake. If small breaks occur, gently fill them.

Alternatively, cut a circle the size of the top of the cake. Roll out remainder to length of circumference of cake (measure with string) and trim to a strip the depth of the cake. Then brush sides of cake with jam and lay on the strip and roll so that the strip adheres. Brush top with jam and apply circle. Gently press the edges together.

Before applying the almond icing, cut the top of the cake level with a sharp knife if it is at all risen in the centre. Then turn it the other way up, so that you ice what was the bottom. This gives you the firmest and most level surface available. The almond icing may be put on the cake as soon as it is really cold – allow 24 hours after baking. It should then be stored in an airtight tin in a dry, cool place until a few days before coating with a layer of glacé icing. Then finish with a layer of royal icing and decorate.

INDEX